Black Caribs - Garifuna
Saint Vincent' Exiled People
and
The Roots of the Garifuna

A Historical Compilation

Edited By

Tomás Alberto Ávila

ISBN: 978-1-928810-28-5

Library of Congress Catalog Card Number: Pending

PRINTING HISTORY
First Edition

Milenio Associates, LLC
61 Tappan Street
Providence, RI 02908
Phone: 401-274-5204
Fax: 401-633-6535
milenioassociates@yahoo.com

Content

St. Vincent Timeline

Svgancestry.com

http://svgancestry.com/index.php/st-vincent-timeline/

1300 - Carib Indians of South America conquer the indigenous Arawak Indians

1498 - 1500 - Island is discovered in the third voyage of Christopher Columbus

1627 - Granted to Britain's Lord CARLISLE

1660 - Declared neutral

1672 - Granted to Lord WILLOUGHBY

1675 - African slaves became the first permanent non-Carib settlers after swimming ashore from a Dutch shipwreck

1718 - La Soufriere volcano eruption

1719 - Yellow Caribs allow French settlement and slaves are brought in to work their estates

1722 - King George I grants the island to the Duke of Marlborough

1722 - 1748 French settle the island

1748 - Declared neutral again in the Treaty of Aix-la-Chapelle

1762 - Captured by British General Robert MONCKTON

1763 - Ceded to Great Britain

24 Sept. 1772 - Start of First Carib War, British forces led by Sir William YOUNG

17 Feb. 1773 - British sign treaty with Caribs giving them the Windward Coast of the island

1778 - French seize the island again

1780 - Hurricane destroys almost all the dwelling houses, the churches, and other buildings

1783 - Treaty of Versailles returns the island to the British

01 Jan. 1784 - France returns St. Vincent to the English following the Treaty of Versailles

1795 - 1797 - France supports Britain in deporting 5,000 Caribs to Roatan Island/Belize, after the Second Carib War

1812 - La Soufriere volcano erupts, many estates destroyed or damaged

1819 - Hurricane - heavy damage to outlying islands

1833 - Becomes part of the Windward Islands

1834 - Slavery is abolished - 18,000+ freed

1840 - Portuguese immigrant workers arrive

1898 - Widespread hurricane damage

1902 - La Soufriere volcano eruption kills 2,000 Vincentians

1935 - Labor Rebellion

1958 - 1962 - Part of the Federation of the West Indies

27 Oct. 1969 - Becomes an associated state

13 Apr. 1976 - La Soufriere erupts again

27 Oct. 1979 - Independence

SOURCE: Various reference books

Address Delivered By Hon. James Mitchell in La Ceiba, Honduras April 11, 1997

Representatives of the government and the people of Honduras, and of the cities of Honduras, representatives of the Garifuna people and the black organization, Garifuna people, people of Honduras, I am very pleased to be here. It is the first time I have come to Honduras. I have visited other parts of Central America - Belize, Guatemala, and Nicaragua. The most important job I have done in Central America was when I helped to supervise the elections in Nicaragua when Violetta Chamorro took power from the Sandinistas. I more recently worked in West Africa to help the transformation of a military government in the Gambia to a newly elected government in the Gambia.

As I travelled from St Vincent yesterday - and it took me only one day - on the plane, I reflected on the history of the Garifuna people, how difficult it must have been for you coming across the sea 200 years ago. It is very funny - as it were -- that we are the only country in the Caribbean that has a human link with a part of Central America in the Garifuna people, between St Vincent and Central America.

I bring you greetings from the government o and the people of St Vincent and the Grenadines. I want to let you know what caused you to be here. Your ancestors fought very hard in St Vincent, then called Yuremei, against the British, and you lost the battle because of the superior naval power of the British. You had friends among the French but they abandoned you. You put up a heavy fight that the British decided they could not let the Garifuna people remain in St Vincent. When your chief, the Caribs Chief Chatoyer died in battle, then the Garifuna people, in the struggle, were demoralized. But however, some of the Garifuna people hid in various parts of St. Vincent and they are still there today to create a link with you the people of Central America.

Now, I want to let you know that the remaining people whom we call the Caribs, were given, by the British, some very isolated and difficult lands on which to live. My political party was founded on the principle of land for the landless and when we took power in 1984 we did the same thing one of our largest plantations was for sale, and it was to be sold to a foreign company. I refused to let the foreign company purchase those lands, and working within the framework of the constitution we purchased those lands. Then we set about getting the lands to the people.

The secret is very simple. A government always has time, and a country is forever. A government has got to find a way to use time to give substance to the people. Therefore we raised bonds, and with our taxes we were able to purchase those lands.

Our government could not afford to give those lands away, but we could afford to give time away. So, we found a framework where all the lands were given to the people and a framework given of time for them to pay for them.

Following that, we were able to get a great deal of international support to develop those lands. I was very pleased that we were able to distribute one-third of the lands to women. Today, all of those communities where we have done our land-reform program are thriving communities, with people having their own homes, good quality homes with electricity and telephones. When we took over those lands, also there were no roads, and that transformation began in 1984, and it is a success in a very short space of time.

I have one message to give you, the first is that it is necessary that secure economic and intellectual independence. That is the way to success. By that I do not mean going to school. You have got to work hard, and discipline yourself. If you are at the bottom, you will never get on the top without discipline. It is important that you understand that, when once you have education, you do not have to be rich. But, if you are rich in your mind, and you are productive, everybody in Latin America will respect you.

At our Independence celebrations this year, we will be establishing, for the first time our national honors. We did not do it before because we were contemplating working with creating a new country united among other islands in the Caribbean. We already have honours which we receive from our sovereign, the Queen, and our national honours will co-exist with the international honours which we receive in our country. In this process, and, to respect the historic origins of our country we will be recognizing the first Garifuna Chief, Chief Chatoyer.

You cannot, in this country, forever live in the past. Nor could we, in our country live in the past. But it is important that we use our history to guide us in the future. For, if you ignore history, it will repeat itself.

Now the future of our region is tied very much with the American Free Trade Area, organized already between Mexico, the United States and Canada. We attend the meeting in Miami, and we are part of the process of preparation for the free trade of the Americas to come into being in the year 2005

While we are working at organizing trade, I want you, the Garifuna people, to realize that that can create opportunities for you to have practical and profitable linkages with the Caribbean. And while it might be very far in the future, nevertheless we must understand what the future holds, and begin to prepare to secure some of that future.

I am very pleased with what I have seen of your organization. Your 200th anniversary has been a good focus of attention. I shall carry back a very important message to the people of St Vincent and the Grenadines, and it is that we have brothers and sisters in another part of the world who in their memories and in their songs and in their culture, think very kindly of St Vincent. While we know that our people came here, we were not aware that there is such a strong sentimental link between Central America, the Garifuna people and our people in St. Vincent and the Grenadines.

I am very pleased that I was able to bring a delegation from St Vincent with me, and the Minister who represents the Garifuna people is here with me today. Honourable Monty Roberts, will you please stand. And also the other members of our delegation so, you could at least see what Garifuna people look like in St. Vincent.

I now conclude by letting you know that you are welcome to Saint Vincent. We have our Independence celebrations in October this year, and I would like to invite your Garifuna Organization to select people to attend our Independence celebration. As long as you arrive in St Vincent, you will be our guests.

It is important that we establish permanent working relations between the Garifuna organization and the organization in St Vincent and the Grenadines. I wish finally to thank the mayor of La Ceiba; I want to thank you, Madam, for your hospitality in your city. I want to thank you to pass on our greetings to the President and Vice Minister, and all of those who made our visit here so welcome.

And I wish to congratulate all those people who have used their leadership ability from the United States Garifuna and here in Honduras to put this show together.

Long live! Thank You

Address By Dr. The Hon. Ralph Gonsalves Prime Minister, St. Vincent and The Grenadines

Chairman Of The Caribbean Community On The Occasion Of The 200th Anniversary Of The Abolition Of The Trans-Atlantic Slave Trade

I have the distinct honour and pleasure of addressing the Caribbean Community on the historic occasion of the Bicentenary of the passage of the Bill by the British Parliament in 1807, that abolished the Trans-Atlantic Slave Trade.

Given the overwhelming significance of this historic moment to us in the Caribbean, it is fitting that we pause for a moment to commemorate and to remember. We must never forget.

So on March 25, 2007, and throughout the rest of the year in our many commemorative activities, we unite as a region and as a people, in a collective moment of reflection, as we remember one of the greatest tragedies in the history of humanity, which denied over 25 million Africans for over 400 years, the basic human right of freedom, the right to self actualization and for so many, denial of even their basic right to life.

As a region, we are collectively engaged in commemorating and paying tribute to all those who triumphed over the anguish of enslavement, of injustice and disenfranchisement, and who helped to bring about the abolition of the nefarious triangular trade that linked Europe, Africa and the Americas from the late 1400s to the late 1800s, in the trading and transportation of human cargo across the Atlantic.

We observe a minute of silence on March 25th, and engage in year-long commemorative activities as mandated by the Eighteenth Inter-Sessional Meeting of the Conference of Heads of Government, which was held in St. Vincent and the Grenadines, in February 2007, in memory of those who survived the horrors of the middle passage, the brutality and dehumanizing experience of slavery and the anguish of displacement from their homeland.

We recall their bravery, we recall their indomitable spirit, that sustained their struggle against the prevailing world order that discounted their right to identity, to citizenship and to develop as a people, as a society and as a continent.

We remember the martyrs and leaders of the slave revolts; we honour the memory of Toussaint L'Overture and Henri Christophe in Haiti, Nanny of the Maroons, Tacky and Paul Bogle in Jamaica; Codjo, Mentor and Kwakoe in Suriname. We honour Bussa in Barbados, Cuffy, Accra and Damon in Guyana, neg marrons Jaco and Bala from Dominica, Joseph Chatoyer in St Vincent and the Grenadines, and the host of others throughout the Caribbean and elsewhere who struggled for their freedom and thereby guaranteed the freedom of generations to come, of which we are currently the beneficiaries.

With the benefit of hindsight, we are able to see that the trans-Atlantic slave trade and the system of slavery, had a profound impact not only on the Caribbean, but on the world, as the economic, political and psychosocial conditions that developed during this period of world history, continue to be at the centre of international relations even today.

Slavery, the slave trade and subsequently indentured servitude were essential elements of a system that generated wealth and economic prosperity for the European super powers, fueled the Industrial Revolution and an economic boom in Europe. Africa on the other hand, was plunged into a state of underdevelopment, social instability and dislocation, persistent poverty, and economic decline, so ably captured in the seminal work of another celebrated activitist scholar, Dr Walter Rodney. The effect on that continent of losing Africa's strongest, brightest and best for hundreds of years is undeniably profound. We cannot afford to forget.

This occasion of the 200th Anniversary of the Abolition of the Slave Trade in the British West Indies also presents many opportunities. It is a time to teach the younger generation of the region, the history, the lessons and the effects, and to ensure that we never again experience this tragedy in old or new forms. It is an opportunity to bring about reconciliation and healing for ourselves and for all the parties in Britain, France, Spain, Portugal, the Netherlands, Africa, South America and the Indian Ocean, among others, who share this experience. But the healing can only come after remembering and acknowledging our respective roles and our collective responsibility for the betrayal, for the atrocities and for the suffering that resulted from African genocide and enslavement. We will not forget.

As a region, we have led the way in focusing the attention of the international community on the Bicentenary, in the spirit of reconciliation and truth, by co-sponsoring a Resolution which was adopted by the 61st General Assembly of the United Nations in 2006, which designated March 25, 2007 as the International Day for the Commemoration of the 200th Anniversary of the Abolition of the Trans-Atlantic Slave Trade. A Special Session of the United Nations General Assembly will be held on March 25, at which Dr. the Hon. Denzil Douglas, Prime Minister of St. Kitts and Nevis will deliver an address on behalf of CARICOM.

The Resolution, which was supported by an overwhelming majority of states, recognizes the slave trade and slavery as among "the worst violations of human rights in the history of humanity," and recalls that slavery and the slave trade were declared crimes against humanity by the World Conference against Racism, Racial Discrimination, Xenophobia and Related Intolerance, held in Durban, South Africa in 2001. The Resolution acknowledges that the legacy of the system of slavery is "at the heart of situations of profound social and economic inequality, hatred, bigotry, racism and prejudice, which continue to affect people of African descent today."

The Resolution honours the memory of those who died through exposure to the horrors of the middle passage and in revolt and resistance to slavery, and recalls the Durban Declaration in emphasizing the importance of the "provision of remedies, recourse, redress and compensatory and other measures" aimed at countering "the continued impact of slavery and the slave trade" and restoring the dignity of the victims and their descendants.

By far, the most crippling effect of slavery and the slave trade has been the ideology and the legacy of racism, legitimized then by the Code Noir in the French colonies; and which is perpetuated in new and insidious forms in our contemporary world. We shall not forget.

However, as we gather on March 25th and throughout the rest of the year in churches, at public lectures, in schools and at ritual ceremonies of commemoration, on Emancipation Day and Independence Day, let us be reminded that we also have much to celebrate as a people. We celebrate our many accomplishments as a great Caribbean civilization that has triumphed over this great adversity.

We celebrate our cultural diversity and the melting pot of races, cultures and peoples who have demonstrated to a divided, globalised world that we can live in peace and harmony. Out of the crucible of our painful past, we have created a neo-people, a model community, and a spiritual and cultural renaissance.

I am indeed grateful for this opportunity to greet the Community as we gather to reflect, to remember, to commemorate, to celebrate, and to act accordingly.

The Caribs

http://members.tripod.com/prejudice/caribs.htm

Introduction

The island of St.Vincent has a mixed population of blacks, Orientals, whites and Caribs. Before the coming of the Europeans and the other races that followed such as the blacks and the Orientals, St.Vincent was settled by Caribs who exists today on the Windward coast of St.Vincent (from Sandy Bay to Fancy) and at Greiggs. The island today has very few pure Caribs, most of them have interbred with the blacks and are now called black Caribs due to the colour of their skin.

This document describes the life of the Caribs before the Europeans arrived, the struggle to regain their lost land that had been taken away by the Europeans in addition to the life of the Caribs has it is placed in today's scenario.

There are many suggestions as to how the Caribs came to live in the Caribbean islands. It seems to most Historians that Pre-historic man from Asia were the forefathers of the Amerindians of the New World. It is hypothesized that during the fourth Ice Age, Pre-historic man from Asia while hunting the giant mammoths, had crossed the frozen Bering Straits and consequently entered into the continent of America, now called the New World (see fig 2). These Amerindians continued the migration southward into Mexico through the Isthmus of Panama and finally into South America (see fig 3). From South America, the descendants formed new tribes that spread northwards into the Caribbean, one of these tribes was the Caribs.

The Caribs migrated across Brazil through the interior of Guyana to the north until the coast of Venezuela and finally to the archipelago of the Caribbean islands in the pursuit of new lands and of Arawaks (an Amerindian tribe who were fleeing from the Caribs), (see fig 3). The Caribs occupied the north-western part of Trinidad, the Lesser Antilles of which St. Vincent is one and the eastern part of Puerto Rico (see fig 4).

The Caribs lived near a water source, here in St.Vincent and in other Antillean islands the Caribs lived on the coast. The reasons for living near the sea were because their diet consisted mainly of fish, the sea was a mean of communication between the Caribs on other islands, it was easy see an oncoming attack from their enemies and their wars always started from the sea. The Caribs did not settle on the larger islands because it was difficult to penetrate the island's interior and they did not need vast amount of lands for farming since they were warlike in nature. The windward side of the islands were developed so as to guard against attacks. The windward of the island often had the roughest waters therefore it was had to enter into the villages by means of the sea unless the coast was well known.

The Carib people were medium in height and lean. They had straight, long, black hair that was worn loose. Their brown skin was always painted with a vegetable dye called roucou. They had flattened foreheads that were considered a beauty. The Carib people were usually naked except for a loin cloth that was worn around their middle. The men were clean shaven since beards were considered a deformity and they were plucked out. They wore bracelets and necklaces made out of amber, shell, agouti teeth, seeds and coral. The men sometimes wore necklaces of their enemies' teeth. Their ears and lips were bore and smooth fish bones and ornaments were placed in them. The Caribs wore small idols around their necks called maboyas. On special occasions the men wore feathered head dresses.

The Caribs life was based on war, they felt that success in battle was the only road for power. War and power was an obsession with the Carib males. Even at the early stage of birth. When a male child was born there was a special ceremony where his father was cut with an agouti tooth, the father was supposed to bear the pain without flinching so that his son would grow up to be brave and strong in battle. The boy was then rubbed down with the fat of a slaughtered Arawak in hope that he would absorb the Arawak's strength and courage. As the boy grew older his education dealt mostly in the making and the using of weapons and making him strong for an initiation ceremony to test his skill that was to come at the age of twelve. Boys tried to improve their marksmanship by being trained to shoot down their meals from on top of trees.

The Carib's boy initiation ceremony was a transitional stage between being a boy and a warrior. On the day of the ceremony the boy was seated on a stool in front of all the warriors. His father explained to the boy, his future duties and responsibilities, after which a bird was beaten against the boy's body until it was dead. The boy was then deeply scratched with an agouti tooth and then rubbed down with the bird that meanwhile had been dipped into pepper. The boy was then given the heart of the bird to eat. During this whole ceremony the boy was supposed to show no sign of pain. He was then sent to his hammock for fast, he was given a warrior's name, taught the language and allowed to go on raids.

The Caribs fighting equipment were rather simple they were made from wood, bone and stone. They had war clubs, bows and arrows that were poisoned so that even a scratch was fatal, fire arrows, wooden swords and knives made of sharp rock. The Caribs fought weaker tribes than themselves, mostly their peaceful neighbours the Arawaks for food and women.

The ubutu, the Carib's war leader, decided the day that the attack was to be made. Each Carib man would collect a stick and make notches in it to count the days until the attack. Their attacks were made in the cover of the night. Before war the Caribs painted and armed themselves (see fig 5). They then worked themselves into a rage and set out for war. Once they set out they never turned back. The Caribs fought in their canoes or piragas from sea. These canoes held up to fifty men. These attacks were always sudden and brutal. They often started with a shower of fire arrows that immediately set fire to the thatched roofs of the enemies. The surprise enemies always flew out their houses to meet the savage Caribs who meanwhile would have grabbed their clubs and arrows and started to beat and shoot their enemies. They kept no order when they fought. When the fighting was over the Caribs that were often the victorious side pile the bodies of their warriors into the piragas because they refused to leave their dead and wounded behind. In the canoes were also the men and women they had taken for prisoners. They often sang songs of triumph as they sailed back home. The Caribs got awarded medals in battle for special courage. These medals were called caracolis, which was a crescent shaped copper medals that they wore around their neck.

The Social struture, the Religion and the Culture of the Caribs.

The Caribs social structure was mobile. The social caste of the Carib community was:

i) the war leader or ubutu

ii) priests and elders

iii) warriors and hunters

All decisions for running the community was made by the men, therefore only men held the ruling positions. The ubutu was always a male whose position was not hereditary. He was chosen by the elders of his village. He had to have been a good warrior, proved that he was physically strong, brave and highly skilled in battle. When he was chosen, he had to carry out a raid, if the raid was successful his positioned was permanent. The ubutu duties were:

1) He was the leader for the raid.

2) He planned and decided when to carry out the raid and who to attacked.

3) He distributed the medals and the loot from the raid e.g. women who were given as slaves or wives to the warriors.

4) He chose the commanders of the piragas.

In times of peace each district was ruled by a headman called a tiubutuli hauthe. The headman supervised the fishing and the cultivation of crops, beyond this he had a very little authority.

Most boys were trained to be warriors, this was discussed earlier in the introduction. A small percentage of the boys were trained to be priests or boyez. The boys were apprentices to an older priest for several years. During this time they often fast and abstain from meat. They then went through an initiation ceremony, if they were successful their teacher would take them to his maboya (idol) where fruit, cassava and ouicou, an alcoholic beverage was offered to the maboya. The priest would then smoke and sang inviting the maboya to enter into the room. When the priest had thought that the maboya had entered, the priest asked the maboya to provide a special maboya to the apprentice if the maboya agreed the apprentice became a full fledged boyez or priest with his own personal maboya to help him perform his duties.

The elders of the villages were well respected. They were taken care of by their families and their relatives. The elders were all ex-warriors. They were the ones who trained the warriors and looked for the qualities in the ubutu since they were experienced.

The warriors were the ones who fought first in line, they were also the hunters for the villages. They were the common villagers.

The Carib males practiced polygamy. Marriages were arranged and girls married at an early age around sixteen to eighteen years. The husband provided a hut and furniture for each of his wives at the time of their marriage. If the wife committed adultery it was punishable by death. It was a custom for an unmarried woman to wear a garter on her right leg, at the time of marriage the garter was removed.

They did not have a family unit but a communal way of living, they were separated based on their sex. The men lived separately in their carbets or houses and the women lived in huts. Boys at the age of four were taken away from their mothers and placed in the carbets, because the men thought that if the boys stayed with their mother too long he would become soft. The women were expected to bear a number of children. If she was barren she was considered a disgrace.

The women and the men had different roles in the society. Men were supposed to be the warriors, priests, leaders, builders of houses and boats, craftsmen and hunters. The women were supposed to do the domestic chores, bring up the children, collecting firewood, bartering produce, weaving, hammock making and cultivating the land.

The Caribs main idol was the maboya. They felt the maboya controlled everything. Each person had his/her own maboya to ward of all evil. The Caribs also had their own good god or chemmen besides the maboya, the chemmen was thought to be stronger than the maboya. They felt when sickness occurred or they had a defeat in battle or death that a hex had been placed on them by an enemy maboya. To ward of these evils, a boyez was called in to carry out a ceremony, for example, if the person was ill, they first cleaned their houses and gifts of fruit, cassava and ouicou were offered to the maboya which were placed on a matoutou, a table for the maboya. The matoutou was placed at one end of the room and stools for each member of the family was placed at the other end. The boyez then entered singing incantations to called upon the patient's good god. The boyez, at this time would strike the ground three times with his left foot. He then proceeded to light a tobacco to smoke. He puffed the tobacco smoke about five times upwards into the air, after which he took the tobacco and broke it into fine pieces. These pieces were sprinkled on the patient. The boyez at this time would have prescribed a mixture of herbs for the patient and asked the family to take revenge on the evil maboya. If the patient was not cured the boyez told them a stronger revenge was needed.

The Caribs believed in life after death, but they had no wish for dying. They preferred to stay on earth to enjoy the materialistic pleasures. They ate healthily and took their medicines regularly. They consulted with piayes or magicians to call upon the devil for them. They tried worshipping the devil thinking they would have longer lives.

When a Carib died, he/she was examined to see if he/she died of sorcery. The body was then washed carefully and painted red. The hair was oiled and combed. The grave for the body was on the floor of he/she house. The grave was round. It was about four feet wide and six feet deep. The body was placed on a stool in the grave, for ten days relatives brought food and water at the grave and a fire was lit around it in order to prevent the body from being cold. At the end of the ten days the hole was filled. There was a ceremony in which, the Caribs danced over the hole. As a sign of mourning relatives cut off their hair. The dead person's possession was burnt. Later a feast was held over the grave, and after which the person's house was burnt.

The Caribs had great respect for the sea. They made sure when they were travelling by sea, they did not eat any crab or lizard or drank any water in fear of offended the ocean spirits. If they were carrying fresh water on their canoes they made sure that the water would not spill in the sea because they thought a storm would brew up, also for this same reason they never ate crab before a sea voyage. If they were passing over places where fellow Carib men had drowned, they threw food in the water in hope that the drown men's spirits would not capsize their boat. When they approached land they precaution themselves from pointing to it or talking about it unless any evil spirit heard and prevented them from landing there.

The Caribs main source of food came from the sea. The Caribs did not eat pig, salt or turtle since they thought it made them stupid. They neither ate much fat. The Caribs were thought to be also cannibalistic. Human flesh was eaten boiled or barbecued. The Caribs did not eat mammee apple since it was considered as a food for the dead. Sometimes soup was made out of agouti bones and ground provisions which were seasoned with pepper sauce, oysters and cassava flour. Fish was often grilled on wooden stakes and served with a sauce called couii. This was often eaten with yams or sweet potatoes. The dish that was the favourite with the Caribs was a stew made out of crab and cassava with a taumalin sauce. Taumalin sauce consisted of lemon juice, pepper, and the green meat in the shell of the crab. Their favourite alcoholic beverage was ouicou.

The Carib houses were rectangular shape. The houses were large about 40ft*20ft. The furniture in the house was rather sparse. There were hammocks, amais, stools, tables in addition to the maboya. Outside the house there was a storeroom in which household utensils, weapons, tools and extra hammocks and beds were kept. The Caribs slept on amais or hammocks. Amais was a piece of cotton folded and both ends were hung from the roof. The hammocks had a small packet of ash placed at the ends that were thought to make it last longer. The stools were made from red or yellow wood that were polished. The tables were made from latainer rushes. At nights the huts were lighted with candles that were made with a sweet, smelling gum.

The Caribs who were considered warlike were rather friendly to visitors. On seeing unfamiliar canoes approaching the island, the posted sentries would announce that there were strangers coming. At this point Carib men got on their canoes and paddled to the oncoming canoes, where they learned the other persons' attentions, if they were warlike the war started at that place if they were peaceful they were taken ashore. The strangers were then taken to the carbet or a tabouii which was the men's house in the village. There they met the leader where names were exchanged. The guests afterwards were taken to a stream where they washed and taken to a clean hut to rest on an amais. Meanwhile, the women prepared a meal for the guests such as roast fish, soup and crab stew. During the meal there were singing and dancing. The music was produced by reed pipes, drums and whistles. The guests were welcome to stay as long as they wished. When the guests left they were loaded with gifts of all sort.

The Struggle of the Caribs to retrieve their land.

The Caribs had many struggles to survive the suppression of the Europeans after they took over their land, they were courageous enough to fight these people in the intentions of getting back their land. The Caribs only wanted to work their land and live in peace with nature. The Carib's lands were being lost to European's sugar plantations. St.Vincent had one of the best sugar lands in the Caribbean. The English had a greed syndrome in which they always tried to get whatever they want not caring who got hurt. Therefore to get maximum amount of land in St.Vincent, they wished that the Caribs would move to Bequia, but their population was too large.

The Caribs passive struggle was in their inside. They had to struggle to keep their culture, identity and family life. They tried to stick together and carry out their old traditions so that they could retain their culture. Although they tried so hard during their wars, when they got separated their culture flagged therefore it did not sustain after the influence of the Europeans. Their lives were not the same.

The Caribs felt there were no compromise for the freedom of roaming wherever they liked, therefore they made the ultimate sacrifice of their life to fight for this freedom. The Caribs dissatisfaction grew when most of their land were given away to the colonists from Barbados, Antigua and United States of America (U.S.A.). The Caribs knew that they would have to fight the English in order to get back their land. They got a chance when they were enticed to rebelled the English in St.Vincent by the Martiniquians. The Caribs destroyed the plantations by setting fire to it and murdering English colonists. These attacks were mostly guerrilla that were made in 1789, at that time the governor of St.Vincent was James Seton.

In 1795, the Caribs began showing alarming signs of activity while contacting the French from Guadeloupe, they were in the contact of Victor Hughes's assistants who were trying to spread the revolution from Haiti. To prevent this, the British sent out ships to patrol the waters of the windward coast in order to stop the French from communicating with Caribs in hope that this will stop their guerrilla warfare.

The government came to know in the first week of March that the Caribs were preparing for war. The body of defence, called the Colonel Militia, was being aided by reinforcements in Martinique. Martinique was in the hands of the English at that time and was the headquarters of the Commander-in-chief of His Majesty troops in the islands. The militia was called to arms. They were drawn up on the Parade Ground now called Victoria Park, to be addressed by the governor who told them their duty. Two days later messages were dispatched to the two main chiefs, Du Valle and Chatoyer, and some other minor ones. The replied the Governor got was that it was too late.

The Caribs planned that Chatoyer whould take the Leeward and Du Valle the Windward. On Sunday the 8th of March, 1795 news came to Kingstown that war had broken out. The Marriaqua Caribs had plundered the Le Croix Estate owned by Mme Croix. The Governor, James Seton immediately dispatched soldiers to go to Marriaqua under the command of his son Brigade Major James Seton and Major Sharpe. They succeeded in capturing eighteen of the Caribs, the others fled.

Meanwhile, further up the Windward coast, another band of Caribs was destroying the estates of Three Rivers. Another set of soldiers was dispatched, this time under the Command of Captain James G. Morgan with reinforcements headed by Lieutenant MacDowall and Keane. The militia of soldiers resumed their march on the windward highway after a night rest at San Souci. This band of soldiers encountered a body of Caribs on a hill, along the road to Three Rivers who opened vigorous fire with their musketry. Before they could retreat, Captain Morgan realized that they were now being attacked from behind as well. The Captain then fled to Kingstown with the lost of thirty-one men.

Du Valle glad with his success, pushed his men onto Dorsetshire Hill where they captured the post and hoisted the flag of the French Republic.

In the meantime, Chatoyer who was the Commander-in-chief of the Caribs, was working his way up to Dorsetshire Hill from the Leeward. The French at Chateaubelair also joined forces with him to fight at the British. Chatoyer approached fighting the English colonists very differently compared to Du Valle. Chatoyer did not destroy the property but directed his fury to the settlers. He did not destroy the properties because he hoped that if they should win the war, the plantations would be intact, so that it could be used. People claimed that while Chatoyer was fighting his way to Dorsetshire Hill, he earmarked Keartons. It is said that Chatoyer capture three young English men from Chateaubelair, Duncan Cruikshank, Peter Cruikshank and Alexander Grant and dragged them to Dorsetshire Hill where he hacked them to pieces on Saturday, 8th of March, 1795, singlehandedly, to display his hatred to the English.

After Chatoyer and Du Valle had united their forces, their next objective was Kingstown. The people of the city on hearing this were alarmed, the Governor immediately moved his office to Berkshire Hill taking a few important documents. Both Berkshire Hill and Sion Hill were strengthening their fortifications. The Caribs meanwhile were strengthening their fortifications at Dorsetshire Hill and Fort Duvernette, which was erected by the French in the support of the Caribs.

The plantations around Kingstown were ordered to be burnt by the Governor, in order to have a clear view of the Caribs approaching Kingstown, who from time to time made appearances at the Redemption Estate and Liberty Lodge. A small body of Caribs had made an attempt to stage an attack at the Government House at which time was situated in Montrose Estate, but they were driven off by the strong guards who were posted there. The Caribs once made an attempt to go to Kingstown en route Sion Hill, but they were driven away by the guns on the fortifications at Sion Hill.

In the second week of March, 1795, two war ships docked into harbour of Kingstown that had reinforcements sent by the English. The ship names were the Zebra and the Roebuck. On the 14th of March, at midnight, forces at Sion Hill divided into four and marched to Dorsetshire Hill in order to destroy it. The force consisted of:

1) detachments of soldiers both from the Zebra and the Roebuck.

2) Sailors and merchants from the harbour.

3) The Company of Forty-six.

4) the detachments of the local militia and armed Negroes at the rear.

The force moved up the hill in the darkness. Only when they were eighty yards from the fort did the Caribs and the Frenchmen who with the Caribs perceived them. The Caribs immediately opened a brisk fire. It was only when the English force was twenty yards away from the fort did they discharged. Most of the Caribs escaped in the darkness, but other Caribs and Frenchmen were harmed and killed. Only five of the attackers were dead and five were wounded. It was on this hill that Chatoyer died that night. He had challenged the Major Alexander Leith to a duel, because, he, Chatoyer was convinced that he could not be killed by mortal hands according to a legend, however this legend did not come to past because he was killed by the Major. The Major did not have much time to enjoy his victory because he was killed by the wounds Chatoyer placed on him. Chatoyer was considered a hero to the nation, although little information exists about him. Most of the information about him is hearsay. However, a rememberance monument has been put up for him at Dorsetshire Hill. There is also a memorial stone for the Major under the large chandelier of the Cathedral in Kingstown.

A few days after the Major and Chatoyer had died, Colonel Gordon, the head of the detachment force went to the town of Chateaubelair that was occupied with the Caribs and the French. He commanded that the town should be burnt down. The Caribs fled. The Chateaubelair Caribs and the Dorsetshire Hill

Caribs met in the vicinity of Calliaqua, where they set up three camps. On the 21st of March, 1795, the important parts of Calliaqua were destroyed by fire set by these Caribs, the sugar mills in Arnos Vale, Villa, Belmont and Fair Hall were destroy by fire a few days later.

On the 5th of April, 1795, reinforcements of trained soldiers, sailed into the Kingstown Harbour on board the H.M.S. Montague. Other ships were soon to arrive such as the Experiment, the Thorn, the Alarm and the Scipio. The soldiers from the Montague, were landed on shore and marched to their quarters in Berkshire Hill.

Captain Lowman made an attempt to attack the Carib camps at Calliaqua upon request by the Governor, on 10th of April. His attempt failed and he had to retreat to Kingstown, the next morning. The only people who were successful in getting rid of the Caribs were the Light Infantry men, some Grenadiers and a detachment of the third battalion of the Sixtieth. They made a spirituous attack that made the Caribs flee in various directions.

Two armed schooners set sailed from the Kingstown Harbour, under the command of Lieutenant Colonel Seton on the 25th of April. These schooners got reinforcements at Chateaubelair, where after, they set sailed to Du Valle's village on the Windward coast. The attack made there on the 26th was quite successful, twenty five houses were burnt and the Caribs' canoes were destroyed.

The Marriaqua Caribs and some other Windward Caribs who were joined with a few French and English slaves, took up positions at the Vigie eastward of the upper Warrawarrou Valley not very far from the Fountain Estate.

Seven bands of Caribs, 800 in all, on the 7th of May were seen advancing to Calliaqua. Calliaqua at this time was occupied by troops under the command of Captain Molesworth. A shot from the English camp was heard by the advancing Caribs that made them stop. A messenger from the Carib was sent to the English bearing a flag of truce. The messenger proposed that Captain Molesworth and his men should surrender. This proposal was rejected. Before any more negotiations should take place the frigate Alarm from Kingstown opened fire on the Caribs and landed 130 men. The Caribs fled in fright. While this incident was occurring in Calliaqua, another band of Caribs assisted by the French soldiers from Guadeloupe, consisted about 300 blacks and mulattoes had captured Dorsetshire Hill. The next day, the Lieutenant Seton made a successful attack on the Caribs near Calliaqua.

Reinforcements for the English arrived from Martinique with the much needed artillery. On the 11th of June, the reinforcement troops were ordered to marched to Marriaqua Valley to meet the Caribs. The troops advanced at night from Sion Hill. The troops were in several columns. The troops stationed themselves at the Agustine's Ridge at the head of the Biabou Valley, at the Iambou Pass near the Mesopotamia sugar works and at Calder Ridge. The attack began at daybreak. The Caribs fled in terror. Sixteen of the twenty-three dead troops of the Caribs were French whites. Among the sixty people who were taken as prisoners was a French Commander. The English lost one English officer, 13 soldiers and 3 militiamen. 3 officers and 55 privates were wounded. The Vigie fell into the hands of the English once again. The English continued to pursue the Caribs by three different routes. The English encamped at the Union Estate, where they waited for supplies from Kingstown. On the 15th of June the supplies arrived and the march continued in quest of the Caribs. The English halted at the Bellevue Ridge and finally they reached the Mount Young Carib settlement. The Caribs escaped and the English proceeded to Grand Sable where they smashed 200 canoes. Seven Englishmen died from fatigue during the march.

On the 23rd of June, English troops were dispatched to Owia aboard two droghers. They arrived at Owia on the 25th and captured it. The English had lost St.Lucia to the French again. This prove to be an advantage for the Caribs since they could have help from the French there. The Caribs made a new stand at Walliabou, but the guns of the Roebuck and the Thorn soon made them withdraw to a position above Chateaubelair where they opened fire upon the town of Chateaubelair, their success was small. Reinforcements from Kingstown soon arrived at Troumaca. The replacment troops included three six pounders and two howitzers. The Caribs soon fled to Morne Garou mountains.

On the 4th of August, an attack was made at Morne Ronde. After fighting for two hours, the Caribs retreated to the village of Du Valle. While going to Du Valle's village they were overtaken by English forces who killed them and took them as prisoners. Guards were posted both at Morne Ronde and at Richmond. The other troops were withdrawn to Mount Young.

At Owia, on the third of September, the Caribs made a raid at Owia. The English suffered a lost. Most of the English soldiers fled through the forest in the direction of Morne Ronde. The H.M.S. Experiment also rescued some soldiers who had taken refuge on a rock of the coast. On the 15th, 500 men from St.Lucia were sent to the Caribs at Owia. These men also brought provisions for them. The troops at Mount Young thought it would be best to evacuate, they arrived at Sion Hill on the 21st of September.

On the 22nd of September, the Caribs gathered at the Marriaqua Valley, and took up stand at the Fairbairn's Ridge. This cut all communication links between Kingstown and Vigie. When the relief troop for Vigie was marching to their position they were unexpectedly charged after by the Caribs. The English fled to Villa and Prospect with the Caribs hot on their trail. They were able to escaped to Fort Duvernette under the cover of the guns. The Caribs obtained most of the supplies the troops were taken to Vigie. The English losses amounted to sixty being killed and wounded.

It was necessary for the government to speak to the forces at Vigie but with the Caribs surrounded Vigie it was virtually impossible. The governor decided to dispatched two Negroes to go to Vigie. They took two different routes. Only one man returned, Thomas Nash. He was given his freedom for a reward and twenty Johannes.

In secret, the Vigie was evacuated and immediately occupied by the Caribs. This made the English more uneasy. On the 29th and the 30th September, reinforcements came on the H.M.S. Scipio. On the 2nd of October a large force of 1650 men attacked the Caribs at Vigie. The attack lasted for a whole day. When night fell the English Commander bidded his troops to retreat. The Caribs not aware of this fled in the darkness for a cover. So once more, the English occupied the Vigie.

The war continued, but it was not favourable to the English to the end of 1795, and 1796 held no brighter prospects. On the 8th of January, 1796, the Caribs launched an attack at the Vigie, the English retreated to Kingstown. The English losses were 135 privates and two volunteers, sixteen officers were wounded and one officer was taken as a prisoner. These events made the colonists feel despondent.

The English started to see promising prospects, when the Major General Hunter arrived from Martinique on the 12th of January, 1796. He soon got acquainted with the problems facing the English in St.Vincent. He set up a detachment group to watch the Vigie. The remainder of the army were post on the hillsides overlooking Kingstown. The Major on hearing that the Caribs were about to attack the Vigie, order it to be deserted on the 14th to Kingstown. The Caribs pleased by the fear the English felt for them, advanced closer to Kingstown, some stationed themselves at Baker's Ridge and the rest at Bow Wood. The Caribs were deciding to make an attack on Kingstown, but they were driven out by Island Rangers who had attacked them after the Caribs had set fire to the Bow Wood House. The English lost 50 men by killing and wounding. Joy spread into the hearts of the colonists when the H.M.S. Brunswick unloaded 300 men at the Kingstown Harbour.

The Caribs were forced to evacuate their position at Baker's Ridge on the 21st of January. The Caribs aimed shots to Dorsetshire Hill that reached the vicinity of Kingstown, however no harm was done. The Caribs retreated to the Vigie, they had lost many fellow Carib men and many were wounded. The wounded were sent to Grand Sable.

The English General Abercrombie had attacked the island of St.Lucia on the 27th of January, and he captured it from the French. This episode had a weakening effect upon the Caribs since they depended on the artillery and the provisions sent by the French from there.

General Abercrombie who had re-established St.Lucia set sailed to St.Vincent to make peace and order. He arrived in St.Vincent on the 3rd of June. The next day a fleet of armed ships disembarked at the Kingstown Harbour. The governor in his welcoming speech to the General commended him on the find artillery he had. The troops from the ships were quartered at Arnos Vale, Sion Hill and Cane Garden. The General recruited his army of 3,960 men and divided them into six sections. Each section was given specific directions where to fight, the first section was to fight at Marriaqua, the second to fight at Calder Ridge, the third to fight at Carapan Ridge, the fourth to fight at Belmont Ridge, the fifth to fight up the Warrawarrou Valley and the sixth who were the reserves were supposed to fight at the rear. Local people acted as guides. They advanced in the night. Between 6 am and 7 am on the 10th of June the Vigie was attacked, both gun shooting and cannon balls were discharged by the troops at Calder and Carapan Ridges and later by the troop at Belmont. At 2 pm all three divisions closed in, they stormed their way to the Vigie. The Caribs fled in terror down the hill, while the English took possession of the Vigie once more. All firing was ceased by both parties. At about 5 pm, when the English decided to start warfare again, Carib bearing a flag of truce approached them. The messenger said that the Caribs were ready to take submission. The next morning the Governor was consulted at 9:00, terms of submission were agreed on by both sides.

This was a blow for the Caribs, although some Caribs still gave trouble, they were finally subjugated. The among the last to give themselves up were Du Valle and young Chatoyer. By 26th of October 5,080 Caribs had surrendered. Most of the Caribs were then sent to Balliceaux and later to Bequia. On the 25th of February, 1797, Caribs were loaded on the H.M.S. Experiment and carry to the Coast of Honduras, stripped out of their homeland. A few Caribs remained, and dwelled in the part island called the Carib Country that extends from Black point to the most northern part of St.Vincent. Sandy Bay and Morne Ronde were the more populated villages. The Caribs tried to live in peace in the most rugged and uncultivated land in along the Windward Coast. The Black Caribs mostly lived in the village of Greiggs that is almost as unfavorable as this area.

Saint Vincent Early History

Known by the Caribs as Hairoun ("Land of the Blessed"), St. Vincent was first inhabited by the Ciboney, a grouping of Meso-Indians. The economy of these hunter-gatherers depended heavily on marine resources as well as the land. They used basic tools and weapons and built rock shelters and semi permanent villages.

Another indigenous group, the Arawak, who entered the West Indies from Venezuela and moved gradually north and west along the islands, gradually displaced the Ciboney. They practiced a highly productive form of agriculture and had a more advanced social structure

and material culture. The peace-loving Arawak fished and collectively formed plots of land. The bountiful harvests and abundant fish, combined with the compact and stable island population, permitted the development of an elaborate political and social structure.

The Caribs, arriving in St. Vincent perhaps no more than 100 years before the Europeans, conquered the Arawak and began a new chapter in Vincentian history. More warlike than their predecessors, the Caribs were extremely efficient at keeping unwanted settlers from their shores. While it is doubtful that Christopher Columbus ever set foot on the island, he may have sighted it on his third voyage to the New World (1498-1500). Heavy Carib resistance prevented St. Vincent from being colonized long after most other Caribbean islands had well-established European settlements. In 1627 Charles I of England granted the island to Lord Carlisle and then, in 1672 Charles II granted it to Lord Willoughby. While the British, French and Spanish disputed possession, the Caribs resisted all these claims.

The first permanent settlers arrived on the shores of St. Vincent in 1635. These new inhabitants were African slaves who survived the sinking of the Dutch slave ship on which they were being transported. The escaped

Africans merged with the Caribs and gradually adopted their language. Referred to as Black Caribs," to differentiate them from the original. "Yellow Caribs," the progeny of this group became the foundation of the Garifuna (which means"cassava eating people") who today populate Belize and Honduras. After several skirmishes both groups had agreed in 1700 to subdivide the island between themselves, the Yellow Caribsoccupying the Leeward and the Black Caribs the Windward.

The British, who claimed Carib land by royal grants, were more despised by the Caribs than the French who were permitted to set up settlements in the early 1700's. The 1748 TreatyofAix -la-Chapelle officially ended the War of the Austrian Succession. This treaty included the proviso that St. Vincent remain officially "neutral." The 1763 Treaty of Paris ceded St. Vincent to the British. During the period 1772-1773 (referred to as the First Carib War), the Caribs engaged in guerrilla warfare and destroyed plantations by setting them on fire. With Carib aid, the French forcibly seized the island in1779, but restored itto Britain in 1783, underthe Treaty of Versailles.

Joseph Chatoyer led a revolt against the British in 1795.

In 1795, with the country under the governership of James Seton, the Caribs began the two years of attack known as the Second Carib War. With the aid of French rebels from Martinique, the Caribs plotted the removal of the British. Chatoyer and DuValle (the two main Carib chiefs) planned that Chatoyer would lead the rebellion on the Leeward side and DuValle would lead on the Windward side. News came to Kingstown on March 8th thatwar had broken out.

Chatoyer directed his fury at the settlers themselves rather than destroying their property. His belief was that the land would be extremely useful to the Caribs after the removal of the British. He worked his way along the Leeward, joined in battle by the French at Chateaublair, to unite with DuValle at Dorsetshire Hill. The amalgamated forces then set their sights on Kingstown.

A battalion of British soldiers from recently arrived warships marched towards Dorsetshire Hill on March 14th. On this night, Chatoyerwas killed by Major Alexander Leith. Considered a hero to the nation, a monument in Chatoyer's honour is placed at Dorsetshire Hill. Battles raged throughout St. Vincent overthe nextyear with both sides bearing heavy losses. The final battle took place at Vigie on June 10th, 1796. After a night of arduous fighting the Caribs approach the British with a truce flag.

Submission terms were negotiatead and during the next four months over 5,000 Caribs surrendered. The Caribs were exiled to the neighbouring island of Balliceaux and in February 1797, the defeated Caribs were loaded onto a convoy of eight vessels and transported to the coast of Honduras. The few remaining Caribs scattered to the north of the island nearSandy Bay where their descendants can still be found.

The plantation economy, based on slave labour, flourished and St. Vincent produced sugar, cotton, coffee and cocoa. In 1812 La Soufiiére erupted and devastated much of the island. After the emancipation of slaves in 1833, indentured labour from Portugal and the East Indies was brought in to rectify the Labour 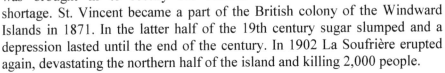 shortage. St. Vincent became a part of the British colony of the Windward Islands in 1871. In the latter half of the 19th century sugar slumped and a depression lasted until the end of the century. In 1902 La Soufrière erupted again, devastating the northern half of the island and killing 2,000 people.

In 1925 a Legislative Council was inaugurated but it was not until 1951 that universal adult suffrage was introduced. St.Vincent and the Grenadines belonged to the Windward Islands Federation until 1959 and the West Indies Federation between 1958 and 1962. Britain granted internal self-government to the isLand in 1969 and as a British Assodated State, Vincentians were responsible for their internal affairs while Great Britain handled foreign affairs and defense.

The Rise And Fall Of The Black Caribs

- By –

I.E. Kirby

And

C.I. Martin

St. Vincent, August 1972

Preface

Few historians have paid any attention to the Black Caribs of St. Vincent, and those who did had good reason to be prejudiced. The first work in which the Black Caribs are extensively discussed is Sir William Young's "An Account of the Black Charaibs in the Island of St. Vincent's," first published in 1795. The monograph was compiled by Sir William Young (Jnr.) from the papers of his father and from his own limited experience of the Black Caribs. Now, Sir William Young (Snr.) was the Chairman of the Commission sent out by the British Government to survey, sub-divide and sell St. Vincent after it had been ceded to the English under the terms of the Treaty of Paris in 1763. In the course of his work Sir. William Young (Snr.) acquired two very substantial parcels of land in St. Vincent, which were subsequently inherited by Sir William Young (Jnr.). In short, the Youngs were so deeply involved in the situation that it would have been extremely difficult for them to write about it in anything but a highly subjective manner. Indeed Sir William's book is a thinly disguised attempt to rationalize the planters' attitudes.

The second work in which the Black Caribs, or rather the wars they urged against the English settlers are extensively discussed is in Charles Shepherd's "An Historical Account of the Island of St. Vincent," published in 1831. Shepherd plainly states in his introduction that he was commissioned by the planters to record their vicissitudes, and so there can be no question as to where his interest lay.

Coke, in Volume II of his "History of the West Indies," originally published in 1810, also devotes considerable attention to the Black Caribs. The good Reverend was not pleased about the reluctance of the Caribs to embrace the proselytising of his Methodist colleagues, and this is inevitably reflected in his work.

More recently, Taylor has made an anthropological study of the Black Caribs of British Honduras. Few people realize that these people are the direct descendants of the

Black Caribs of St. Vincent. It is hoped that this booklet will help to make the link clear, assure the Black Caribs that we in St. Vincent have not forgotten them and have at least striven to tell the story of their ancestors with some degree of objectivity.

Introduction

The story of the Black Caribs cannot be fully appreciated without a clear grasp of some of the geographical details of the Caribbean area, particularly the location of such places as Bequia, St. Vincent, St. Lucia, Martinique, Barbados and Honduras. The Caribbean Sea together with the Gulf of Mexico form an almost complete rectangle. On the northern, southern and western sides are North, South and Central America, respectively. The last named of course, includes, among other countries, British Honduras and Guatemala. On the eastern side, there is the chain of islands known as the West Indies stretching from North America (Florida) to South America (Venezuela). At the southernmost end of the chain, immediately adjacent to Venezuela, is Trinidad, then comes Grenada and this is followed by St. Vincent. Between Grenada and St. Vincent are a group of very small islands called the Grenadines. Most of these Grenadines, including Bequia, the northernmost, and its neighbours to the east, Balliceaux and Battawia, are part of the State of St. Vincent. Directly east of St. Vincent is Barbados, while immediately to the north is St. Lucia, and this is followed by Martinique. The prevailing winds in the area are the North-East Trades and these touch at Barbados first and then come on to St. Vincent and the Grenadines. Thus, ships drifting from Barbados almost invariably make a land fall in St. Vincent or the Grenadines. One final point about the geography of the area that it is worth bearing in mind is that it is hurricane prone, these violent storms being most prevalent between June and September. These storms have played no mean part in the history of St. Vincent.

The recorded history of course, begins with the arrival of Columbus in the West Indies. The inhabitants that he found in these islands are believed to have come up the Chain from Venezuela, their original home being the Orinoco basin. The Europeans on their arrival found that St. Vincent contained far more Caribs than any other island. Some historians have attributed this to the Caribs' liking for St. Vincent's rugged terrain and good fishing grounds. Since other islands in the chain have these characteristics too - in fact there are others more favoured in this respect than St. Vincent - it is more likely that when the Europeans arrived, only the advance guard of the Caribs had got as far as St. Kitts, the main wave had only reached St. Vincent where they were gathering in preparation for the next move northwards. Be that as it may, the arrival of the Europeans put paid to any such plans.

The mountainous nature of the island's terrain and the large number of Caribs inhabiting it combined to make the Europeans give St. Vincent a fairly wide berth, and in the Treaty of Aix-La-Chapelle in 1748, St. Vincent was declared to be neutral. It is, however, not accurate to say, as some historians have done, that the Caribs were left unmolested. Raleigh visited the place in 1595 and subsequently spread stories about the cannibalistic nature of its inhabitants. The English monarchs were continually granting the place to one duke or another. A Frenchman, M. DuBlanc, even declared war on the Caribs and as we shall see later, the Caribs had to repel two serious efforts at settlement, one by the English and the other by the French.

Despite all this, the Caribs in St. Vincent not only survived but also prospered. They came to be regarded as the warriors who would assist their fellow Caribs in other islands in the struggles against the Europeans. It is reported that they possessed some large canoes capable of carrying up to 60 warriors. These they would launch and sail with amazing dexterity for the islands where their assistance was needed. It is clear, too, that when the Caribs in the other islands were defeated and had to flee, it was to St. Vincent they came.

For instance, Van der Plas suggests that the Bayabous, a tribe of Caribs, were forced to flee their native Guadeloupe and settle near to a river midway on the east coast of St. Vincent, thus giving the place their name Biabou, which today is a large village about 13 miles from Kingstown, the capital of St. Vincent.

Probably the Caribs might have survived even longer had they not made the fatal mistake of inviting French priests to live among them. It appears that a French sailor had enticed two young Caribs, one of them the son of an influential chief, on to his ship and sold them as slaves in Tortuga. General Poincy ordered the boys to be returned to St. Vincent and in turn, they were sent to St. Kitts to thank him. While there, they met a French priest, Père Aubergeon, who spoke the Carib language and they invited him to come to St. Vincent and spread the gospel. Père Aubergeon arrived in St. Vincent in 1653, where he estimated the population of the Caribs to be about 10,000. Later Aubergeon was joined by another priest, Père Geuimu. It was customary for each priest to be accompanied by a lay assistant and one or two slaves. Previously it has been suggested that the headquarters of these missionaries was Barrouallie, but our researches however indicate that it was nearer to Chateaubelair.

It is clear from all accounts that the French priests made little impact on the Caribs; in their own phrase, they laboured "bien inutilissime." The organization, or rather, lack of organization of Carib society made the propagation of the gospel extremely difficult. The Caribs were fiercely individualistic, with chiefs emerging mainly in time of war. The difficulties, too, of reconciling the precepts of the French priests with the practices of their other countrymen who sought to take away the Carib lands and enslave them must also have made the Caribs somewhat skeptical. Matters came to a head when, in 1654, the Caribs, at an inter-island council, resolved to drive the French from the islands. One of their first acts was to massacre the French priests and their assistants in St. Vincent. In reprisal the French sent an expedition in three men-of-war to deal with the Caribs in St. Vincent. For eight days they systematically destroyed the Caribs, their villages and whatever little cultivation they had.

This was not the only disaster to befall the Caribs as on July 13, 1653, the island had been struck by a violent hurricane. Moreover, the negroes from Africa had by this time made their appearance with consequences that were to be extremely far-reaching.

The precise origin of these negroes has been difficult to determine. The available evidence, however, suggests that they may have got here in three different ways. The first group or groups were apparently captured and enslaved by the Caribs. For almost a century, before efforts were made to colonize the Lesser Antilles, usually by the French or English, the Spaniards were carrying slaves from Africa to Santo Domingo. The Caribs had a habit of luring the Spanish ships into rocks and shoals by giving incorrect directions to their crews. Once the ships had been wrecked, the Caribs would kill the crew and take over the cargo, be it gold, eau-de-vie or slaves. Later, when the French and English settled most of the Lesser Antilles, leaving St. Vincent and Dominica to the Caribs, the latter would make excursions from their two islands and carry off slaves from the French and English plantations. Several documents attest to the presence of negroes in St. Vincent at an early date. Armand de La Paix, a Dominican missionary writing in 1646 refers to them. In the British Calendar of State Papers, 1661-1662, St. Vincent is referred to as being "all Indians and some negroes from the loss of two Spanish ships." Lord Willoughby, too, described St. Vincent as covered with woods, Indians and Blacks, and Phillip Warner stated in 1676 that St. Vincent had some 3,000 negroes and no island as many Indians.

The second major source from which the negroes may have come is a Dutch ship carrying slaves from the Bight of Benin, West Africa, to Barbados. The ship foundered off the east coast of Bequia in 1675. The records do not indicate why the ship foundered, but it is reasonable to suppose that it might well have encountered the hurricane that struck Barbados in August 1675. It is significant that "Janet," a hurricane that struck Barbados in 1955, also devastated the Southern Grenadines.

Ironically enough, though the negroes would have been chained below deck and one would expect them to be unable to help themselves, they appear to have been the only survivors. They managed to reach Bequia where they were looked after by the Caribs they found living there. Subsequently they came across to St. Vincent and were absorbed into the Yellow Carib community.

The third and probably the most important source from which the negroes came was Barbados. It has already been mentioned that most of the Lesser Antilles, including Barbados, were colonized, while St. Vincent and Dominica were left to the Caribs. The slaves in Barbados did not take long to discover that a boat or even a raft drifting from Barbados would end up in St. Vincent where they could once more enjoy their freedom in the island's thickly wooded mountains. To a lesser extent, the slaves in St. Lucia, probably noting how quickly the Carib canoes covered the 28 miles between St. Vincent and St. Lucia, also used this as an escape route. As a result, the negroes found their numbers enormously swollen by this wave of "illegal immigrants" from Barbados and St. Lucia.

By 1700 the negroes were well established. Labat, a French priest, delightful travel writer, and master-spy visited the island in 1700. His comments on the situation are not only well put in his inimitable laconic style, but they are also extremely illuminating. Below, they are quoted verbatim:

"Our vessel was no sooner anchored than it was filled with Caribs and negroes come to see us and to ask for brandy. All these gentlemen were rocoued - that is, painted red, and wore - most of them, at any rate - a little strip of cloth over their parts. This uniform attire does not prevent the Caribs' being easily distinguished from the negroes; the latter having fine kinky hair like wool, whereas that of the Caribs is black, long, straight, and very coarse. But even were this indication lacking, as would be the case if all their heads were shaved, it would still be easy to know them by the look of their heads, by their eyes, their mouths, and their corpulence, in all of which respects the ones differ greatly from the others."

He continued:

"This is the centre of the Carib Republic: the place where the savages are most numerous - Dominica not approaching it. Besides the savages, this island is also inhabited by a very great number of fugitive negroes, for the most part from Barbados, which, being to windward of Saint Vincent, gives the runaways every possible facility for escaping from their masters' plantations in boats or on piperis or rafts, and taking refuge among the savages. The Caribs formerly brought them back to their masters, when they were at peace with them, or took and sold them to the French or to the Spaniards. I don't know for what reason they have changed their method, nor what has induced them to receive these negroes amongst themselves and to regard them as belonging to one and the same nation."

It is reasonable to assume that the vast majority of 'migrants' were male. At the same time there is evidence to suggest that there was a surplus of women among the Yellow Caribs, as it was their custom to collect women as booty in war and add them to their households. In fact, the main reason why Carib men spoke one language (Carib) and the women another (Arawak) is that many of the women were captive Arawaks and their female descendants. Naturally the negroes helped themselves and this soon led to friction between the negroes and male Caribs. The latter resolved to kill the male children born to negroes, who objected vigorously. In the ensuing skirmishes, the

Caribs got the worst of it and were forced to, if only temporarily, live and let live.

The children produced as a result of this union between the Carib women and the negroes have been aptly described by Raynal, as having preserved more of the colour of their fathers than of their mothers, being tall and stout in contrast to the stocky appearance of the Caribs, and speaking with a vehemence close to anger. They were to become known in history as the Black Caribs, to distinguish them from the Amerindian, or original Yellow Caribs.

The French Interlude

The population of the Black Caribs continued to grow inexorably through both natural increase and a constant flow of runaway slaves from Barbados. As a result, they tended to encroach more and more on what the Yellow Caribs considered their preserves. The latter, however, had by now learnt, to their cost, that they were no match for the Black Caribs and so sought assistance from the Governor of Martinique.

In 1700, the Governor responded by dividing the island into two sections. He drew a line called Barre de l'Isle in the vicinity of the present Colonaire, giving the western half to the Yellow Caribs and the eastern to the Black Caribs.

The arrangement appeared to suit all parties admirably without any of them realizing what the other really had in mind. The Black Caribs did not merely accept the Governor's ruling, they held it sacrosanct and were prepared to defend their territory, which subsequently became known as the Carib Country, against all comers. The arrangement appealed to them as it gave them the eastern coast, where the runaway slaves from Barbados invariably landed. They would, therefore, be in a position to welcome these additions to their number and prevent them from falling into the hands of the Yellow Caribs, who were now prepared to sell them as slaves to the French.

The Yellow Caribs, for their part, saw the French as protectors and suppliers of "eau de vie." They wanted the western coast since it would facilitate intercourse with the French in Martinique and St. Lucia. The French had, in the first place, suggested the division as they intended to settle surreptitiously among the Yellow Caribs, all the while paying lip service to the Treaty of Aix-La-Chapelle and assuring the English that the island was in fact neutral territory. The Yellow Caribs of course went out of their way to encourage this, so that one day they could join with the French and get rid of the Black Caribs.

By 1719, the Yellow Caribs felt the time had come to put their plan into operation. The French were enthusiastic since they saw considerable advantage in the scheme for themselves. Their surreptitious settlements would then not be confined to the western sector, but could be extended over the whole island. Moreover, if they could reduce the Black Caribs to submission without killing too many of them, they would obtain an ample supply of slaves at little cost. And so, the Governor of Martinique gave the project his full support and sent Major Paulian with 400 volunteers to do battle with the Black Caribs.

Paulian's strategy was to join the Yellow Caribs who could at least serve as guides in the difficult terrain that was, and still is, St. Vincent, and rout the Black Caribs. The plan failed dismally. In the first place, the Yellow Caribs reneged on their commitment. No doubt they realized that Paulian's small and untried force would be no match for the Black Caribs, so rather than join the French, lose, and be exposed to the full vengeance of the Black Caribs, they kept out of the battle altogether.

In the second place, the Black Caribs, probably for the first time in the Caribbean but certainly not for the last, embarked upon what centuries later became known as guerilla warfare. They refused to meet the French in open combat. During the day they would be on the defensive, hiding out in the mountain fastness except to climb coconut trees and "pick off" the leaders of any expedition that ventured into their strongholds. At night they would go on the offensive, descending in small groups from unexpected areas on any Frenchmen they could find. Major Paulian and many of his followers were killed and the remainder retreated to Martinique.

The French hushed up the whole incident, no doubt because it perhaps did not have the sanction of the metropolitan Government, but also because they did not want it known that they had been beaten by the Black Caribs, whom everyone thought were very unsophisticated. The Black Caribs, for their part, extracted war damages from the French and boasted about it. They, however, still allowed the French to settle in increasing numbers, though only in that section of the island that the Governor of Martinique had allocated to the Yellow Caribs. One Frenchman, M.Perain, Secretary to the Governor of Martinique, had the temerity to build a house, not on the lands of the Black Caribs, but on Yellow Carib lands immediately adjacent. The Black Caribs burnt the house and destroyed the plantation.

Once the French had come to accept the ascendancy of the Black Caribs as an established fact, their method of settlement enabled them to live and let live with both Yellow and Black Caribs alike. Unlike other European colonists, the French did not see themselves as amassing a large fortune in St. Vincent in the shortest possible time and retiring to the Mother Country to live happily thereafter. Rather, they considered St. Vincent as their home where they should earn a living and spend the rest of their days. Consequently, they were not interested in large sugar plantations, but preferred to practise diversified agriculture, growing indigo, cotton, tobacco and a little sugar in small holdings. These holdings extended deep into the interior and even today one can see the remains of the very small sugar factories used by the French in such remote places as Lammies, Riguad and Nugent.

The restriction of the French settlements to the area allocated to the Yellow Caribs does not by any means imply that they had no impact on the Black Caribs. On the contrary, the French presence affected the Black Caribs directly and indirectly.

It was the custom of French settlers who came to St. Vincent to bring their slaves with them. This posed a problem for the Black Caribs since it was virtually impossible to distinguish between many of them and the slaves, particularly between the children. The Black Caribs sought to deal with the issue by ostensibly adopting more and more of the habits of the Yellow Caribs. The most significant of these was the practice of flattening the skulls of their babies or small children by compressing their heads between two pieces of board, which they tightened progressively at both ends. Labat, in discussing the effect of this habit on the Yellow Caribs, noted that their foreheads were flat and sloped backwards so much that it appeared that they could look at the sky without raising their heads.

They buried their dead, too, like the Yellow Caribs, in a round hole about four feet in diameter and six feet in depth. The body was propped up in the same position the Caribs used when squatting around a fire, the elbows, resting on the knees, and the palms supporting the cheeks. These burials usually took place under the floor of the huts in which the relatives normally lived.

Long before the arrival of the French, the Black Caribs had adopted and/or inherited the Yellow Caribs' extensive use of the cassava root in their diet. They used it as a type of bread, as a beverage and for meat preservation and seasoning. Of course, the Yellow Caribs' habit of killing their male enemies in war and carrying off the females as additional wives was too good a practice for the Black Caribs not to adopt.

There were more direct ways in which the French settlers affected the Black Caribs. Since the French had no legal right to be here and could hardly defend themselves against the Black Caribs, they made every effort to try to be on good terms with them. Sir William Young goes as far as to say "they (the French) helped to conciliate them (the Black Caribs) by occasional hospitalities at Martinique, and they gave them presents and supplied them with arms; they sent missionaries amongst them to dazzle them with ceremonies and entertain them with festivals, and they availed themselves of the enthusiastic temper of a wild and free people, to promote a communion of interests and passions, under covert of religion."

As we shall see later, the Black Caribs definitely acquired the French taste for wine instead of rum and became quite proficient in the French language and French manners. One forever hears of them coming to "faire bien leur complements" even when they are up to mischief. Coke, who has maligned them so much, admits they were very lavish in entertaining guests and took it amiss if visitors did not partake of their hospitality, usually helpings of eggs, cassava bread and a bowl of punch. The most obvious impact of the French presence on the Black Caribs was of course the latter's adoption of French names; one finds Black Caribs with names like Pierre Gateau, Taussé, Laimont, Guerin, Anselm, Thuriau, Laline, Bruno, Chatoyer and, of course, Jean Baptiste.

A few of the Black Caribs did, like the French, establish small farms where they grew cotton, indigo and tobacco, which they traded with the French for arms, ammunitions, tools and ornaments. The place today known as Duvallé (De Volet), or Windsor Forest, was the site of a cotton plantation owned by Duvallé, the brother and deputy of Chatoyer, paramount chief of all Black Caribs. He operated this farm with some nine slaves. Sir William Young, when he visited St. Vincent in 1791 entertained Chatoyer, Duvallé and six of their sons. He thought very highly of Duvallé, referring to him as the most enlightened of his people "who may be termed the founder of civilization among them." One hopes that his 'civilization' was not based on his ownership of slaves.

Conceivably, the Black Caribs may well have abandoned their purely fishing and hunting way of life to become yeoman farmers had it not been for circumstances that forced them to become instead perennial guerilla fighters in a desperate bid for survival

The Advent Of The English

It has been indicated that French settlement in St. Vincent had been a surreptitious affair. The English, however, sought to clothe their own intrusion with an aura of legality. Consequently, when discussing their role in St. Vincent, mention must inevitably be made of royal grants, treaties, agreements and the like. It appears that St. Vincent featured in at least four royal grants. Charles I granted it to the Earl of Carlisle in 1627, who made no attempt to colonize it. On Carlisle's death, Charles I granted it to Lord Willoughby, who died not long after. In 1672, St. Vincent was given to Sir John Atkins, who may or may not have been Lord Willoughby's brother. All these noblemen appeared to have taken little concrete action to capitalize on their grant. There appears to have been only two major expeditions. In 1686, Colonel Edwin Stede sent a Captain Temple to stop the French from obtaining wood and water in St. Vincent, and in 1708 a definite attempt at colonization was made, but the settlers were driven off by the Caribs with the support of the French under one Coullet. The final, and the most relevant royal grant, for our purposes, occurred in 1722, when George I gave St. Vincent and St. Lucia to the Duke of Montague.

The Duke wasted no time in trying to take possession of his islands. In the same year, he sent out a Captain Uring as his deputy Governor, with seven ships and a man-of-war as convoy. Their purpose was to establish colonies in both islands. They first tried St. Lucia, but were driven off by the French, who had settled there illegally. They then negotiated with the Governor of Martinique whence the French settlers had come to St. Lucia, and both sides agreed that St. Lucia should be evacuated. Uring then went on to Antigua but sent the man-of-war and a sloop under Captain Braithwaite to see if it was practicable to make a settlement in St. Vincent.

On his arrival here, Braithwaite's first contact was with the Yellow Caribs, the chief of whom he found sitting with about 100 guards, some of whom had muskets, and others, bows and arrows. A Frenchman, who acted as interpreter, was also present, and after the usual courtesies had been extended, Braithwaite returned to his ship. Next day, Braithwaite was again invited ashore and on this occasion he found that the chief of the Black Caribs had arrived, with 500 men all armed with muskets.

To Braithwaite's amazement, the Chief of the Black Caribs needed no interpreter since not only he, but also some of his sub-chiefs spoke fluent French. Braithwaite entertained the leaders on board his sloop where they liberally imbibed the wine he provided, but spurned the rum. Apparently the festivities went on until spirits were high and, as is usual in such circumstances, both sides began talking what was more or less the truth, but which perhaps was better left unsaid. The English declared that the real purpose in coming to St. Vincent was to try to effect a settlement. This elicited from the Chief a reply that turns out to be the earliest policy statement we have from the Black Caribs, and goes a long way to explain what superficially appears to have been paradoxical behaviour by these people in their dealings with Europeans.

The Chief declared that it was just as well that Braithwaite had not mentioned anything about settling in St. Vincent while he had been ashore. For in that case, not even he as Chief could have saved him from the wrath of the other Black Caribs. He went on to state that a Dutch Ship had recently tried the same thing but had had to retire very quickly. Moreover, two French ships had the day before come over from St. Lucia, bringing arms and ammunition and warning them that the British wanted to force a settlement and to enslave them. The French had also assured them of their support in any undertaking to drive out the English.

The Chief made it quite clear that although they were friendly with the French and under their protection, this was only a matter of expediency since they trusted no European and would never put themselves in a position where a European could harm them. The French, the Chief claimed, no doubt in reference to the war damages that they extracted from Paulian's ill-fated venture, had only obtained their good will by providing them with large presents. This did not mean they distrusted the French any less than other Europeans. The Chief closed by asking Braithwaite to treat his remarks as an act of friendship and to hoist anchor as soon as possible and get out of here. As soon as the Black Caribs had gone ashore, Braithwaite did just that. As a farewell salute, the English ordered a discharge of cannon, the Black Caribs answered with a fusillade of regular volleys of small shot, which in Braithwaite's opinion, was as fine a series of volleys as he had ever heard.

The English were no less reticent about Captain Braithwaite's adventure than the French had been about Major Paulian's expedition. Many of their writers have either ignored it or glossed it over so glibly that it is still widely believed that English efforts at colonizing St. Vincent only started after the Treaty of Paris in 1763. Under the terms of the Treaty, St. Vincent was ceded to the English, and as Southey aptly observes, no notice was taken of the existence of the Black Caribs. As soon as the treaty had been signed, a commission under the chairmanship of Sir William Young was sent out to survey, sub-divide and sell the land. English settlers began pouring in from North America, Antigua and, of all places, Barbados, from which many of the Black Caribs or their ancestors had come. The attitude of these settlers was quite different from that of the French. They had no interest in St. Vincent as such, it was simply a place where they did a brief sojourn to amass wealth in the shortest possible time and return to England to enjoy it. The way to do this was to obtain a large tract of land, grow sugar cane on it with an army of slaves, and process the cane into sugar in large mills powered by wind and water and latterly by steam. This implied the end of small scale diversified farming, which the French settlers had practised. The flat and coastal lands were to be devoted to the growing of sugar cane, while the inland valleys were reserved for growing ground provisions and later, breadfruit to victual the army of slaves.

The change was not only one of the tenure system, it was also a psychological one. The English had deluded themselves into believing they had a legal right to the place. It is amusing to see Sir William Young trying to convince his readers that the mere fact that the Caribs did not cultivate all the land was sufficient to give the

English a good title to it. Apparently, the Black Caribs system of tenure was a communal one. Each "family," or, more accurately, clan of Caribs had its own territory, the boundaries of a particular territory being delineated by the island's numerous rivers. Thus, one finds references being made to the Caribs of Grand Sable, of Massarica, of Rabacca, of Macaricaw, of Byera, of Coubamarou, of Yambou, of Colonaire, of Cramacrabou, of Owiawarou and of Point Espagnol. Each territory had its own chief, and a chief of chiefs appears only to emerge when the Caribs were on the warpath. The Chief of Chiefs was Joseph Chatoyer of whom we shall hear more. His consigliari, or chief adviser, was Jean Baptiste. Within his territory a member of the clan, usually the females, could cultivate plots, which some did, but not in a systematic or contiguous manner.

Apart from the conviction that the land was theirs, the get-rich-quick attitude generated so much greed among the English that there was little question of living and let live. It was each man for himself and the devil take the hindmost. As one or two of the more far-sighted English settlers foresaw, given the rapacity of their countrymen and the determination of the Black Caribs to hold on to their island, at least their section of it, it was not possible for the Black Caribs and the English to live in St. Vincent at one and the same time. One or the other would have to be removed.

To make matters worse, the best sugar lands in St. Vincent have always been in the heart of the Carib Country, (which is) that section of the island allocated to the Black Caribs by the Governor of Martinique in 1700. This area, stretching from the Byera River to Rabacca, the whole of which was then called Grand Sable, was the most densely populated area in the Carib Country. No clearer evidence of the area's suitability for sugar is needed than to note that long after the sugar industry ceased to be a viable proposition in the rest of St. Vincent, the crop was profitably grown and processed in that area. The industry only ceased to operate in 1962, when the area was once again racked by disputes.

The incompatibility of the desires of the Black Caribs on the one hand, and those of the English settlers on the other, was not immediately obvious to all. It was not until some thirty years after the commissioners had begun to sub-divide the island that the issue was finally resolved. The French suffered a great deal. With their slaves they numbered about 4,000 and were exporting annually some 30,000 pounds cocoa, 50,000 pounds of coffee and 13,000 pounds of cotton at this time. The English took over their farms and the French either had to repurchase them or leave the island, which many of them did. In the case of the Black Caribs, though the Treaty of Paris had made no mention of them, the English Government had specifically instructed the Commissioners "not to molest them in their possessions nor to attempt any survey of their country without previous and express orders from home." Both the commissioners and the settlers sought to get around this injunction.

The commissioners tried first to get the Caribs to become subjects of the English king, and to confine their activities to the lands they had cleared, handing over the rest to the commissioners to be sold. Chatoyer is reported to have asked Commission Chairman Young what king he was talking about. When this ruse failed, they tried to persuade the Black Caribs to evacuate St. Vincent and go and live on Bequia. Someone must have told Sir William Young that he could not, on the one hand, say that some of the ancestors of the Black Caribs - the shipwrecked Mocoes - had been forced to leave Bequia since there was not enough food there for them, and then turn around now, when the Black Caribs had become so numerous, and recommend their return to Bequia. This line of action was therefore speedily abandoned.

The commissioners then tried to deal with the Caribs through Abbé Valladores. One year after Labat's visit, around 1701, the Jesuits had closed down their missionaries in St. Vincent altogether. Contrary to what Van der Plas states, they evidently re-opened them soon afterwards, no doubt hoping that the gospel could be more successfully preached among the French and Black Caribs than it had been among the Yellow Caribs. Valladores was one of the missionaries and the Black Caribs had appointed him as their agent to negotiate with the English. They soon discovered Valladores had been thoroughly brainwashed by the English, and their confidence in him misplaced. He was slated for assassination but fortuitously escaped. The Black Caribs considered the subversion of their own agent Valladores to be the last straw and started to take reprisals for trespass on their land by destroying houses and plantations which had sprung up on their land contrary to the instruction of the commissioners by His Majesty's Government.

The commissioners now wrote home to the English Government; to paraphrase their letter would be to do injustice to it and it is reproduced in full below:

"The instructions we now have from your Lordships are, in our humble opinion, as proper as any that could have been devised for the purpose of settling the windward part of the country; but experience now shows us that it will be impossible, without imminent danger to the colony, to complete any settlement or arrangement with the Charaibs, let the terms proposed be ever so tender or advantageous, without a force sufficient to restrain and awe them into obedience; for which purpose it will be highly necessary to have a considerable military force on the island, before we again attempt to carry our instructions into execution, as we find their numbers greatly exceed what we formerly apprehended.

"We have the greatest reason to think that suffering the Charaibs to remain in their present state, will be very dangerous, and may at some period prove fatal to the inhabitants of the country, as their situation, surrounded with wood, makes any access to them, for the purpose of executing justice, impracticable; and they will from thence be capable of committing all outrages unpunished; or harbouring the slaves of the inhabitants for this island, as well as of all the neighbouring islands; of sheltering amongst those, vagabonds and deserters from the French, and in case of a rupture with France, it is probable they will join in distressing the inhabitants, and in an attempt to conquer the country."

Before a reply could even be received from the Government in England, the commissioners and settlers took it upon themselves to hire an armed sloop to patrol the waters of St. Vincent, not only to prevent the Black Caribs from consorting with the French, but also to reduce the possibility of the Caribs making forays on the plantations on the coast. On August 24, 1769 the armed vessel came upon four large canoes on the channel between St. Vincent. Each canoe contained about 20 armed Caribs and, it is said, was loaded with kegs of ammunition. The commander of the sloop ordered the canoes to hove to and approach in single file. The Black Caribs ignored this and continued to advance together, whereupon a shot was fired in their midst, which was answered with a volley of musket fire. The cannon fire continued and the canoes were sunk one by one.

The Caribs, despite these reverses continued to swim with their cutlasses in their mouths determined to board the English vessel on which two men had been killed and one wounded. Whereupon the captain of the sloop, deciding discretion was the bettor of valour, broke off the encounter and sailed away. He reported hopefully that all the Caribs must have perished. We shall never know if they did, but this seems unlikely since all accounts whether written by admirers or detractors note the amazing dexterity of the Caribs in water. What can be said with certainty is that this incident shows how strongly aggrieved the Caribs must have felt and the courage they were prepared to display in any encounter with their enemies.

While the commissioners were prepared to ignore the proclamation to a certain extent, they were not willing to go as far as the settlers. The latter sought to circumvent the commissioners by purchasing land direct from the Black Caribs. They were fully aware that, given the communal nature of their system of tenure, no single Carib could give a good title to land. They hoped, however, having got some title or other, they could convert it into a good title by having one of their contacts in high places in England intervene on their behalf. This attempt at by-passing the commissioners reduced the whole disposal of land by the commissioners to such a ridiculous farce that it is reported that three times as much land was sold as there was land in St. Vincent. One enterprising gentleman from Grenada, we are told, bought some 69,000 of the 85,000 acres that is St. Vincent.

The immediate cause of the outbreak of hostilities between the settlers and the Black Caribs was the sequel to the grant of 4,000 acres to General Monckton by the British Government. The General fought with Wolfe in Canada and had been in charge of the land forces when Rodney captured Martinique and St. Vincent in 1762. It was this expedition that had led to the cession of St. Vincent and some other islands to the British Government under the Treaty of Paris. The grant of 4,000 acres represented the General's reward for such gallant services. The land itself was situated north of the Couboumarou (Stubbs) River, and the General sold it to two speculators, Baillee and Gemmeltz who in turn sub-divided it and resold (it) to eager planters. It did not take long for these planters to discover how well suited to sugar cane the land was, mainly because of its fertility and easy topography.

The lesson was not lost on others who realized that the adjacent lands must be equally good or even better because of the easier gradients. This land was, of course, well within the Carib country, and when the settlers attempted to make incursions into it, they were vigorously opposed by the Black Caribs. All sorts of subterfuges were tried in an effort to allay the well-founded suspicions of the Black Caribs. One example of this is the effort to convince the Black Caribs that the survey parties that frequently visited the Carib country were there expressly for tracing a road that would facilitate the movement of produce by the Black Caribs. The Caribs themselves were not so easily duped and realized that after the road would come the troops to protect the inevitable settlers. The Black Caribs, therefore, constantly harassed the surveyors and this was construed, or perhaps misconstrued, as an act of aggression against His Majesty's Government.

Two regiments were ordered from North America to join those as could be spared from the neighbouring islands to subdue the Caribs. If they could not be subdued they were to be rounded up and transported to a place where they could no longer be a threat to the extension of the plantations in the island. Major General Dalrymple, the commander of the expedition, who in the eyes of the settlers acquitted himself admirably, was not able to subdue the Caribs until February 1773, almost one year after he had been ordered to do so.

Fortunately for the Black Caribs, not all Englishmen were blinded by the quest for quick riches through sugar cultivation. There were many who thought the Black Caribs had been wronged. Bryan Edwards was of this opinion and wrote to that effect. Sir William Young was obviously very disturbed by Edwards' observation for he went out of his way to discuss it in one of the rare footnotes in his monograph on the Black Caribs. He argued thus:

"Mr. Bryan Edwards, the elegant and able author of the History of the West Indian Islands, accurate and learned in other respects, hath been misinformed on the subject of the treatment of the Charaibs, the Charaib war, and on many particulars relating to St. Vincent's, consolation is, that the history of the West Indies cannot stop at a second edition."

As far as we are aware, Edwards never did commit any other opinion to writing.

It is perhaps worthwhile recording that on the one hand, Bryan Edwards' work, probably more so than any other contemporary historian, has stood the test of time, and after almost 200 years, is widely quoted. On the other hand, it would have been very difficult for the Sir William Youngs (father and son) to have been impartial on this subject, since they derived considerable pecuniary and other benefits from their association with St. Vincent. Sir William Young (Snr.) acquired most of what is possibly the best land on the Leeward side of the island, Pembroke Estate, a property of 1,000 acres, more or less. He also owned the Villa Estate on the southern side of the island, now the centre of the tourist business. There is a legend that one day, Sir William Young was being driven in his carriage, drawn by two magnificent white horses, when he met Paramount Chief Chatoyer who expressed admiration for the beasts. Sir William, in a fit of generosity offered them to him. Chatoyer in turn looked across the strait and pointed to the island and told Sir William he was more than welcome to it if he so desired. Today we still call the island Young's Island. Sir William Young (Jnr.) inherited these properties from his father and in later years became Governor of Tobago.

The British Government, too, seems to have agreed with Edwards' view and had some misgivings about Major Dalrymple's expedition. There was a feeling that the Caribs were an honest and peaceful people whom the avarice of the settlers had driven to fight for their freedom, and even their survival. As a result, a commission of enquiry was set up. They concluded that Dalrymple's expedition 'was founded on injustice and reflected dishonour on the national character, a violation of the natural rights of mankind and totally subversive of that it gloried to defend." As a result, orders were issued to put an end to the campaign and to offer honourable terms of peace to the Caribs. The terms of the treaty, which were printed in the St. Vincent Gazette of 1773, are set out below:

I.   All hostile proceedings to cease; a firm and lasting peace and friendship to succeed.

II.   The Charaibs shall acknowledge his Majesty to be the rightful sovereign of the island and domain of St. Vincent's; take an oath of fidelity to him as their King; promise absolute submission to his will, and lay down their arms.

III.   They shall submit themselves to the laws and obedience of his Majesty's government, with power to the Governor to enact further regulations for the public advantage as shall be convenient. (This article only respects their transactions with his Majesty's subjects not being Indians, their intercourse and customs with each other, in the quarters allotted them not being affected by it.) And all new regulations to receive his Majesty's Governor's approbation before carried into execution.

IV.   A portion of lands, hereafter mentioned, to be allotted for the residence of the Charaibs, viz. from the river Byera to Point Espagnol on the one side, and from the river Analibou to Point Espagnol on the other side, according to lines drawn by his Majesty's surveyors, from the sources of the rivers to the tops of the mountains; the rest of the lands, formerly inhabited by the Charaibs, for the future to belong entirely to His Majesty.

V.	Those lands not to be alienated, either by sale, lease, or otherwise, but to persons properly authorized by His Majesty to receive them.
VI.	Roads, ports, batteries, and communications to be made as his Majesty pleases.
VII.	No undue intercourse with the French islands to be allowed.
VIII.	Runaway slaves in the possession of the Charaibs are to be delivered up, and endeavours used to discover and apprehend the others; and an engagement in future, not to encourage, receive, or harbour any slave whatever; forfeiture of lands for harbouring; and carrying off the island a capital-crime.
IX.	Persons guilty of capital crimes against the English are to be delivered up.
X.	In time of danger to be aiding and assisting to His Majesty's subjects against their enemies.
XI.	The three chains to remain to his Majesty.
XII.	All conspiracies and plots against his Majesty, or his government to be made known to his Governor, or other civil magistrates.
XIII.	Leave (if required) to be given to the Charaibs to depart this island, with their families and properties, and assistance in their transportation.
XIV.	Free access to the quarters allowed to the Charaibs, to be given to persons properly empowered in pursuit of runaway slaves, and safe conduct afforded them.
XV.	Deserters from His Majesty's services (if any), and runaway slaves from the French, to be delivered up, in order that they may be returned to their masters.
XVI.	The chiefs of the different quarters are to render an account of the names and number of the inhabitants of their respective districts.
XVII.	The chiefs, and other Charaibs, inhabitants, to attend the Governor when required for his Majesty's service.
XVIII.	All possible facility, consistent with the laws of Great Britain, to be afforded to the Charaibs in the sale of their produce, and in their trade to the different British islands.
XIX.	Entire liberty of fishing, as well as the coast of St. Vincent's as at the neighbouring keys, to be allowed them.

XX.   In all cases, when the Charaibs conceive themselves injured by his Majesty's other subjects, or other persons, and are desirous of having reference to the laws, or to the civil magistrates, an agent, being one of his Majesty's natural born subjects, may be employed by themselves, or if more agreeable at his Majesty's cost.

XXI.   No strangers, or white persons, to be permitted to settle among the Charaibs, without permission obtained in writing from the Governor.

XXII.   These articles subscribed to and observed, the Charaibs are to be pardoned, secured, and fixed in their property, according to his Majesty's directions given, and all past offences forgot.

XXIII.   After the signing of this treaty, should any of the Charaibs refuse to observe the condition of it, they are to be considered and treated as enemies by both parties, and the most effectual means used to reduce them.

XXIV.   The Charaibs shall take the following oath, viz.

We A.B. do swear, in the name of the immortal God, and Christ Jesus, that we will bear true allegiance to his Majesty George the Third, of Great Britain, France, and Ireland, King, defender of the faith; and that we will pay due obedience to the laws of Great Britain, and the Island of St. Vincent's; and will well and truly observe every article of the treaty concluded between his said Majesty and the Charaibs; and we do acknowledge, that his said Majesty is rightful Lord and Sovereign of all the Island of St. Vincent's, and that the lands held by us the Charaibs, are granted through his Majesty's clemency.

On the part of his Majesty,

W. Dalrymple

On the part of the Charaibs,

Chatoyer

Doucre Baramont Lalime,

Junior Broca

Saioe

Francois Laron Saint Laron

Anisette

Clement

Bigott

Matthieu	Jean Baptiste
Jean Louis Pacquin	Dufonte
Gadel Goibau	Begot
John Baptiste	Boyordell
Lonen	Dirang
Boyudon	Simon
Du Vallet	Lalime,
Boucharie	Senior
Deruba Babilliard	Bauamont
Canaia	Justin Bauamont

What strikes one immediately about the whole treaty is how a Black Carib, more versed in the French language and institutions, could be expected to grasp the import of a document which required not only a sound knowledge of the English Language but also of English Law. Article XI mentions three chains that even today few people realize is a reference to a measurement from the shoreline delineating the area reserved for His Majesty's forces to establish forts and other military structures.

More seriously, let us look at Article XXIV. How could a Black Carib who did not believe in the Englishman's God and might never have been aware of His relationship with Jesus Christ, swear by them to an allegiance to His Majesty George II of Great Britain, both Britain and George III being nebulous entities to them? How could they be expected to heed the articles of a treaty, the language of which was alien to them and the spirit of which was contrary to all their instincts?

No one could seriously expect the terms of the treaty to endure. For one thing it formally reduced the area the Caribs considered theirs. The boundary having been shifted some ten miles from the present Stubbs to Byera. At the same time the best sugar lands, the original Grand Sable were still in the hands of the Black Caribs. Sooner or later the avarice and ill Judgment of the English settlers was bound to assert itself.

The Second Carib War

What Major Dalrymple's expedition and the treaty did for the Black Caribs was to give them a more realistic assessment of the forces that could be brought to bear against them. Hence they were able to evolve a more coherent strategy in trying to cope with these forces. The elements of this strategy were simple. Two conditions had to be met before they could carry out a successful onslaught on the settlers. First, the English military forces must be engaged overseas and so reduce the possibility of troops being sent to assist the settlers, as had happened in the case of Major Dalrymple.

Secondly, they must get the support of the French who would provide not only arms and ammunition but also troops.

When conditions were not favourable they should make conciliatory gestures to the English, such as prosecuting the French settlers before English courts and tribunals; sending their women folk to the English Sunday Markets to sell produce; operating lighters needed to transport sugar from shore to ship, and enjoying the hospitality with which people like Sir William Young tried to bribe them. In general, be at their friendliest while waiting for the opportunity to present itself. When conditions were favourable they would, with the French, descend not only on the English but also on such Frenchmen as had English sympathies with a view to annihilating all their enemies completely.

About 1779, the Black Caribs got the opportunity to put their strategy into practice. Great Britain was engaged with three of the great powers of Europe and also in the American colonies. Moreover, the settlers in St. Vincent were at loggerheads with the Governor Valentine Morris in one of those numerous feuds that punctuate the course of British colonial history. On this occasion, the quarrels seem to have been about the imposition of export duties, the French settlers and Carib lands. The slaves, too, were absconding in droves.

To make matters even more favourable for the Caribs, a Colonel Etherington had been sent out with some raw recruits to garrison the colony. The man is reported as having been a drummer who had been promoted to Colonel all too rapidly. He too had been infected with the get-rich-quick germ and no sooner had he arrived, than he obtained an estate well within the Carib lands on the Leeward side, probably in the area which is now called Top Hill. Apparently, he employed the usual methods to get land from the Caribs - first, he got one or more Caribs to agree to a transfer, and when the Governor who opposed it was away, Etherington persuaded the President of the Council to approve the transfer. Later, the Lords of the Treasury in the United Kingdom, no doubt at the instigation of Etherington's contacts there, ordered the Governor to confirm the title under the Great Seal. Etherington may have thought that he had outwitted the Black Caribs, but in the end, his action rebounded on him and on the settlers. It gave the Caribs a good pretext for recommencing hostilities and when they did, they and their allies found the settlers in no position to resist, since Etherington had been using the troops to develop his plantation and had completely neglected the island's defenses. One wonders if this was not what Chatoyer envisaged all along and so turned a blind eye to Etherington's action.

The Caribs began by going over to Martinique and informing the French of the dissension among the Governor, the Assembly and the Militia. They also let the French know that the keys to Wilkie's Battery (probably the site of the present Grand View Hotel) had been lost. The Caribs themselves may well have engineered the keys' disappearance since this was to have so profound an effect on the subsequent encounters. The French were delighted with this intelligence and immediately dispatched 5 armed vessels, four of which had been captured from the English while the other was French built. On board there were over five hundred troops under M. LeChevalier du Rumaine. They left St. Lucia on the night of the 10th June but because of bad weather did not arrive off Grand Sable until the 15th. M. Percin de la Roche in the French ship was detailed to land at Grand Sable, where he and his 45 men were to join the ever-ready Caribs. They were not able to land at Grand Sable, but did so at another spot, probably Byera Beach, and immediately captured Fort Colonaire. The Caribs then began to plunder the English plantations in this area, but were restrained by the French. The French considered this pillaging a waste of valuable time, as it was their plan to continue the march to Kingstown. And there join the forces from the other ships. Three of these had sailed along the coast, two anchoring in Young Bay (Villa) while the third proceeded to Warrawarou (Great Head).

As has already been mentioned, these ships were British built having in fact been captured from the English. The settlers were convinced that they were British merchantmen coming from Antigua to take sugar to England. Their anxiety to make the first shipment of sugar for the year must also have predisposed the settlers to think this way. They went so far as to forbid the gunner at Hyde's Point (Ratho Mill Point), who thought otherwise to fire on the ships. One settler, Mr. Collins, was so imprudent as to even board one of the ships and, totally confused, was taken prisoner by the French.

Another gentleman who had strenuously resisted Governor Morris' efforts to fortify his bay, that is Great Head Bay, was seized and stripped almost naked by the invading French. The fact that his underwear seemed to be of an unusual variety added to his discomfiture.

M. Du Rumaine and his 500 troops advanced on Kingstown and decided to attack the fort there. As they began to advance they saw about 600 Caribs shouting loudly in their usual manner - M. Percin de la Roche with his army of Frenchmen, free negroes, mulattoes and Black Caribs had arrived. They had overrun the Windward side from Fort Colonaire, which had been their first conquest.

Governor Morris wanted to make a last stand at Sion Hill. He was about to fire his only cannon, when Etherington snatched the fuse away from him, thus preventing any firing. Etherington reasoned with some justification that if they did not oppose the French, the terms of capitulation would be easier as they in fact turned out to be. Under the terms of the Treaty, the Governor, officers, and soldiers were to be taken to Antigua and exchanged for French prisoners. As for the settlers, they now had to pay for the upkeep of the French troops. They complained bitterly about this, though they ought to have considered themselves lucky, for it was the French who restrained the Black Caribs from massacring them. In any case, when the island was restored to the British in 1783, the amounts paid to the French were deducted from the arrears of taxes due to the British Treasury during the French occupation. The restoration itself took place in January 1784 and was part of the Treaty of Versailles.

With the departure of the French the Black Caribs who had seized every opportunity to vent their spleen on the English, once again had to eat the humble pie and resort to their conciliatory gestures. The English welcomed these gestures and let bygones be bygones. This is not as stupid or altruistic as may appear at first sight, as the settlers wanted to remain in St. Vincent and eventually get hold of the Grand Sable area, but by their own admission, they were mortally afraid of the Black Caribs, since the latter's excesses knew no bounds when once their anger was aroused.

The ideas that inspired the French Revolution crossed the Atlantic and were disseminated by French Agents throughout the Caribbean. Trouble commenced thus at St. Domingo in 1789 and very soon reached Martinique, where all the forces of law and order broke down. The Caribs were aware of all this but did not consider it meet to revolt just yet since they were not certain of French support. All this changed when in 1794 the arch-revolutionary Victor Hugues contrived to being about a successful uprising in Guadeloupe. He then recruited agents whom he sent to St. Vincent and other islands to work on French settlers there. Many of these were only too glad to get an opportunity to get back at the British by inciting the Black Caribs to revolt. The type of propaganda they spread among the Caribs is reported in Shepherd and is here quoted verbatim:

"Behold your chains forged and imposed by the hands of the tyrannical English! Blush, and break those ensigns of disgrace, spurn them with becoming indignation, rise in a moment, and while we assist you from motives of the philanthropy and zeal for the happiness of all nations, fall on these despots, extirpate them from the country, and restore yourselves, your wives and children to the in. heritance of your fathers, whose spirits from the grave will lead on your ranks, inspire you with fury, and help you to be avenged." The Caribs gleefully embraced the doctrine. But one should not take these professions of philanthropy by the French too seriously. Some, if not all of them, must have hoped that English and Caribs would destroy each other and leave the island to them. This was an exercise in which both the French and the Caribs sought to use each other.

Martinique, then being in the hands of the English, it was agreed that arms and ammunition would be sent from Guadeloupe. The plan was for the Caribs of the Leeward under Paramount Chief Chatoyer, and those of the Windward under deputy Duvallé to converge on Kingstown, join forces with their French allies and massacre all whites regardless of sex or age. They would then fan out across the country to ensure total elimination of all the English and their supporters. The deadline for the uprising was the night of the 10th of March, 1795 to coincide with similar uprisings in other islands where Hugues' agents had already laid the groundwork.

The plan went awry, and the deadline was not adhered to, probably because of poor communications and also because overriding factors caused the uprising to start in Grenada at an earlier date. This gave the President of the Council in that island an opportunity to forewarn his colleagues in the other islands. The news reached St. Vincent on March 5th, and the Governor immediately placed the troops on the alert and got the defenses of Kingstown in a state of readiness. During the course of the next few days, English settlers in Marriaqua and Massarica (South Union) areas told the Governor that they had been reliably informed that a Carib uprising was imminent. The Governor contacted Chatoyer and Duvallé, and requested their presence at a meeting of the Council fixed for the following Tuesday. This was a rather strange coincidence since it was the very day that had been fixed for the commencement of hostilities. The Caribs replied with the now famous sentence, "It is too late, it might have been sent sooner." The heads of other clans were also contacted and they professed complete ignorance of any form of disorder, planned or otherwise.

The Caribs realized there was no time to lose and started the uprising on Sunday March 8th with the burning of Madam La Croix's estate at Evesham Vale. To this day, the area is called La Croix and the remains of an old sugar mill can still be seen there. The campaign was to be a long end bitter one, and impressed itself so firmly on the minds of the settlers that they commissioned an historian, Shepherd, to record it, in almost overwhelming detail, for posterity. Broadly speaking, there were three phases of this second Carib War, which is described in British Colonial history as the Brigands War, though who exactly were the brigands in the whole affair is a moot question, the answer depending to a great extent on where one's sympathies lay. The first phase began with the burning of the La Croix estate and ended with the death of Chatoyer on the night of March 14th. During this phase, the Caribs were well organized and very much on the offensive. The second phase was more a war of attrition, with the Caribs resorting to guerilla tactics, biding out in widely separated areas and pouncing on the settlers when the opportunity arose. This phase came to an end with the arrival of General Abercrombie in June 1796, when the English went on the offensive and set out in systematic and ruthless manner to get rid of the Caribs. Here no attempt shall be made to examine the vagaries of the second phase which be followed in all its labyrinthine details in Shepherd's "Historical Account of the Island of St. Vincent." Attention is concentrated on the first and third phases.

The burning of Madame La Croix's property did not go unheeded. The settlers sent out a detachment from the militia to investigate. Later that same night they came upon some huts occupied by some Carib and French families who were in the throes of celebration and in an advanced state of intoxication. This put them at a disadvantage, and it was not until they were almost surrounded by the troops that they realized what was happening. However, most of them still managed to escape, only a handful being taken prisoner.

In the North Windward, Duvallé had not been idle for, by the next day, he had devastated the countryside, burning all sugar works, killing all the English and their sympathisers, even their cattle. His progress was made infinitely easier as a result of the fate of the first English soldiers who had been sent into the area. They were cunningly ambushed by the Caribs in the South Union area and almost wiped out. The few who managed to reach Kingstown had to use elaborate detours and avoid the main highway. The stories they told of the treatment meted out to their late colleagues were sufficient to daunt the stoutest heart. Many settlers simply fled from their plantations on the Windward coast long before Duvallé could reach them. He himself reached Dorsetshire Hill on the morning of the 12th. There he pulled down the British Flag and raised the new flag of the French Republic. No time was wasted and with what can only be described as herculean efforts, the Caribs dismantled the fort at Stubbs Bay and dragged a 12-pounder, which weighed about 3,000 pounds and a small four-pounder, all the way to Dorsetshire Hill. By the night of the 14th, they had the four-pounder mounted.

Chatoyer, in the meanwhile, was heading for Kingstown from Chateaubelair. En route, he was joined by the French settlers, some of whom subsequently said they had done so under duress. Unlike Duvallé, he did not destroy property, but reserved his fury for the settlers. His idea seems to have been to keep the properties intact so that he could operate them after he had won the war. It is claimed that he had earmarked Keartons, as it was called then and still is, for himself. Much has been said of how Chatoyer took three Englishmen captive and on arrival at Dorsetshire single-handedly hacked them to pieces, all the while giving vent to his hatred of the English. Much has also been said of how the Caribs killed an estate manager by running him through the rollers of a cane mill. But one has to try and see all this in its proper perspective. After all, these people, at least some of them, were descendants of runaway slaves from Barbados. Now, one punishment meted out by English settlers to slaves caught attempting to run away was boiling in molasses. Chatoyer eventually joined Duvallé on Dorsetshire Hill.

The Governor with his staff and documents took refuge in the Fort at Berkshire Hill. Reinforcements arrived from Martinique, which, as was previously mentioned, had fallen to the English. A force comprising these troops, the local militia and some negroes stormed Dorsetshire Hill on the night of March 14th. A vigorous skirmish ensued, with the Caribs well on the way to carrying the day. Chatoyer, for his part, had, by this time, become fully convinced of the truth of the legend that he could not be killed by mortal means. He allowed his vanity to run away with him and he made the fatal mistake of challenging Major Leith to a duel. Leith was a trained army officer and would obviously have been proficient with the sword. Chatoyer, who had put himself at this disadvantage, was killed. For Leith, it was, however, a pyrrhic victory, as he died soon afterwards, it was said, from the exertions of the war. His mortal remains lie under the chandelier in the Anglican Cathedral in Kingstown.

No objective assessment of Chatoyer as a person or military leader has ever been made. It is difficult to do so now with the limited information available. Not only nearly 200 years have passed, but even the archaeologist would be hard put to unearth much information since two series of volcanic eruptions, one in 1812 and the other in 1902, have literally wrought havoc with even the topography of Chatoyer's home and headquarters, Morne Ronde. We do not have a clue as to his final resting place. Nevertheless, there are a few indications, which even the passage of time and natural disasters cannot obscure.

In the first place, the Caribs were a fiercely individualistic people living in clans, each clan having its own chief, and there is evidence to suggest that the chieftaincy was not an hereditary institution, but rather one is led to believe that the chief was an individual who had distinguished himself in war or in other respects, and consequently held in high regard by all others. The literature is replete with references to feuds among the Black Caribs, some of whom were only too glad to live near the English to protect themselves from their countrymen. Further, the institution of Chief of Chiefs was not known among them except in times of emergency. Yet, Chatoyer appears not only to have been the paramount military chief, but also the civilian one. For example, Sir William Young and his family whose status, if anything, was not subordinate to that of the local Governor, by his own admission went out of his way to cultivate the friendship of this man, which suggests he must have been considered the ranking civilian among the Black Caribs.

In his domestic affairs he was undoubtedly a remarkable person, as all written accounts of him are adorned by the reproduction of the famous painting showing him with his five wives. That this is the only contemporary painting of the Black Caribs suggests that the phenomenon of multiple wives in a single household must have impressed itself on the mind of the English whose culture afforded them but a single wife.

In war he must have been an outstanding commander for his forces included not only his fellow Caribs, but also French troops. Neither they nor his fiercely individualistic countrymen would have subordinated themselves to him in war, had he not been an outstanding General.

In heat of battle, unlike Duvallé, he did not destroy property for the sake of vandalism, but sought to preserve it so that he could use it in the future. This may be construed as self-interest; nevertheless it does show much foresight.

But perhaps the most pointed indication of his generalship was what happened to his troops on his death. Most of the French immediately forsook the Carib cause and with maximum speed tried to seek refuge at Layou. Unfortunately most of them, including M, DuMont, the Secretary of the conspiracy, never made it. They were caught, hanged and committed to the tide. The Black Caribs were evidently dumbfounded at this event, the death of the invincible Chatoyer. They retreated to their villages and took some time to recover from the shock. Henceforth, the very character of the war assumed an entirely different complexion.

As already mentioned, this the second phase of the Carib War was one of guerilla type activity and fluctuating fortunes. The Caribs were evidently trying to conserve their numbers, and at the same time, decimate those of the settlers to such an extent that they could once again make an all out attack on the enemy with reasonable hope of success. This was not to be since the English, being relieved on other fronts, mainly those involving the Great Powers, were able to devote adequate numbers of their professional soldiers to the task of suppressing the uprising. Lieutenant General Sir Ralph Abercrombie was dispatched to the Eastern Caribbean, and his arrival in June marked the beginning of the third and final phase of the war.

Abercrombie set about his task in a thoroughly professional manner. Before coming to St. Vincent he called at St. Lucia and captured that island on March 17, 1796. As far as the Black Caribs were concerned, the most crucial term in the list of conditions under which the French in that island surrendered was that all white, and free coloured, persons were to be extradited to England as prisoners of war. This meant that in a single stroke the Caribs lost their main source of arms, ammunition and additional personnel. Further, most of the non-Vincentian French fighting with the Caribs had lost their home base. This must have been a severe blow to the morale of the Black Caribs and they may have realized that the end of the road must be in sight. Nevertheless, they used their considerable wiles to postpone the inevitable for as long as possible.

Abercrombie first arrived in St. Vincent on June 3rd and after a short sojourn to Carriacou to attend to some similar business, returned on the 7th. He threw 6 columns with a total of about 4,000 men in the field against the Caribs. Their first success was at Vigie where the Caribs surrendered on June 10th. In adversity the Black Caribs did not forget their friends. They specifically requested that such French and free mulattoes as were fighting with them be included in the terms of the military surrender. The terms of surrender took some time to be negotiated and many of the Caribs used the opportunity to slip away and create as much havoc as they could in the Colonarie and Mt. William areas. Against overwhelming odds, they could not keep it up and again sent a flag of truce to the fort at Mt.Young, now called Chester Cottage.

They tried to convince the English that they had been at war, and everything that had been done was done in the spirit of war. If they had burnt the English houses and canefields, the English had in turn burnt their canoes and destroyed their provision grounds. The war was over and both sides should revert to the status quo. The English replied that there was no room for negotiation and unconditional surrender their only hope for survival; otherwise, all their forces would be unleashed on them. The Caribs argued that they could not recall any act on their part that would justify such extreme measures and requested time for their chiefs to consult.

In the meantime, planters asked their agents in London to suggest that the Caribs be removed from St. Vincent. The memorandum submitted in England was signed by no less a person than one of the ubiquitous Youngs, Sir William Young (Jnr). The Governorin-Council ordered the banishment of the Caribs to the Bay Islands of Honduras, whose capital is still Roatan. The Caribs, however, were not going so easily. When the answer to their request for a truce was sent, it was found that they had vanished from their normal haunts. No further military action was taken against them and once again they began to visit Kingstown to sell ground provisions and baskets.

A meeting of citizens chaired by the Governor was called to decide what effective measures could be taken against them. It was agreed that the Caribs would surrender and be taken to the Grenadine Island of Balliceaux where adequate water, food and shelter would be provided until they could be sent to Roatan. Several of the Carib chiefs were taken to Kingstown where they were officially informed of the plan and were given 4 days in which to inform their people and communicate their acquiescence. The alternative was the reopening of the war. They promised to comply, but again many of them did their disappearing act and only about 280 were embarked from Calliaqua on July 20th for Balliceaux.

The troops were now sent to bring them in, but the Caribs would beckon the troops on and fire on them. This was not the type of humour that appealed to Abercrombie and his men, and they dealt with the Caribs in no uncertain manner. Grand Sable was literally reduced to ashes. Over 1,000 huts, many canoes including the Carib men-of-war and their enormous stores of provisions were put to the torch. The Caribs still would not give in, but resorted to hiding in the woods. This proved frustrating to the troops until they hit on the idea of destroying all provision grounds and sending two Caribs back from Balliceaux to tell those in hiding how well they were being treated in the camps at Balliceaux. These tactics had the desired effect. At last, in early October, most of the Black Caribs, some 5,080 of them including Duvallé, Chatoyer's son and many women and children, gave themselves up. They consoled themselves that they were not the first, nor would they be the last people to be defeated in war. They had fought a good fight and been beaten by a great nation. The Caribs were taken to Bequia and made to embark on the transports, which set sail for Roatan on March 11, 1797.

This was not the end of the Carib story in St. Vincent. The Yellow Caribs who numbered only a few hundred and had not been involved in the long drawn out hostilities were given a reservation at Old Sandy Bay, which, like all reservations, proved inadequate. The first Government to take any interest in these people removed them to their present home, New Sandy Bay, a much less inhospitable area. Such of the Black Caribs as did not surrender, the most elusive ones, went into the bush mainly in the Upper Massarica Valley now known as Greggs. Later they were given a reservation in this same area at the foothills of Petit Bonum. Others on the Leeward side were given an impossible area at Morne Ronde and near the Lariki River, where only iguanas seem able to survive. The Black Caribs in the latter areas fled in terror before the 1812 eruption of the Soufriere, both Morne Ronde and Lariki lying directly in the path of mud, dust and ash coming from the volcano. Afterwards they were given lands at Rose Bank and Windsor Forest. A few migrated to Trinidad in 1812.

Epilogue

The Black Caribs did not remain long in Roatan. At the invitation of the Governor of Honduras, they soon crossed into that country. There, many of them got embroiled in the wars of the day, between royalist and republican forces. When the royalist forces eventually lost, some of the Caribs who had served with them were forced to flee to British Honduras, mainly to the Stann Creek and Punta Gorda areas. There, Thomas Young in his "Narrative of a Residence on the Mosquito Shore during 1839, 1840 and 1841" provided the first written account of the Black Caribs in their new homes.

Young highlighted their great facility for language, noting that many of them spoke Spanish, French, Creole and English, besides Carib. A century later, Taylor was to tell of having met a Black Carib schoolteacher who spoke Carib at home, Spanish and Mayan in the village and taught in English and Mayan at school.

Young went on to describe them as being peaceable, friendly, ingenious, industrious, extremely loud of dressing up and anxious to obtain an education. It is hardly likely that in the space of less than 50 years, the character of a people could have undergone so drastic change. No doubt the Black Caribs had always been like that, but the rapacity of the English planters in St. Vincent had brought out the worst aspects of their character. Young predicted that 50 years after he wrote, the Black Caribs would become very numerous, friendly, but jealous of their rights.

The prediction turned out to be extremely accurate. In 1949 when Douglas Taylor did his study of the Black Caribs, he found that there were some 30,000 Black Caribs living in 25 settlements in three different countries: the

Republic of Honduras, British Honduras, and Guatemala. Trujillo, in the Republic of Honduras, is still considered their 'capital,' though they also predominate in the towns of Punta Gorda, Stann Creek, (British Honduras) and Livingston (Guatemala). It has also been observed that Black Caribs are to be found in Nicaragua, Costa Rica and Yucatan

They have never lost their identity, remaining unto this day, a distinct race. Inter-marriage, on the rare occasions it has taken place, has been mainly to the Miskito Indians of the Republic of Honduras who, like themselves, are descended from runaway slaves and Indians native to Central America. They continue to speak Carib, though this has never become a written language. Cassava still plays a major role in their diet and the implements used to process are much the same as the ones used by their Indian ancestors in St. Vincent.

As had been the case in St. Vincent, the Black Caribs of Central America rarely live far from the coast. If one were to speak of a Carib country today, it would be the littoral stretching from the Black River in the Republic of Honduras to Stann Creek in British Honduras. Their great skill as seamen, which so amazed even their enemies in St. Vincent, has been handed down from generation to generation. The ships that ply the coast between Honduras and Florida are manned mainly by Black Carib crews. This is not to say they have not moved into the other fields such as mahogany logging and grapefruit canning. They are also to be found in the public service in British Honduras, particularly the teaching service. It has been estimated that some 75 per cent of the rural teachers are Black Caribs. One, having risen to the highest level in the British Honduras civil service, joined the staff of the University of the West Indies and is now with the World Bank. He and his father, who stated that his grandmother was among those banished from St. Vincent, visited this state recently to see what they would find out about their ancestors. In recent years, many others have attended the University of the West Indies. Long before this, some of them had become priests and politicians. The charge that they are looked down on and discriminated against in British Honduras is beginning to wear a little thin. In the polyglot population of that country, the Black Caribs are playing a prominent part.

Very often comparison is made between the progress the Caribs in Central America have made as against the retardation of those in St. Vincent. What is generally not recognized is that we are talking of two different sets of people. In St. Vincent, when we speak of Caribs, we usually mean the Caribs of Sandy Bay. These are not Black Caribs at all, but the direct descendants of Indo-Caribs or Yellow Caribs as they are called. Their physical characteristics attest to this. Labat and others writing three centuries ago, observed that the Black Caribs in fact inherited more of the negro characteristics than those of the Indians. All observers in Central America have come to the same conclusion.

The few Black Caribs who escaped exile to British Honduras, as was mentioned, lived in the Greggs Mountains and were later given a reservation at the foot of these mountains. There, they merged with the descendants of the slaves and in a very short while, the difference in origin was quickly forgotten. Most Vincentians do not even know there was a Carib reservation or settlement at Greggs. However, when Taylor writes that the Black Caribs in British Honduras are outspoken and almost aggressive in interpersonal relations, no one who knows the people of Greggs in St. Vincent will for a moment deny that they are indeed the true descendants of the Black Caribs and the cousins of those in Central America.

Bibliography

Coke, Thomas, History of the West Indies, Vols. London, 1970.

Edwards, Bryon, The History, Civil and Commercial of the British West

Indies.Vols. London, 1818-1819.

Labat, Jean-Baptiste, Voyage aux Isles de l'Amerique, Vols. Paris

The Fall of the Planter Class in the Caribbean, 1763-1783, New York, 1963.

Shepherd, Charles, An Historical Account of the Island of St. Vincent, London, 1971.

Southey, Thomas, Chronological History of the West Indies, Vols. London, 1968.

Taylor, Douglas Macrae, The Black Carib of British Honduras. New York, 1967.

Van der Plas, Gualbart, The History of the Massacre of two Jesuit Missionaries in the Island of St. Vincent. Kingstown, 1964.

Waters, Ivor, The Unfortunate Valentine Morris Chepstow, U.K., 1964.

Young, Thomas, Narrative of a Residence on the Mosquito Shore during the years 1839, 1840, 1841. London

Young, Sir William, An Account of the Black Charaibs in the Island of St. Vincent's., London, 1971.

The Brigands's War in St Vincent: The view from the French records, 1794-1796

Curtis Jacobs

In memory of George Louison 1941-2003

Background to 1794

The Brigands' War - also called 'The Second Carib War' - took place in the Eastern Caribbean, particularly in the Windward Islands, between 1794 and 1798. Today, it is an almost forgotten episode in the history of the then mortal struggle between Britain and France throughout the eighteenth century, for control of this sub-region of the Caribbean.

The origins of this conflict, however, go back even further then the eighteenth century and into the very beginning of the European presence. Whereas the Spaniards quickly subdued the indigenous peoples of the Greater Antilles of the west Caribbean, those of the eastern Caribbean had held up the advance of European colonisation for two centuries. After the original Spanish colonisers had effectively passed from the scene, the indigenous peoples found themselves in a three-cornered contest between the rival colonialisms of Britain and France. This lasted from around 1625 to 1796.[1]

St Vincent was caught in the middle of this conflict. By the end of the seventeenth century, however, a new people had emerged on the island. According to Shephard, around 1675, a slave ship was wrecked on the coast of what is known today as Bequia. The survivors of this shipwreck were then accepted by the indigenous peoples who then inhabited the island. Through inter-marriage between the two peoples, a new people appeared. They were called the 'Black Caribs' as distinct from the 'Yellow Caribs,' the original inhabitants.[2]

These indigenous peoples and their African-descended cousins succeeded in keeping the Europeans at bay for a time, to the point where both British and French were forced to recognise St Vincent as one of several 'Neutral Islands' at the Treaty of Aix-la-Chapelle.[3] At the end of the Seven Years' War (1756-63), the British right to St Vincent was conceded by the French, along with Grenada, the Grenadines, Dominica, and Tobago. Together, they were called the 'Ceded Islands', which Britain organised as the 'Government of Grenada' in 1763.

The Seven Years' War was probably the most decisive of the Anglo-French colonial wars of the eighteenth century. The French lost to the British in India, North America (Canada) and the eastern Caribbean. However, the vanquished French never lost interest in these territories and only waited for time and circumstance for the opportunity to regain them.

If the French had, albeit grudgingly, accepted British rule of St Vincent, the so-called 'Black Caribs' did not. They challenged the British at every opportunity, even to the point of attacking those officials sent out to survey the land and organise the territory.

It was not surprising that open warfare broke out between the indigenous peoples and the British, who, under military pressure, were forced to propose terms of peace, which, were signed on 17 February 1773. This treaty was based upon the treaty between the British and the Maroons of Jamaica several decades before. Under the terms of the 1773 treaty, the indigenous people recognised George III as their sovereign. They were also required to come to the King's assistance in times of emergency. These terms would assume great legal significance more than twenty years later, but for the moment, the treaty confirmed the loss of some "4,414 squares of good land." They however retained their right to exist as an independent nation and to an area of reduced territory in the northern third of the island.[4]

Five years of uneasy peace followed, lasting until the War of the American Independence broke out in 1776. After France's entry into the war against the British, the indigenous peoples rose against their British rulers and assisted the French in recapturing the island in 1779. Under French rule, their lands were restored to them and in return helped the French in successfully resisting a British attempt to recapture the colony in 1780.[5] Like the French of Grenada in 1783, the indigenous peoples and their French colonists were abandoned to the tender mercies of the British, to whom France ceded St Vincent at the Treaty of Versailles, which ended the War of the American Independence.

The restoration of British power in 1784 only served to exacerbate the tensions between the Black Caribs and British. The British rebuilt the military posts that had been constructed up to 1779 and which had been destroyed. The Caribs then revolted and it was only after reinforcements were brought in from Grenada that calm was restored.

British entry into the French Revolutionary War against France in 1793 made for renewed conflict in St Vincent. Matters came to a head in 1794, with the arrival of Victor Hugues and a small force from France. The French arrived off the coast of Guadeloupe in June 1794, only to find that the British under Grey and Jervis had already captured France's entire eastern Caribbean Empire.[6] Hugues managed to land on Guadeloupe and captured the colony after fierce fighting. From this position, Hugues began to not only recapture lost French territory but also to take the war to the British. The period of Hugues's attempt to recapture territories lost to the British and to capture British territory, is called 'The Brigands' War.' William Dyott, a British Lieutenant whose first active service was in the Grenada theatre of Brigands' War - and who later became a General and aide-de-camp to King George III - described the 'brigands' in 1796 as "emancipated slaves and whites of extreme democratic principles."[7]

Hugues was officially sent out to the Windwards to implement the 'le Decret du 16 pluviôse' in France's colonies in the eastern Caribbean. This decree was, in effect, the ratification of the unilateral declaration of Sonthonax in St. Domingue of August 29, 1793. Faced with invasion by the British and threatened by internal enemies, the French Commissioner declared emancipation of the some half million enslaved Africans in the still French colony. This created an army of more or less similar size to resist the red-coated British invaders.

When Sonthonax's decision came before the French National Convention on the 16 day of pluviôse of the French Revolutionary calendar (February 5, 1794), the situation had changed. The British had invaded France's colonies in the eastern Caribbean. The Convention not only ratified the decision taken in St. Domingue; slavery was declared abolished in all of France's colonies and all persons domiciled therein, regardless of origin, Citizens of the Republic of France.[8]

This is the decree that Hugues was sent out by the French National Convention to implement in the Windward Islands - Les Îles Du Vent - from 1794. To aid him in this task, Hugues brought several powerful weapons: a printing press and a guillotine, which, according to the British military historian Sir John Fortescue, was the only guillotine that operated outside of France during the revolutionary period.[9]

Hugues's real objective, however, was to regain France's empire in the eastern Caribbean. In order to accomplish this task, Hugues adopted the strategy of recruiting to his cause those people and groups that had long had grievances living under British rule, and reviving long-standing relationships that existed between groups and the French. In St Vincent, the French faced the situation where there were people with whom they had maintained long-standing friendships and were also discontented with British rule. These made for a close alliance in 1794-95.

Hugues, however, was the representative of a country and government that on one level, had been locked in a struggle with Britain throughout the eighteenth century, and despite France being in the throes of revolution during this period, had not abandoned their ambitions for territorial expansion.

On the other hand, the groups nursing long-standing grievances over British rule were not, in the first instance, concerned with France's colonial ambitions. Their immediate aim was the redress of their respective grievances.

The documents that have survived show the complicated nature of the relationships that Hugues was required to cultivate and maintain as he strove for France's survival as a colonial power in the Caribbean. His situation was rendered even more uncertain after July 1794 - the revolutionary month of 'Thermidor' - when the leader of the Jacobins and his mentor, Maximilien Robespierre, fell from power and was himself executed on the guillotine. During the fourteen month period called 'The Thermidorean Reaction' Hugues faced the situation where the government in France had changed but in the colonies the government remained Jacobin. Had Hugues been in France, he would have certainly followed Robespierre, Saint-Just and Couthon to the guillotine. In the eastern Caribbean, however, he managed to maintain an aggressive French presence while France itself the Revolution was over and events were moving towards reaction. As such, his situation did not receive as high a priority in Paris as his British counterparts did in London.

The French documents on the period of 'The Brigands' War' are, collectively, one of the remaining frontiers for historians of the Anglophone Caribbean. In France itself, they lie in the Centre d'Archives d'Outre Mer (C.A.O.M.) at Aix-en-Provence, in pristine condition, strong evidence that they have not been studied much by historians during the last 200 years. They make interesting reading for several reasons. The first is that they were meant for the eyes of Frenchmen only. The authors of these dispatches knew that these documents were never certain to arrive safely in France. The British navy controlled much of the Atlantic, and French ships were likely to be captured before they reached France. As such, the language appears to have been deliberately garbled so as to confuse readers unfamiliar with the French language. While that was a useful technique to confuse the British, for researchers in the twenty-first century they present special problems of deciphering first, translating second.

The documents that relate to the French involvement in The Brigands' War are comprised of two main groups. The former is that set of dispatches between Guadeloupe and Victor Hugues and the revolutionaries at St Vincent. These documents are, in the main, are concerned with the keeping the Vincentians supplied with sufficient arms, ammunition and money. The latter are comprised of those from Guadeloupe and Paris. These are, in the main, reports of developments in the colony, and the progress of the French efforts to bring this territory under French control.

The documents consulted for the present paper are, for the most part, drawn from the latter. Time and circumstances did not permit an examination of the former in time for the present conference. They relate, for the most part, to the period June 1794 to August 1796. This covers the major period of The Brigands' War in St Vincent (March 1795 to June 1796).

The Brigands' War: 1795-96

The evidence strongly suggests that, although Hugues's agents had made contact with the major groups dissatisfied with British rule in St Vincent (and Grenada), the immediate drive to revolutionary violence did not arise from the instructions from Hugues himself. The actual impulse came in fact from Grenada. Fédon's Rebellion broke out during March 2-3, 1795. Within twenty-four hours, the revolutionaries had captured the Lieutenant Governor and members of the upper echelons of Grenada's colonial establishment. The Acting Governor, Mackenzie, immediately sent out messages of distress to all neighbouring colonies, both British and Spanish.

Seton, the Governor of St Vincent, upon receipt of the news from Grenada, immediately summoned Chatoyer and other leaders of the Carib community to a meeting. This was undoubtedly in accordance with the 1773 Treaty, which required the Caribs to come to the King's assistance in times of emergency. Unknown to Seton, Chatoyer and his followers were themselves planning similar revolutionary action to their Grenadian counterparts. Chatoyer and his followers, thinking that their plot had been discovered, stalled for time and later declined to accept Seton's invitation, all the while accelerating their own plans for armed revolution.[10]

Shephard observes that the Caribs' joining the war on the side of the French against the British was the subject of doubt, particularly during the period immediately preceding Hugues's arrival in June 1794. This proclamation from Hugues, demonstrates the appeal that the French overtures had upon the Caribs after June 1794:

LIBERTY - LAW - EQUALITY

The Commissioners, delegated by the National Convention to the Windward Islands, to General Chatoyer, chief of a free nation [i.e., the Caribs of St Vincent].

The French nation in combating with despotism is allied to all free people: it desires nothing but liberty. It has always sustained the Caribs against the vile attempts of the English. The time is arrived when the ancient friendship between the French people and the Caribs ought to be renewed. They should exterminate their common enemy, the English.

We swear friendship and assistance in the name of the French nation to you and your comrades... Attack! Exterminate all the English in St Vincent; but give means to the French to second you. We have nominated citizen Toraille Captain, and citizen Michael Mather Lieutenant of the Infantry of the Republic.[11]

This was a general proclamation. According to Dubois, Hugues appointed Chatoyer, Chief of the Caribs, general in the army of France. In this message, Hugues declared the French position on what was perhaps the most important issue before the Caribs since the start of British colonial rule:

Victor Hugues leur avait envoyé des emissaires pour les inciter à la révolte et nommé général leur chef: "Chatouillet" - Dites à notre frère le général Chatouillet que la nation Française leur rendra les terres que les Anglaises ont usurpées sur eux.[12]

Victor Hugues had sent emissaries to incite them to revolt. "Tell our brother general Chatoyer that that the lands usurped from him by the English will be returned by the French nation."

Taken together, Hugues drew upon the historical ties that existed between the French and the Caribs, and the prospect of even closer ties. However, from the standpoint of his quest to conquer the island from the British, Dubois may have lost sight of the fact that the Caribs possessed issues and resources of their own. The issues of equality and that of land tenure were longstanding grievances of the Caribs. They stood to be redressed whether or not the French had decided to make war against the British during the period of the French revolution. The Caribs' decision to cast in their lot with the French was a strategic alliance with a major European nation to settle grievances of long standing. With the 'decree of pluviôse' France had created the archetype of the first super-state. As the National Convention had declared all persons living in all of France's colonies Citizens of the Republic of France, she had extended her boundaries beyond the 'natural' ones of the Pyrennes and the Rhine. The Republic was extended to any colony, as Hugues declared "conquered or to be conquered." In this declaration issued by Hugues and Lebas in both French and English, the French intentions were clearly stated:

Time and the defeat of the English forces in Guadeloupe have weakened the remembrance of the heinous crimes, by which the vile Satellites of George had sullied the Windward Islands... we hereby give solemn Notice to the Commanders in Chief of the British forces in the Windward Islands, That, from and after the Date of this our Declaration, the Assassination of each and every Individual Republican (of whatever Colour he is, and in whatever island it may happen) shall be expiated by the Death of two English Officers our Prisoners. The Guillotine shall, in the first Notice thereof, perform this Act of Justice.[13]

Like Boukman in St Domingue, Chatoyer apparently did not live for long after the outbreak of the revolutionary struggle on March 10. He who lit the torch of revolution was believed killed on March 14. Duvallé had assumed command. In this Proclamation, published on "le 11 germinal, l'an 3" (March 31, 1795), Hugues, Goyrand and Lebas informed the entire Windward Islands that:

...ARRÊTENT que la nation Caraïbe ayant des traités avec la nation française, à laquelle elle a été constamment attachée, et qu'en vertu des pouvoirs a nous donnés, avons nommé le citoyen Duvalay (leur chef) officier des armées de la republique française, conjointment avec les citoyens Torailles et Michel Mathieu, republicains Français, leur enjuignons d'user de représailles envers les Anglais dans les Îles Saint Vincent, etc. etc., après leur avoir signifié le présent arrêté par un parlementaire.[14]

The outbreak of hostilities in both Grenada and St Vincent was something of which Hugues and Lebas advised France. In these dispatches, the two colonies, conceded by France to Britain in 1783, occupied a special prominence. In this dispatch to the President of the National Convention, Hugues and Lebas reported:

...La Guadeloupe, Ste. Lucie ont été conquises: St. Eustache & St. Martin sont sous la protection de la République Française. la Grenade St. Vincent & la Dominique ont été attaquées, les anglaises tremblent; et une quantité immense de prises remplissent nos ports.[15]

It does not require an expert in French to tell what Hugues reported to Paris: Guadeloupe, St Lucia have been conquered: St Eustatius and St Martin are under the protection of the French republic. Grenada, St Vincent and Dominica have been attacked; the English are trembling, and an immense quantity of prizes fill our ports.

This was excellent news to the men at Paris. This may have prompted Defermont, under the auspices of the Committee of Public Safety, to inform the Convention on August 15, 1795 that:

L'étendard tricolor flotte à St. Lucie, à la Grenade, à St. Dominique; à St Vincent nous avons reveillé les sentiments des Caribes qui ont déjà exterminé une partie de leurs oppresseurs... Les Anglais sont abhorrés dans toutes les Colonies.[16]

The reference to the large number of prizes was also an indication of another important aspect of Hugues's presence in the eastern Caribbean: his 'revolutionary piracy.' This policy was particularly directed towards the United States of America. As a French patriot, Hugues did not take lightly to the Americans' friendly neutral support of Britain during the French Revolutionary War:

On his own initiative, Hugues declared war on the United States, accusing them of selling arms and ships to the British. 'The very name of America,' he announced, 'inspires only scorn here. The Americans have become the reactionary enemies of every ideal of liberty, after fooling the world with their Quaker play-acting. We shall have to remind this treacherous nation that but for us, who squandered our blood and our money to give them their independence, George Washington would have been hanged as a traitor.'[17]

Using a small fleet, Hugues began to capture all ships that he and his captains regarded as enemies. The prizes were a source of revenue to the cash-strapped rulers at Paris. In the dispatch, Hugues seems to be demonstrating his usefulness to France's Thermidorian rulers in a period where Hugues, a Jacobin, was already a relic of a past regime.

Hugues sometimes used news from one island to inform and inspire their fellow revolutionaries in other islands. In this dispatch to the Grenada revolutionaries, dated "25 ventôse, 3r. année" (10 March, 1795) Hugues informed them of the proceedings in St Vincent:

Courage, freres et amis.... Exterminez les anglais, ils sont les Ennemis du genre humain... frappez fort. Saint Vincent et Sainte Lucie sont attaqués; Bientôt les anglais le seront partout; il faut que nous En effacions jusqu'au nom.[18]

Courage, friends and brothers... Exterminate the English, they are the enemies of humankind... strike hard. St Vincent and St Lucia have been attacked....

The enthusiastic reception that the dispatches received in France notwithstanding, all was not completely well with the operations in the Windward Islands. There were tremendous logistical difficulties associated with keeping the revolutionary movements in these islands. This had been subject of several dispatches to Paris. In this dispatch, dated "30 brumaire, 4 année Républicain" (November 21, 1795), Hugues explained the problem to his superiors in some length:

St Vincent et le Grenade no sont poins encore en notre pouvoir. Nous savez que lorsque les attaquames notre progres n'etoit que de faire une diversion a fin d'obliger nos ennemis a diviser leurs troupes et de favoriser par ce moyen la conquête de Ste. Lucie. Nous avons continué de les tenir en échec dans ces deux iles qui sont le tombeau des forces qu'ils ne cessent d'envoyer d'Europe. Ils en attendent encore qu'on dit devoir être considérables. Nos armées les leurs sont toujours en presence; Si les notres eprouvens en revers, elles se hatent de la preparer par une victoire. C'est ainsi qu'affaiblissant nos ennemis nous Sommes parvenus a garantir la Guadeloupe d'une nouvelle invasion. Tandis que nous occupions les anglais a défendre St Vincent et la Grenade nous eussions pu les attaquer a la Martinique. Tel étois notre projet; nous vous l'avions annoncé et il eut été effectué S'ils n'eusseus pas tenu la mer pendant tout l'hivernage. Neamois [sic] cet obstacle n'etoit pas insurmontable. Une autre motif nous a determiné a retarder cette enterprise; elle est hardie, il y a plus elle est téméraire. L'enthousiasme qui a contribué au Succés de toutes celles espece nous ayant paru se refroider par tes différens rapports que les anglo-americains faisoient du evenement (nous n'avez pas oublié que nous sommes restés 10 mois sans recevoir de vos nouvelles) qui se sont succédés en france [sic] par l'assurance que la nouvelle legation dans l'amerique Septentrionale tournois a son arrivée du prochain rapport du Decret du 16 Pluviose, par la vente que les anglais font des nous qui deviennent leurs prisonniers, chose qu'ils n'avoient pas faite jusqu'a present.[19]

From the number of issues that are referred to in this extract, this dispatch must rank among the most important. It does not require expert knowledge of the French language to understand the issues at work. Hugues's aims not only included the French re-conquest of Martinique and St Lucia, but also the conquest of Grenada and St Vincent. The importance to which Hugues attached to the latter is shown in the amount of space that St Vincent and Grenada occupied in his dispatch. The attacks on these two colonies were also in part a diversion to induce the British to draw some of their strength from Martinique, which they still held. This action, as the extract shows, was timed to be put into operation during the winter months, where it was usually logistically difficult for the British to send reinforcements out to the region.

The extract also shows Hugues's resourcefulness and sophistication in striving to maintain an aggressive French presence in the eastern Caribbean when national politics was slipping into reaction, and when his government lacked both the will and military resources necessary to devote to this cause. The French Commissioner was busily creating enough diversions for the British in order for them to scatter their forces throughout the archipelago. The conquest of the British territories of Grenada and St Vincent was secondary to Hugues's ultimate objective: to regain France's Antillean empire in "Les Îles du Vent."

Hugues's projects were undertaken during a period where even his position as relic of the defunct Jacobin regime was in serious doubt. Hugues was perhaps on his guard every occasion that a French ship appeared on the horizon.[20]

This dispatch shows how a local political conflict became inextricably enmeshed and subsumed in the diplomatic and military struggle between the two foremost western European nations of the time for the mastery of the Windward Islands. For Chatoyer, Duvallé and the Carib nation of St Vincent and the wider Windward Islands, the conflict was an opportunity to seek redress of the burning issues of the day in the face of the British threat to their existence. For Lebas, Hugues and those at Paris, it was, at the very least, "une diversion a fin d'obliger nos ennemis a diviser leurs troupes et de favoriser par ce moyen la conquête de Ste. Lucie;" at most, "une reconquête."

But things were not going as well as Hugues and Lebas would have liked. In this dispatch, dated "le 20 Messidor, l'an 3e" (8 July, 1795), Hugues and Lebas reported to the President of the French National Convention the loss of Soulhat:

...a St Vincent, nous allons faire un effort pour nous en assurer la Conquête; le commandant Soulhat... nous vous annoncions les blessures dans notre dernier, a été tué dans une attaque générale, mais nous esperons avoir notre revanche ainsi que le Dominique.[21]

In the paragraph immediately following the above, Hugues also addressed the matter of the operations in St Vincent and Grenada (which occupied the paragraph immediately before that of St Vincent) into perspective:

Le Comité de Salut public sentira que toutes ces diversions étoient absolument nécessaires pour diviser les forces de terre et de mer trop considérables de l'ennemi, et que ce n'est qu'on portant la guerre chez eux que nous pourrons reconquerir en entire toutes nos possessions.[22]

The two colonies of St Vincent and Grenada, on the face of it, occupied pride of place in the considerations of the French in the eastern Caribbean, that is to say, next in order after Martinique, Guadeloupe and St Lucia. In the dispatches to Paris, particularly between 1794 and 1796, showed this interest. They were always reported on immediately after the best-known French colonies. During the War of the American Independence, Grenada and St Vincent were captured by an improved French navy. As in the case of Grenada, the evidence strongly suggests that the French local officials were dissatisfied with the return of the two colonies at the negotiation table at Treaty of Versailles in 1783, which brought an end to the War. This importance was seen in this message sent to the British commander in Grenada in late 1795 by Charles Joseph Sugue, the French administrator of Grenada:

...a War, maintained by a System unknown in the Annals of the World, has given France two fine Colonies, those which she had lost under a cowardly and pusillanimous Government, will soon return to her power.[23]

These two colonies were obviously important to the French. They nursed ambitions to regain them since the end of the Seven Years' War. They both had communities that were discontented with British rule, and which took every opportunity to aid their French brothers and allies, particularly in times of war. In both colonies, they were subjected to intensified persecution after British rule was restored in 1783.

During the period of the Brigands' War, the contest between the rival colonialisms of France and Britain came to a head. In 1794, the French brought abolition to the eastern Caribbean. In St Domingue, where the Africans were in revolt since 1791 and had been emancipated since August 1793, the 'Decree of Pluviôse was the ratification of Sonthonax's unilateral decision. In the eastern Caribbean, the implementation of this decree meant nothing short of social revolution. Hugues's message of immediate and unconditional emancipation and automatic citizenship of the French Republic was a heady, powerful and almost irresistible to the enslaved masses and free coloureds living under conditions of institutionalised social inequality.

On the other hand, the French had imperial concerns that were not abandoned, even during the period of revolution and reaction at the end of the eighteenth century. Groups that decided to ally themselves with France in this struggle with Britain saw their concerns relegated to second place.

To complicate matters, Hugues tenuous position after the fall of Robespierre meant that he and his fellow Jacobins owed their allegiance to no immediate earthly authority, except a loyalty to themselves, or perhaps a devotion to the service of France itself. Hugues's adoption of 'revolutionary piracy' may have brought him riches, but at the same time slowed the reinforcement of Grenada and St Vincent to a trickle.[24]

The Brigands's War dragged on throughout 1795. Military operations mostly took place when there were reinforcements arrived from outside for both sides. The British were planning a major counter-offensive since August. However, a series of unfortunate delays prevented the arrival of the expeditionary force in the Caribbean - under the command of Abercromby - before March 1796. It had been nearly two years since Hugues arrived and seized the initiative from the British, and they were about to regain it for good.

During the period after Abercromby had received his original instructions and before his departure for the Caribbean, his orders changed at least four times. As he prepared to leave Britain, St Domingue has lost pride of place as the most important objective. That 'honour' had gone to two colonies in the eastern Caribbean:

Expulsion of the brigands from Grenada and St Vincent was now Abercromby's first objective. The capture of Demerara and St Lucia became the second objective. Guadeloupe, however, the center of French military activities and revolutionary propaganda in the West Indies, was left untouched.... St Domingue was similarly consigned to the background.[25]

St Vincent had become second only to Grenada in the considerations of the British political and military directorate. In the British counter-attack, the eastern Caribbean was the first objective.

When the fleet had arrived safely at Barbados, Abercromby did not go directly to Grenada and St Vincent. Instead, he sent in enough soldiers to have a holding operation in Grenada and concentrated his attention on St Lucia. This was an important strategic move. From late 1795, Hugues had delegated responsibility to Goyrand (pronounced "Gwa-Ran") who operated in St Lucia. Most of the day to day operations of the French forces were directed by this Commissioner, with Hugues still having overall control. St Lucia was one of the main sources of supplies to the two islands due south. Securing St Lucia would cut off the revolutionaries' main supply lines.

It took a month, and some 500 men lost, to bring St Lucia under control, but in the end, the British secured the surrender of Goyrand. After the conquest of St Lucia, the reduction of St Vincent and Grenada were but a matter of time.

From his headquarters in Guadeloupe, Hugues was able to obtain intelligence of remarkable accuracy. On the developments in St Vincent, Hugues reported to his superiors:

Le renfort de St Vincent est aussi de 1500 hommes, leur arrivée a été la Cause d'une succession de chocs très meurtriers, où, quoi que les avantages aient été partagés, les Anglais perdent beaucoup plus de monde que nous. Afin d'espérer une diversion utile a Ste. Lucie, nous avons donné l'ordre d'en venir hier aux mains et de harceler continuellement l'Ennemi.[26]

This dispatch from Hugues and Lebas is dated "le 24 floréal an 4." This corresponds to May 13, 1796. Hugues is clearly on the defensive. The British have put into the field an almost overwhelming superiority of force. All the French could hope for was to "harceler continuellement l'Ennemi" to "continually harass the enemy." This, however, only applied to Grenada and St Vincent. Through Hugues's heavy involvement in 'revolutionary piracy,' he did not pay as much attention to reinforcements to the two still [officially] British colonies as Guadeloupe. The ease of the British invasion showed the limitations of this policy. On the other hand, Guadeloupe, Hugues's headquarters, was strengthened with his recruiting of some 4,000 well-trained black and coloured troops since his arrival in June 1794. Security there was so tight that the British, despite several attempts, were unable to obtain information on the internal situation in Guadeloupe.[27]

Hugues, on the other hand, seemed able to gather intelligence almost at will. He was able to able to advise his superiors of the strength of the British, particularly when the expeditionary force arrived in the Caribbean in early 1796. In his dispatch of "24 floréal an 4" he informed Paris that "Cent quarante Batiments dont Sept Vaisseau de ligne, beaucoup de frégattes, de Corvettes et Quatre vingt Transporte se sont presentés devant Ste. Lucie et ont débarqués huit à dix milles hommes parmi lesquels Deux Légions d'Émigrés," on "le 7 floréal" (April 26, 1796).[28]

Within St Vincent, however, matters were not progressing to the satisfaction of Hugues and the other French commissioners. In a document dated "le 21 messidor an 3" (that is to say, July 9, 1795), entitled, "Notes Sur la Situation ou j'ai laissé les Îles du Vent a l'Epoque de 21 messidor, jour où j'ai quitté la Guadeloupe,"[29] a now unidentified French official wrote the following entry under "St Vincent:"

Cette Ile a été attaquée par 50 Républicains auxquels S'étoient joints Les Caraïbes.

Le Commandant Chaulat chargé de cette expédition y a Laissé La vie ainsi que tous ses malheureux frères d'armes. Les Caraïbes que s'étoient Déclarés en faveur des français sont réfugiés dans le bois ou ils sont réduits a la plus affreuse misère. Les anglais les considerant comme des sujets.

From this dispatch, one obtains details of the French military involvement in St Vincent. The brunt of the fighting was obviously borne by the Caribs, with the French having a limited number of personnel, that is to say, up to that period of the Brigands' War. The final sentence, however, is an indication of the legal situation into which the Caribs were placed when they decided to bear arms against their British rulers. The observation that the British considered them - that is to say, the Caribs - "British subjects," pointed the way in which the Caribs were treated at the cessation of the internal war.

It was one thing to be dissatisfied with British rule. It was quite another matter to openly associate with subjects of another country with whom His Majesty was at war. This was, in British law, high treason:

Entering into the service of any foreign state without the consent of the King, or contracting with it any other engagement which subjects the party to an influence or control inconsistent with the allegiance due to our own sovereign, such as receiving a pension from a foreign prince without the leave of the King, is at common law a high misdemeanour and is punishable accordingly.[30]

This is known as "Serving or procuring others to serve Foreign States." Chatoyer, Duvallé and other Carib leaders had unambiguously accepted commissions in the French Revolutionary armed forces. They had also openly given aid and comfort to His Majesty's enemies, the French, during the period of The Brigands' War. But, in the case of the Caribs, there was another matter. One of the terms of the Treaty of 1773 required the Caribs to come to His Majesty's assistance in times of emergency. The Caribs had also failed to observe this term.

By the time of The Brigands' War, British jurisprudence on the question of treason had reached a high degree of sophistication. Bellamy, in his work, *The Law of Treason in the Later Middle Ages*,[31] in tracing the evolution of the law of treason from the thirteenth century, writes that during that period there was a strong tendency to punish such offenders with such punishments as disembowelment, burning, beheading and quartering.[32] East explains why, in British law, the authorities took a very dim view of high treason:

High treason, which by the very term denotes treachery or breach of faith, is a violation of the allegiance which is due from the subject to the king as sovereign lord and chief magistrate of the state. It is... the greatest crime against faith, duty, and human society, and brings with it the most fatal dangers to the government, peace and happiness of the nation.... This offence, therefore, which includes felony, is the highest known to the law, and subjects offenders to the greatest ignominy and punishment.[33]

These considerations lay behind the French official who was the author of the report. It was the precise dilemma faced by the Grenada revolutionaries: were they French Citizens, or were they British subjects? From the proclamations of the French, it was obvious that they were regarded as Citizens of the Republic of France. For the British, they were subjects who had borne arms against their natural sovereign. The French military and civilian personnel were treated as honourable enemies on the battlefield. For the Vincentians, the British treated them as traitors.

After St Lucia was re-captured by the British and left under the command of Brigadier (later General Sir John Moore), the British moved to St Vincent in early June. Putting into the field nearly 4,000 men, the British were able to first secure the surrender of the French forces, then the Caribs a few days later. In these operations, as in St. Lucia, the British cause was aided by the services of a crack German mercenary army called the "Lowenstein Jagers."[34] This corps was specially suited to mountain warfare, and first distinguished themselves in the capture of Morne Fortun☐ in St Lucia.[35] In St Vincent, they were no less successful. Their presence did not escape the attention of Hugues and Lebas. In this dispatch dated "le 5 fructidor l'an 4me," (August 22, 1796), Hugues and Lebas informed their superiors of their presence:

C'est ici le moment de vous parler d'un essai que nous ...de faire; quelques allemands du corps de Lowenstein servant dans l'île St. Vincent à la ... du gouvernement britannique ont été faits prisonniers de guerre, ils sont laboureurs, nous leurs avons offert la liberté et de l'emploi dans la culture...[36]

By the time that Hugues and Lebas had prepared that dispatch, official French involvement in The Brigands' War in St Vincent had been at an end for nearly two months. Apparently, the French had had them taken to Guadeloupe, where they were made labourers. The Caribs were left in the lurch, and faced harsh retribution at the hands of the vengeful British. On 15 June, they sued for peace. Shephard comments:

It was utterly impossible for the English to come again to any terms of accommodation with these perfidious and deceitful people; it was a principle of their religion to wage inexpiable war, and such was their attachment to their old, and inseparable allies, the French, that they were ever ready to co-operate with them in any acts of sanguinary violence.[37]

By October 1796, some 5,080 Caribs had surrendered to the British, including Young Chatoyer, son of Joseph Chatoyer, who was killed early in the war. In February 1797, the survivors were transported from Bequia to Roatan Island, in Spanish held territory in Central America.[38] Their embarkation at Bequia was, in a way, symbolic. It was off the coast of that island that their ancestors had been shipwrecked more than a century before. In 1804, an Act was passed in the St Vincent legislature that re-vested in the Crown the lands that they held at the time of the Treaty of 1773. By rising in rebellion, the Caribs had forfeited all claims to their lands. The Caribs remaining in St Vincent were later pardoned by an Act of the Legislature in 1805, but they lost all claims to the lands that they formerly occupied.[39]

After the end of the French Revolutionary and Napoleonic Wars in 1815, the French never made another attempt to bring St Vincent under their rule. They had by then been left behind in the struggle with Britain to be the dominant colonial power in the Caribbean. France lost much of her colonial empire in the Caribbean after 1800. They were reduced to Martinique, Guadeloupe and Cayenne, the latter on the South American mainland.

In the face of this loss to the British, French political and military historians have shown a marked disinterest in the period where their nation presented a strong but ultimately unsuccessful challenge to the British in the Caribbean. As such, the records of this period remain, in pristine condition, in the archives of their overseas territories at Aix-en-Provence in southern France. Together, they comprise a rich repository of material for students of Caribbean history. This observation is, of course, not new. At the height of the Second World War, Lowell Joseph Ragatz made this observation in an article, "Early French Records at the Archives Nationales."[40] In this work, Ragatz told British West Indian historians of the presence of this rich trove of information. Perhaps, with declonisation and independence of the post-1945 period, such advice fell largely upon deaf ears.

The present paper is a work in progress. It is but the beginning of an investigation into the French records on Caribbean history. There is much to be done. Missing - at least - are the dispatches that passed between directly between the French at Guadeloupe and the revolutionaries in St Vincent. With access to these records, a new and fascinating chapter in the history of the eastern Caribbean will be opened.

Notes

[1] An excellent overview of the period from 1493-1796 is given by Gerard Lafleur, 'The Passing of a Nation: The Carib Indians of the Lesser Antilles,' in Gerard Lafleur, Susan Branson, Grace Turner, *Three Papers in Caribbean History (Barbados Jamaica Trinidad and Tobago)*: Canoe Press, University of the West Indies, 1996), 3-20.

[2] Charles Shephard, *An Historical Account of the Island of Saint Vincent* (London: Frank Cass and Company Limited, 1971), 22.

[3] Lowell J. Ragatz, *The Fall of the Planter Class in the British Caribbean 1763-1833* (New York: Octagon Books, Inc., 1963), 111.

[4] Lafleur, *The Passing of a Nation*, 13.

[5] Lafleur, 14.

[6] In fact, on the very day that Hugues and his party left France, April 23, 1794, France had lost her last colonial possession in the Windward Islands. See Colonel Dubois, 'Le Robespierre des Colonies...Victor Hugues 1762-1826,' *Revue Historique de L'Armée* (Martinique - Guadeloupe - Guyane: Ministère des Armées, Paris, Dix-Neuvième Année - Numéro 1, Février 1963) 91.

[7] R.W. Jeffrey (Ed.) *Dyott's Diary 1781-1845* (London: Archibald Constable and Co. Ltd., 1907) Vol. 1, 97.

[8] Robin Blackburn, *The Overthrow of Colonial Slavery* (London: Verso, 1990). See also C.L.R. James, *The Black Jacobins: Toussaint L'ouverture and the San Domingo Revolution* (New York: Vintage Books, 1963) 139-43.

[9] John Fortescue, "The West Indian Rebellion, Part I," *Macmillan's Magazine* (London: Volume 70, 1894).

[10] Shephard, 57-65.

[11] Lionel Mordant Fraser, *History of Trinidad* Volume I (London: Frank Cass & Co. Ltd., 1971) 88-9.

[12] Colonel Dubois, "Le Robespierre des Colonies... Victor Hugues 1762-1826", *Revue Historique de L'Armée* (Martinique-Guadeloupe-Guyane: Ministre des Armées, 1963) 97.

[13] Thomas Turner Wise, *A Review of the Events, Which have happened in Grenada, from the Commencement of the Insurrection to the 1st of May* (St. George's, Grenada, 1795) 9-10.

[14] ARRÊTÉ. Les Commissaires délégués par la convention nationale, aux îles du vent, le 11 germinal. L'an 3.

[15] Hugues and Lebas to the President of the National Convention, 2nd Floréal, l'an 3 (April 21, 1795).

[16] Cited in Fraser, *History of Trinidad* Vol. I, 89. Fraser quotes *Moniteur*, 9th August, 1795.

[17] David Mitchell, *Pirates* (London: Thames and Hudson, 1976), 164. Mitchell seems to be quoting Alejo Carpentier, *Explosion in a Cathedral* (London: 1963).

[18] Archives Nationales, Col. C10 A4: dossier 5, Pièce 246. Hugues to Nogues and La Vallée, 25 ventôse, 3r. année.

[19] Archives Nationales, Col. C7A 48, 39-40, Hugues et Lebas au Comité du Salut Public, le 30 Brumaire 4 année Républicain.

[20] This is discussed in *Explosion in a Cathedral*.

[21] Hugues at Lebas au Président de la Convention Nationale, le 20 messidor, l'an 3e de la république française.

[22] Hugues et Lebas, le 20 messidor, l'an 3.

[23] Charles Joseph Sugue to General Nicolls, 13 Brumaire, 4th Year of the French Republic, one and indivisible, cited in Henry Thornhill, *A Narrative of the Insurrection and Rebellion in the Island of Grenada from the Commencement to the Conclusion* (Barbados: Mr. Gilbert Ripnel, 1798) Appendix VII.

[24] Michael Duffy, *Soldiers, Sugar, and Seapower: The British Expeditions to the West Indies and the War against Revolutionary France* (Oxford: Clarendon Press, 1987) Ch. 9.

[25] Roger Norman Buckley (Ed.), *The Haitian Journal of Lt. Howard, York Hussars, 1796-1798* (Knoxville: The University of Tennessee Press, 1985), Appendix xxxiv.

[26] Hugues et Lebas au Ministre de la Marine, le 24 floréal, an 4 de la république française, une et indivisible.

[27] W.O. 1/85, 146.

[28] Hugues et Lebas au Ministre de la Marine, le 24 floréal, an 4 de la république français, une et indivisible.

[29] Archives Nationales, Col. C748, 236, sender and recipient unknown.

[30] Edward Hyde East, *Pleas of the Crown 1803* (London: Professional Books Limited, 1972) 81.

[31] J.G. Bellamy, *The Law of Treason in the Later Middle Ages* (Cambridge: Cambridge at The University Press, 1970).

[32] Bellamy, 23.

[33] East, *Pleas of the Crown*, 48.

[34] For a discussion of the work of this mercenary army that served in the British Expeditionary Force, see Wolf-Dietrich Sahr, "Die Lowensteiner Jager: Auszuge aus einem Kapital deutsch-karibischer Geschichte," *Wertheimer Jahrbuch*, Verlag des Historischen Vereins, Wertheim, 1989.

[35] Duffy, Ch. 9.

[36] Hugues et Lebas Au Ministre de la Marine & des Colonies, "le 5 fructidor l'an 4me de la République française une et indivisible."

[37] Shephard, 160.

[38] Shephard, 172.

[39] Shephard, 178-9.

[40] Published in the United States of America, 1941.

The Second Carib War

By Suzanne Burnette

Archivist & Developer - SVGancestry.com

Peace and tranquility were hard to come by in early St. Vincent. If hurricanes and earthquakes were not enough to shake up the growing population, restless natives were another. Those natives were called Caribs, and St. Vincent had been their home for hundreds of years before European discovery. It was a home they were not willing to give up without a fight, despite the onslaught of settlers eager to use the land for profitable sugar cane production. First it was the French, then it was the English, who gained control of the island in 1763. But before the passing of a decade, the Caribs and English would go to war. The First Carib War ended in a stalemate in 1773, when the English forces (led by Sir William Young) conceded the windward coast to the Caribs. It was not an easy concession for the English, since it was well-known that these "Carib lands" were the best suited for growing crops.

Despite that, the peace held between the English and the Caribs until 1795. From 1779 to 1783, the island had returned to French control but was restored to Britain by the treaty of Versailles. By the spring of 1795, St. Vincent's governor, James SETON, had received word some Carib chiefs were planning an attack. His response was a call to arms for the island's colonial militia, with reinforcements from English regiments. SETON called the militia together on the Parade Ground now called Victoria Park, and assigned them their duty. Two days later, messages were sent to the two Carib chiefs CHATOYER and DU VALLE. However, negotiating another treaty was not on their minds, and the fighting soon began.

The Caribs had planned for CHATOYER and his fighters to attack from the Leeward side of the island, with DU VALLE and company coming from the Windward side. The news reached Kingstown on Sunday the 8th of March, 1795, that war had broken out. The first strike reported was that the Caribs at Marriaqua had plundered the Le CROIX Estate owned by Mme Le CROIX. Governor SETON wasted no time dispatching soldiers to Marriaqua. Troops led by his son Brigade Major James SETON and Major SHARPE, succeeded in capturing eighteen of the Caribs, but the others got away.

At the same time further up the Windward coast of the island, another band of Caribs was reported to have destroyed estates at Three Rivers. More soldiers were sent, this time under the command of Captain James G. MORGAN with reinforcements headed by Lieutenant's MacDOWALL and KEANE. The soldiers rested for the night at San Souci before resuming their march on the windward highway. It was not long before they encountered a group of Caribs on a hill, along the road to Three Rivers, who opened fire with their muskets. Before they could retreat, Capt. MORGAN realized that they were now being attacked from behind as well. Suffering heavy casualties, they returned to Kingstown with thirty-one fewer men. This victory gave Carib chief DU VALLE something to celebrate. He and his men captured the post at Dorsetshire Hill, and replaced the Union Jack with the flag of the French Republic.

While on the way to Dorsetshire Hill, other Carib forces captured three young Englishmen at Chateaubelair. They were identified as Duncan CRUIKSHANK, Peter CRUIKSHANK and Alexander GRANT. By the time Chief CHATOYER reached Dorsetshire Hill, his rage for the English was in full force. The three captives bore the brunt of CHATOYER's rage. It is said that he single-handedly hacked them to pieces. This is reported to have taken place on Saturday, 08 March 1795.

After Chatoyer and Du Valle had united their forces, their next objective was Kingstown. The people of the city on hearing this were alarmed, the Governor immediately moved his office to Berkshire Hill taking a few important documents. Both Berkshire Hill and Sion Hill were strengthening their fortifications. The Caribs meanwhile were strengthening their fortifications at Dorsetshire Hill and Fort Duvernette, which was erected by the French in the support of the Caribs.

The plantations around Kingstown were ordered to be burnt by the Governor, in order to have a clear view of the Caribs approaching Kingstown, who from time to time made appearances at the Redemption Estate and Liberty Lodge. A small body of Caribs had made an attempt to stage an attack at the Government House at which time was situated in Montrose Estate, but they were driven off by the strong guards who were posted there. The Caribs once made an attempt to go to Kingstown en route Sion Hill, but they were driven away by the guns on the fortifications at Sion Hill.

In the second week of March, 1795, two war ships docked into harbour of Kingstown that had reinforcements sent by the English. The ship names were the Zebra and the Roebuck. On the 14th of March, at midnight, forces at Sion Hill divided into four and marched to Dorsetshire Hill in order to destroy it. The force consisted of:

1) detachments of soldiers both from the Zebra and the Roebuck.

2) Sailors and merchants from the harbour.

3) The Company of Forty-six.

4) the detachments of the local militia and armed Negroes at the rear.

The force moved up the hill in the darkness. Only when they were eighty yards from the fort did the Caribs and the Frenchmen who with the Caribs perceived them. The Caribs immediately opened a brisk fire. It was only when the English force was twenty yards away from the fort did they discharged. Most of the Caribs escaped in the darkness, but other Caribs and Frenchmen were harmed and killed. Only five of the attackers were dead and five were wounded. It was on this hill that Chatoyer died that night. He had challenged the Major Alexander Leith to a duel, because, he, Chatoyer was convinced that he could not be killed by mortal hands according to a legend, however this legend did not come to past because he was killed by the Major. The Major did not have much time to enjoy his victory because he was killed by the wounds Chatoyer placed on him. Chatoyer was considered a hero to the nation, although little information exists about him. Most of the information about him is hearsay. However, a rememberance monument has been put up for him at Dorsetshire Hill. There is also a memorial stone for the Major under the large chandelier of the Cathedral in Kingstown.

A few days after the Major and Chatoyer had died, Colonel Gordon, the head of the detachment force went to the town of Chateaubelair that was occupied with the Caribs and the French. He commanded that the town should be burnt down. The Caribs fled. The Chateaubelair Caribs and the Dorsetshire Hill Caribs met in the vicinity of Calliaqua, where they set up three camps. On the 21st of March, 1795, the important parts of Calliaqua were destroyed by fire set by these Caribs, the sugar mills in Arnos Vale, Villa, Belmont and Fair Hall were destroy by fire a few days later.

On the 5th of April, 1795, reinforcements of trained soldiers, sailed into the Kingstown Harbour on board the H.M.S. Montague. Other ships were soon to arrive such as the Experiment, the Thorn, the Alarm and the Scipio. The soldiers from the Montague, were landed on shore and marched to their quarters in Berkshire Hill.

Captain Lowman made an attempt to attack the Carib camps at Calliaqua upon request by the Governor, on 10th of April. His attempt failed and he had to retreat to Kingstown, the next morning. The only people who were successful in getting rid of the Caribs were the Light Infantry men, some Grenadiers and a detachment of the third battalion of the Sixtieth. They made a spirituous attack that made the Caribs flee in various directions.

Two armed schooners set sailed from the Kingstown Harbour, under the command of Lieutenant Colonel Seton on the 25th of April. These schooners got reinforcements at Chateaubelair, where after, they set sailed to Du Valle's village on the Windward coast. The attack made there on the 26th was quite successful, twenty five houses were burnt and the Caribs' canoes were destroyed.

The Marriaqua Caribs and some other Windward Caribs who were joined with a few French and English slaves, took up positions at the Vigie eastward of the upper Warrawarrou Valley not very far from the Fountain Estate.

Seven bands of Caribs, 800 in all, on the 7th of May were seen advancing to Calliaqua. Calliaqua at this time was occupied by troops under the command of Captain Molesworth. A shot from the English camp was heard by the advancing Caribs that made them stop. A messenger from the Carib was sent to the English bearing a flag of truce. The messenger proposed that Captain Molesworth and his men should surrender. This proposal was rejected. Before any more negotiations should take place the frigate Alarm from Kingstown opened fire on the Caribs and landed 130 men. The Caribs fled in fright. While this incident was occurring in Calliaqua, another band of Caribs assisted by the French soldiers from Guadeloupe, consisted about 300 blacks and mulattoes had captured Dorsetshire Hill. The next day, the Lieutenant Seton made a successful attack on the Caribs near Calliaqua.

Reinforcements for the English arrived from Martinique with the much needed artillery. On the 11th of June, the reinforcement troops were ordered to marched to Marriaqua Valley to meet the Caribs. The troops advanced at night from Sion Hill. The troops were in several columns. The troops stationed themselves at the Agustine's Ridge at the head of the Biabou Valley, at the Iambou Pass near the Mesopotamia sugar works and at Calder Ridge. The attack began at daybreak. The Caribs fled in terror. Sixteen of the twenty-three dead troops of the Caribs were French whites. Among the sixty people who were taken as prisoners was a French Commander. The English lost one English officer, 13 soldiers and 3 militiamen. 3 officers and 55 privates were wounded. The Vigie fell into the hands of the English once again. The English continued to pursue the Caribs by three different routes. The English encamped at the Union Estate, where they waited for supplies from Kingstown. On the 15th of June the supplies arrived and the march continued in quest of the Caribs. The English halted at the Bellevue Ridge and finally they reached the Mount Young Carib settlement. The Caribs escaped and the English proceeded to Grand Sable where they smashed 200 canoes. Seven Englishmen died from fatigue during the march.

On the 23rd of June, English troops were dispatched to Owia aboard two droghers. They arrived at Owia on the 25th and captured it. The English had lost St.Lucia to the French again. This prove to be an advantage for the Caribs since they could have help from the French there. The Caribs made a new stand at Walliabou, but the guns of the Roebuck and the Thorn soon made them withdraw to a position above Chateaubelair where they opened fire upon the town of Chateaubelair, their success was small. Reinforcements from Kingstown soon arrived at Troumaca. The replacment troops included three six pounders and two howitzers. The Caribs soon fled to Morne Garou mountains.

On the 4th of August, an attack was made at Morne Ronde. After fighting for two hours, the Caribs retreated to the village of Du Valle. While going to Du Valle's village they were overtaken by English forces who killed them and took them as prisoners. Guards were posted both at Morne Ronde and at Richmond. The other troops were withdrawn to Mount Young.

At Owia, on the third of September, the Caribs made a raid at Owia. The English suffered a lost. Most of the English soldiers fled through the forest in the direction of Morne Ronde. The H.M.S. Experiment also rescued some soldiers who had taken refuge on a rock of the coast. On the 15th, 500 men from St.Lucia were sent to the Caribs at Owia. These men also brought provisions for them. The troops at Mount Young thought it would be best to evacuate, they arrived at Sion Hill on the 21st of September.

On the 22nd of September, the Caribs gathered at the Marriaqua Valley, and took up stand at the Fairbairn's Ridge. This cut all communication links between Kingstown and Vigie. When the relief troop for Vigie was marching to their position they were unexpectedly charged after by the Caribs. The English fled to Villa and Prospect with the Caribs hot on their trail. They were able to escaped to Fort Duvernette under the cover of the guns. The Caribs obtained most of the supplies the troops were taken to Vigie. The English losses amounted to sixty being killed and wounded.

It was necessary for the government to speak to the forces at Vigie but with the Caribs surrounded Vigie it was virtually impossible. The governor decided to dispatched two Negroes to go to Vigie. They took two different routes. Only one man returned, Thomas Nash. He was given his freedom for a reward and twenty Johannes.

In secret, the Vigie was evacuated and immediately occupied by the Caribs. This made the English more uneasy. On the 29th and the 30th September, reinforcements came on the H.M.S. Scipio. On the 2nd of October a large force of 1650 men attacked the Caribs at Vigie. The attack lasted for a whole day. When night fell the English Commander bidded his troops to retreat. The Caribs not aware of this fled in the darkness for a cover. So once more, the English occupied the Vigie.

The war continued, but it was not favourable to the English to the end of 1795, and 1796 held no brighter prospects. On the 8th of January, 1796, the Caribs launched an attack at the Vigie, the English retreated to Kingstown. The English losses were 135 privates and two volunteers, sixteen officers were wounded and one officer was taken as a prisoner. These events made the colonists feel despondent.

The English started to see promising prospects, when the Major General Hunter arrived from Martinique on the 12th of January, 1796. He soon got acquainted with the problems facing the English in St.Vincent. He set up a detachment group to watch the Vigie. The remainder of the army were post on the hillsides overlooking Kingstown. The Major on hearing that the Caribs were about to attack the Vigie, order it to be deserted on the 14th to Kingstown. The Caribs pleased by the fear the English felt for them, advanced closer to Kingstown, some stationed themselves at Baker's Ridge and the rest at Bow Wood. The Caribs were deciding to make an attack on Kingstown, but they were driven out by Island Rangers who had attacked them after the Caribs had set fire to the Bow Wood House. The English lost 50 men by killing and wounding. Joy spread into the hearts of the colonists when the H.M.S. Brunswick unloaded 300 men at the Kingstown Harbour.

The Caribs were forced to evacuate their position at Baker's Ridge on the 21st of January. The Caribs aimed shots to Dorsetshire Hill that reached the vicinity of Kingstown, however no harm was done. The Caribs retreated to the Vigie, they had lost many fellow Carib men and many were wounded. The wounded were sent to Grand Sable.

The English General Abercrombie had attacked the island of St.Lucia on the 27th of January, and he captured it from the French. This episode had a weakening effect upon the Caribs since they depended on the artillery and the provisions sent by the French from there.

General Abercrombie who had re-established St.Lucia set sailed to St.Vincent to make peace and order. He arrived in St.Vincent on the 3rd of June. The next day a fleet of armed ships disembarked at the Kingstown Harbour. The governor in his welcoming speech to the General commended him on the find artillery he had. The troops from the ships were quartered at Arnos Vale, Sion Hill and Cane Garden. The General recruited his army of 3,960 men and divided them into six sections. Each section was given specific directions where to fight, the first section was to fight at Marriaqua, the second to fight at Calder Ridge, the third to fight at Carapan Ridge, the fourth to fight at Belmont Ridge, the fifth to fight up the Warrawarrou Valley and the sixth who were the reserves were supposed to fight at the rear. Local people acted as guides. They advanced in the night. Between 6 am and 7 am on the 10th of June the Vigie was attacked, both gun shooting and cannon balls were discharged by the troops at Calder and Carapan Ridges and later by the troop at Belmont. At 2 pm all three divisions closed in, they stormed their way to the Vigie. The Caribs fled in terror down the hill, while the English took possession of the Vigie once more. All firing was ceased by both parties. At about 5 pm, when the English decided to start warfare again, Carib bearing a flag of truce approached them. The messenger said that the Caribs were ready to take submission. The next morning the Governor was consulted at 9:00, terms of submission were agreed on by both sides.

This was a blow for the Caribs, although some Caribs still gave trouble, they were finally subjugated. The among the last to give themselves up were Du Valle and young Chatoyer. By 26th of October 5,080 Caribs had surrendered. Most of the Caribs were then sent to Balliceaux and later to Bequia. On the 25th of February, 1797, Caribs were loaded on the H.M.S. Experiment and carry to the Coast of Honduras, stripped out of their homeland. A few Caribs remained, and dwelled in the part island called the Carib Country that extends from Black point to the most northern part of St.Vincent. Sandy Bay and Morne Ronde were the more populated villages. The Caribs tried to live in peace in the most rugged and uncultivated land in along the Windward Coast. The Black Caribs mostly lived in the village of Greiggs that is almost as unfavorable as this area.

Chatoyer's Artist: Agostino Brunias and the depiction of St Vincent

Lennox Honychurch

Introduction

1st National Hero

Joseph Chatoyer led a revolt against the British in 1795.

In 2002, the paramount chief of the Black Caribs of St Vincent, Chatoyer, (Chatawe), was declared the National Hero of St. Vincent. The visual representation of Chatoyer as a nationalist icon of an independent Caribbean state in the 21st century was set in place by the paintings and engravings of him, which were done by an Italian artist, Agostino Brunias, in the 18th century. Today his paintings and engravings sell for thousands — and in the case of the larger paintings for hundreds of thousands of dollars — in the auction houses of London and New York. His art was escapist as it was romantic, it distorted the harsh realities of slavery in St Vincent and the Lesser Antilles so as to satisfy his absentee planter clientele and yet in its detail it reveals aspects of Caribbean heritage that are impossible to glean from the texts of documentary archives. Historic illustrations in the tourism literature of St Vincent today still use Brunias' engravings to depict an idyllic plantation society in tune with the demands of the tourism product which, in matters of history prefers a selective memory in the same way that the plantocracy favoured a selective depiction of reality.

Agostino Brunias was born in Rome in 1730 and was hired by the leading 18th century architect Robert Adam to work with him in England, doing decorative murals and drafting designs for the stately homes that Adam was building across Britain. During this period Brunias made the acquaintance of William Young, who in 1764 was appointed President of the Commission for the Sale of Lands in the Ceded Islands, which included St Vincent. In this position Young purchased property on the island including land on the west coast along the borders of what the British chose to declare as Carib territory. Brunias traveled with Young as his personal artist recording the Commissioner's progress and the visual context of his exploits. Yellow Caribs, Black Caribs, enslaved Africans and the free 'people of colour' of St

Vincent all become subjects of Brunias' brush. This paper seeks to place these images in the context of their times so that they can be better understood today.

Recording an Adventure

Agostino Brunias began his art studies in Rome at the Academia di San Luca, where he won 3rd prize in the second class for painting in 1754. Like many other Italian artists of the period he immediately found work, painting scenes of the classical ruins and doing souvenir portraits for wealthy British visitors who were sightseeing in the city during the mid-eighteenth century as part of their "Grand Tour" of Europe. This was an extended expedition, a mixture of early tourism and education in the field, that was undertaken by wealthy young British gentlemen, and occasionally ladies, often accompanied by tutors or experts in classical history and art. Brunias was noticed by the Scottish architect Robert Adam, who as part of his tour was sketching Roman architecture, admiring Palladian buildings and collecting ideas that he would later use to great effect in designing and constructing some of the most fabulous stately homes in England.

Adam is considered to be the greatest British architect of the later 18th century and was equally if not more brilliant as a decorator, furniture designer and the leader of neo-classical and neo-Gothic taste at the time. Adam offered Brunias a job as a draughtsman and decorative artist in the studio that he had set up in Rome during most of the four years, from 1754 to 1758, that he was on his Grand Tour. He said of Brunias that he had been "bred a painter" but was "converted into an architect" by his French assistant cum guide, Charles-Louis Clerisseau and himself. "He does all my ornaments and all my figures vastly well." In 1758 Adams took Brunias and most of his studio staff along with him to London where he set Brunias to work doing architectural drawings and painting friezes, ceilings and decorative murals in Adam houses across the country.[1]

It was during one of these commissions that Brunias was introduced to Sir William Young, who, in December 1764 was preparing to go out to take up an official position in the recently captured islands of the Southern Caribbees, as they were called at the time. Early in 1764, Minister George Grenville nominated Young to be the first Commissioner and Receiver for sale of lands in the ceded islands of Dominica, St Vincent, Grenada and Tobago. These islands had been granted, or ceded, to Britain under the terms of the Treaty of Paris, signed in 1763 that ended the Seven Years War. They were to be governed as a group with headquarters in Grenada.

1. Family of Sir William Young by Johan Zoffany, R.A. (1733-1810).
Walker Art Gallery, Liverpool.

Sir William's meeting with Brunias coincided with a falling out between Brunias and Adam over living conditions, pay and what appear to have been complaints by Brunias about the lack of accreditation of his work.[2] In the circumstances Brunias readily acceded to Young's offer to accompany him to the Caribbee Islands as his personal artist. It was an attachment that allowed him an honourable escape and an opportunity for adventure. He was to act as the recorder of Young's progress. In effect he would do in the Caribbean, what he had done for the English tourists in Rome; providing in paint, snapshots of their experiences and souvenirs of the places they had visited, in those days before photography.

2. Sir William Young, 1st Bart (1725-1788) & Sir William Young 2nd Bart (1750-1815)

In late 1764 Sir William Young and his entourage, including Agostino Brunias, set sail for Barbados on "the first of six West Indian voyages made by Sir William in his public employ." In all, Young was away from his family for eight years from 1764 to 1773. The Board of Land Commissioners, of which Sir William was President, had its first meeting in Bridgetown on 10 January 1765. It was here that Brunias did his first sketches on the islands and one in particular, which was later made into an engraving "Barbados Mulatto Girl".[3] With their preliminary business done, the Commissioners set sail again to dispose of Britain's latest conquests. The sales of land commenced in Tobago on 14 May 1765, at St Vincent on the

28th May and on Dominica in June. Sir William purchased some of the best pieces of real estate on all three islands. 'Insider trading' was obviously not an issue in the 18th century.

3. The Barbadoes Mulatto Girl

Sir William juggled his duties as Commissioner of Lands and his post in Dominica with periodic visits to his estates in St Vincent and Tobago. Brunias accompanied him on these trips, which included social calls on Grenada, St Kitts and Barbados. Young recorded "110 voyages of a like nature performed in the course of nine years amongst the ceded islands on the service of the Commission for the sale of lands."

4. Ile Saint-Vincent. Levée en 1773 après le traité fait avec les Caraïbes. Traduit de L'Anglais. Paris, Le Rouge, rue des Grands Augustins, 1778.
Click on image to see larger version

Artist in the field 1765-1768

Once he set up his easel in the tropics, Brunias readily adapted to his new environment. Forested mountains, rivers, unusual plants and scenes of Creole life replaced the vine covered ruins of the Eternal City peopled by colourful Italian peasants. These were the recurrent images that he and other Italian painters had produced in response to the market thrown up by the Grand Tour. In the West Indian case, the clientele was rather similar, for absentee planters living on their accumulating wealth in Britain wanted pictures of their properties and sugar works as evidence of their investments and interests across the Atlantic. While other visiting artists to the West Indies were sketching the forts, ports and rural plantation scenes of the sugar-rich islands, Brunias was looking closely at the people around him. There were the indigenous Caribs and enslaved West Africans who were being transported to St Vincent in increasing numbers as British plantations were established after 1763. Thomas Atwood, who was a resident magistrate, attorney and Dominica's 18th century historian, describes a most diverse white population in these new colonies. "English, French, Spaniards, Italians, and Genoese, who are natives of those countries in Europe, or their issue, born in the West Indies; which are called Creoles, to distinguish them from Europeans."

In the stratified British colonial society that quickly fell into place on St Vincent and the other ceded islands, Brunias was an outsider on several levels. He was not an Englishman or a Scotsman, both of which nationalities were in the vanguard of settlement; he was a Roman Catholic in a colony that discriminated against the mainly French Roman Catholic minority in preference to members of the established Church of England, the church of the State; and his status as a draughtsman placed him just one rung above the level of Sir William Young's white servants. The other Italians already in the islands made their living mainly as contract lumbermen clearing virgin forest for the opening of plantations. Just as Adam referred to Brunias as his draughtsman, so did Sir William. His son notes Brunias' presence in his father's entourage obliquely when he lists the costs of "deputies, extra clerks, draftsman and contingencies in the islands of Grenada, Dominica, St Vincents, Tobago, Becuya and the Grenadines."

His social equivalents in St. Vincent were the "free people of colour", the mainly French mulattoes who, along with yeoman farmers from France had settled in St Vincent among the Caribs prior to the conquest by the British. Those who stayed on were either owners of small coffee estates in the hills or petty tradesmen in Kingstown. It was among these people that Brunias pursued his social life and it was among their type that he eventually sired a family in Dominica. He related easily to them and this is clearly reflected in his art. A white face is seldom seen except if painted by special commission as in "Pacification with Maroon Negroes" where British soldiers form the right half of the picture while the Black Caribs stand on the left. One exception to this tendency is the face of Brunias himself, which he slips into one of his many paintings of washerwomen, depicting himself as a voyeur hiding in the bushes. And perhaps it is he who makes an appearance again as the white man standing in the doorway of a hut observing "A Cudgelling Match between French and English Negroes in the Island of Dominica"

With Young as his patron he had the time and facilities that are ideal to the artist. The Commissioner did not have a reputation for skimping on his luxuries, even in the frontier setting of the "the ceded islands", which were then the Empire's newest and rawest possessions. Here it was said, "he lived in the style of a prince". He had his own traveling musicians and brought out his personal servants from England along with his silverware, linen and furniture. He imported deer to provide him with venison and peacocks to parade across the lawns of his villa overlooking Calliaqua Bay on St Vincent and later at Government House in Roseau, Dominica. The Villa area in southern St Vincent is named after Sir William's residence, which was unusually sumptuous in its décor, boasting a grand ballroom and paintings by Brunias, all of which were destroyed in 1795 during the second "Carib War". But that was some thirty years in the future. Of that earlier period there is the legend of Chief Chatoyer passing through Villa Estate and admiring two of Sir William's fine horses, which the Commissioner immediately gave to him. In return, Chatoyer is said to have "looked across the strait and pointed to the island and told Sir William he was more than welcome to it if he so desired."[4] Brunias features Young Island in one of his engravings.

Even in his official affairs Sir William ensured that the finer trappings of the British aristocracy were transported across the Atlantic and planted upon rain-drenched volcanic islands amidst the bland brutishness of a colonizing plantocracy. Years later, his son, also named William, recalled of his father that "He recommended, he solicited; he invited to settlements in a wilderness, with the voice of music, and fine arts; he made jovial parties of colonisation...and few who ventured within the charm of his society could not long resist his example or his persuasions, to enlist in the undertaking...and his bounteous entertainment, necessarily unremitting, from a succession of unprovided friends (for in enterprises of hazard all are friends) was to be defrayed at the charge of the individual first Commissioner."

Young was made Lieutenant Governor of Dominica in 1768 but soon the planters there were demanding their own separate Assembly, and not for the first time was a federated government of the Caribbees broken up. Sir William was chosen to be the first Governor of the new government and was sworn in on 17 November 1770. However his main private interests at the time were in St Vincent. The contrast between pioneers hacking their way into a jungle frontier over rain-drenched volcanic peaks and the ornate furniture, chandeliers, crystal, paintings, entertainments and fine wine lavishly provided by an 18th century Man of Sensibility gave this enterprise an aura of exoticism that is reflected in the work of Brunias.

The subjects of his paintings and engravings include dancing in St Vincent and Dominica, women washing clothes in the rivers, cudgeling matches or 'stick licking', market scenes and expensively dressed free people of the 18th century. His near-nude washerwomen on the luxuriant banks of streams add a prophetic touch of the primitive Gauguin to the style that Brunias followed. Pictorial accounts of maroons, the escaped slaves who had taken to the hills, and the Black Caribs of St Vincent, particularly the chief Chatoyer, occupied his attention. Brunias worked on watercolours, sketches and oil paintings in the islands. These originals on canvas, wood or paper were then taken to England where they were redesigned as engravings. It was a period when there was great demand in Europe for engraved prints on all subjects. Many of the figures seen in his paintings can be identified in the prints rearranged in various ways to suit the different medium. In most cases the original images are reversed when transferred to the metal plate and printed. Some of the characters appear several times. Two women as flower girls turn up again as spectators to a dance or may be observed in the corner of a group promenading along a riverbank. Most of them were published in the years after his term with Young was over, while several were produced after they were both dead. Most are dedicated with great flourish to his patron and other colonial personalities associated with the islands.[5] A number of Brunias works on paper were included in a sale at Christies auction house in 1785. These were used freely by the engravers and printers who got their hands on them, so that many of the "Brunias prints" published may have had little input from the artist himself in the final process.

Engravings made up from various paintings by Brunias were used to illustrate the important plantocratic account of Britain's exploits in the region, '*The History Civil and Commercial of the British Colonies in the West Indies*' by Bryan Edwards. These prints appeared in the second edition (1794) and later editions (1801 and 1818-1819). The images conveyed by his engravings complements Bryan Edward's text, which used a combination of history and contemporary reports to launch an unabashed defence of slavery so as to counter the growing voices of opposition coming from the Abolitionists in England at the end of the 18th century. James Pope Hennessy called it the "Myth of the Merry and Contented Slave".

"Its components can best be envisaged as a series of vignettes in the mode of the lovely coloured engravings of slave festivals based on the pictures of the eighteenth-century painter Agostino Brunyas (sic). In this fictive slave existence turbaned Negroes and Negresses sang as they worked the cane or cotton fields by day, spent the night drinking, dancing and making love, reared their families of sportive piccaninnies, and liked and respected the white masters, their indolent whey-faced wives and their spoilt children." He argued that this was a theory, effectively conveyed by Bryan Edwards, which swept back to Europe and was long believed there. To illustrate this view, Hennessy uses the engraving of "A Negro festival in the island of St. Vincent". The same print is used by Eric Williams in his magisterial history of the Caribbean, '*Columbus to Castro*', to argue a similar point. Brunias' "Negro Festival" is in effect a propaganda piece.

A Negro Festival

5. Negro Festival in the Island of St. Vincent.

Although it is described as taking place in St Vincent, this engraving combines scenes produced elsewhere on the islands. In the left hand corner of the picture a drummer and female tambourine player reappear from similar scenes painted in Dominica and St Kitts. A dancing couple performs what may be the 'Bélé', now called 'Belaire' in Trinidad. They too can be observed in at least three of his other paintings of the period. A white sailor or overseer asks a decorous Mulatress to dance or at least gestures towards the dancers. To the right a slave lays out plates of pineapples, pears, plums and grapes, symbols of the tropical bounty readily available from the island. This is taken from a Carib basket, a hint of the trade in handcraft, which was carried on between the St Vincent Kalinago and the colonists. In the background are slaves, all dressed in resplendent fashion, partaking of a feast. Luxuriant vegetation and craggy cliffs rise behind the festive gathering.

6. Negroes Dance in the Island of Dominica (or St. Kitts)

7. Negre et negresse de la Martinique dansant la Chica. Par de J. Lachaussee d'apres S.G. Saint-Sauveur (d'apres Agostino Brunias) 1805. Click on image to see larger version

As in his other paintings Brunias records the costume of the time in magnificent detail, but gives what some believe to be an exaggerated conception of the dress and conditions of the age. In a wider study of his prints one can follow the social order of fashion, beginning with the issued denim or chambray livery or 'livre' of the field slaves through to the extravagant material and colours of the freed slaves and mulatto planters. This, and other Brunias prints show the different styles of tying the madras head kerchiefs, of wearing the accordion pleated petticoats, strapped bodices and silk foulards. The detail of their jewelry gives evidence of a considerable trade and creativity in gold and other metal work.

8. Mulatto Promenade.

Mode of dress is still a subject of importance and much debate in the West Indies and is a direct result of historical systems. Without social or educational means of showing their status over others the only way that free blacks could exhibit their superiority was to imitate their former white masters to the extreme and one of the ways this could be done was through clothes. It is well recorded that free blacks and 'people of colour' went to great lengths to outshine the issued wear of the field slaves and factory hands. But the British travel writer Quentin Crewe commenting on Brunias' paintings two hundred years later felt that "however good they are, there is an element of mockery in his paintings, which so often depict black people aping white manners."

However there was a desperation to declare their position as free people, to use fashion to counteract, and indeed to protest, against the social restrictions imposed upon them. This may well have contributed to the excesses of which Thomas Atwood commented: "The free people of colour are remarkably fond of dress and dancing; for the enjoyment of both which they will sacrifice everything that is valuable in their possession... their ladies being usually dressed is silks, silk stockings and shoes; buckles, bracelets and rings of gold and silver, to a considerable value."

9. Negro Festival in the Island of St. Vincent.

This is vividly represented in the controversial "Negro Festival in the Island of St Vincent", which perhaps more accurately represents a party of "free people of colour" than the slave festival that the term "Negro" or "Negre" (synonymous with "slave") indicated in the 18th century. But this is splitting hairs, for whatever the source, it has conveyed its misleading message of merriness and contentment of the enslaved for over two hundred years.

The Fruit Market

10. The Fruit Market at St. Vincent.

The Sunday market was a focal point for plantation society in St Vincent. Apart from its obvious commercial appeal it provided a significant moment of liberation for the enslaved. It allowed them to engage in enterprise for their own benefit, selling produce from their garden plots to obtain money with which to purchase sundry goods such coloured cloth, jewelry and basic utensils for personal adornment and use. In other paintings Brunias has featured more crowded market scenes but in this engraving, "The Fruit Market at St Vincent" it appears more as an encounter with vendors on their way to the main market in Kingstown. As in the engraving of "a Negro festival", Brunias uses fruit and luxuriant vegetation on the right of the picture to conjour up an image of tropical plenty. A melon is proffered to a mulatto mistress and her companion while a man, most likely her slave carrying her basket, observes the transaction. Two other vendors, baskets loaded with fruit, are nearby.

In the background across the bay stand the unmistakable outlines of Young Island and the rocky outcrop of Fort Duvernette, in homage perhaps to Sir William's ownership of these landmarks. This print can be studied in conjunction with a rare watercolour sketch by Brunias showing two of the characters who appear in the picture. Painted on paper, it is entitled in French Creole, "Madame épis Mouchier", (Mistress with head tie) and shows the identical couple that appear in the print. Because of the engraving and printing process they stand in the opposite direction to which they had been painted. These original figures were copied and inserted into the picture by the engraver Brown and published by Thompson in 1804, eight years after Brunias' death. Such scenes of mulatto ladies accompanied by or engaged with black slaves are a common feature of Brunias' work.

11. Madame □pis Mouchier (Mouchw□). Watercolour sketch. Click on image to see larger version

12. The Fruit Market at St. Vincent. Click on image to see larger version

The Aboriginals

13. Couple Cara□be des Antilles. Sebastien le Clerc (1637-1714)

Engraved 1667.

Brunias did several paintings of Caribs in Dominica and St Vincent and these have become important sources of information on the remnants of indigenous culture, as it existed on the islands in the 18th century. One of these interesting oil paintings shows a group of Caribs outside their huts in St Vincent displaying artifacts and adornment that can be related to descriptions of similar scenes given in ethnographic texts of the Caribbean published by French writers during the previous century.

The most influential of these were the engravings of Le Clerc, which illustrated Jean Baptiste Du Tertre's '*Histoires generales des Antilles habittees par les Francaise*'. Jean Jacques Rousseau noted the accounts of the Caribs contained in this book in formulating his theories on the ideal of the 'Noble Savage'. This concept was taken up in the work of Brunias as he portrayed the last of the Caribs during the peak years of Enlightenment thought in the latter half of the 18th century.

While on a visit to England c. 1775-1784 Brunias reworked scenes of Carib life. At Stowe House in Buckinghamshire, for instance, he did "wall paintings of Caribbean aborigines" in the Ante Library, but by the 1870s there was no evidence of them, so they had apparently been painted over. These murals must have drawn heavily on the sketches that he had done among the 'Yellow Caribs' St Vincent.

14. Caribs of St. Vincent. Oil painting.

On the outskirts of the pioneer British settlements such as those of Sir William Young in St Vincent, particularly along the Leeward coast, there were members of the original Kalinago, the inheritors of the previous Native Caribbean cultures on the island. The colonists knew them as the 'yellow' or 'red' Caribs. In "A Family of Chairaibes drawn from the life in St. Vincent" Brunias provides us with an ethnographic study of the people and their material culture. The engraving and the painting are almost identical.

15. A Family of Charaibes drawn from life in St. Vincent. Oil Painting.
Click on image to see larger version

16. A Family of Charaibes drawn from life in St. Vincent. Print. In Bryan Edwards' *History Civil and Commercial of the British West Indies*, 1801, 1818, 1819, T. Miller Publ. Cheapside, London. Click on image to see larger version

Two types of hut stand in a forest glade, which provides the backdrop for six adults and two infants who display various tools and utensils. The larger hut, a *taboui*, in the Island Carib language, was of a type used up into the 1950s while in the background stands the open-ended *mouina* with a hammock strung across it. The Kalinago appear in their tribal finery of beads, earplugs, decorated aprons and hair ornaments. From the left one woman arrives with her loaded *pegal* greeted by a man carrying a bow and several arrows. In the centre a woman lowers a clay bowl, *chamacou*, onto a wicker stand, *mattoutou*. A woman seated on a wooden stool displays the reed bark leg straps that were woven on at marriage so as to enlarge her calves and was considered to be a mark of female beauty. A baby suckles her while another eats from a small bowl. A man drinks from a calabash, *mouloutoucou*, and as in the pictures of the Black Caribs he carries a knife slipped into his loincloth. Identifiable plants are the heliconia or balizier, *baliri*, to the left and a native palm, in the centre. Apart from the specific botanical specimens, Brunias painted trees in the manner of temperate oaks and elms rather than tropical rainforest vegetation. Such a pristine gathering, free of European trade goods, may not have existed in the 1760s and Brunias may have pieced together elements of what was left of the culture at the time. However it still is a valuable ethnographic record of Vincentian Kalinago and it is an image that has been reworked by other artists in the generations that followed.

Chatoyer and the Black Caribs

In the first years of settlement Sir William Young was aware that he had to woo Carib friendship, at least until the British had the upper hand. During the first three years of settlement, 1765-1768, there appears to have been much interaction between Young and the Caribs and it is during this period that Brunias had his greatest access to them. Several paintings of Chatoyer are done during this interlude, the most famous being versions of Chatoyer and his five wives. Sir William records giving the chief numerous gifts and holding 'vins' or feasts for his entertainment. But there was growing apprehension among the Caribs as colonization progressed. The relationship changed as they saw the plantocracy's greed for more land transgress any earlier assurances they may have been given as to the security of their own farming and hunting territory. It is a subject well covered in the literature of the period elsewhere and it needs to be taken into account as a background to this section of this paper.

17. Chatoyer and his Wives.

As the situation in St Vincent deteriorated Governor Young suddenly left his post in Dominica in 1772 rushing to St Vincent to "assist with the Carib War" and to protect his estates there. The Dominican Assembly was none too pleased by his departure and refused to pay him, arguing that, "His salary was conditional on his actual residence and must be forfeited because of his absence." Regardless of this Young participated fully in the so-called "First Carib War" of 1772-1773. At first he attempted negotiation, but when conflict broke out, he adopted the hard line view, which included, among other possible solutions, the idea of transporting the Black Caribs away from St Vincent.

18. Pacification with Maroon Negroes. Oil Painting.

Like the "Negro Festival", the engraving entitled "Pacification of Maroon Negroes" has been the centre of some controversy. The original painting from which it is taken depicts, what is believed to be the climax of the First Carib War, when in February 1773 a treaty was made between the British and the main Black Carib chiefs, Chatoyer prominent among them. British soldiers are encamped on the right, while the eleven men due to take an oath of allegiance to King George III stand to the left listening as an interpreter, probably Chatoyer's chief advisor, Jean Baptiste, explains the terms dictated by the British. As demanded in Article 2 of the treaty to "lay down their arms", the guns, swords and bows of the Black Caribs lie on the ground between them. At the extreme right a British officer holds a map of St Vincent, which would have had the respective boundaries of Carib and plantation land delineated on it. Another officer reads from a paper, which contains the twenty-four articles of the treaty. There is some disagreement as to who is the senior officer seated with his arm extended in a classic gesture of peace. Some have it to be Major General Dalrymple leader of the expedition of 1772. Others are convinced that it is Sir William Young himself, painted as heroic peacemaker by his loyal artist. A comparison of Sir William, painted by Zoffany and Sir William as painted by Brunias would favour the view that it is Young. But by the time the painting was transferred into an engraving it could be any white official and in its printed form this scene took on a life of its own. It has been used to depict scenes of maroon confrontation in Jamaica and Dominica as well as at its point of genesis in St Vincent. In Bryan Edwards' history it is captioned "Pacification with Maroon Negroes" without any direct reference to the text, which mainly covers the Jamaican maroon campaigns. Printed at the time of the Haitian revolution and its aftermath it became also a symbol of British order and control in comparison to the disastrous French collapse in St Domingue. Brunias had once again provided visual reinforcement of the security and contentment under British rule at a time when the British Empire was expanding its vision to India and Africa beyond its early focus in the West Indies.

19. Pacification with Maroon Negroes. Print. In Bryan Edwards' *History Civil and Commercial of the British West Indies*, 1801, 1818, 1819, T. Miller Publ. Cheapside, London. Click on image to see larger version

Patron and Artist

20. Sir William Young by Johan Zoffany and Agostino Brunias. Click on image to see larger version

Sir William Young was back in England at the end of 1773 and his office of Receiver and Governor closed on 1 October 1774. It was concluded by his family that "the adventure in the ceded islands had proved so expensive and indeed ruinous" to him. Brunias stayed on in the islands for a while after Young's departure in 1773 and then returned to England in about 1775 and visited the continent. During this visit he exhibited and sold paintings, mainly to absentee planters resident in Britain. He transferred details of his paintings into engravings and returned for a time to his former occupation of carrying out commissions in the grand houses that Adam had constructed, this time using Caribbean rather than classical themes. He exhibited three of his West Indian paintings at the Royal Academy exhibitions of 1777 and 1779.[6] At this time he was living in London's West End. He was at two addresses during this period, 20 Broad Street, Carnaby Market; and 7 Broad Street, Soho.

He kept in touch with his patron and eventually returned to the Caribbee Islands in 1784 where he produced a set of botanical drawings for the newly appointed curator of the St Vincent Botanic Gardens, Mr Alexander Anderson. This return coincided with the declaration of peace between the French and the British following five years of war during which time Dominica and St Vincent had been occupied by the French: Dominica from 1778 and St Vincent from 1779. Both were returned to British rule by the terms of the Treaty of Versailles in 1783. All of this had happened during Brunias' absence in Britain. Sir William died in England on 8 April 1788 leaving estates in Tobago, Betsy's Hope in Antigua and Calliaqua and Pembroke in St Vincent. The title went to his son, also William, who inherited his plantations and died in Tobago in 1815. In his will, written and registered in St Vincent, Sir William the elder, bequeathed to "Mr Brunias, one mourning ring" and fifty pounds Sterling. After his job in St Vincent, Brunias was again in Dominica where he spent the rest of his life continuing to paint surrounded by the family, which he appears to have begun just before his departure in 1775. Brunias died in Roseau on 2nd April 1796 at the age of 66 and was buried in the old Roman Catholic cemetery that

surrounded the church dedicated to Notre Dame du Bonne Port, Our Lady of
Fair Haven.[7]

21. Painted buttons from the coat of Toussaint L'Overture.
Click on image to see larger version

His work continued to be admired and copied long after his death. A set of
painted buttons on a coat said to have belonged to Toussaint L'Ouverture, the
liberator of Haiti, are replicas of Brunias prints miniaturized on each button,
probably in France. French engravers in the 19th century copied his work
freely and this has caused some confusion in verifying authenticity. In 1854 a
Paris journal: "*Manuel de l'amateur d'estampes*" mentions an exhibition of
certain of his prints. In the 1980s there was a renewed interest among a select
group of international collectors, which resulted in a marked rise in the prices
paid for his works.

Negre et negresse de la Martinique dansant la Chica. Par de J. Lachaussee d'apres S.G. Saint-Sauveur (d'apres Agostino Brunias) 1805. Click on image to see larger version

West India Washer Women in Oils, Engraving and Reproduction. Click on image to see larger version

Conclusion

On the surface it may seem out of place that one should find a romantic among the crude gaggle of planters and merchants scrambling for the material riches of the 18th century West Indies. His work has classical qualities: figures, regardless of what they may be doing, fighting or washing, are poised with seemingly elegant ease in settings characteristic of the period. It is this Rousseauesque neo-classicism in Brunias' work that makes his prints such popular and enduring works of art. But it is a deceptively partial view of the plantation society which Brunias recorded, for his work almost purposefully ignores the seedier, brutal side of the Caribbean experience in the latter half of the 18th century that would have been all around him. There are no scenes of slavery in action, no depiction of gangs cutting sugar cane or ladlers and tenders of the furnaces processing sugar in the mills. The iron neck braces and gagging metal masks padlocked upon the head as punishment that are described on the streets of Roseau and Kingstown by others at the end of the 18th century are nowhere to be seen in Brunias' work. He was indeed no conscience-stricken Goya, but rather an artist with his eye on a particular market for his craft, producing a decorative form of art that would not upset his clients.

The style of Agostino Brunias touched the intellectual spirit of the age, where a branch of Enlightenment thought conceived of the Noble Savage set in an idyllic tropical paradise. It was at the same time and in a similar spirit that William Hodges, one of the artists who traveled with Captain Cook, was painting his scenes of the Pacific where noble native chiefs, dancers, and warriors astride decorated canoes in coral lagoons, were placed against the spectacular backdrops of the sunset tinted mountains of Tahiti and Raratonga. They were recording a culture that the very expeditions upon which these artists had embarked would ultimately destroy. Brunias' paintings of St Vincent likewise caught images of a pre-conquest culture destined for destruction.

In Britain his work complimented the transformation that was taking place in the gardens of the same stately homes where his paintings and engravings were displayed. Formal gardens were being transformed into pastoral landscapes dotted with artificial lakes and classical follies designed to evoke a rural idyll. This was far removed from the grime and squalor of the coal mines and factories of the Industrial Revolution that were emerging along the borders of those same estates, the stately homes of which Brunias was decorating. The lavish adornment and pastoral landscaping on one hand and the "dark satanic mills" of industry on the other were both, in several cases at least, a reinvestment of profits from the slave-based plantations of the West Indies. In the art of Agostino Brunias, as in the enterprise of his time, the relationship between the late 18th century plantations in the West Indies was linked to the powerful forces of British wealth and to the enjoyment of the fruits of that wealth. One of those pleasures was to enjoy the work of a painter who skillfully, some would say immorally and without conscience, used the demands of the market and the prejudices of society to his own advantage.

Phonecard.

Perhaps such esoteric academic analysis may be forcing us to be too critical. In the popular culture of the post-independent islands where he once worked, Brunias' depiction of 18th century plantation life has become a source of inspiration for Crop Over Kadooment bands, restaurant signage, Plantation Inn dancers and museum souvenirs in Barbados; costumes from his prints are copied by nationalist village cultural groups in Dominica. In St Vincent the national hero is depicted on everything from walls to telephone cards in the image that Brunias gave us, while tourism and other literature is illustrated with his work. By creating a visual and romantic icon of Chatoyer as the 'noble savage', the idyllic aboriginals and the 'merry slaves' of St Vincent, perhaps Agostino Brunias, the Grand Tour artist of Rome, has struck a cord of escapism from history and from truth, that, dare we admit it, still lingers to this day.

Footnotes

[1] Prominent among these stately homes are Syon, Osterly, Stowe, Saltram, Audley End, Kedleston and Harewood. Brunias had a hand in the decoration of those constructed or renovated between 1758 and 1764 and again when he was back working in England from about 1775 to 1784.

[2] Adams was known to scratch out Brunias' signature and to leave the space blank or even, it was alleged, replace it with his own so as to get credit for the work. Six years before, another of Adam's assistants, a Belgian from Liege, Laurent-Benoit Dewez, escaped across the channel to Europe fearing that Adam was planning to make a slave of him.

[3] Today a copy of "A Barbadoes Mulatto Girl" is sold as a souvenir by the Barbados Museum. The Cunard Gallery at the Museum is lined with a fine array of visual records of people, places and events; probably the best collection of West Indian prints in the region. Many of Brunias' engravings can be seen there.

[4] L.E. Kirby and C.I. Martin, *The Rise and Fall of the Black Caribs*, Caracas 1985. p.46.

[5] These bear dedications to such officials as Sir John Frederick; General Dalrymple who clashed with the Black Caribs in 1772-1773 and Charles O'Hara, Crown Surveyor in Dominica during the 1770s and later a Brigadier General who was a partner in the group that owned Rosalie Estate on Dominica's east coast.

[6] The programme of an exhibition of paintings at the Royal Academy in London in 1777 mentions one painting by Brunias: 'A Negroes Sunday Market in the Island of Dominica'. In 1779 they also hung 'A View of the

town of Roseau in the Island of Dominica' and 'A View of the river of Roseau in the Island of Dominica.'

[7] In the baptismal records of the Roseau Cathedral an entry was found noting the baptism of "Edward and Augustin two illegitimate children born on the 1st October 1774 of Louis Bruneas and a free mulatto woman". A watercolour done by Brunias during that time depicts a mulatto woman wearing a fashionable pink 'grand robe' with a red bordered head tie, under which he wrote, "Ma Coummier", which means in Dominican French Creole, "The godmother of my child". This woman appears again in an oil painting of mulattoes promenading on the banks of the Roseau River. In the tax returns of 1827, giving lists of produce and slaves on Dominica, we find in the parish of St Paul, a small estate owned by Elizabeth Brunias, which was worked by 11 slaves who produced 1,225 lbs of coffee. An estate house and surrounding yard typical of a property of this size appears in his painting of "A Creole scene in Dominica". Standing in the main door of the house is a lady who appears to be the mulatress mistress of the place. Is there any connection? Is Louis Bruneas anything to do with Agostino Brunias? The French always spelt his surname with an 'e'. Are they one and the same person? Is the Elizabeth Brunias of 1827 a daughter of the painter, or did he in the end marry "the free mulatto woman" who was the mother of his children? And if so, are the present-day Bruney families, who trace their origins to land around the hillside village of Cochrane in the parish of St Paul in Dominica, the descendants of this 18th century artist, traveler and chronicler in paint of our island's history? These are just some of the loose ends still to be explored in piecing together a fuller account of this colourful life.

Bibliography

Atwood, Thomas 1791 *The History of Dominica*, London.

Breton, Raymond 1665 *La Dictionnaire Caraïbe-Française*, Gilles Bouquet, Auxerre, France.

— 1667 *Grammaire Caraïbe*, Gilles Bouquet, Auxerre, France.

— 1877 *Grammaire Caraïbe, Catéchisme Caraïbe*, Nouvelle edition, L'Adam & Charles Le Clerc, Paris.

Davies, John 1666 *The History of The Charriby Islands*, London. (Transl. fr. Charles Rochefort 1665).

Du Tertre, Jean-Baptiste 1667 *Histoire generales des Antilles habitees par les Francais*, T.Jolly, Paris.

Edwards, Bryan 1794, 1801, 1818, 1819 *History Civil and Commercial of the British West Indies*, T. Miller Publ. Cheapside, London.

Geracimos, Ann 2000 'A Mystery in Minature', *Smithsonian Magazine*, January 2000, Washington. http://www.smithsonianmag.si.edu

Gullick, Charles, J.M.R. 1976a *Exiled from St Vincent: The development of Black Carib Culture in Central America up to 1945*, Progress Press, Malta.

— 1976b 'Carib ethnicity in a semi-plural society', *New Community* Vol. 5 No.3

— 1979 'Ethnic interaction and Carib Language', *Journal of Belizian Affairs* No.9

— 1984 'The changing Vincention Carib population', in Crawford M. et al. *Human Biology* Vol 53, 1981.

— 1985 *Myths of a Minority*, Van Gorcum, Netherlands.

Honychurch, Lennox 1975 'Agostino Brunias, a precursor of Gauguin' *The Bajan and Southern Caribbean Magazine*. Bridgetown, Barbados. June edition.

— 1997 *Carib to Creole: A History of Contact and Culture Exchange*, unpublished thesis, University of Oxford.

Hulme, Peter 1992 *Colonial Encounters: Europe and the Native Caribbean*, Routledge, London.

Hulme P. & Whitehead N. 1992 *Wild Majesty: Encounters with the Caribs from Columbus to the Present Day*, Oxford University Press, Oxford.

Kiple, Kenneth and Kriemhild C. Ornelas 1996 'After the encounter: Disease and demographics in the Lesser Antilles', in *The Lesser Antilles in the Age of European Expansion*, ed. Robert l. Paquette and Stanley L. Engerman, University Press of Florida, Gainsville, pp. 50-70.

Kirby L. E. and C.I. Martin, 1985 *The Rise and Fall of the Black Caribs*, Caracas, Venezuela.

Labat, Jean Baptiste 1724 *Nouveau Voyage aux isles de l'Amerique*, 8 Vols. Cavalier Pere, Paris.

— 1931 *Memoirs of Pere Labat*, transl. and abridged by John Eaden Constable, repr. Frank Cass & Co. London 1970.

La Borde 1674 *Voyage qui contient une relation exacte des caraibes sauvages des Antilles de l'Amerique*, Louis Billaine, Paris.

Ober, Frederick 1880 *Camps in the Caribbees: The adventures of a naturalist in the Lesser Antilles*, Lee & Shepard, Boston (also David Douglas, Edinburgh).

Pope Hennessy, James 1967 *Sins of the Fathers: A Study of the Atlantic Slave Traders 1441-1807*, Weinfield and Nicholson, London.

Rochefort, Charles de 1658 *Histoire naturelle et morale des iles Antilles de l'Amerique*, A. Leers, Rotterdam.

Smith McCrea, Rosalie 2002 'Disordering the World in the 18th Cenury, The Duplicity of Connoisseurship: Masking the Culture of Slavery, or, The Voyage of the Sable Venus: Connoisseurship and the Trivializing of Slavery', *The Society For Caribbean Studies Annual Conference Papers*, Sandra Courtman, ed. Vol.3, http://web.archive.org/web/20050211102408/http://www.scsonline.freeserve.co.uk/olvol3.html

Young, Sir William, 1st Bart. 1764 *Considerations which may tend to promote our new West India Colonies*. New Bond Street London.

Young, Sir William, 2nd. Bart. 1795 *An Account of the Black Charaibs in the Island of St. Vincent's*, London.

— 1807 *The West India Common Place Book*, Richard Phillips, London.

Manuscripts

Rhodes House Library, Oxford.

The Young Family Papers: MSS.W.Ind.t.1, Sir William Young, 1st. Bart. Commissioner of lands of the Ceded Islands and first Governor of Dominica. Correspondence relating to the Estates of Sir William Young 2nd. & 3rd. Barts. in the West Indies and Claims for compensation 1768-1835, 6 Vols. The North MSS (The papers of Lord North, Earl of Bute): William Patterson report on the Neutral Islands, 12 May 1761,ff.40-51(1),ff.65-67. Some Hints on the Settlement of the Ceded Islands, ff. 196-198. Thomas Curlett, Letter on Productivity of the Ceded Islands, f.198 Instruction for the Councel appointed for fforreigne plantations, 1 Dec.1660, ff.1-5.

Joseph Chatoyer

SVG Hero

Ministry of Urban Development, Labour, Culture and Electoral Matters
Culture - Culture General Administration

The Black Carib wars against the English were in three phases. It was during the closing stages of the second phase that Chatoyer, the great Carib Chief, met his death.

In March 1795 Duvallier, the Windward Carib Chief, pulled down the British flag at Dorsetshire Hill and made his headquarters there. Chatoyer eventually joined Duvallier at Dorsetshire Hill where he took command. However, on the night of 14th March of that same year, the English stormed Dorsetshire Hill to fight against the Caribs.

Chatoyer, by this time, was convinced that he could not be killed by mortal means so he challenged Major Alexander Leith to a duel. Leith was a trained army officer and as such, he was a good swordsman and so Chatoyer was killed in the duel. The French account of the duel says that while Chatoyer was getting the upper hand over Major Leith, an English soldier shot the Carib Chief in the back. No matter how Chatoyer was killed, the limited information available on him indicates that he was a great leader. We know that his home and headquarters were at Morne Ronde on the North Western end of the island however, there is no clue as to his final resting place.

To become a chief of the Caribs, one had to distinguish oneself in war or in other respects. Chatoyer appears not only to have been the paramount military chief, but also the civilian one. In war Chatoyer was an outstanding leader. His forces included not only his fellow Caribs but also Europeans who were French troops. Neither the French nor his fiercely individualistic countrymen would have respected him had he not been an outstanding general.

During battle Chatoyer did not destroy property for the sake of vandalism, as Duvallier had done on the Windward side of the island. Instead, Chatoyer preserved it so that he could use it in the future. This action shows remarkable foresight. Chatoyer, despite the great odds against him, was able to defeat the English twice. He was able to mould his army into a remarkable fighting force. The strategies he used, to inflict blows on and to negotiate with the English, indicate he was a man of great character.

Perhaps the most pointed indication of his leadership was what happened to his troops: when he died most of the French soldiers immediately forsook the Carib cause and fled to Layou. The Caribs themselves were so shocked at their leader's death that retreated to their villages. From then on the very character of the Carib war took on an entirely different complexion.

It is possible that had this great man Chatoyer lived, the English might not have been able to so quickly suppress the Caribs and transport them from their homeland to Central America. Chatoyer remains a hero even though his Carib empire has long been destroyed.

The most recent development in this quest for reclaiming identity and reconstructing their history took place on March 14, 2002 when the Great Carib (Garifuna) Chief, Chatoyer, was declared first National Hero of St. Vincent and the Grenadines, and the day made a national holiday. Chatoyer, who is also revered bythe Garifuna people in Central America, was Paramount Chief at a very critical period in the struggle to retain the independence of St. Vincent and to preserve the lands on which his people lived. He died in 1795 during the battle that led to the final defeat of the Caribs. The recognition of the importance of the Carib Chief to the life and struggles of his people has long been recognized. The British have established a monument in a prominent place in the Anglican Cathedral to their Major Leith who, it was alleged, had killed Chatoyer in a duel. The account of his death given by the British has been disputed, and is believed to have been part of efforts at psychological warfare.

Chatoyer was also immortalized in a play, the "Drama of King Shotaway" , that was performed in NewYork in 1823, twenty-eight years after his death. The play was written by Mr. William Henry Browne. It is believed that he was a Garifuna member who had experienced the battle of 1795 in which Chatoyer was killed. Mr. Browne is regarded as the Father of BlackTheatre in the United States of America and this play is said to be the first about a black person.

The recognition given on March 14 to this leading figure in the history of the Garifuna/Black Carib people will undoubtedly focus attention on his and his people's contribution to the history of St. Vincent and the Grenadines. They had held the might of Europe at bay for centuries, St. Vincent being among the last of the Caribbean countries to be colonized. It will also contribute to restoring the confidence and reconstructing the identity of a people who had been victims of a colonial past and who have had over the years to face the accusation of being cannibals that had been widely propagated in colonial history.

The Black Carib/Garifuna population in St. Vincentthat remained following the exile, had for long lived on the margin of society, many of them in communities that had been devastated by volcanic eruptions in 1812 and 1902 and had, to all intents and purposes, been cut off from mainstream Vincentian life. A lot has changed over the years, a result of political developments and the growing consciousness of the people. The reconnection of the people, among other things, will help in the reclaiming of their history, identity and pride; and in reconstructing and restoring their central place in the eady history and development of St. Vincent, or Yuremi as it is known in Garifuna language.

The history, artifacts and other symbols of the Black Caribs (Garifuna people) are essential parts of the history and culture of St. Vincent and the Grenadines. Many of the forts and places where the different encounters took place, remain and tell their own story, among them the cannons at Fort Charlotte that point inland. Beside the information they provide to the Vincentian people, they also add to the rich heritage and cultural-tourism infrastructure. Sections of the Central American Garifuna community are developing a case for reparations and are seeking 'symbolic' citizenship of this country.

The story of the Garifuna people is a unique one that needs to be told, since among other things, it is pivotal to understanding their position in Central America and also the history of St. Vincent and the Grenadines; and indeed the rest of the Caribbean region in which St. Vincent was one of the last outposts of Carib resistance.

The Last Stand of the Black Caribs on Saint Vincent

By James L. Sweeney [1]

Perhaps the one of the most important historic events in Eastern Caribbean history and also one of the most fascinating was the defeat and exile of the last independent indigenous group in those islands, the Black Caribs, by the British in the Second Carib War, 1795-1796. This war was part of a regional conflict between the French islanders and their allies against the British, called the War of the Brigands. This regional war was in turn a part of the larger conflict between the British and Revolutionary France.

For France the conflict in the Eastern Caribbean was a sideshow that helped divert British power from the main conflict in Europe. For the French settlers and Caribs on St. Vincent, who sought to expel the British from their island, it was a fight for survival. For the British Empire the goal of the conflict was to expand and secure British power in the Caribbean, defeat their French rivals for empire, and counter the values of the French Revolution. The more parochial goals of the English planters on St. Vincent were to defend their plantations and the capital of Kingstown from marauding French and Carib attackers, who were seeking to push them off the island, and to then defeat them and expel the Black Caribs from the prime sugar cane growing lands that they still held.

The general outline of Vincentian history is consistent with the history of the Western Hemisphere and much of the rest of the world that was controlled by European colonial powers.

It follows with a succession of indigenous groups, colonization and conquest by Europeans, the introduction of new population, indigenous resistance, removal, extermination, or depopulation of the indigenous groups, conflict between rival colonial powers, and eventual control by one power. After long tenure the greatly altered society is then granted autonomy and independence in the late 20th century, but the lasting effects of colonialization linger.

While the history of St. Vincent follows the general pattern of colonial history for the region, and for similar territories world wide, it does have its unique aspects. Among these is the prolonged resistance of the indigenous inhabitants, the Caribs, to occupation by the European powers. The Caribs were among the most successful Native American groups in resisting conquest. Their last strongholds in the Eastern Caribbean were on Dominica and St. Vincent. St. Vincent was the last of the Windward Islands to be totally subjugated. This was not accomplished until 1797. By contrast other islands, such as Barbados and St. Kitts, were settled, and successfully controlled nearly a hundred and fifty years earlier by the British ("Caribbean Time Line").

Another unique aspect of St. Vincent's history was that the first important contact between the indigenous Caribs and the Old World was not with Europeans, but rather with Africans. African refugees came largely from slave ships that wrecked on the reefs or as escapees by boat and raft from the slave islands of St. Lucia and Barbados to St. Vincent and the nearby Grenadine Islands. Others were captured in raids on the European held islands or purchased as slaves by the Caribs. These people intermarried with the Caribs, and adopted their culture. Eventually the resulting Black Carib group developed out of this blending of African and Carib cultures. With the continuing migration of escaped slaves to St. Vincent the population that was of mixed ancestry eventually predominated. These were the people who eventually led the final resistance to the British takeover of their island in 1796.

The difficulty of putting down the resistance of first the Caribs, and later the Black Caribs meant that St. Vincent was one of the last of the Lesser Antilles to become part of the Sugar Empire that dominated the Caribbean economy for nearly two hundred years, and was a great source of wealth for the colonial nations of Europe. The slowness of the introduction of the sugar plantation economy to St. Vincent meant that large-scale slavery was also late in being introduced into the islands. This did not occur until the sugar lands controlled by the Black Caribs were taken over after the last Carib War ended in 1797. As slavery was abolished in St. Vincent in 1832, large-scale production of sugar on plantations by large numbers of African slaves was a phenomenon that lasted just over a generation on St. Vincent.

Caribs

The best known of the indigenous groups that once occupied St. Vincent and the Grenadines are the Caribs. These people arrived about 1200 AD from the mainland according to carbon 14 dating (de Silva xv). They moved up the island chain from the mainland as far as Eastern Puerto Rico, displacing, exterminating, and incorporating the Arawak population. They had a tradition of war and raiding, especially for women. The origins of their drive into the islands from the mainland may have been similar to their predecessors, the Siboney and Arawaks, but the French missionary, Fr. Adrien Le Breton, who lived among them from 1693 until 1702 recounts an oral history told to him by Caribs that explains the tradition of why they left the mainland to conquer the islands of the Lesser Antilles. According to the story the Caribs had been slaves or subjects of mainland Arawaks, and had been freed in the 11th Century. From 3 that point they had spread into the

Caribbean, driving out or incorporating the island Arawaks already there (de Silva xix).

The term Carib was not originally used to designate the people of the Lesser Antilles, and as with the Arawak, it would not have been used by the people themselves. Linguistically and culturally the Carib were not really very different from their Arawak victims. Fr. Raymond Breton lived among the Indians of Dominica from 1641 to 1655 and reported that the Island Caribs called themselves Kalinago (Davis 1) or Callingo for the men and Callipunam for the women (Johnson 2). The term Kalinas has also been used for these people (de Silva xxii). Today anthropologists prefer to designate them Kalina (Johnson 2). To refer to all the people of the Lesser Antilles as a single ethnic group probably makes about as much sense as labeling all the contemporary people of Western Europe as a single group. Though they spoke a language from the same basic language family, and had similar origins on the mainland of northern South America they were as different from each other as Spaniards would be from the Italians, French, and Portuguese at the time.

The origin of the term Carib may have for its basis accounts based on the writing of Christopher Columbus himself. In conversations with the Taino (Arawak) inhabitants of Hispaniola Columbus was told of the Caniba or Canima of the small islands to the southeast, who raided the peaceful people of the larger islands, and ate their flesh. These people also found their way into the underworld of the local mythology (Davis 1). Columbus recorded what the Taino told him about these people. In Cuba on November 4, 1492 he learned that the Caniba "had but one eye and the faces of dogs" (Davis 1).

It seems that the name Carib has it origins in these encounters with the Taino and Columbus. The Taino word *Caniba* means manioc people or people of the manioc clan, and is the root word for both Caribbean and cannibal (Davis 1). Apparently the Spanish hispanicized *Caniba* into *Caribas* or *Caribes* (de Silva), which became Caribbees, Charibs, or Caribs in English, and Caraibes in French (Johnson 1). Van der Plas gives an alternate explanation. He claims that the Arawaks of the mainland, whom the Caribs had rebelled against, moving first to Tobago, and then up the chain of islands to the north, may have called them Carib, meaning rebels. They called themselves Callingos. St. Vincent was called Youlou or rainbow, a diety, the Mainland Caribs, Balouemhounum, and the Island Caribs, Oubaohonum (11). According to Adams the Callingos said the word Carib meant devastator, and was given to them by their Arawak enemies, and then adopted by the Europeans (6). The first explanation seems the most logical, though the term may have had multiple meanings in different contexts.

The Caribs did contribute other words to the English vocabulary though the Spanish. The term cacique is widely used in the Americas to signify a chief.

Buccaneer is the name used for the European freebooters of the times, who raided Spanish shipping. The name is derived from the Carib word *boucan*, which is a system for curing meat over an open fire on a raised wooden platform. When the freebooters were not raiding Spanish ships or settlements they made a living hunting the wild cattle of Western Hispaniola, curing the meat on *boucans*, hence the name *boucaneers*. Cigar, hammock, and hurricane are words borrowed from the Caribs (Hoebel 572, de Silva 9).

The word cannibal, eater of human flesh, was derived from Caniba or Carib. This may prove to be a misnomer. In James Michener's 1989 epic historical novel, Caribbean, he graphically depicts the invasion of a peaceful Arawak village by grizzly Carib warriors, who murder the men, to be dismembered for the cooking pot, and capture the women and children. The boys are to be fattened up for the pot, and the women used as slave wives and concubines.

Others depict the Caribs as ruthless marauders, and murdering cannibals who followed the hapless Arawaks up from the Amazon basin, and ate their way up the chain of islands to Puerto Rico ("Caribs" 1). The peaceful Arawaks, or Tainos, were only saved from inevitable annihilation, rape, dismemberment, and being eaten by the Caribs through the intervention of the Spanish, who managed to eliminate them before the Caribs got the chance. This view of the Caribs is today being challenged by a closer look at the cannibalism myth by revisionist historians and anthropologists.

Were the Caribs cannibals? This myth seems to have begun with Columbus, and the stories that were related to him by the enemies of the Caribs, the Tainos of the Greater Antilles. A review of documents from the early explorations of Europeans in the Lesser Antilles reveals evidence of low-scale raiding and slave taking, but no reliable evidence of cannibalism (Davis 1).

The stories of cannibalism by the Island Caribs made their way to Europe, and became part of the European view of what they considered a savage people. Shakespeare's Caliban, was a cannibal slave (Johnson 1). De Foe's Robinson Crusoe lived in fear of cannibals, and rescued Friday from the cooking pot.

Perpetuating the cannibal myth served a political and economic purpose. In the 16th century, Pope Innocent IV declared cannibalism a sin deserving punishment by force of arms (Salisbury 1). Free Indians, who were potential Christian converts, were not supposed to be forcibly enslaved, and were protected by the Spanish Crown and the Church. In 1503 Queen Isabel issued a decree protecting Indians from capture, arrest, harm, or evil to their persons or possessions (Johnson 2). Of course, this was largely ignored in the Americas. An edict in 1511 defined Caribs as any Indians who were hostile to Europeans, behaved violently, or consumed human flesh. These people were deemed without souls, and liable to be enslaved (Davis 1). Queen

Isabela decreed that only cannibal Indians could be enslaved. This gave the Spanish an economic interest in lumping as many Caribbean Indians as possible into the Carib designation, thereby making them potential targets for capture and enslavement (Salisbury 1). Uraba la Cosa may have deliberately misled the Queen to justify his 1504 voyage of plunder and slaving along the South American coast (Johnson 3). Perpetuating the cannibal myth ensured political and moral support for Indian slavery, and eased those with any conscience by relegating the Indians to less than human status. This myth lingers with us today.

In 1595 Sir Walter Raleigh encountered the island, and had reports of cannibalism. An earlier French vessel's crew had been devoured. More likely they had been boarded, murdered, and robbed, perhaps for liquor. The tales of cannibalism may have been a way to keep aggressors away from the islands (Van der Plas 4). The violence by Caribs against Europeans was largely a reaction to violence, and enslavement by the Spanish, and others against them. Vengeance was an important motivator in Carib warfare. Vengeance for past depredations at the hands of Europeans led to raiding and violence against European settlements from the 1500's on in the Antilles. Some of these were successful in driving Europeans out of the islands, at least for a time.

There is little evidence for Carib cannibalism. In response to the allegation that Caribs were cannibals in earlier days the French priest, Pere Labat, who lived with the Caribs of Dominica, and knew them well, wrote "'If they were cannibals in those days, why are then not cannibals now? I have certainly not heard of them eating people, whether Englishmen with whom the Carib are nearly always fighting, or Allouages Indians of the mainland near the Orinoco with, whom they are continually at war'" (Johnson 3). Other Europeans with experience living with the Caribs relate no examples of cannibalism that mirror that depicted by Michener.

There are examples of ritual cannibalism. Caribs believed in sympathetic magic, the idea that they could acquire strength and courage by simply biting and chewing on the cured limbs of an enemy killed in battle. Caribs would carefully preserve the appendages of a few chosen fallen enemies, and hang them from the roofs of their meetinghouses as war trophies. This is similar to the taking of scalps in North America, by both Indians and some colonials, and the taking of heads by other warlike people in the Americas and elsewhere, including at times European fighters. Some Americans in Vietnam are alleged to have taken Viet Cong ears as trophies. Pere Rabat describes an account of ritual cannibalism.

To arrange a war party an old woman enters the *carbet* (meeting house), and harangues the guests to excite them to vengeance. She recounts the wrongs that they have suffered at the hands of their enemies and recites a long list of their friends and relations what have been killed. When she sees that they are properly heated by drink and showing signs of fury, she throws the *boucanned* (cured) limbs of some of their enemy into their midst. The Indians thereupon fall on the limbs, cutting, tearing, biting, and gnawing them with all rage . . . . (de Silva 32).

Similar stories are told by a 17th Century Dutchman who lived with mainland Indians similar to the Caribs, and by Luisa Navarrete, a 16th Century Kalina slave on Dominca. After successful raids one or two male captives would be ritually killed in a victory ceremony, and pieces of their flesh were put into a pot. An arm or leg was preserved to remind them of the hatred of their enemies (Johnson 2). Young boys were initiated by being rubbed down with the fat of a slaughtered Arawak in hopes that they would absorb the Arawak's strength and courage ("Caribs" 2). While these practices may seem gruesome, the Europeans of the time had their own brutal tortures for captured escaped slaves, heretics, and rebellious Indians that rival or surpass that of their Indian enemies. While cannibalism was decried in Europe as heathen, Europeans of the time thought nothing of consuming "medicines" made from the dead bodies of executed prisoners or the desiccated flesh of Egyptian mummies (Salisbury 1).

There is no archaeological evidence for large-scale cannibalism in the Caribbean. The best conclusion is that, with the exception of possible isolated circumstances and the ritual cannibalism described above, the Caribs were no more cannibals than their European and Indian enemies. The myth was perpetuated for the purpose of those who benefited from promoting it and by the lack of knowledge of the reality of Carib life by everyone else.

The fact remains that a people called the Caribs by Europeans occupied, and controlled much of the Lesser Antilles Islands for at least four hundred years until finally exterminated or removed by the Europeans. They fought valiantly, and sometimes successfully to resist European domination and the last to be defeated were the Caribs of St. Vincent. But by the 18th Century these were a changed people, caught between big power politics and warfare, and at times manipulating it to maintain their sovereignty, and even being changed genetically through the infusion of European and especially African peoples into their population.

What is known of traditional Carib culture and how they used the land on St. Vincent when they were in control has been preserved by the writings of French missionaries, and others, and the work of archaeologists. Caribs practiced the slash and burn agriculture common to the Circum-Caribbean peoples (de Silva 12). They grew cassava, potatoes, yams, cotton, tobacco, beans, corn, and other Native American crops. The women did the farming. Fish were an important part of the diet. The men and boys hunted birds, land crabs, agoutis, manicous (fox-like animals, possibly possums), and collected conch, saving the shells for horns to signal their arrival on peaceful voyages. They collected the wild foods of the reef and forest. Feral goats and pigs left by the Spanish were hunted using javelins and hunting dogs. They hunted other types of animals, using specialized types of arrows, blunt ones for birds. Some birds were tamed, and kept as pets, or as future meals (de Silva 17-18).

They were excellent mariners. They built huge piraguas or ocean going dugout canoes, up to fifty feet long and seven feet wide, carrying fifty warriors each. They were reinforced with thwarts, side planks on the gunnels, caulking, ribs or seats, used stone ballast, and sails. Long voyages were made, up and down the island chain, from the South American mainland up as far as Florida, and as far west as the Greater Antilles. Most islands are within sight of each other and require less than a 24-hour passage between them by piragua. Raids were conducted by piraguas (de Silva 26).

Before a raid a more or less democratic meeting was held in which the women participated. War or peace was decided in these meetings (de Silva 29). The motivation for war was revenge, and the capture of women, food, and slaves. An *ubutu* or war chief would decide on the day of the attack. The Caribs were armed with war clubs, wooden swords, stone knives, bows, poisoned arrows, and fire arrows ("Caribs" 2). All were made of wood, stone, or bone. Prior to leaving for the attack they would paint themselves, and get worked up into a frenzied state. They would then paddle out to attack a usually weaker people. Attacks were made under cover of night, and were sudden and brutal. It began with a hail of fire arrows into the thatched roofs of their victims. As they exited their homes they were set upon with war clubs and arrows. After a victorious battle they returned in their canoes with their own dead, and with captured men and women ("Caribs" 2). The men were destined to be killed in ritual celebration, or kept as slaves, while the women became wives or concubines, being distributed by the *ubutu*.

Carib villages were built along the coast high up so lookouts could be posted in case of attack. The favored location was on the rugged Windward Side of the island, which gave the advantage to the defenders who knew the rare coves and safe landing beaches. In the event of attack those that lived closer to the forest could flee into the jungle for safety. The villages usually consisted of 50 to 60 families, headed by caciques. The authority of the *ubutu* was during wartime. In peace the *tuibutuli hauthe* supervised fishing and farming. The *boyez,* or shaman, handled the magico-religious duties, and dealt with illness, often attributed to witchcraft. Elders and retired warriors were respected, and played an important role in decision-making. Marriage was polygynous. The sexes were segregated residentially. Women had their own separate huts and males, from age four, lived together in *carbets,* or large men's houses. They slept in hammocks. Infants had boards tied to their heads to flatten them for beauty. Clothing consisted of a small cotton loincloth, body paint, and ornaments, feathered headdresses for special occasions ("Caribs"). There may have been between 9,000 and 10,000 Caribs on St. Vincent during the early period of contact with Europeans. This was later augmented by refugees from the islands conquered by Europeans, especially the French and British.

The initial contact with Europeans was minimal. The Spanish were not much interested in the Lesser Antilles, with their aggressive natives and no gold. They preferred the more populated and rich lands of Meso-America and Peru. The Caribs of St. Vincent were initially successful in resisting European encroachment on their island by a combination of aggression toward outsiders, and forming alliances with them when expedient. Other islands sought aid from St. Vincent and Dominica, the Carib strongholds, in times of trouble. When the French attacked Guadaloupe, St. Vincent sent hundreds of warriors to help, but they were defeated. Refugees fled to Dominca, and some to St. Vincent. When the French invaded Martinique in 1635 the Caribs sent 1500 warriors from Dominica and St. Vincent, but were defeated again. This began a long-term hatred of the French by the Caribs. Guerilla warfare continued from 11 1636-1639. In one raid the Caribs loaded 800 warriors into 15 piraguas, and attacked the French from St. Vincent and Dominica (de Silva).

The Caribs would trade with the Europeans for goods, but steal wine, incurring French retribution, massacre, and the destruction of whole villages (Van der Plas). In 1639 the British became the target of Carib raids on Antigua and Barbados after attempts to enslave Caribs on Dominica by trickery. Caribs burned plantations, and massacred settlers and turtle hunters. French and British colonists' attempts to settle St. Vincent were repelled by the Caribs in the early 17th Century (Van der Plas).

The first outsiders to successfully settle on the islands were not French or English Europeans, but rather Africans, whose descendants may have made up the majority of the population by the time the French and English gained a toehold on the island in the 18th Century. The African connection becomes mixed up with that of the Caribs to the point that it is hard to distinguish between Africans and Caribs by the beginning of the 18th Century. From that point on the term Carib was used almost interchangeably for the people of St. Vincent who were living in indigenous fashion, culturally Carib, whether of Indian, African, or of mixed descent.

Africans in St. Vincent

The first outsiders to permanently settle St. Vincent were from Africa. This began as early as the beginning of the 17th Century, when captured, escaped, or purchased African slaves entered the island, and became an important part of the Carib population. This is somewhat analogous to the Seminole experience in Spanish Florida.

Historians have speculated about pre-Columbian contact between West Africa and the Caribbean. Edgar Adams sites Ivan Van Sertima's *African Presence in Early America* and Harold G. Lawrence's (Kofi Wangara) *Mandinga Voyages Across the Atlantic* as books that address the unconfirmed idea that West African explorers from Mali in the early 14th Century may have been the first from the Old World to contact people in the Caribbean. Apparently Prince Abubakari of Mali outfitted two voyages in 1307 and 1312. One consisted of 200 vessels, and the other of 2000. The purpose was to explore lands to the west (Adams 4). Beyond that not much else is known, but it is possible that West Africans, by plan or by accident, may have made it across the Atlantic. Whether this actually occurred, and can be confirmed, is anybody's guess. It is also possible that the occasional fishing or trading dugout may have been driven across the Atlantic, and into the islands of the Caribbean.

No significant evidence of any pre-Columbian African contact with St. Vincent exists. The first likely Africans to arrive on St. Vincent were unwilling passengers on European slave ships from Africa. This began quite early. As soon as Europeans brought Africans to the New World some escaped to St. Vincent, some were shipwrecked on the coast, and in the Grenadines, and some were captured or otherwise acquired by the Caribs, and brought to the island.

St. Vincent received African refugees as early as 1635 when two Spanish ships carrying slaves were lost in the area (Adams 5). Father Vasquez Espinosa wrote in the 1620's of five hundred shipwrecked Africans stranded in the Grenadines when a Portuguese slaver ran into the islands. The Africans dispatched the Portuguese. Their fate is unknown, but they may have joined the Caribs on St. Vincent. Raiding Caribs often captured Africans in their attacks on European plantations, settlements, and shipping. These people were brought back to St. Vincent where the women became Carib wives and the men slaves or were freed, eventually to marry Carib women, adding to the mix in the population. Caribs and Africans had a common enemy the Europeans that sought to enslave them and take their lands. They often made common cause against their oppressors. By 1672 it was estimated that six hundred runaway slaves were living with the Caribs on St. Vincent and Dominica. Besides these runaway slaves, known as Maroons, and the people of mixed African/Carib ancestry, the Caribs held an increasing number of Africans as slaves.

The growing numbers of slaves, free Africans, and mixed Black Caribs became a destabilizing force. The Windward side of St. Vincent attracted escapees from Barbados, who could steal a boat or make a raft, and ride the currents for a couple of days and wind up free on the eastern shore of St. Vincent (Muilenburg 2). In 1675 the Dutch ship, *Palmira*, was wrecked by a hurricane on Bequia in the Grenadines (Adams 6). The surviving African captives were from a notoriously warlike tribe known as Mocos. The Caribs transported them to St. Vincent where they were difficult to control. Those of African descent were beginning to outnumber the indigenous Caribs. Maroons in the mountains sought women, held by the Caribs.

The Caribs resorted to a drastic measure to regain control over a minority they had adopted into their midst that was quickly becoming the majority. They began killing African males at birth, while sparing the females. The Africans revolted, killing some of the Caribs, and withdrawing to the mountainous Windward Coast, where the Maroons had established themselves (Muilenburg 3). The Governor of Martinique intervened in the dispute between the two groups, and offered to arbitrate. He drew a line called the "Le Barre de l'Isle", which divided up the island between the two groups. The native Caribs, known as the Yellow or Red Caribs, received territory on the Western or Leeward Side of the island, while those of African and mixed descent, known as the Black Caribs, received the Eastern or Windward half. Despite this agreement harmony between the two groups was never completely restored. They would cooperate against outside invasions, intermarried, and shared a common language and culture, but from this point on the Black Caribs dominated affairs on the island. Some Yellow Caribs migrated to the mainland, Trinidad, or Tobago. By 1730 there were about 6,000 free Africans and 4,000 Caribs on the island (Adams 6). By the end of the 18th Century when the British fought a series of violent wars against the Caribs of St. Vincent, they were largely fighting the Black Caribs, as the Red Caribs' numbers had dwindled down to the hundreds, though this has been disputed by some observers, such as the French revolutionary officer, Moreau de Jonnes, who lived among the Red Caribs during part of the Second Carib War. Moreau De Jonnes places them in the majority of the Carib population and includes them as active participants in the fight against the common British enemy.

How the ethnicity of Caribs is defined may differ between observers, often for political reasons. Sir William Young identified the Black Caribs as African colonists and considered them identical to the Maroons of Jamaica. He also labeled the Red Caribs as the true indigenous people of the islands and numbered them at just a few hundred. He claimed that the Black Caribs usurped the lands of the rightful indigenous owners, the few remaining Red Caribs, raided them for women, and therefore had no rightful claim on the lands. This was a convenient claim in that the British crown was perfectly willing to step in and replace the Black Caribs by taking over the lands they had occupied for generations. William Young was an advocate for the removal of the Black Caribs from St. Vincent, plantation owner, and son of the first Sir William Young, a land commissioner appointed by the crown to distribute land for sugar cane plantations from the islands captured at the end of the Seven Years War. He wrote the book about the beginning of the Second Carib War most often cited in accounts of the times. He was also the official that signed the removal order to expel the Black Caribs from St. Vincent in 1797. Moreau de Jonnes, a French gunnery officer, on the other hand, lived among the Caribs, was sympathetic with their cause, and while he wrote about his experiences decades after they were over, he did become the premier statistician of France, so his account of the relative numbers of Red to Black Caribs might be considered more accurate. Moreau de Jonnes says that physically it was not difficult to distinguish between Red and Black Caribs or between Black Caribs and African slaves.

The new group of mixed African/Carib people, the Black Caribs, called themselves the Garifuna (plural Garinagu), or cassava eaters. They lived much like their Yellow (Red) Carib cousins, were tough fighters, resisted the settlement of Europeans, routing the French in 1719 when they sought to exploit tension between the two Carib groups by invading the island unsuccessfully (Muilenburg 3). They later had good relations with the French, traded with them by sea, learned French, and were allied with them during conflicts with the British. Culturally then Black Caribs were indistinguishable from their Yellow or Red Carib cousins. They practiced skull deformation by tying boards the foreheads of their infants, buried their dead in a flexed fetal position, spoke the same language, and had the same material and non-material culture as the other Caribs, having assimilated their culture over generations. Their practicing Carib culture and exhibiting Carib cultural traits effectively set them apart from the African slaves on the French and English plantations on other parts of the islands. The Black Caribs sometimes held Africans as slaves, sometimes captured escaped African slaves to be sold to the plantation owners of the French islands or returned to their owners on St. Vincent for reward. They also harbored some and incorporated them into Carib society. The British viewed the Black Caribs as "African colonists" or Maroons and not as indigenous. The Black Caribs viewed themselves as indigenous to the island and part of the overall Carib nation. While there were sometimes conflicts between the Red and Black Caribs and they lived on opposite sides of St. Vincent, they also shared a common culture and language and would meet together in a common island-wide national council in times of crisis to cooperate against common enemies. Moreau de Jonnes witnessed one of these councils on his first visit to St. Vincent at the beginning of the Second Carib War to warn them of a British plot to despoil their lands. This council included the important chiefs of both the Red and Black Carib groups.

European Encroachment

The French and British had been vying for control of the West Indian Sugar Islands from the early 17th century. The Caribs of St. Vincent had been able to trade one side off against the other, and use their rugged terrain and warlike reputation to keep both nations largely out of St. Vincent, a rich prize with soil ideal for sugar cane, until the late 18th century. In fact St. Vincent was the last of the Windward Islands to fall under colonial control. The French wanted to keep out the British, and the British wanted to keep out the French, while the Caribs, both Black and Yellow (Red), wanted both groups to leave them alone. The Caribs traded with and raided the Europeans, and allied themselves against one side or the other when it was convenient. Eventually they allowed a few French owners of small plantations to settle on the Leeward Side with their slaves, and were influenced by French culture and language. While there were some tensions, the less intrusive French presence meant for a more cooperative relationship between the French, headquartered in Martinique, and the Caribs, loosely ruled by their chiefs in island councils when the need to cooperate arose.

Some of the chiefs and notables among the Caribs learned French, sent their children to study with the French in Martinique, took to occasionally wearing European dress, and copied the European plantation system. It is said that the most famous leader of the Caribs, Chief Joseph Chatoyer, had his own sugar cane plantation and slaves at the main Carib town of Grand Sable, and was as comfortable having dinner and doing business with a European governor at Government House as he was trekking through the jungle in a loincloth with his several wives in tow. There was a certain amount of cultural trade-off between the French and Caribs, leading to the exchange of traits between cultures. There are French words that have made their way into the modern Garifuna language, along with some from Spanish, and a few from African origins.

By 1756 war resumed between France and England in Europe, leaving the French a relatively free hand in St. Vincent. The French settlers had amicably acquired possession of much of the island, and lived peacefully with the remaining Caribs. Toward the end of the Seven Years War, General Monckton and Rear Admiral Rodney were sent in 1762 to St. Vincent and other islands, to capture them from the French and to hold them as bargaining chips in peace negotiations. The French were expelled from Canada, but regained some of the lost sugar islands, including Guadeloupe and Martinique. Some British politicians felt that Canada should have gone back to France, and the more valuable (at the time) sugar islands should have been retained by the British. The British did keep St. Vincent and Dominica, ending the effective neutrality of those islands in the Treaty of Paris of 1763.

They also gained Grenada and Tobago, which effectively gave them control over the Grenadines, which had been under French sway previously.

At this point the English were determined to colonize the island of St. Vincent, and develop it for sugar cultivation. The lands already cultivated by the French and Caribs were to be acquired by purchase or otherwise. New lands, held by the Caribs exclusively, were to be acquired, and the Caribs and Blacks removed from the terrain so the lands could be cleared for the cultivation of sugar cane by enslaved African laborers. As it happened, the best sugar lands were those of the Black Caribs in the Northeastern Windward Side. The Black Caribs did not recognize the sovereignty of the British over their lands.

A period of British encroachment on Carib lands, accommodation to gain time by the Carib leaders, and then conflict took place over the next thirty-five years. During this time the French supported Carib resistance to British expansion by actively sending agent provocateurs and arms to the Caribs, and in time of conflict reinforcing Carib fighters with French soldiers from Martinique.

It is interesting to look at parallels between the French in Canada and the Caribbean. The French in Canada had generally good relations with the native populations, lived and traded amicably with them, and used them as allies in time of war against the British. The same can be said for the relations between the French and the Caribs on St. Vincent. The French had been living among them for a generation before the English gained control of the island. The French continued to support the Caribs as allies after the British occupied the island and, as in Canada, a large portion of the European population remained French after the British occupation, while the Caribs were much more familiar with the French language than with English. It seems the colonial policies of the British and French in North America and the Caribbean were similar. After initial conflict, the French sought friendly relations with the native populations, living among them and trading with them, while the British preferred removal of the natives and confiscation of their lands, to be replaced by plantations run by the British with the labor of captive Africans.

After the British occupation of the island in 1762 and their sovereignty confirmed in the Treaty of Paris in 1763 they set about promoting the island as ideal for development as a sugar production center. The fertility of the islands that had been under sugar cane cultivation for the previous hundred and twenty years was diminishing, and the relatively unexploited and fertile volcanic soil of St. Vincent was a resource that the British sought to exploit. The problem was the best lands were under the control of the Black Caribs, who continued to have the support of the dispossessed French. The island was now constitutionally, in the minds of the British at least, a colony of

Great Britain. The problem of Carib occupation of potential sugar lands had to be addressed.

Sir William Young the elder circulated a pamphlet advocating investment in the new sugar lands opening up on St. Vincent. He was appointed to head a commission to arrange the orderly sale and distribution of the new lands, and their settlement. This commission studied the problem of acquiring the Carib lands and removing the Caribs so the lands could be distributed to sugar planters. In the British view, uncultivated land was a waste of resources. The Carib pattern of subsistence was based on small garden plots scattered throughout the jungle. The jungle was vital as a resource for protein and the wild foods that were collected by the Caribs. It was also their source of security in time of war. They were also dependent on the clear streams that gushed from the forested mountains. Destruction and clearing of these lands for sugar would eliminate their means of subsistence, their security, and their traditional way of life.

This was not clearly understood by the British who sought to purchase the land owned by the Caribs, but not farmed. The British endeavored to move the Caribs to small plots or offer them substitute lands, perhaps including those located on Bequia, that were less suitable for sugar production. This would, of course, make the Caribs destitute and destroy their culture. The British planned to offer the incentive of British citizenship if members of the Caribs cooperated. The plan to remove the Caribs to Bequia was dropped in 1766, when it was discovered that the island lacked the streams considered essential for life by the Caribs (Adams 30).

In 1768 new instructions were issued for the acquisition of Carib lands, purchase of their cleared land, and their resettlement on lands "sufficient for their support, and . . . adapted to their manner of living" (Adams 36). The Caribs were to be given five years to resettle and build a new dwelling. Prices for cleared land were set, and the Caribs were to receive property rights with certificates for the new lands awarded. All this seemed reasonable from the British point of view, as they sought to make St. Vincent profitable as a sugar-producing island. The fact remains that the Caribs were given no input into this process and were in effect being evicted from lands they had controlled for generations. Provisions were also made for separate arrangements for "the remains of the native, or Red Charaibs, desire for their security to be separated and settled apart from the free Negroes" (from the Commissioners Instructions in Adams 36-37).

The instructions were printed in both English and French, as many Caribs spoke French. Abbe Valadares was appointed as a liaison between the British land commission and the Caribs. He went to an important Carib settlement, Grand Sable, to explain the British plan to the leaders of the Caribs. A young Chief Joseph Chatoyer, who was the cacique of Grand Sable and who would later play an important role in Carib resistance, presided over the meeting with Valadares. The bottom line of the British proposal was the eventual forced removal of the Caribs after five years. Some of the chiefs went along with the plan, while others protested. A general sentiment was that they recognized no British king and would deal only with the French governor in Martinique. Abbe Valadares was advised to withdraw. The English had to go back to the drawing board in their plans for the orderly acquisition of Carib lands.

The English believed that the Caribs were divided on the question of removal. Chatoyer appeared to be the leader of those most amenable to the removal plan. In actuality the appearance of division was an apparent delaying tactic. While the British regrouped, the Caribs began preparing for resistance. The commission was busy distributing land on other ceded islands so activities on St. Vincent were suspended until 1769 (Adams, Fraser, and Muilenberg).

The British marked out new roads they intended to build. The Caribs realized that any road into their territory could be used for military purposes against them. The roads were allowed to proceed only as far as the Colonaire River, the boundary established in the land agreement between the Red and Black Caribs in previous generations. The British road builders were stopped at the Yambou River by the Caribs, and called on military assistance before continuing any more road construction (Adams 31).

When the project was restarted in 1769 military personnel accompanied the road surveyors, and a barracks was built for them. Captain Wilkie and forty soldiers took up their position in May of 1769. The Caribs stormed the barracks and removed the roof. The captain halted further operations, and awaited instructions from the Governor. The Caribs were not happy with the outcome, and surrounded the soldiers with a force of three hundred, cutting them off. A force of local military and militia came to rescue Captain Wilkie. The Caribs released the surrounded forty soldiers when the Carib chiefs were promised that the commissioners would be advised not to interfere in their country or build any more roads. This was a false promise, and was only made to rescue the soldiers. The British sought help from England (Muilenburg, Adams).

The Black Caribs were also preparing, procuring arms and ammunition from the French. The English patrolled the channel between St. Lucia and St. Vincent and intercepted four large canoes loaded with kegs of gunpowder, and twenty men each. The canoes rushed the patrol cutter and shots were exchanged. The dugouts were disabled with cannon fire, but the eighty Caribs swam, cutlasses in their teeth, toward the cutter. The captain withdrew leaving the Caribs to their fate (Muilenburg 4).

A land sale scandal occurred in the interim, and the British government had to rescind all such land sales, including those made by some Caribs (Adams 33). As a consequence, Chief Chatoyer and forty of his leading people met with the commissioners in 1771. The matter of the sovereignty of the British crown was raised and the Caribs declared that they recognized neither French nor British sovereignty and were independent of both. They also had the promise of the French to support them in protecting their territory from British encroachment (Adams 33).

The establishment of new, successful sugar plantations on lands previously awarded to General Monckton for his success in the occupation of St. Vincent in 1762 brought a rush of new planters to the island seeking lands. The Caribs were determined to sell no more land within their boundaries to the planters. The British decided to carve new roads into Carib territory by force of arms. They obtained the required forces in 1772, and sought assurances that the French in Martinique would not intervene on the Caribs' behalf. The French governor responded that while he could not commit the French to war against the British by openly supporting the Caribs, he also could not prevent private citizens from selling them arms (Adams 35).

It all came to a head in September 1772 when, with the British troops assembled, the British offered the Caribs one more chance at reconciliation, which was refused. The First Carib War was then fought at great cost to both sides for five months. The Caribs were effective guerrilla fighters, and knew the territory well. The strategy of British Major General Dalrymple was to establish military posts in Carib lands so as to isolate the Caribs and control their movements. Despite resistance, the Caribs could not overcome the superior military supply and weaponry of the British, and were forced to surrender in January of 1773. They had faced 2,273 British soldiers, among whom 150 were killed or wounded and 110 died from disease. There was criticism in Britain of the campaign, and orders were issued to offer an honorable peace to the Caribs (Adams 36).

A treaty of "firm and lasting peace and friendship" (from the treaty text in Adams 37) was signed by Darlrymple and twenty-five chiefs, including Chatoyer, who was to play an important role in the Second Carib War. The treaty ended hostilities, forced the Caribs to recognize British sovereignty, avoided dealing with the French, allowed forts and roads in Carib territory, and ceded the coastlands to the Crown. The treaty only delayed future confrontations.

The defeat of the Caribs was a major setback in their attempt to maintain their sovereignty and their lands. They lost a large portion of their territory, and were forced to accede to British sovereignty, but they did not give up the desire to expel the British from the island. The French shared this continuing animosity toward the British interests, though their goal was also to take over the sugar lands claimed by the Caribs. Both the Caribs and the French knew that their mutual cooperation would be necessary to achieve these goals, despite their different and conflicting objectives. War between France and Britain began again in Europe in 1778 and included French support for the American Revolution. This offered both the French and the Caribs an opportunity to regain ground lost to the British in St. Vincent. The Caribs invited French agents to the island as spies, including Percin de la Rocque, who was arrested and jailed by the British, but escaped (Adams 45).

The state of the British military on St. Vincent was quite weak at this point with some troops being sent to the war in Europe. Lieutenant Colonel Etherington of The Royal Americans took charge of the defense of the island, but spent most of his time on his estate, acquired under questionable circumstances, supposedly with the help of Chatoyer. In June of 1779 the French invaded the island. La Roque and about 600 men took the Windward Coast with the help of the Caribs. Another 450 men landed without opposition near Kingstown in ships mistaken for British merchant vessels. Etherington convinced Governor Morris not to the resist the French, and the island was surrendered without much fighting. The British soldiers were taken to Antigua and exchanged for French soldiers (Adams 45).

The British made one feeble attempt under General Vaughan and Lord Rodney to recapture St. Vincent and were turned back by the combined forces of the French and Caribs in 1780. The French appointed Lieutenant Governors to rule St. Vincent from Martinique, including la Roque. The French remained in control for four years until the terms of the Treaty of Versailles of 1783 returned St. Vincent to the British on January 1st, 1784. During the French occupation relations with the Caribs were often tense, as they sought to destroy the British sugar plantations protected by the French.

The British now felt relatively secure in their control of the island, but new challenges still lay ahead. The Caribs were still in possession of some of the best sugar lands, especially around one of their main villages, Grand Sable, which was Chatoyer's hometown. The French Revolution of 1789 presented another threat to the security and advancement of the British designs in St. Vincent. New ideas out of revolutionary France spread to the Caribbean. One result was the slave uprising in Haiti, leading to its eventual independence. A slave revolt also occurred on Guadeloupe. The French began to stir up sentiment for revolution among the French, Mulattos, and Caribs on those islands recently occupied by the British. The French Jacobin governor of Guadeloupe, Victor Hugues, played a role in advocating revolution on St. Vincent, and promised the support of the French Republic if the Caribs and French settlers took action against their British oppressors. The ideas of the equality were taken to heart by many of the French leaders of the revolution at the time. Cynics saw this as simply a way to exploit tensions to help in defeating the British by creating a diversion in the Eastern Caribbean. The French forces in the Caribbean were known as Brigands by the British and consisted largely of freed slaves and French privateers, who were as much motivated by desire for pillage and profits, as by the ideals of the French Revolution. Part of this wider conflict involved the taking of American ships trading with the British by French privateers.

Hugues' plans were for a coordinated rebellion on Grenada and St. Vincent, but had to be changed. The military state of the British on St. Vincent was very weak at this point, and it was an ideal time for the Caribs and their French allies to strike. Word spread from Grenada of the planned attack and Governor Seton requested a meeting with the two top chiefs of the Caribs, Chatoyer and Duvalle. The response was that it was too late to negotiate.

The Second Carib War began on March 8th, 1795 with the burning of the La Croix estate. The militia was called up under the command of Governor Seton's son to respond, and captured 18 Caribs. Duvalle, known as Chatoyer's brother, pushed his forces down the Windward Side of the island, burning estates as he advanced. Chatoyer, on the other hand, killed colonists and their workers as he advanced down the Leeward Side, but spared the property, anticipating future use for it. Duvalle advanced on the post at Dorsetshire Hill, capturing it and hoisting the flag of the French Republic. Chatoyer held the rank of a French general and his French and Carib forces joined him on Dorsetshire Hill for the final assault on Kingstown. He had captured three young Englishmen and brought them with him, and is alleged to have personally hacked them to pieces to show his hatred for the British ("Caribs" 6).

In the capital at Kingstown, Governor Seton was making ready for the defense of the town and the government. Two war ships had arrived in the harbor with reinforcements of British soldiers, and a force of soldiers, sailors, merchant mariners, slaves, and island militia in four columns advanced up the hill under cover of darkness for a surprise attack under on March 14th, 1795 (Adams 56). The Carib and French forces were caught by surprise and driven from the hill, saving the capital.

There are several versions of how the Paramount Chief, Chatoyer, was killed. The most dramatic involves a duel between Chatoyer, by then in his fifties, and Major Alexander Leith, forty-six years of age. The duel is supposed to have ended with Chatoyer's death by Leith's hand. Leith later died at the end of the war. Other stories have Chatoyer being killed in ambush, or bayoneted, by five militiamen, as he moved to attack Leith. His body was not displayed by the victors in the battle, and its burial place has never been found, so the real story behind his death will remain a mystery. The government of St. Vincent in 2002 honored Chatoyer as the first national hero for his leadership and resistance to British tyranny. Each March 14th, the day of his death, is now remembered as a Vincentian national holiday. An obelisk has recently been erected in his honor on Dorsetshire Hill. Major Leigh's death and his killing of Chatoyer was remembered by the colonists with a plaque in St. George's Cathedral in Kingstown, now hidden under a rug by modern Vincentians.

This defeat and the death of Chatoyer did not end the war. The fighting continued on for more than a year. The fighting was a seesaw affair, with victories and losses on both sides. The French had recaptured St. Lucia and could easily supply the Caribs and French forces on St. Vincent from there. The British continued to reinforce St. Vincent with more soldiers. When they retook St. Lucia, and destroyed many of the Carib piraguas on St. Vincent it was harder for the Caribs to get re-supplied by their French allies. The Caribs nearly took Kingstown again, but failed.

In June of 1796 a British force of nearly 4,000 advanced on the Caribs in six sections supported by cannon. British forces included slave rangers led by Leith and German mercenaries. The Caribs were routed and submitted under a flag of truce. Some resisted further, but by the end of October 1796 over 5,000 had been captured or surrendered to the British. Among the last to surrender were Duvalle and Chatoyer's son ("Caribs" 9).

Exile

At the war's end the Caribs were starving and destitute. They were to become exiles from their own country. Similar to the removal of other Native American peoples in North America, such as the Indians of the South East and the Trail of Tears, the Caribs were rounded up and expelled to lands unwanted by the British. The Black Carib Trail of Tears was a watery one, as they were loaded on ships and exiled to Roatan Island, thousands of miles from their homeland on St. Vincent.

At the conclusion of the war most of the Caribs were held on the small Balliceaux Island, where more than half died of disease. The approximately 2,000 remaining Caribs were exiled to Roatan Island, off the coast of Honduras in 1797. Their descendants are now known as the Garifuna, and number in the tens of thousands. There are 200,000 in Honduras alone (Conley 1). Others live all along the Central American Caribbean Coast and in the United States. They still view St. Vincent as the motherland. Some have recently been visiting the island in an attempt to reconnect with their roots, and in so doing reintroduce a lost culture to the people of St. Vincent.

Not all the Black Caribs died or were exiled in 1797. A small number moved to the most remote and rugged part of the island and their descents still live there today. Greiggs was their most important settlement. Today they have largely forgotten their Carib culture and language, and have assimilated into the mostly African Vincentian society. There were only a few hundred Red Caribs remaining in St. Vincent during the Second Carib War. Those that did not participate in the war were settled at Sandy Bay on the Northeast Coast, where their descendants still live today, mixed in with the largely African descendant population. There is little visible trace of the once proud Carib nation, Black or Red, on St. Vincent today.

On March 11, 1797, 722 men, 806 women, and 720 children were embarked on ten ships, escorted by the *H.M.S. Experiment,* leaving from Bequia Island in the Grenadines, and bound for Roatan Island off the coast of Spanish Honduras (Adams 58). These forlorn passengers were the remnants of the approximately 5,000 Black Caribs that were rounded up and imprisoned on tiny Balliceaux Island in the Grenadines after their defeat in the Second Carib War on St. Vincent in 1796. These captives spent nearly nine months on Balliceaux, where most died. The remaining 2,000 odd survivors were being transported to Roatan as exiles. This action ended resistance to total British sovereignty over St. Vincent and the rich undeveloped sugar lands, once controlled by the Black Caribs. The way was open for the British to establish an extension of the Sugar Kingdom on the former Carib lands of St. Vincent. The expulsion of the Caribs also meant that the French no longer had allies on the island with which to plot their recapture of it. From 1797 on, the French were unable to make any serious challenge to British sovereignty over St. Vincent and the Grenadine Islands.

What happened to the once feared Black Caribs who had been able to resist European conquest for so long? After being rounded up and held on Balliceaux, the British exile fleet took the remaining 2,248 captives to Roatan. The voyage took 31 days, including a ten day stay on Jamaica for repairs and provisioning. The British defeated the Spanish garrison on Roatan to open the way for the exiles on April 12th. On the way the Spanish captured one of the British ships with 289 exiles on board, and took the ship to the Spanish port of Trujillo on the mainland of Honduras. The British sent three ships to bombard the town, and the ship was released with is prisoners back to the British. On the way to Roatan it hit a reef entering the harbor, and sank. What happened to the 289 Black Caribs aboard has not been recorded. The group that was eventually left off on Roatan to perish or survive was numbered at 2,026 (Adams 58). The Spanish later removed most of the survivors to Trujillo where they became farmers, and did fairly well. Some were used as woodcutters by the Spanish in Belize. Some were drafted into Spanish military service, fighting on the losing side in the wars of independence. This compelled some to move again, into another exile in Belize, a time now celebrated by their descendants as Settlement Day. Today these people are known as the Garifuna, and they make up an important part of the population of the

Caribbean coasts of Honduras, Guatemala, and Belize. There are also thousands now living in the United States. To these descendants of escaped African slaves and Carib Indians, St. Vincent is "Yurumein," or Homeland, and it holds a very special place in the hearts of the Garifuna people.

Back on St. Vincent some of the Black Caribs were able to flee into the mountains, and avoid capture by British soldiers. They settled on the edge of La Soufriere volcano, and have suffered from its eruptions over the years. A Black Carib woman named Fanny Greigg came out of hiding to recover a captured child from the British. They were impressed with her bravery, and allowed her to mark out a boundary for a reservation where the tiny remnant of the population could live in freedom. Their descendants still live in the town of Grieggs, marked out by this Carib woman ("Symbols of Independence").

What of the original inhabitants, the Yellow or Red Caribs? There were only a few hundred left during the last Carib War. Many of them did not participate in the conflict, and were not exiled. These few were resettled in the old Black Carib territory at Sandy Bay on St. Vincent, and have today largely disappeared as a recognizably separate group. Much was made by the British of the domination of the Yellow Caribs by the Black Caribs, and their apparent take over of Yellow Carib lands. This was done partly to justify the British taking the Black Carib lands. There is some contradiction between sources on the relative numbers of Yellow Caribs and Black Caribs during the last Carib War. The British writers Young and Anderson, who were justifying the British expulsion of the Caribs, claim that only a few Yellow Caribs remained. French historian Alexander Moreau, who was an eighteen year old French agent working with the Caribs during the war, claims that the Yellow Caribs were still in the majority, and that both groups cooperated with a kind of national council, where all indigenous leaders were present. Moreau witnessed the aftermath of a British massacre of the Carib village where he had once lived, with the homes burned and the inhabitants hacked to pieces, including the 18-year-old Carib girl Eliama, with whom he had fallen in love, and her father the chief (Adams 61). It is likely that the political and national differences between the French and British have distorted the historic accounts of the times for their own purposes. It may well be that the line between Black Carib and Yellow Carib was not as clear in the minds of the Caribs as it might have been in the minds of their British conquerors.

Of the French who had settled the islands before the British, and remained during the last Carib War, some were killed along with many of their 3,000 enslaved African laborers, during the war, others fled the islands, or were bought out after the war, and some remained to live under British rule. Those, like young Moreau de Jonnes, who were captured by the British in the war, were expelled to the French islands.

With the removal of the Caribs from the best sugar lands on the Windward Side of St. Vincent the British could now develop and exploit these lands. The Carib threat was gone and defenses against the French were strengthened, such as Ft. Charlotte, on a ridge 600 feet overlooking Kingston harbor that was completed in 1806, and Fort Duvernette, next to Young Island, completed in 1800 to defend Calliaqua Bay. Roads and tunnels were built into the sugar lands, and the lands were distributed to prospective sugar barons.

Garifuna Diaspora

The Black Caribs on Roatan, now known as the Garifuna, at the end of the 18th century were now a people without a country. The British had left off over two thousand exiles on Roatan, with food, supplies, utensils, seeds for planting, and fishing gear. The Garifuna were having a difficult time getting started on the island and asked the Spanish in Honduras to transport them to the mainland. On May 17th, 1797 the Spanish brought the Garifuna to Trujillo on the northern coast of Honduras, where they thrived as farmers, and helped the struggling Spanish, unfamiliar with the tropical agriculture of the Caribbean. According to legend, the Garifuna (for "Cassava Eaters") on the exile ships hid cassava inside their clothing. It was kept alive by their sweat on the crowded ships. They were able to plant it on Roatan, and continue to use it as a basic stable.

Some of the Caribs living with the Spanish were conscripted into the military and served with distinction. The commander of the fort defending access to Lake Isabel in Guatemala at San Felipe was a Garifuna. Garifuna spread along the Caribbean coast of Central America from Nicaragua to Belize, fishing and farming. The first Garifuna to arrive in Belize came as woodcutters, working for the Spanish in 1802 near Stann Creek and Punta Gorda.

During the Central American wars for independence from Spain the Garifuna found themselves again on the losing side. When Honduras became independent, sentiment against Spain and those who fought for Spain were strong. Many Garifuna who had supported Spain during the independence movement fled to Belize, which was under to control of the British. They joined those who had already settled there earlier. This mass migration from the Spanish territories to Belize is remembered annually in the Garifuna towns of Belize as Garifuna Settlement Day, a major holiday. It is celebrated each year on November 19th, even by Garifuna Belizeans living in the United

States. The Guatemalan government officially recognized the importance of the Garifuan community with a visit of their president to the Garifuna town of Livingston on Guatemala's Caribbean coast on Settlement Day in 1996.

During the early 1900's the banana industry came to northern Central America. There were banana plantations, processing plants, and ports all up and down the coast from Belize City to Trujillo in Honduras. Many Garifuna settled in towns near the banana companies to work on the plantations or at the ports and processing plants. In the 1940's this industry was hit hard by a disease that attacked banana plants, and many of the companies were forced to shut down, throwing people out of work. Many Garifuna turned to the seafaring business and immigrated to North America and other parts of Central America.

During World War II Garifuna served in the merchant marines of Britain and the United States. Some then settled in the large U.S. port cities of Los Angeles, New York, and New Orleans. Large numbers of Garifuna have migrated to the United States in recent years and can be found all over the country. The United States is now the country with the second largest population of Garifuna after Honduras.

The Garifuna Today

Today the Garifuna live scattered in small coastal communities from Belize to Nicaragua. Many suffer from poverty, malnutrition, poor housing, and lack of education. The majority are not literate or only semi-literate in the national language of their host country. Most speak

Spanish, and many of the younger Garifuna are losing their native language altogether. English is also spoken by many Garifuna.

There are 43 towns and villages that are home to the Garifuna along the Caribbean coast. Generally they stay out of the mainstream politics of their host countries. They are often discriminated for their cultural and language differences from the mainstream of Central American societies. There are Garifuna who have made distinct contributions to their communities and nations, as educators, doctors, and community leaders. Many of the younger people are migrating to the cities for education and economic opportunities, where some are losing their unique cultural identity.

Those that migrate abroad to North America or elsewhere often go to school, work, raise families, and then return to their home village or town on the Caribbean coast to retire. This will probably be less likely with the younger generation being raised abroad, away from the memories of life in the Caribbean. Some will not learn the traditions of language of their ancestors and will assimilate into the mainstream of their adopted homes. This is a major concern of Garifuna leaders, who have established international organizations to preserve the unique Garifuna identity, language, and culture, despite the lack of a Garifuna homeland. There are even calls by some for reparations from Britain, modeled after those given to indigenous peoples in North America that would lead to the development of education, health, housing, and economy of the Garifuna living in northern Central America.

Note

1. The author, James Sweeney, Ph.D., completed graduate studies at California State University, including his thesis entitled *History as National Myth: The War of the Brigands or the Second Carib War*, from which this paper is derived. He teaches with Central Texas College-Asia and will also be teaching with the University of Maryland University College-Europe.

References

Adams, Edgar. People on the Move: The Effects of Some Important Historical Events on the People of St. Vincent and the Grenadines. Kingstown, St. Vincent and the Grenadines: R&M Adams Book Centre, 2002.

"Caribbean Timeline." Dominica Home. 19 July 2002 Dominica Web. 8 Nov. 2003 http://condoo.com/genresources/historical.htm

"Caribs" 8 November 2003 http://members.tripod.com/prejudice/caribs.htm

Conley, Pamela. "The Garifuna: A Changing Future" Your Guide to Eco Travel. March 2000 <http.//web.archive.org/web.20020616165843>

Eastern Caribbean Territories. Pages 2-5, 8 November 2003 www.cs.indiana.edu/~gkandasw/numismatics/britishCaribbean.html

Davis, Dave D. "Rumor of Cannibals" Archaeology. January/February 1992 p. 49. 8 Nov. 2003 <http://muweb.millersville.edu/~columbus/data/art/DAVIS-D1.ART>

De Silva, Mark ed. Adrien Le Breton (1662-1736). The Caribs of St. Vincent: Historic Account of St. Vincent, the Indian Youroumayn, the Island of the Karaybes. Kingstown: Mayreau Environmental Development Organization, 1998.

Fraser, Adrian. Chatoyer (Chatawae) National Hero of St. Vincent and the Grenadines. St. Vincent: Galaxy Print Ltd., 2002.

Hoebel, E. Adamson, and Thomas Weaver. Anthropology and the Human Experience fifth edition. New York: McGraw-Hill Book Company, 1979.

Johnson, Kim. "The Story of the Caribs and Arawaks" Race and History. 29 March 2003 <www.raceandhistory.com/Taino/>

Michener, James. Caribbean. New York: Random House, 1989.

Muilenburg, Peter T. "Black Carib Bastion of Freedom" Americas May 1999 vol. 51. InfoTrac Web 30 December 2002.

Salisbury, David F. Exploration. "Brief History of Cannibal Controversies" 15 August 2001 http://exploration.vanderbilt.edu/news/news_cannibalism_pt2.thm 8 November 2003.

St. Vincent and the Grenadines Ministry of Tourism and Culture.

Life in St. Vincent and the Grenadines 2002-2003. St.

John's, Antigua: West Indies Publishing, 2002.

Van der Plas, D. Gualbert. The History of the Massacre of Two Jesuit Missionaries in the Island of St. Vincent 24 January, 1654. Booklet in the Kingstown Public Library.

Return to March 2007 Newsletter:

http://www.diaspora.uiuc.edu/news0307/news0307.html

Our History

Saint Vincent & The Grenadines Hotel Association

http://svghotels.net/index.php?page=history

The first people to discover St. Vincent (or "Hairoun" as it was first known) and The Grenadines came in small craft from South America. First came the Ciboney, long before the ancient Pharaohs held sway over the Nile; then the peaceful Arawaks, who brought rudimentary farming and fishing skills with them. Shortly before the Europeans "discovered" the West Indies, the Caribs over-took their Arawak predecessors and worked their way north through the Caribbean islands.

There is some dispute as to whether Columbus ever laid eyes on St. Vincent, but the island's reputation was well known. Any Europeans unfortunate enough to set foot on the island, whether through design or disaster, were not warmly received. It took more than 200 years after Columbus for the Europeans to establish any kind of permanent settlement.

St. Vincent's mountainous, densely forested geography allowed the Caribs to resist European settlement here longer than on almost any other island in the Caribbean. In fact, after the Caribs were defeated on other islands, survivors made their way to St. Vincent and swelled tribal ranks even further.

During that time, the Caribs were joined by slaves who had escaped bondage on Barbados and followed the prevailing trade winds westward to St. Vincent, as well as those who had survived shipwrecks near St. Vincent and Bequia. The mixed progeny of the island warriors and the freed Africans (who became known as Black Caribs), with their common distrust and hatred for the Europeans, proved to be a formidable foe.

Reportedly, as the tribes of the Black Caribs increased, the original "Yellow" Caribs were pushed off their lands. Fearing complete domination, the Yellow Caribs allowed the French to construct a settlement on the island in 1719. With the French came slaves to work their plantations. The Black Caribs took to the thickly forested hills and continued their resistance.

As late as 1748, St. Vincent still was considered too troublesome to deal with so in the Treaty of Aix-la-Chapelle it was officially declared neutral by Britain and France. However, in 1763, after the First Carib War, the British decided to claim the island (and its extraordinarily fertile soil) for themselves.

In 1779, the French took over the island with hardly a shot fired. Reportedly, the conquest of the island took place because all of the British soldiers were working in the northern part of the island on the Governor's plantation, and, to compound matters, no one could find the key to the gun battery. Not surprisingly, the island surrendered in almost a matter of moments without a struggle.

With the Treaty of Versailles in 1783, St. Vincent was brought back into the British fold. However, neither the Black Caribs nor the French had given up just yet. With French backing, the Black Caribs went on the offensive in 1795 in what is now called the Second Carib War or "Brigands War."

Tribal forces under a chief named Duvallier made their way down the windward (eastern) coast of the island, burning British plantations and reportedly putting the planters themselves through the crushing gears of their own sugar mills. Meanwhile, various tribes under the leadership of a famed Carib chief, Chatoyer (also known as Chattawar) pushed British forces down the leeward (western) coast toward Kingstown. The two met in the hills above the capital.

Unfortunately for the Caribs, Chatoyer was killed when British forces stormed Dorsetshire Hill. His dream of providing an island home for the remaining Carib population died with him. However, the Black Caribs fought on valiantly for another year. Finally, by 1797, the British had tipped the battle in their own favour and forced the remaining Black Caribs to choose between annihilation or surrender.

They chose the latter. Their villages were destroyed and their crops decimated. The 5,000 Black Caribs were then rounded up and unceremoniously shipped off to what is now Honduras and Belize, where their descendants still thrive. The few Yellow Caribs left on the island withdrew into the nearly inaccessible northern region of the island, near Sandy Bay, where their descendants live today.

In 1871, St. Vincent became a part of the British colony of the Windward Islands. In 1969, it became a British Associated State, which allowed for full internal autonomy, while foreign affairs and defense were handled by Britain.

Ten years later, on October 27, 1979, St. Vincent and The Grenadines became a fully independent state within the British Commonwealth.

The History of Black Carib Deportation & Migration Through Central America

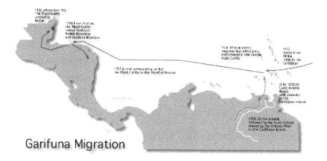

Garifuna Migration

The Garífuna history has been one of constant migration and miscegenation. One of the Garífuna ancestors, the Arawak Indians, migrated from Guyana, Surinam and Venezuela around 160 A.D and settled in the Greater Antilles Islands in the Caribbean. A second ancestor, the Carib Indians, also abandoned their settlements in the Orinoco Delta in 1220 A.D. and seized the Lesser Antilles. The Carib and Arawak then mixed and engendered the Island Carib, who settled predominantly on Saint Vincent Island.

When the Spaniards arrived in the early 1500s, they introduced foreign diseases and an oppressive system of forced labor that disseminated local populations.

African slaves are therefore imported into the New World beginning in 1517. Many slaves escape from European plantations (*cimarrones*). Others survive two shipwrecks off the coast of Saint Vincent Island in 1635. Both are taken in by the Island Carib and their offspring are called the Black Carib, commonly known today as the Garífuna or Garinagu.

Over the next 150 years, a series of wars erupt between the Spaniards, French, British, and Black Carib. Treaties are made and broken and alliances are formed and dissolved in this all-out race for control of the land and its inhabitants. Finally, the British emerge as the victors in June of 1796. They unleash a massive man hunt, trapping and banishing 4,644 overly "rebellious" Black Carib to Baliceaux Island - where they are held on a 464 m. high cliff! Others manage to escape to South America and to the neighboring Antilles Islands. This adds to the African Diaspora.

Of those deported, the lighter-skinned "Yellow or Red Caribs" are classified as "benign" and returned to St. Vincent. Today, many Creole-speakers on St. Vincent are descendants of the Yellow/Red Carib. The remaining 2,026 captives are left on Honduras' Roatan Island with limited food and supplies on April 11, 1797. The Spaniards transport the Garífuna to the mainland and rescue them from potential starvation. The Garífuna return the favor, supplying food for the entire colony - which is dying of hunger because Spanish farming practices are not suited to the tropics.

The Garífuna soon tire of Spanish authority. As early as 1802, they join British woodcutters to log mahogany or smuggle contraband trade along the Belize, Guatemala, and Nicaragua coastlines. But a mass migration does not happen until 1832, when the Garífuna are charged with treason for supporting the Spanish royalists' failed insurrection against the Federation of Central American States. Many Garífuna flee to the remote Mosquitia region. Others, under the leadership of Alejo Beni, set sail for Belize and found the settlement of Dangriga. Today this city holds the largest Garífuna population.

Those who remain in Honduras after Central American independence tend to work on the banana plantations at the turn of the XX century. When the market collapses before World War II and banana companies shut down their operations, many Garífuna are forced to look for alternative work. Some join the U.S. and British merchant marines, who were looking for new recruits to replace those who had left for war. After completing their service, many Garífuna settle in England and the U.S., and others return to their communities with fantastic tales and fancy merchandise. This intrigues younger generations and women to seek better opportunities abroad.

Today, approximately, 300,000 Garífuna live around the world. Of this number, the largest concentration of Garífuna peoples, 100,000, are found in Honduras. Around 90,000, nearly the total Garífuna population in Honduras, are living in the U.S. They are primarily located in Chicago, Houston, Los Angeles, Miami, New York, and New Orleans. Many Garífuna have migrated to the U.S. because of the limited economic opportunities available in their hometowns. Today, many Garífuna communities in Honduras are kept afloat by money sent from relatives working in the U.S. Grandmothers and mothers, in particular, wait on this money to take care of the children left in their custody. New, concrete houses can now be built and furnished with televisions, stereos, and other luxuries. Dreams can be achieved. But families can be torn apart. Communities can be drained of bright leaders and entrepreneurs. And customs, values, and social structures can be altered.

The Black Carib - Garífuna

Early History

The story begins in South America, where people who spoke Arawak-an Amerindian language fashioned a culture based on yuca or cassava farming, hunting and fishing in a dense forest cut by many rivers. By the year 1000 AD some of them had moved up the Orinoco River to the Caribbean Sea and it's islands, where they established a new way of life. Later other people, whom history has called "Caribs", moved into the Caribbean out of the same areas.

They traded with the Arawaks, sometimes raiding their settlements, and eventually they pushed them out of the smaller islands, taking their women as wives and killing or enslaving the men, according to stories told to Columbus. The mixture of Carib and Arawak created a new people who have been called "Island Carib". They were one of the two main racial components of the modern Garinagu, who continue to speak the language of the Arawaks.

In the 1500's many Europeans visited the Caribbean islands, and soon they came to live on some of them, bringing Africans as slaves to carry out much of the agricultural and other work. The Island Caribs fought fiercely to protect their islands, but succeeding in holding only two Dominica and Saint Vincent, or Yolome (Yurume), as they called it. In 1635 two Spanish ships carrying slaves to the West Indies were ship-wrecked near St. Vincent and the slaves on board scaped and took refuge among the Carib Indians. The Caribs welcomed and protected the Negro refugees, and in time allowed them to marry the Caribs. The Africans then adopted the languages, culture and traditions of the Yellow Island Caribs. The intermarriage brought about a rapid growth of hybrid mixture of African and Yellow Indians Caribs. From this union arose a half-bred race possessing some Caribs and African characteristics to which the name Garifuna or Black Carib was given. Some of the African customs were preserved and blended with those of the Caribs. Out of this union came a new people who began to compete with the Island Carib for land and power. These were called Black Caribs by the Europeans to distinguished them from the others, who were called Red or Yellow Caribs. Today they are more often known as Garifuna (or Karaphuna, in Dominica) which is closer to the original word by which they called themselves so long ago. More correctly they are called Garinagu.

By the 1750 the Black Caribs of St. Vincent were numerous a nd quite prosperous. They had war-chiefs, some with several wives who did most of the farming. The men hunted and fished and made trips to nearby islands to trade tobacco and baskets for arms, munitions and other European manufacture goods. Some began to grow cotton for export, using captured

African slaves to supplement their wives labor. French settlers lived in St. Vincent then too, but there was enough land for all, and few problems arose. In fact the Caribs found it to their advantage to trade with the French not only on St. Vincent, but on neighboring islands such as Martinique, St. Lucia and Grenada.

But in 1763 the British started coming to St. Vincent in large numbers and over the next several years they tried everything they could think of to get the Black Caribs to give more of their fertile lands to them so they could plant sugarcane. They tried persuasion, trickery, purchase and finally by 1772 provoke the Caribs to open war fare. The French sympathized with their Black friends, and help them to try to get rid of their common enemy, the British. For 32 years the struggle continued on and off again, and both sides had many losses.

Finally in 1795, the British determined to end the conflict and take over the entire island. They brought in special troops and put on a major military camping. Their own slaves helped them fight the Black Caribs, for they had accepted their master's views and were frightened of what they saw as a dangerous "primitive" people. By the summer of 1796 the French had had enough, and surrendered but the Carib continued fighting. The British burned their houses, canoes and crops and eventually, sick and nearly starving the Caribs surrendered too. A total of 4,644 men, women and children were taken prisoners and sent to the island of Baliceau until it was decided what to do with them. While there, under dreadful, dreadfully crowded unsanitary conditions, more than half of them died from a terrible disease, probably Yellow Fever. Black and white British troops, who also suffered the disease, did not died in such large numbers because they were better nourished, or because they had become immune through exposure to their African childhood.

In February, 1797, the order came to send all surviving Black Caribs to the island of Roatan, just off the Honduran coast, where other rebellious blacks had been sent previously. At the same time, they returned the so-called "Red" or lighter skinned" Caribs to Saint Vincent. By this time the two populations were very mixed. Single families would have had some light and some darker-skinned individuals: thus it's likely that forced separation according to skin color only made the situation more tragic.

On March 11, 1797 the order came to send all the captured Black Caribs, along with some other non-Carib black people, British troops and supplies, were loaded onto eight ships. Captain James Barrett, commander of his Majesty's Ship Experiment, took the lead, and they set off westward accross the Caribbean Sea toward Roatan, with a stop over of about 10 days in Jamaica for repairs and to load fresh water and meat. As they neared Guanaja, one of the ships was captured by the Spanish and taken directly to

Trujillo with 289 Garifuna aboard. After the convoy had landed and secured the surrender of the Spanish fort at Port Royale (Roatan) on April 12, Captain Barret ordered three ships to go in pursuit of the captured ship, the "Prince William Henry". Upon reaching Trujillo, the English bombarded that town, but did not succeed in taking it. Eventually a truce was reached, and the Prince William Henry was released with all it's prisoners still aboard. Unfortunately, however, it struck a reef entering the harbor at Roatan and sank. No one knows how many, if any, of those aboard survived.

Although the British left them with food supplies, tools, fish hooks and lines, cuttings and seeds, it would have been very difficult to have cleared and planted before the rainy season began-specially because the people were weak and miserable from their long ordeal. Therefore, they begged the Spanish on the main land to come to Roatan and rescued them. On May 19. 1797, the Spaniards did that, and thus became the master of the Bay Island again. They also acquired a new labor force, for once the Garinagu had moved to Trujillo, the men worked as soldiers and fisherman. They also cleared land so the women could plant food crops for themselves and for sale. In this way they provided enough food for the entire European coastal population, which had been near starvation before that because they did not know how to live and produce food in the tropics, and their traditional crops did not do well in the acidic soils found there.

Soon after arriving inn Trujillo, some of the men began to explore the coast line as far as Belize in one direction and Nicaragua in the other. Longwood and mahogany were major exports then, and the British woodcutters were please to give work to any Garinagu who would venture to Belize. The Miskito people (then called Sambos) who lived east of Trujillo in what is know as the Mosquitia, were allies of the British and bitter enemies of the Spanish. They were friendly to the Garinagu at first, and offered them advice and assistance. By 1807, the Garinagu became disgusted or disappointed with Spanish rule and many of them left Trujillo, settling tiny villages on the "Costa Arriba" as far as the Patuca River and perhaps beyond. Others moved north and west to what they called La Buga or La Boca-the mouth of the Rio Dulce(Livingston), as well as to Dangriga (then Stann Creek), where some of their fellows had been working sin 1799.

Woodcutting and smuggling were the main occupations of the British in Central America at that time, and the Garinagu soon became known for their skills in both activities. There canoes were likely to be seen anywhere on the coast and it's many lagoons, and their small settlements dotted the entire shoreline wherever work could be had. they clustered about Omoa and Trujillo in Honduras, near San Felipe in the Gulf of Dulce and Livingston and Santo Tomas in Guatemala, as well as what the British came t call "Carib Town" in Belize. Once known as Stan Creek, it was renamed Dangriga to honor the Garifuna people in 1975. Woodcutting near Limon, Black River(now Palacios), Bruce and Caratasca Lagoons also drew Garinagu settlers. No until the beginning of the fruit industry toward the end of the 19th century did they lived near La Ceiba and Tela. They always settled villages where the woman and children stayed while the men traveled as necessary to gain their livelihood, though in the early days the women sometimes went with the men into the bush camps.

The Spanish frequently used Garinagu as soldiers, even after the independence of Central American states in 1821. In 1832, however the Garinagu backed the loosing side in an effort to overthrow the president of the Central American Federation, Francisco Morazan, and they were forced to fleet from the settled Central American areas. Most went Belize or the far Mosquito shore. After that their military activities were sharply reduced, although a few continue to serve in their several national armies, even today.

Ethnological studies have proven that the Garifuna, are the only black people in the Americas to conserve their native culture. Throughout more than 300 year, the Garifuna culture has undergone constant change as the Garifuna people respond to the new demands placed on them through contact with other cultures. They still share a great deal with the Indian of the Amazon such as language, yucca, fishing, circle dancers and several religious practices and beliefs. However, their African ancestors have also left a deep mark in their dances, oral traditions, drum styles and agriculture.

In 1974 the Garífunas had a population of approximately 77,000 and had established a total of 51 communities, 43 of which were located along the shore of northern Honduras from Puerto Cortès in the west to Río Paulaya in the east. In effect, almost every village along the coast of northern Honduras was inhabited primarily by the Garífunass, whose population in Honduras alone was 61,000 in 1974. The Garífunas have maintained an ethnic unity primarily because they continue to speak as a mother tongue a common language (along with English and Spanish) called Garífuna, which derives from native Island Carib Culture. The Garifuna are spread out in villages all along the Honduras' Atlantic coast in the departments of Cortés, Atlántida, Colón and Gracias a Dios.

Recent History

After the independence of Central American nations, more woodcutter move in to the Mosquitia. Garinagu were expert wood cutters, but they also had generations of experience with the sea and everything related to it. They transported people and goods the length of the shore between Belize and Bluefields. Along the way they fished and carried contraband items, including arms and secret messages for various of the almost continual revolutionary and counter revolutionary movements. If caught they said they were merely fishing. They had learned from the Europeans in the West Indies how to fool the authorities and operate outside the law in order to advance their own interests.

By the end of the 1800's mahogany was no longer so profitable for various reasons. The wood in Belize, Guatemala and the Mosquitia had been plentiful, but over cutting had reduced the Honduran, which thus reduced it's value, even though the cost of cutting and transporting it were the same as for others. Besides, fine woods from Asia and Africa were now increasingly available at lower prices in Europe. Cutting and sawmill operations gradually shut down.

Fruit, especially bananas had been exported for some time from the Bay islands and later from the area around La Ceiba. By 1900 there were more than 100 companies exporting bananas from the Central American coast, and Garifuna were involved in growing the fruit and helping to load it. Small schooners sailed along the coast, buying a few stems here and there in what was known as "Poquitero"(small scale) trading. Later three large companies either absorbed or drove most of the others out of business; they planted their own plantations and built railroad lines so they could more easily transport the fruit to the coast line. They concentrated their shipping at Punta Castilla near Trujillo, La Ceiba, Tela and Corte in Honduras, Livingston (and later Puerto Barrios) in Guatemala and Belize City.

Garinagu clustered around these ports with their families as the men sought and found jobs with the companies or in related industries.

Just before World War II, the banana industry in Central America was hurt by plant diseases and events in Europe, both of which caused prices for the fruit to fall. When the United States entered the war, the companies began to reduce their operations along the coast. They closed Punta castilla completely in 1942, pulling out all the railroad lines in the area. This was a major blow for the Garinagu, for they had come to depend on the opportunities. the well stocked commissary with it's favorable prices, and the railway for transportation to many of their villages. The later was more reliable in bad weather than their own canoe transport.

Many Garifuna men made a major job switch at that time, taking advantage of the enormous increase in the merchant marine of the United States and Britain and the fact that too few men were available for that work because so many had entered military service. Hundreds of Garinagu, along with other Central American and Panamanian men signed up as sailors and soon made a new reputation for themselves. Their work took them to ports all over the world, and they came home with stories and goods which made younger men eager to follow their brothers, fathers and uncles. Some settle permanently in the lands they visited-specially in cities such as New York, London, Los Angeles and New Orleans.

Soon there were Garinagu employed in a variety of occupations in those cities. Many worked in the docks, and large numbers in the food service trades-a specialty for which they had become known in the merchant marine as well. At first it was mostly men who travel in search of work, but in ht 1960's large number of woman also began to find it to their advantage to work outside their countries. Traveling was nothing new of course, for both men and women had been accustomed to going long distances along the Central American coast to see relatives, attend wakes, go to school, trade, or find jobs. But the new migration present new challenges.

The people quickly learned how to manage in New York-how to get appropriate papers or to find work, how to get appropriate papers or do without them, how to get help from public assistance programs, how to find a place to live, and so forth. There may be as many as 50,000 Garinagu now living in New York City alone and perhaps another 10,000 across the United States in far flung cities as Washington, Chicago, Saint Louis, and Los Angeles. London England also has a sizable community, mostly from Belize.

For those who choose to stay overseas, there are many rewards. Immigration in most industrial nations have been welcomed, for usually they'll work for less money than citizens. But even small wages have looked good to those whose living costs are modest and who have been without work in their own countries. And once again, Garinagu enjoy a reputation for being good workers.

In spite of the cold weather, which no tropical people really enjoy, life in the United States has been generally good. Not only are the Garinagu able to live better than they did at home, but the vast majority send money, regularly or irregularly, to help support those left behind.

They have discovered how to use the available health facilities, free education and adult classes, food stamps and other means of public assistance. They have found living spaces in many different neighborhoods which they've transformed with love and hard work into comfortable homes. Some, of course, live more luxuriously than others. Local stores and markets sell most of the foods they've always eaten: plantain, yuca, yams, mangoes, avocados rice and beans as well as more more modern processed convenience foods which they like but can seldom purchase in Central America. They will cross the city to buy fresh fish in the early dawn before going to work.

Language is not a problem, for in addition to their native tongue, all Garinagu today speak either standard English or Spanish. Both New York an Los Angeles are today practically bilingual cities, therefore even those with no English are not at a disadvantage. Many have cars, and some have purchased homes. Some of their members have professions-there are Engineers, doctors, butchers, bankers and barbers. Others work in the garment industry, either in the factories and marketing outlets, or by sewing piece work at home. Still others do domestic work by the day or as live-in help. College graduates have become more common and some have gone to post graduate programs as well.

Most Garinagu, just as in the home villages, socialize primarily with each other during their nonworking hours, visiting each other's houses, playing soccer, cards or dominoes in neighborhood parks, drinking and some times dancing Punta and other traditional dances. They have both new and old holidays to celebrate, Belizean Settlement Day in November 19 being one of the most important. As at home, they occasionally have John Anoe dancers entertain at Christmas time.

There are traditional curers working in the United States, but major rituals to placate the ancestors are said to be best held in Central America. Many Garinagu however have found comfort and help in the rituals of other Afro-Americans living in New York. Some of the elements of these have been taken back to villages and have found a place in curing practices here.

Garinagu try to visit their home villages from time to time, specially at Christmas and Easter, and almost all return for major family crises, such as the death of a parent. To do this, they sometimes borrow from each other or pool their resources in ingenious ways. They may take back inexpensive goods to sell at home, and thus pay their tickets.

But there are social and cultural sacrifices of such migration. Children born in the United States, seldom learn to speak their native tongue well and many don't speak it at all. They know nothing of their heritage, and often are embarassed or ashamed by the elder's beliefs in the spirit of the dead, or gubida and the powers of the Garifuna "Priest" called a buwiye A return visit to Central America may be an agony-they dislike the food, are uncomfortable with the lack of the things they are use to in the USA.

Life in Central America

The Garinagu who stay living in Central America, scratch out a living as best as they can. In addition to traditional occupations of farming and fishing, some sell lottery tickets, cold drinks, fruits, make clothes for sell to the community, tend small stores or make and sell bread.

Many of those that stay behind are able to make a living because of the help they get from abroad. Older people in particular, are very dependent upon these checks, and the women depend on them to support their households, to buy food for the children left in their care, including some of their own. It's common to see grandmothers taking care of their adult children, and their grandchildren.

With decline in jobs all along the Caribbean coast and Central America, it's provable that many of the smaller villages would have ceased to exist long ago were it not for the international migration. Honduran were the first to go, follow by the belizeans and finally, Guatemalan Garinagu.

Those of Nicaragua have migrated in fewer numbers, yet have have lost more of the cultural features which made them distinct from other afro peoples living in the Atlantic coast of such country.

In Honduras the smallest villages between Trujillo and Plaplaya at first appear untouched by modern life. But one finds in most of them some new concrete block houses. Most of them are constructed with money sent back by the immigrants. More importantly, however are the retirees (pensionados) who are now returning to live out the remainder or their lives where they were born. The men specially, prefer to come home again. They spend much time on the street, relaxing in front of their houses, on the beaches, playing card and just plain gossiping.

Their retirement checks in U.S. dollars give them comfort and security. In Central America they live quieter life, and spend time, painting, repairing and generally improving their houses, and proudly displaying their possessions. They are good role models for the younger men, for they have been successful in their working lives.

Older women unlike the men, like to be with their children and grand children, and although they too like to gossip in public places, and participate in local organizations, many of those who migrate and spend much time abroad, often prefer to stay in the U.S. cities with their loved ones. They usually care for their grand children there as well as in the villages.

Money and ideas from outside have had other influences on the home villages . More people have possessions , such as radios, refrigerators, televisions, gas stoves and other home appliances, which tend to improve their lives.

n addition to changes in consumption patterns, there have also been spiritual effect. All observers agree that the number of ancestors rites has increased over the past 20 years. The cost of putting on a major dugu is very expensive. Since large number of friends and relatives attend this rites, it can be said that money from abroad spent in this way provides a social benefit for the entire village. The rituals serve to remind them of their common origins, mutual problems, and spiritual and ethnic unity. Families reinforce their loyalties to each other, and many who were desbelievers in their youth, come to appreciate the deeper meaning of their traditional celebrations in middle or old age. These rituals are private, soul-wrenching deeply religious affairs and they are definitely not dying out. Rather the migration seems to have increased the number and elegance of the traditional ceremonies.

Today there are three primary countries in Central America in which Garinagu live. And although they share a common heritage, their loyalties to their nations have had some affect. They are not by any mean alike. In New York It can be seen that they have grown apart. They tend to live in different parts of the city, they hold separate activities and celebrations and their values and aspirations are different, even though some of their leaders would like to see a more unified front. In part their failure to achieve this seem related to political and economic events in their countries of origin.

The social positions of Garinagu with the different countries varies as well. In Honduras and Belize they have become a visible and politically aware minority. Their members live not only on the rural coastal cities, but in the capitals as well, where many of them have achieved high governmental and other positions. Some, as in Belize and Honduras have become elected officials. Garifuna teachers are to be found in large numbers in both countries.

Guatemala on the other hand is a very different story. Perhaps because there's today really only one Garifuna community-Livingston containing no more than 3,000-4,000 Garinagu, the country pays little attention to them. They are not perceived as Indians, nor are they Ladinos the two primary ethnic categories in that country. Since Livingston itself is isolated, so are the people. Although a small number have migrated permanently to Guatemala city, most have sought to leave for New York or elsewhere in the U.S.. For the most part, they have not participated in the recent Guatemalan political struggles, apparently preferring migration to a reform which may take generation.

Livingston boast few of the large, attractive and well built modern houses seen in Honduras and Belize. There are no Garifuna retail store, that occupation being dominated by the chines and more recently Indians from the highland. Most of the money coming into the community, is spent in material and personal gratifying artifacts.

School statistics in all three countries show that Garifuna kids leave school earlier than do member of other ethnic groups in the same communities, but here are smaller percentages of them studying in Livingston than elsewhere.

Because Livinstonians did not begin going to New York until the 1960's a generation later than the Hondurans, there are as yet few retirees. One wonder how many will choose to return at all.

The Future

Migration has provided a temporary solution to the problem of joblessness to the Garinagu, for a long time but this is not likely to continue forever. Nor is it the best way to provide a good life for more and more Garinagu. The immigration changes being instituted in the United States, will make it more difficult for future migration. It hereford seems that Garinagu must find ways to improve their situation at home, and their national governments owe it to them to help in this. Even migration to cities within Central America, which will certainly continue, is not a solution, for there will not be enough jobs there either.

The smaller towns and villages must find ways to improve their ability to provide useful goods and services for themselves and sale to others. The people must be helped to bring modern techniques into their agricultural and fishing activities so as to produce a surplus for sale. Garinagu should be encouraged to make ereba for sale in major cities and perhaps even export it to Miami and New York. Machinery for grating the cassava and improved stove have already been introduced into some of the villages. New varieties of cassava chips for feeding cattle could be processed and sold. Other specialty agricultural products might also be encouraged.

But the people can not be expected to return to the last century. To be successful and happy, they must learn about agronomy, marketing. bookkeeping, advertising, legal procedures and other skills used by modern farmers. In Belize few Garifuna have joined in a new cacao growing community near Belmopan. As Garinagu in the towns accumulate capital, they may choose to invested at home, thus improving their local standards of living.

They will need service specialists such as master electricians, plumbers, masons, engineers of various kinds. They will be able to efford other amenities such as town bands or orchestras, beauty parlors, libraries and so forth. Garinagu are not "primitive"; their ancestors have been part of the Western civilization for more than 2 centuries. Even though they tend to drop out of school too early, they enjoy a higher rate of fundamental literacy than some other ethnic groups in their countries, and most homes, even in the smaller villages have some well thumbed books.

But at the same time they have traditional customs and values some of which they would like to preserve. Their religious beliefs, which they have successfully blended with the more formal teachings of Christianity, especially Roman Catholicism, emphasize the concept of life after death, continuity of family lines, and mutual assistance. These are values worth saving in the modern world.

Garinagu's artistic expression occurs mainly in music and dance. Although most of their seasonal celebrations have been heavily influenced by Europeans customs, they are the only ones left in Central America who dance the intricate and fascinating "John Canoes" during the Christmas and New Year holidays.

Garinagu's should be encourage to maintain their traditional dances, and special talents as both performers and composers should be recognized. Some Garinagu have not been satisfied with merely preserving the traditional styles; but have found their joy in inventing new songs and dances to enrich all our lives. Punta Rock has provided a setting of the creativity of the Garifuna. Garifuna productions have been presented around the world, by the Ballet Folklorico Garifuna of Honduras.

For more than 300 years the Garinagu have been developing their culture. It has constantly changed in response to new demands which have been placed upon them and as they have come into contact with new peoples. They still share much with the Indians of the Amazon forest (language, ereba, round dances, some religious practices and beliefs, emphasis in fishing), but their African ancestors have left a strong mark as well (punta, John Canoe, many folk tales, drumming styles, plantain, sacrifice of roosters and pigs).

Europeans have added to and modified all of these most notably in their household furnishings, religion, foodways, dress styles, and folklore. Where other societies have simply given up their special character as they have modernized, the Garinagu have retained much of the old as they have adopted the new. As a result, many of the things they themselves believe are old and traditional were not known to their ancestors.

Perhaps Garinagu have been able to retain their ethnic identity precisely because they have been able to change their cultural patterns as needed. They have changed willingly, quickly and jet insisting all along that the new is really Garifuna after all. In other words their adopted customs became their very own, and thus valuable to them. Intermarrying with non-Garinagu has been no problem; the later are simply incorporated into the group, provided they are willing. Historical and biological evidence shows that among their ancestors are Indians from both South an Central America, Africans from many tribes(the Yoruba, Ibo and Ashanti tribes of West Africa from Ghana, Nigeria and Siera Leon), and Europeans from several different countries, which may herein lies another source of their survival strength.

Garinagu have proved that modernization need not involved a sacrifice of all that is dear, yet neither must people be excluded from the benefits of the modern world, because they refuse to give up all their traditions. The Garinagu survival may serve to help other ethnic groups understand hoe they may have the best of both worlds-people whose own culture seem in danger of dissapearing, as well as those who believe they must turn their backs or everything new in order to preserve the old.

Bibliography

Breton, Raymond (1877) *Grammaire caraibe, composée par le p. Raymond Breton, suivie du Catéchisme caraibe.* Maisonneuve, Paris. - from 1635 manuscript

Cayetano. Sebastian R Garifuna history, language and culture of Belize and C.A. November 1, 1989

Davidson, William V. Historical Geography of the Bay Islands, Honduras. Southern University Press, 1974.

Gullick, C. J. M. R. (1985). *Myths of a Minority.* Assen: Van Gorcum Press.

Gonzalez, Nancie L. (1988). *Sojourners of the Caribbean: Ethnogenesis and Ethnohistory of the Garifuna.* Urbana: University of Illinois Press.

Humphrey, Chris. *Honduras Handbook.* Moon Publications, 1997.

Kerns, Virginia (1983). *Women and the Ancestors: Black Carib Kinship and Ritual.* Urbana: University of Illinois Press.

Lehman, Jeffrey. *Gale Encyclopedia of Multicultural America.* 2nd ed., vol. 1. Gale Research, 1995

Whitehead, Neil L. (1988). Lords *of the Tiger Spirit.* Leiden: Foris Publications Holland

Garifuna Re-Settlement in Central America: Nicaragua, Honduras, Guatemala and Belize

By Sebastian R. Cayetano

(From the book Garifuna History, Language & Culture, 1989)

Since Garinagu are a coastal people, shortly after they arrived and established new homes, and manioc cassava fields, and built their canoes in Honduras, they also began a pattern of spreading and establishing village communities along the Caribbean coastline. Up to relatively recent times two Garifuna settlements were found in Nicaragua--Orinoco and La Fe, both located on Pearl Lagoon.

In Honduras, it is estimated that there are about 42-46 Garifuna settlements, the largest being Trujillo with a population of about 10,000; followed by other communities--Pieda Pintada near La Ceiba, then others running from west to east--Masiga, Travesia, Bajamar, Saraguina, Rio Tinto, Tornabe, San Juan, La Ensenada, Triunfo de la Cruz, Nuevo Go, Cayo Venada, Rosita, Monte Pobre, Corozal, Sambo Creek, Nueva Armenia, Salvado Lislis, Rio Estaban, Guadaloupe, San Antonio, Sante Fe, Cristales, Rio Negro, Barranco Blanco, Barra de Chapagua, Santa Rosa de Aguan, Barra de Aguan, Limon, Rio Zarco, Punta Piedra, Cusuna, Ciriboya, Iriona Viejo, San Jose de la Punta, Sangrelaya, Cocalito, Dugamacho, San Pedro, Batalla, Pueblo Nuevo, Buena Vista, and Plaplaya (Gullick 1976:111).

In Guatemala there are three communities, the town of Livingston Labuga; Chawecha, and Sampuli. In Belize, there are six communities, the major town Dangriga (population 7000), Hopkins, Georgetown, Seine Bight, Punta Gorda Towm (2300) and Barranco. I must also note here that Garifuna spread is no longer confined to the shores of Central America, for since the late sixties Garinagu have also migrated to the United States, where there is a sizable population of roughly twenty to fifty thousand Belizeans now living in America. These Garinagu have settled in the state of California, particularly in Los Angeles, and in Chicago and New York.

In contrast, in Dominica today there are 6,000 Yellow Carib Indians who live on the Salibya Carib Reserve, whereas in Saint Vincent-Yurumein--the Garifuna motherland, there remains but a small population of 3,000 and they are to be found in Sandy Bay and Greggs. It is estimated that there are about 300,000 Garinagu throughout the world today. (Gonzalez in Krohn 1987)

Garinagu in Honduras: Two Brutal Massacres of Garinagu Only twenty-six years after their arrival in Honduras Garinagu found themselves embroiled in Honduran politics. Evidently many males had joined the army and had

---

159

become good soldiers. Unfortunately for them, many supported the Spanish Royalists who were then the ruling colonial power. Morazan was leader of the Honduras Ladinos who opposed and fought against Spanish domination from 1823-1832. He was victorious; Spain lost the war, and consequently bitter reprisals befell the Garinagu.

hey were hunted and massacred. To escape the atrocities, Alejo Beni, his second-in command Yurumein, 28 other adults and a dozen children secured two doreys and left Roatan for Belize, where they arrived and settled in Dangriga on 19 November, 1832. (Flores 1979:67)

In 1823, the Federation of Freedom for Central America, under the leadership of Mexico, began. The Ladinos of Honduras, under Morazan, went to war against Spanish domination of their country. Unfortunately the Caribs chose to fight on the side of their hosts, Royalist Spain against the revolution which lasted until 1832. When Spain lost the war, terrible reprisals were inflicted upon the Caribs, bringing to mind, the West Indies all over again. It was then that Alejo Beni fled the country in dories with a large number of Black Caribs, across the Gulf to Belize colony, where they asked for, and were granted political asylum by the Governor of that era. (Flores 1 979:24)

The Garinagu who remained behind in Honduras continued their existence by farming and fishing; growing crops of yams, bananas, cassava, plantain, yucca, etc. This was primarily the women's occupation, and fishing and the running of contraband was the males' responsibility. In 1867, the American-owned United Fruit Company built a railroad from Puerto Cortez, to the Gulf of Honduras. This was to facilitate the shipment of bananas, coffee, cattle, lumber, and cotton.

Garinagu soon found themselves labourers in these industries, for they were dependable workers (Flores 1979:25). Despite total illiteracy among the majority, they worked as gangs in the loading and unloading of ships, clearing of forests for banana plantations, became merchant seamen, the more lettered among them became office clerks and managers. In the 1890's Garinagu continued to be employed on the railroads, banana farms, on the docks and in the machine shops. It is ironical and indicative of the strong suspicion and discrimination Garinagu faced then, and still do now face in that Republic, that while United Fruit Company employed 90% Garinagu, Honduras government hired only 1% compared to every 100 Ladino employed. In contrast to the Garifuna of Belize, education of Honduran Garifuna is only a recent development.

Then on June 19th, 1937, came the blackest day in San Juan Village. It was the day Teniente Remiro invaded San Juan Village with about 200 armed soldiers to achieve the second Honduran Garifuna Massacre. He declared by reading a letter: "You Morenos (Caribs) of this village have been found guilty of the crime of treason against the country by the HighCommand and Tribunal of the Republic of Honduras. And are hereby sentenced to death as revolutionaries by a firing squad on this day, June 1 9th, 1937. We are here to carry out that order in the name of E1 Supremo, our Glorious Leader and President Dictador Tiburcio Andino Corias 1932-1945." Men, women and children were routed from their homes at gunpoint and led to the village square, where the men, numbering 22 in all and including their informant Garifuna Yeureudi, were made to dig their graves themselves, then stood before the firing squad in innocence, before the very eyes of their horrified wives and children. The 22 men were all shot, then buried as the proclamation had read; only one, a personal friend of one of the soldiers, was allowed to escape--Maestro-Musico Hernandez. He fled to Belize and lived to relate that horror. With the help of a sea captain, the women and children remaining eventually escaped to Belize, to found the Village of Hopkins. (Flores 1979:41)

As Garinagu become increasingly educated in Central American, the emphasis appears to lie on cultural preservation, rather than on economic self reliance. To this end, since 1980, Garifuna programs are heard on national radio in Belize and Honduras, but very little in Guatemala except for occasional political and religious propaganda. In Belize since 1966, and in Honduras just recently, drama groups have formed and staged national and international performance in Garifuna. Famous among these are "Teatro Garifuna Loubavagu" directed by Rafael Murillo, and "Garifuna Ballet Folklorico de Honduras" directed by Rene Crisanto Alvarez, both Honduran, and the Belizean internationally acclaimed Warigabaga Dance Group directed by Roysus Bregal and Mrs. Phyllis Cayetano.

Recently in Honduras, Garinagu and other minority Blacks gathered and formed "Organisacion Fraternal Negra Hondurena:" (OFRANEH) to champion the cause of Honduran Blacks. So far OFRANEH, headed by a Gaifuna--Santos Centeno Mena, President--has hosted three visits of the National Garifuna Council of Belize, headed by President Fabian Cayetano in the years 1986, 1987, and 1989.

These delegations, initially involving 22 persons, then 15, and then 10, have brought us closer together for greater understanding and for the sharing of common problems and concerns. Interestingly, and perhaps typically Garifuna, almost all Garifuna organizations that concern culture in Belize, Honduras and Guatemala are headed by women. It is a further indication that Garifuna culture is passed on from generation to generation through its women, and this has been so since way back in Saint Vincent.

Labuga-Livingston - Dept. de Isabal - Guatemala

In 1804 a Carib Shaman by the name of Marcus Sanchez Diaz founded the town of Labuga, Livingston at the mouth of the Rio Dulce opposite the modern Puerto Barrios. It was first called Labuga (mouth of the River). (Gullick 1976; Flores 1979) In Labuga, Garinagu lived by fishing and farming, as do all in Central America. Many of the children did not attend school until recently, and the people, although in the majority, are ruled by Ladinos. In the early 1980's the Save the Children Christain Fund, an international organization, extended its operation to the Garifuna Community of Puerto Barrios.

It promised to be of great benefit to our poverty stricken people there; it was to provide financial assistance to farmers and fisherman alike, and sewing machines to Garifuna women. It also initiated a feeding program to upgrade the nutritional intake of malnourished children. It was an ambitious program. A Garifuna association was formed called Asso Garifuna for Garifuna Association. Its first elected leader was Luis Franzois.

Under his leadership there was frequent contact with Belize National Garifuna Council. In 1986, Asso-Garifuna sent a delegation to the second National Garifuna Convention sponsored by National Garifuna Council in Georgetown Village. On the 15th of May, Garinagu in Livingston celebrate the Feast of San Isidro, the Patron Saint of Farmers. Belizean Garinagu also join in this celebration, and occasionally accompany Garifuna priest for the celebration of the mass in Garifuna at the church in Laguga. But New Year's Day, 1989, will always be sadly remembered in Livingston, Guatemala.

On the eve of the last New Year's Day, December 31, 1988, a ferry boat owned by a Guatemalan Ladino which ferried people between Livingston and Puerto Barrios, capsized and sank and drowning with it 103 passengers of which 33 were Garinagu from Labuga and Barrios. The boat sank in calm still waters; it was the result of overload--it is estimated that about 300 passengers were on board. However, the ferry boat in which they were traveling actually capsized while being towed by a Guatemalan government army boat. Eyewitness reports confirmed that scores of persons fought for their lives as they scrambled from the ill-fated ferryboat. Furthermore, the carelessness of the captain of the tug boat added to the loss of so many lives. Again, this clearly illustrates the antipathy and condescending attitudes in which Garinagu-Morenos are perceived by the Ladino authorities of Guatemala. When a check of survivors was made, only then was it discovered that the Spanish Ambassador to Guatemala and some Americans from U.S.A. were among the victims. This incident created great international embarrassment for the Guatemalan Government, particularly the armed forces.

As the accident occurred, there was a demonstration of solidarity coming form the Garifuna of Belize, Guatemala, Honduras and as far away as St. Vincent, the Garifuna motherland. The Caribbean Organization of Indigenous Peoples-COIP Secretariat in Belize--was happy to serve as a medium for the galvanizing of regional concern on the tragedy that befell our brothers and sisters. (COIP Indigi-Notes 1989:12)

The Arrival of Garinagu to Belize (British Honduras) 1802: Dangriga Settlement 1832

The first indication of their presence in the settlement comes from the minutes of a Magistrate's meeting of August 9, 1802, recording the decision "that the admission of Caribs into the Settlement rests with the Superintendent" (Burdon 11 :57). There was considerable opposition to their being admitted into the Settlement. On December 17, 1802, one Andres Cunningham Esq. addressed the Magistrates:

Saying that though he does not wish to be classed with "Drunken men, Childish men, and Hysterick Women" he sees great danger in the presence in this Settlement, so far from any assistance of numerous 'Charibs,' he believes to the number of 150, stating that everyone is aware of the atrocities committed by these people in Granada, St. Vincent etc. and points out that with Christmas approaching, when the brains of the best servants will be inflamed with liquor, the danger of an insurrection led by these people will be considerable. Requests that the Magistrates will hold a special meeting and consider the propriety of expelling these people from the Settlement. (Burdon 11 :60-61 in Hadel 1976:562) (Gullick 1976:29)

Garinagu arrived in Roatan Honduras on 12th April, 1797; and five years later in 1802, they made a series of landings on the shores of Belize. Between August 9 and December 17, 1802 an estimated 150 Garinagu had been seen in the British Colony. Their unwelcome but inevitable presence created a ferment within the colonial magistracy that the expulsion of theCaribs was sought. The Garinagu, however, lingered on, and soon enough somebody must have come to regard the Caribs as sufficiently trustworthy to make them responsible to man the lookout post on Cay Corker. Yet, the British fear of Garinagu kept them under great suspicion, not unlikely due to the possible circulation of Young's Book of 1795 about the events in Saint Vincent--the atrocities committed by the British and Garinagu upon each other--though Young's reporting of the events was extremely biased in favor of the British.

Be that as it may, the Caribs were needed in Belize Settlement and were eventually admitted for reasons of cheap labour since the labor shortage was becoming acute. In 1807, the slave trade was abolished and the desertion of slaves to the Spanish territory of Guatemala had become a serious problem

(Hadel 1976:563). Then in the year 1811, the High Constable was directed by the magistrates to:

. . .warn all Charibs who could not produce a permit or ticket from the Superintendent, to quit the Settlement in 48 hours. Notice to be given to all Charibs arriving through the Non Commissioned Officer to whom they report at the Fort upon arrival, that they would subject themselves to Imprisonment by remaining in the Settlement more than Forty Eight Hours, without leave in writing from the Superintendent, as the Magistrates considered them a most Dangerous Peoples. (Burdon 11:146 in Hadel 1976:563)

Garinagu truly suffered overwhelming obstacles throughout process of being accepted by the Baymen; nonetheless, through their resolve they stood their ground and, somehow, providence was on their side. Passage of the Abolition Act in 1833 and emancipation in 1838 worked in favour of these refugees.

Consequently by 1835, 500 Caribs were stationed in Dangriga, and by then, the attitude of the Baymen was more conciliatory, though for purely monetary motives rather than humanitarian. During that year 1835, Thomas Miller, Clerk of the Courts Keeper of the Records, was sent on a mission to England to define the Status of Belize as a British Colony. Here is what he wrote:

There are about 2,000 Charibs settled near Truxillo, 160 miles from Belize. They are quiet, industrious and attached to the British. About 500 of these persons have already sought British protection and are now settled 30 miles to the Southward of Belize. They migrated there voluntarily during the late civil dissension in Central America. and have attached themselves with fidelity to the British, carrying on a constant traffic by sea with Belize, in plantains, maize, poultry, etc. The men in great part hire themselves by the year to mahogany cutters. There seems to be no reason to doubt that the Charibs still remaining at Truxillo might be induced to join their countrymen in Honduras. (Archives R. 11:79-80 in Hadel 1 976:564)

The modern history of the Catholic Church in Belize begins m 1832 when a Franciscan priest from Honduras, Fray Antonio, came to minister to Honduran refugees who had settled in the Mullins River area. Fray Antonio returned to Honduras in 1836 and was replaced by Fr. Rubio from Bacalar and the first Belizean Catholic Church of modern times was built in Mullins River. Four years later in 1840 two Yucatecan priest, Frs. Sandoval and Rivas, established a residence and opened a chapel on the south side of Belize City. They ministered mainly to resident Latin merchants and to the Catholic Caribs of the South. (Buhler 1976:7)

The role of the Catholic Church and Jesuit missionaries and their attitude towards the Garifuna in Belize Settlement contrasts starkly with that of the British settlers. It seems accurate to say that the Garifuna refugees in Mullins River area were escapees who had fled Honduras alongwith Alejo Beni, and he came along to minister to his church followers. This relationship or outreach also marked the beginning of the three-way power sharing that has charactierized the Belizean society.

In Belize today, the British have gone, yet somehow ensuring that the Creoles were left in charge of the Civil Service while the Mestizo in the West and North controls the economy through the Agricultural sector. Garinagu were left to pursue and to predominate in the educational field, largely through the Catholic Church.

There was once a settlement of Belgians in the eastern part of Guatemala and Fr. John Genon, S.J. of the Belgian Province, went to Guatemala in 1843 to work with his countrymen. When the Belgian settlement scheme collapsed, Fr. Genon asked permission of the Jesuit General to work among the Carib people of Guatemala to whom he had become very much attached. In 1855 he set up his residence in Livingston and used this as a base to evangelize the Carib Settlements of the Central American coast. In 1862 the Jesuit Superior in Guatemala sent two priests to help him in his work and Fr. Genon took advantage of this increased manpower to shift the scene of his own work in Punta Gorda. He had a plan of uniting all of the Central American Caribs into one ecclesiastical jurisdiction of mission. Such a plan would have crossed the national boundaries of Belize, Guatemala, and Honduras and the Jesuit General in 1862 decided to limit Fr. Genon's work to the Caribs of Belize. In that same year the Jesuit residence of Punta Gorda was established and Fr. Genon was put in charge of the area from Redcliff-Barranco to Stann Creek Dangriga. (Buhler 1976:1 2)

Throughout the 1800's Garinagu in Belize continued to consolidate their settlements; some of the men hired out for work at the mahogany camps seasonally, while off season they fished and cleared plantation plots for the women to do their cassava cultivation and other root crops and staples.

By the turn of the century in 1913--the Jesuits had opened schools from as far back as the 1800's--they had experienced success in the school work of Carib teachers whom they had earlier employed. It was at this point that Fr. Herman J. Tenk, S.J. was assigned to Punta Gorda where he recruited large numbers of young Garinagu men as teachers and catechist. It was under Fr. Tenk that many of the young men left their southern coastal homes to carry education and the Catholic faith throughout all parts of Belize. (Buhler 1976:75)

In recognition of their teaching ability, and as part of their gradual acceptance as neighbours in Belize, Anderson was able to write the following about Garinagu.

The Caribs of British Honduras ... are a very distinctive type and excellent seamen and provide many of the best school teachers in the colony. (Anderson 1958:24 in Hadel 1976:567)

As the church became increasingly established in Belize, the roles of Garinagu, Mestizo and Creoles became an important factor, and in 1934, Rev. Philip B. Marin, popularly known as "Father Marin." became the first Garifuna to be ordained a Roman Catholic priest. His ordination paved the way for the ordination of Fr. Oswald Peter Martin as the first Belizean Catholic and Garifuna Bishop of Belize just forty-eight years later on October 7, 1982.

Garinagu in Belize from 1900-1990

The Period 1900-1920

For ease of chronological reference, I have arbitrarily elected to divide the next ninety years into four twenty-year, and one ten year, period. The twentieth century is marked by Garifuna interaction with other Belizeans from all walks of life. Garinagu have finally begun to play an important and enduring role in the life of Belize as educators and evangelists. This is a role for which they were thoroughly gifted--they have a natural facility to acquire languages. Most are multilingual, speaking as many as six languages. Personally, I find it a rewarding yet humbling experience to be able to speak all the six languages of Belize, namely Garifuna, Kekchi, Mopan Maya, Creole, Spanish and English. Having fully realized that English was the language of the colony, the Jesuit missionaries undertook the task of educating the citizenry in that language.

Garinagu wasted no time in acquiring English as a second or third language, without forsaking their native vernacular. Consequently, they were not only prepared to staff primary schools, but were also prepared, given the necessary military training, to join Britain and Allied forces in the First and Second World Wars. Indeed, between the years 1914-1918, Garifuna men were recruited as soldiers and many fought in the military campaigns of North Africa. Being in the battlefront of Europe and Africa revealed certain insights previously unknown to them. Additionally, in the fighting and in their interactions with the Europeans, their view of the world changed and also their self image. So that on their return home to Belize at the end of the war, they began to question their state of poverty and neglect.

The Period 1920-1940 - Thomas Vincent Ramos

This period seems to have been dominated by the work and zeal of Thomas Vincent Ramos who was born on 17 September 1887 at Tulin, Puerto Cortes in the Republic of Honduras. Ramos married Elisa Marian Fuentes in 1914 and they migrated permanently to Dangriga, Belize around 1920. While in Belize, Ramos became a school teacher but he was also a visionary leader. He founded the famous Carib Development and Sick Aid Society (C.D.S.) and later Carib International Society (C.I.S.). Both organizations spread and were established in all Garifuna communities throughout Belize, and the C.I.S. had affiliations as well in Guatemala and Honduras.

Thomas Vincent Ramos had serious concerns about the systematic neglect and the need for improvement of the health facilities for Garinagu in Dangriga. This translates as concern for the sick and proper burial of the dead. Up to that time, there was not a single Garifuna nurse working in the entire Stann Creek Distirct. So Ramos lobbied and agitated that Dangriga get its native nurses to serve its citizens in the Dangriga Hospital. The colonial authorities finally capitulated and granted the request.

But T.V. Ramos was also concerned with promotion and preservation of the Garifuna cultural heritage, and to that end, he dedicated his talent, time and effort so that in 1940, as leader and spokesman, along with Pantaleon Hernandez and Domingo Ventura, T.V. Ramos approached the Governor of the colony and requested the establishment of a Public and Bank Holiday in observance of the Garifuna arrival to Belize on November 19th. The request was granted and official celebration of the 19th November as a Public and Bank Holiday began in Stann Creek District on November 19, 1941. Two years later in 1943, Punta Gorda. or Toledo District, was also given the Holiday, and in 1977, Garifuna Settlement Day became officially a Public and Bank Holiday throughout Belize.

The Periood 1940-1960: The Credit Union Movement: 1939-1945

Second World War

World War II broke out in September 1939 and throughout the war, Garinagu men were recruited along with other Belizeans to help defend democracy and freedom on the side of Britain, U.S.A. and other Commonwealth Nations. Around this same time, some men were engaged in the dredging of the Panama Canal that links the Atlantic Ocean to the Pacific.

One of the side effects of the Second World War on our Garifuna communities was that it tied our people to permanent wage labour with heavy reliance on a money economy which they could least afford. this was secured by way of the considerable and handy remittances sent to mothers and children at home by the soldiers at the battlefront.

Remittance began to be perceived as favorable and desired long after the war was over. It is granted that Garinagu were involved in part-time wage labour even while still on the island of St. Vincent--they hired themselves to the French in exchange for savages, and when they arrived in Belize they hired out to the mahogany contractors seasonally.

But they never forgot to return home to cut down the plantation for the year's supply of ground food, cassava, plantains and other staples. In 1942, Reverend Marion Ganey S.J. arrived in Punta Gorda, and being aware of the proverty and destitution of his parishioners, decided to organize them into a Credit Union.

The following year, 1943, Fr. Marion Ganey and his Garifuna followers began operating the Saint Peter Claver Credit Union, the first of its kind in Belize. Holy Redeemer was established by Fr. Sutti in May of 1944 in Belize City (Buhler 1976). In 1943, trade unions were legalized in Belize and the General Workers Union became the biggest and most active labour movement in the country. It had members and affiliations in Dangriga among Garinagu who worked at the Pomona Citrus factory. December 31 st, 1949 witnessed the devaluation of the British Honduran dollar which up to that time was trading at par--one to one with the U.S. dollar.

This event led to the birth of the Belizean Nationalist Movement headed by Leigh Richardson, John Smith, Phillip Goldson, George Price and Nicholas Pollard. Between 1950- 1952 the labour union leaders also became the leaders of the political movement which in 1952 became the People's United Party, and shortly afterward George Price emerged as leader, a position he continues to hold to this day. In 1954, under the leadership of Mr. Price, universal adult suffrage was achieved, thereby enabling all citizens of Belize over 21 to vote, a right which they had been denied. (Shoman 1987)

The following year, 1955, the great Garifuna leader and man of vision T.V. Ramos died and was laid to rest in Dangriga on the 14th November. A torchlight parade is conducted every year on November 13 in honour of his contribution to the Garifuna people and Belize. Along with Alejo Beni, T.V. Ramos is hailed as one of Belize's great patriots.

The Period 1960-1980: Rebirth of Interest in Garifuna Culture

Garinagu in Belizean Politics: elected 3 representative then 2 now 1

In the political arena, the General Elections of 1961 resulted in the election of three Garinagu into political office--David Mckoy, Catarino Benquche and Faustino Zuniga. But the same year, October 30-31, 1961, Hurricane Hattie struck Belize and destroyed Belize City and Dangriga.

It was an economic ruin for Belize. Shortly thereafter, Belizeans, Creoles and Garinagu began migrating to the United States where they reside mostly in New York; Los Angeles, California; and Chicago. It is estimated that there are about 20,000 to 50,000 Belizeans in U.S.A. In 1988, remittances to Belize totaled $10 million dollars.

Then in 1965 a great and concerted effort was launched to revive C.D.S. through a convention held in Georgetown Village under the leadership of Simeon Sampson, Godsman Ellis and Dennis Gonquez. The ruling government saw this alliance of Garinagu as a serious threat--reminiscent of the 1 800's--so every effort was made to destroy the movement.

But nobody has ever succeeded in destroying the Garifuna spirit; it may be delayed, but not destroyed, for the God of Creation and the Ahari in Seiri are always on his side. A few years later, Hon. David Mckoy, Minister of Labour and Social Services, organized the visit of three Vincentian Caribs to Belize. That meeting in 1967 was of historic importance since it marked the first of such encounters between Garinagu of the Caribbean and those on the Central America mainland. But even the year previous, Mrs. Phyllis Cayetano, Miss Chica and Roysus Bregal had formed the Waribagaba Dance Group 1 966.

As we approached the decade of the 1 970's, it appeared that the lull of the 1960's was over for 1972 marked the birth of the "Queen of the South" contest, currently referred to as Miss Garifuna Belize National Contest. The winner of that first contest was Mrs. Jovita Casimiro of Barranco Village. The pioneers or founders of this cultural pageant were Dr. Theodore Aranda, Mrs. Phyllis Cayetano, Sister Jean Martinez, Mr. Austin Flores, and others.

The Government could see that Garinagu were committed to press on with their culture, consequently in 1977 the Government of the People's United Party declared Garifuna Settlement Day a Public and Bank Holiday throughout Belize. The decision was greeted with joy and interpreted as a serious move towards the national recognition of Garinagu and their contribution towards the development of Belize.

The General Election of 1979 resulted in Dr. Theodore Aranda assuming leadership of the United Democratic Party, a post he held to November 1982. This has been the highest political office held by a Garifuna in Belize. The only irony is that just a month earlier, a Garifuna had been elevated to the Bishopric of the Roman Catholic Church of the country. Perhaps the difference was that the appointment of bishop was made by the outgoing Bishop Robert L. Hodapp and confirmed by Pope John Paul II of the Vatican.

The Decade of the 1980's-1990's

The Birth and Dominance of Belize National Garifuna Council.

The exciting decade of the 1 980's was ushered in by the commencement of Garifuna Half Hour Programmes on Belize Radio One on Sunday July 15, 1980. This was the result of untiring efforts by Sebastian Cayetano and Sr. Jean Martinez. Garifuna Half Hour injected further dignity, self respect and pride in Garifuna throughout Central America. Because the program was aired in the Garifuna language, Garinagu were encouraged to write their own language for the first time; this was to ensure that the programmers delivered the requests over the radio waves in the desired vernacular. Today~ we have two time slots--half an hour on Sundays from 1:30-2:00 and 45 minutes on Thursday morning from 5:156:00 A.M.

December 5, 1981 witnessed the official formation of the National Garifuna Council of Belize (N.G.C.). The main task of the Garifuna Council is the coordination and enhancement of economic, cultural and social development of Garinagu in Belize. All six Garifuna communities in Belize are founding and active members of the Council. N.G.C. presently organizes the Miss Garifuna Belize Cultural Pageant, and the annual Garifuna convention held yearly, beginning in 1985 in Hopkins Village. The 1990 convention is sheduled for Dangriga. Founding members and executive leaders of the N.G.C. were Mrs. Phyllis Cayetano, President; Anthony Ogaldez, Vice-President; Sebastian Cayetano, Secretary; and Jerris Valentine, Treasurer. Mrs. Cayetano held the post for three years and in 1984 Fabian Cayetano was duly elected President, a post he still holds. Under Fabian's leadership, the Council has grown nationally and internationally .

Garinagu will remember triumphantly the date of October 7, 1982 when Father Martin was ordained Bishop Oswald Peter Martin, Bishop of Belize and Belmopan. It has been one of God's greatest blessings on the Garifuna people, whose sons and daughters fought the elements to spread education and bring enlightenment to all Belizeans, particularly those who lived in the most inaccessible and remote corners of Belize. Hon George Price dissolved the National Assembly and called elections of December 14, 1984. Although two Garinagu were duly elected to Office--Hon Simeon Sampson and David

McKoy--the People's United Party to which they belong suffered a massive defeat, winning only seven out of a total 28 seats. Rt. Hon. Manuel Esquivel, leader of the United Democratic Party (U.D.P.) became Belize's second Prime Minister. While the U.D.P. was in power, Silas Cayetano J.P. became Senator and Mrs. Doris Garcia was appointed President of the Senate. Interestingly, there were now four Garinagu in the National Assembly, two elected and two appointed.

With due credit to Rt. Hon. Manuel Esquivel and his Cabinet Secretary Carlos Perdomo, the National Garifuna Council was always warmly received and welcomed to the Prime Minister's Office in Belmopan and Belize City. During the reign of the U.D.P., Mr. Edmund Zuniga of Punta Gorda was appointed Permanent Secretary in the Ministry of Defence; for the first time, a Garifuna finally achieved the position of Permanent Secretary in Belize in 1988.

The year 1985 witnessed the unveiling of a monument to honour the Carib Chief and Freedon Fighter, Joseph Chatoyer, in Saint Vincent. In March of the same year, N.G.C. held its National Garifuna Convention in Hopkins Village at which the former Deputy Prime Minister, Hon. Curl Thompson, was guest speaker. The atmosphere at the convention was cordial, and much was achieved through discussions. Without a doubt there was no fear of reprisal whatever; of course the leaders then did not hold any key government positions, unlike the scenario in Georgetown in 1965 under P.U.P. and in 1986 still under U.D.P. On both occasions, the two policital parties felt threatened by our coming together. But they need not have. Belize is our home and we are interested in the development of Belize and all its people, including Garinagu.

Dr. Joseph Palacio, an anthropologist and Resident Tutor of the University of the West Indies, Belize Campus, had always expressed a desire to sponsor and participate in Cultural Projects. Now that dream had been twice translated into living reality. For in 1987, Dr. Palacio and myself organized and launched the first Cultural Retrieval Project in Hopkins Village with 35 Garifuna youths. This was a great success; several skills in craft production were taught by our very able Garifuna craftsmen and women. Our greatest discovery was that our skills could be taught in a formal group setting--a new incentive to teachers, directors and students alike.

In the same year, from August 13-17, 1987, the Toledo Maya Council and National Garifuna Council became founding members of the Caribbean Organization of Indigenous Peoples (C.O.I.P.) at a conference held in Kingstown, St. Vincent. The theme of the conference was Caribbean Indigenous Revival: Towards Greater Recognition and Development.

That first meeting, sponsored by Canadian University Services Overseas (CUSO), paved the way for the establishment of a COIP Secretariat in Belize with Dr. Palacio as its coordinator. Just recently from November 13-20, 1989, another conference of the COIP was held in Belize City, Belize. Since 1981, N.G.C. had been drafting, and revising its Constitution or Bylaws. This constitution was finally legalized after its registration at the Registry's Office on April 27, 1988. This year's Seine Bight convention was a tremendous success, according to N.G.C. President Fabian Cayetano.

From July 18-28, N.G.C. led a successful 10 person delegation to Honduras where we visited ten Garifuna Honduran communities on the north coast around Trujillo and actually landed on the island of Roatan. Our Garifuna brothers and sisters proudly welcomed us into their homes, their only regret that our visits were too short. We also were very happy about the exchange of information and the well attended meeting and Garifuna Mass we had with them in Cristales, Trujillo, La Ceiba, Griga, Funda, Lawan, Limon, and Marugurugu.

On August 20-25, Dr. Palacio and I directed Cultural Retrieval Project II. This time we employed nine crafts instructors--four males and five females-- and there were 60 participants, predominantly mature women who are members of various kinds of income generating activity. This was a remarkably successful project from the points of view of students, teachers, and directors. Even more rewarding, the entire proceedings were video by Fred Campbell, a video technician assigned this responsibility from Newfoundland. The video cassettes are retained by COIP Belize Secretariat, but are available for viewing by any and all interested persons .

General Elections held September. 4, 1989 returned only one Garifuna, Dr. Theodore Aranda, into the House of Representatives, who was named to the Cabinet position of Minister of Health and Urban Development in the People's United Party Government of Rt. Hon. George Price. In addition, Conrad Lewis and Soloman Lewis, both of Hopkins Village, were appointed Senators, one of the P.U.P. and the other of the np.

Conclusion

The lessening of prejudices against Garinagu has been due to the birth of the nationalist movement in which they have actively participated. As well, the Garifuna Punta Rock music composed by Pen Cayetano during the 1980's has had great appeal to Belizeans, and it has served to play down the stereotypes that have existed previously. But lest we forget, it is necessary herein to comment on the prejudice and, in my consideration, undue and exaggerated discrimination suffered by Garinagu under the British colonial authorities and the Creoles who replaced them, and then later by Catholic authorities who condemned Dugu Garifuna traditional healing ritual. My summation is that Garinagu have had to undergo four stages, or levels, of acceptability before achieving total acceptance into Belizean society. Firstly, before being accepted as Carib neighbours, they had to achieve acceptance as citizens; next they had to achieve the status of acceptance as brothers and sisters before accepted as Belizeans; and even as recently as this year, Garinagu are still discriminated against, especially on the job and in promotion within certain employment sectors. Unfortunately, it seems, the more sophisticated Belizeans become, the more subtle becomes the discrimination.

It is long overdue that we find a permanent cure for this disease, and eradicate it completely from our system. Belize is in its infancy and it desperately needs all the strength and talent and energy of its citizenry to push it forward. Garinagu and Creole alike--who share a common African ancestry, and who arrived in St. Vincent perhaps on the same ship, around the same time--have much more to gain by uniting together than by perpetuating the old stereotypes.

A tink a si wha new Belize weh di Creole man, di Mestizo, di Garifuna, an di Mayan, no separate as a lis dem, but instead all da Belizeans.

"All a wi da wan" di Creole man sey. "Todos son hermanos." Asi dice el Mestizo. "Ubafu lun Garifuna." A wanda wth dende mean? When Maya man sey "Koten waye da ie temple ie wha sho yu. Who sey me sey Coolie Indian no de? Go da Punta Gorda, check out Yahbra, da time fi si di new Belize. (Philip Lewis; Belizean Poets Part 3)

On November 11, 1989, history was made in Belize City, with the converging of close to one thousand Belizeans on Bird's Isle to witness for the first time the selection from among seven constestants of Miss Garifuna Belize. At the time of this writing, I understand that Miss Dangriga won the coveted title.

The year draws to a close, and we move into the 1 990's with hope and confidence of greater things to come, and the celebration and observance of four Bicentenaries beginning in 1992, with the observance of 500 years of Columbus' discovery of the New World--the Americas, and the Caribbean in 1492. This will be followed in 1995 by the Bicentenary of the Assassination of Joseph Chatoyer, founder of Garifuna civilization, in St. Vincent in 1795; then in 1997, the observance of 200 years since the Deportation of Garinagu; and lastly, remembrance of Garinagu arrival in Belize from 1802 to 2002.

Acknowledgments

I take this opportunity to thank Dr. Geoffrey O'Gardy for his kind consent and patience in the supervision of my labour of love--my paper on Garifuna History and Language. I also wish to thank Lucille Donnelly for her patience and editing suggestions, and in typing of this manuscript. To my readers, I add only: enjoy, and learn about the Garifuna story as told by a Garifuna.

I must certainly acknowledge my appreciation to Her Excellency Dr. Dame Minita Gordon, Governor General of Belize, for her sponsorship of my 1987 Scholarship; to Dr. Howard E. Petch, President of the University of Victoria, Canada, for his willingness to initiate it; and to Mr. Cled Thomas, Administrative Registrar, for his excellent supervision of the financial requirements of the scholarship.

I offer my special thanks and gratitude to my wife Isabelle, and to my children, Carlos, Isani, and Emeri, for their forbearance and I was absent from home organizing and other Garifuna communities; and understanding during those times Garifuna activitiesin Belize City while in Victoria, British Columbia, Canada, pursuing my studies.

A Re-consideration of the Native American and African Roots of Garifuna Identity

by

Dr. Joseph Palacio

Resident Tutor
University of the West Indies School of Continuing Studies
PO Box 229, Belize City,

Belize, Central America
uwibze@btl.net

Paper Presented at:

Professional Agricultural Workers Conference (PAWC)

58th Session, Tuskegee University

December 3-5, 2000

Theme: Land, Community, and Culture–African American and Native American/Native Alaskan Connections

Tuskegee University, December 3-5, 2000.

Introduction

The topic of cultural identity is probably one of the most complex social issues that was unresolved in the last century and which all of us will have to be deal with during this 21st century. The problem about cultural identity is that too many people are talking about it and all of them want to be correct. The state tells you what you are; people in your neighbourhood tell you what you are. Nobody listens to what you are saying about what you are. What is even worse is that your children and grandchildren may no longer believe you when you tell them what they are.

Nowhere is this question as complicated and conflictive as the topic of intermixture across bloodlines. My topic is the blending of Native Americans and descendants of maroon Africans which led to the formation of the nation called Garifuna (previously called Black Carib in English). At first I review some of the theories that have been proposed to explain the blending. Secondly I compare some historical moments in the formation of the

Garifuna with the Black Seminoles in the southeastern United States to arrive at commonalities that underlie such intermixture and the larger conditions that provoke them. Thirdly, I focus on some cultural traits that the Garifuna acquired through their traumatic experience on the Eastern Caribbean island of St. Vincent, where they were formed. Finally, I refer to my findings to show what lessons can be derived for the hemispheric Indigenous Peoples movement.

Theoretical Perspectives on the Formation of the Garifuna

First a brief description of the Garifuna people. They number over 200,000 and are found in communities along the Caribbean coast of Central America primarily in Honduras but also in Belize, Guatemala, and Nicaragua. There are also large communities in United States cities, mainly New York, Chicago, and Los Angeles. They are quintessentially the products of the European colonial enterprise in the Caribbean. They are the result of the intermixture of Africans with Native Americans–called Caribs. The Africans and their descendants were fleeing from European chattel slavery and the Caribs had already been decimated from wars, diseases, and their forced abduction by Europeans. They have a language that is primarily Arawakan, diet typified by Caribbean foods, including several varieties of marine and coastal items. They also have a specific kinship system, religion, and wide-ranging artistic expression. As the largest nation in the Caribbean deriving from the intermingling of its first peoples with others, the Garifuna are an anomaly. Everyone thinks that they are so strange that they need to be explained.

Here are some reasons. They are not a plantation derived creole culture, although they live in the Caribbean sub-region. They did not originate from slavery but more so in resistance to the slavery of both Africans and Native Americans. They did not originate in Central America but are found there. They have black skins but are mixed both biologically and culturally. So the riddle keeps coming back–what are they?

If they were to be asked this question, they would appear surprised and answer that they are people, who don't have to be explained anymore than others should be. Furthermore they would add that they proudly share both Native American and African blood. But this hypothetical answer has not been sufficient to quench the thirst of curiosity coming from observers, researchers and laypersons alike, who in turn have come up with many answers. One is the historically documented fact that their African origin comes from a shipwrecked slaver, from which scrambled hundreds onto the island of St. Vincent in the mid-1600s. Additionally many others escaped from plantations on St. Vincent itself not to mention neighbouring plantation strongholds like Barbados, St. Lucia, and Martinique.

The rise of anthropology to prominence in the United States during the last century saw its practitioners applying their own ways to explain the Garifuna enigma. Under the influence of his advisor Melville Herskovits, Douglas Taylor saw the Garifuna displaying African cultural survivals in their assertiveness as against the reticence of American Indians (Taylor 1951). His main concern, however, was the language and folklore, which revealed the overwhelming Indian component of the culture. Nancie Gonzalez was also impressed with the assertiveness of the Garifuna as field informants. She subsequently found West Indian Afro-American traits among them Gonzalez (1959: 300-307), although her main focus was not on their dual origin but on their trajectory in Central America.

A Guyanese Africanist, Ivan Van Sertima, found evidence through various sources of the actual presence of Pre-Columbian Africans in St. Vincent, among other parts of the New World (1976). So, for him the answer took the African explanation. Van Sertima was under the 1970's influence to restore to Africans and Afro-Americans "facts" that the white academic establishment had deliberately denied them. This thesis together with his erroneous findings continues to confine him to the periphery in western epistemology. For a detail rebuttal see Haslip-Viera et al 1996: 419-441. In keeping with the swinging pendulum within academic circles, there should now be a thrust to strengthen their Indian origins to counter Van Sertima. I can hear the Garifuna answering should they be asked their opinion at this conjuncture. "We have told you before. We are ordinary people. If you are so keen to find out about our origins, find out about other peoples with similar origins and compare for yourself."

The Garifuna and Black Seminole – some commonalities

I will follow the hypothetical advice of our Garifuna listeners and do a brief comparison on the maroon history of the Black Seminole and the Garifuna. I rely on a paper that Rebecca Bateman had published on this topic in 1990 entitled "Africans and Indians: a comparative study of the Black Carib and Black Seminole". My aim is to paint a broad picture of the experiences of these two brave peoples at some of the bitterest moments in their history and pinpoint some specifics that are unique to the Garifuna.

For both peoples the story begins in the 18th century, a period when Britain lost her United States colonies but still maintained vital interests in Florida, further south throughout the Caribbean rim land, and circling north through the Eastern Caribbean. Not only was the region rich in lands producing sugar, cotton, coffee, and cacao that would enable Britain to recoup her loss of the American colonies; it was also a strategic passageway for heavy boat traffic and trade with the Spanish colonies. There were several factors, however, that had to be overcome. The first was Britain's recurring wars with Spain and France fought mainly on the Continent but the spoils included territories within the Caribbean. The second was the recalcitrant slaves, which were becoming more restive especially under French provocation during the latter years of the 18th century. Closely related to the problem of the slaves were the remaining Caribs in the Eastern Caribbean who continued their periodic insurrections. Despite all of these obstacles, there were moments when there seemed a masterpiece of good luck. An example of this took place with the 1763 Treaty of Paris, when Britain received Flroida from Spain and from France it also received St. Vincent, Dominica, and Tobago. The last three were potentially wealthy plantation territories in the Eastern Caribbean.

Reaping the fruits of these newly gained possessions, however, was not going to be any easy task. In St. Vincent there were two groups of Caribs to be dealt with. One was the original Yellow Caribs who had inhabited the island from Pre-Columbian times. The other was the result of intermixture between Caribs and escaped slaves called Black Caribs by virtue of the colour of their skin. Such intermixture had occurred from the 16th century during frequent Carib raids on European plantations but had increased since the 18th century with the escalation of plantations throughout the islands together with the resultant high numbers of fleeing escapees. As the yellows decreased so did the blacks increase exponentially. After several skirmishes both groups had agreed in 1700 to subdivide the island between themselves, the yellows occupying the leeward and the blacks the windward. From now on I will use the term 'Garifuna' to refer to the Black Caribs.

Rather unfortunately for the British the windward side was the more fertile and less rugged portion ideally suited for sugar plantations. Furthermore, the Garifuna were most possessive of their lands and resisted all efforts to hand them over to the British peacefully. Despite numerous offers from the British to compensate them in cash, allow them access to the oceans for fishing, to relocate them within the island or away at British expense, and to grant them the status of Free Negroes, the Garifuna refused steadfastly (Kirby and Martin 1972). Between 1763 and 1790 through various ruses the British were able to whittle away on some lands but the rightful owners were finally determined not to yield one more square centimetre of the last portion of their entire 6000-acre territory. The final pleas from the British for re-consideration went unanswered. In fact, the Garifuna were already in full preparation for war with the aid of the French.

The one significant factor to note from this episode was that the British treated the Garifuna as a nation with full autonomy and jurisdiction over their territory. Indeed, the Garifuna regarded the land as their heritage from their ancestors, for which they had fought and from which they would not part. The other nation that was intimately involved with its own vested colonial interests was the French. The third nation, the Yellow Caribs, gradually lost their earlier influence and joined with the Garifuna at moments during the military struggle, the alliances of kindred overtaking whatever animosity might have existed between them earlier. In short, the multi-national conflict saw contradictory political jurisdictions joining in battle, the sharpest divide being between the Garifuna and the British.

The Second Carib War 1795-1796 was much more definitive in destroying the military power, morale, and the people themselves than the First Carib War of 1772 to 1773. After viciously extricating men, women, and children from their hideouts, the British left 4,338 at Baliceaux, a small desolate island holding station before sending them in exile to Roatan in Central America, a distance of about two thousand miles. For more information on the final routing and travel see Kirby and Martin (1972), Gonzalez (1988: 39-50), and Marshall (1973: 4-19).

The experiences of forced relocation and maroonage among the Black Seminole are far more convoluted than those of the Garifuna partly because there were far more people involved and covered a larger space and time. Readers are encouraged to consult Bateman (1990:1-24) for more information. The relationship between the escaped African slaves and native peoples had started as far back as the 17th century when Spanish-controlled Florida promised asylum to escapees from the British North American colonies, who converted to Catholicism. The black refugees found several settlements of different Southeastern peoples, including members of the Creek Confederacy. The latter actually formed the Florida Seminole nation by the mid-eighteenth century.

There are some comparisons that we can draw at this point between the Garifuna and the Black Seminole. One is that the amalgam that formed the Florida Seminole contrasts with the one nation, the Yellow Caribs, who were the hosts of the Africans. Secondly, the groups making up the Seminole were refugees from a previous homeland. Again, the Yellow Caribs had been long-term residents of St. Vincent and were not in the process of consolidating themselves into nationhood as the Florida Seminole. A third contrast is that both the escapees and the Florida Seminole had extensive plantation experiences by the time they intermarried. This exposure to a strong creolizing influence seemed to have been absent, especially among the founding African population of the Garifuna. The African episode in the early formation and evolution of the Garifuna and the Seminole certainly needs more study.

Finally, the impression one gets is that the fleeing Africans who joined the Caribs were mainly males as against the cross-section of men, women, and children among their counterparts in Florida. All of these elements inevitably contributed to a stronger and more lasting bonding that attended the formation of the Garifuna nation. It is a case where the simpler the elements the easier the bonding. The one Indian anchor of the Garifuna made for a deeper Indian root for them than in the case of the Black Seminole.

Of course, the ruling government authorities provided the context for the intermixture. It is worth giving them a brief overview. The salient point here is that Florida, and especially its northern part including the Panhandle, was frontier territory between often conflicting jurisdictions, who conveniently used both the Indians and blacks for their own ends. At first, Florida was Spanish bordering on British territory. Between 1763 and 1783 it came under British control. This was also during the American War of Independence when hundreds of blacks and Indians moved south into British territory. In 1783 Florida again reverted to Spanish control. In 1821 it was eventually ceded to the United States. It was during the U.S. jurisdiction that both the Seminoles and the blacks experienced the greatest military violence. One sorry episode was during the Second Seminole War from 1836 to 1842, also dubbed the costliest Indian war in U.S. history.

This war started further problems in the formation of the Black Seminole in different parts of the United States, where the extreme racism of the federal government has influenced their cultural identity together with their relations with other Indian peoples. This contrasts with the experience of the Garifuna in Central America, where there was no federal government to provide cash retribution and welfare allowance but also neither to impose stringent legalistic intrusions into their resettlement, movement, and status. On the other hand, the relatively little scope of government intrusion gave the Garifuna a greater opportunity to develop their cultural identity with a certain amount of integrity not available to the Black Seminole. Further below I will say a further word of the type of government-Garifuna relations that exists in Central America.

Past Experiences and Cultural Identity among the Garifuna

In this part of the paper I turn to the Garifuna not as the product of two races but as one people chastened by the bitter events in St. Vincent. It is tempting to ask the question what effect did the defeat and exile of their ancestors have on the formation of their cultural identity. I am doing this for two reasons. The first is my assumption that an experience *that* traumatic must have left some scars, which they have been attempting to heal. My other reason is my observation that there are distinct differences between the descendants of the Yellow Caribs in St. Vincent, whose ancestors had participated less in the Carib Wars and had not been exiled, with the Garifuna found today in Central America. There is far greater atrophy in traditional cultural identity among them than in Central America. For this topic I include kinship, land, and personality traits under cultural identity. Let me also say that my views here are more reflective of initial thoughts around some research that I am currently doing in Belize.

It is not the first time that this kind of cause-effect processual analysis has been done for the Garifuna. Two such studies are by Nancie Gonzalez (1988), who focuses on themes that include spirituality, the socio-economy, and domestic relations and Gullick (1985), who focuses on the formation of ethnic worldviews. My own current effort circumscribes events surrounding their military defeat, subsequent massacre, and humiliating exile as the causative factors. It is necessary to say at the outset that any extrapolation of cause-effect relations in this case will have to be tempered by the radically different socio-political contexts within the two settings, St. Vincent and modern day Central America. Indeed, an awareness of these two extreme conditions will help us appreciate even more the resilience of people as they form their own cultural traits.

In St. Vincent the Garifuna were a primitive hunting and gathering society, where territoriality harboured the natural resources essential for daily life and community solidarity. They lived in dispersed uxorilocal household groups under the control of a headman. When not engaging in wars, bringing in food from the land as well as rivers and sea, or assisting his wife in swidden agriculture, he spent time in the men's house with his sons, sons-in-law, and other male relatives (Gonzalez 1988: 148-154). A group of the households belonged to one of the several "tribal" subdivisions headed by a leader, who exerted more authority during war than peace. The territories claimed by these groups were separated by natural geographic features, such as rivers and mountains. The entire nation functioned as one big unit during the several raids and wars fought against Europeans. At such moments men from St. Vincent would join fellow warriors from other islands as reinforcement. During the other times there were frequent squabbles and skirmishes among the several territorial groups (Kirby and Martin 1972).

Today the Garifuna live in developing states that deliver many of the services that they had had to provide for themselves, such as territoriality, security from the enemy, public access ways among the communities, and other basic needs. Most especially, the state guarantees their basic civil rights, negating the need to engage in feuds among themselves. In all the four countries the Garifuna are recognized as ethnic minorities, often held in opposition to indigenous peoples that originated within the immediate sub region. They have minimal control over lands adjacent to their communities and no political autonomy. They are among the poorest of the poor in countries that have to face the overwhelming challenges of a globalizing economy. Three of the four countries–Guatemala, Honduras, and Nicaragua–are still undergoing painstaking reconstruction after the civil wars fought a decade ago. As a result the needs of the minority Garifuna have to be postponed given their powerlessness and dwindling resources in the national treasuries.

With the poor conditions traditionally overcoming them, the Garifuna have left their communities in large numbers to migrate as far north as the United States. These massive movements to various surroundings so different from their Central American habitat present challenges in attempting to find links that originated one step further back in St. Vincent. My belief, however, is that the links can be found. Some are easily identified while others demand the fine teeth of social science research methodologies.

What are some of these linkages that we can find within the wealth of Garifuna cultural identity? It is not surprising that we start with Chatoyer. The aura around him is a beacon that draws the attention of everyone. In introducing themselves to each other Garifuna men and women say, "We are all the grandchildren of Chatoyer." In Belize his memory is venerated. Indeed, one of the largest festivals in the country, November 19th, was started to uphold his bravery in alleviating the suffering of Garifuna ancestors.

Not only is Chatoyer a hero in the subliminal sense, the existence of his descendants actually carrying his flesh and blood has always been a part of the collective consciousness in the town of Dangriga and several villages in southern Belize. I came across this information by interviewing the granddaughter of the granddaughter of Joseph Chatoyer's daughter, who had been known as Gulisi. My informant led me to others who indeed had heard about Gulisi as a daughter or some close relative of Joseph Chatoyer. The study uncovering the wealth of information I collected about genealogy and memories of life in St.Vincent and Honduras has already been published (1999:1-24).

The significance of the Gulisi account for our current analysis on linkages is threefold. The first is to pinpoint continuity in oral tradition between St. Vincent and Belize covering thousands of miles and over 200 years. The second is that she appears as an outstanding mother figure paralleling the father figure that her father maintains. The third is that the genealogy investigation revealed information about the descendants of Gulisi pioneering settlements in several communities in southern Belize. A closer examination reveals that their descendants have retained their family leadership quality, becoming success stories in business, politics, education, Garifuna spirituality and Roman Catholic clergy, among other fields.

The Gulisi story brought out the extended nature of Garifuna kinship ties that goes beyond communities and national boundaries. It is a very strong nucleating force stretching across time and space as it coagulates the peoplehood of the Garifuna. This is a point that still needs further analytical refinement. Certainly the term "kinship" as used in English is inadequate by virtue of its traditionally limited use to persons within family groups and communities but not as a primal coercive force for cultural identity and peoplehood. The term used in Garifuna is *iduheguo*. A derivative of the term, *iduhenyu,* is used by the Garifuna to refer to fellow Garifuna wherever they are.

Closely related to the bond of Chatoyer and *iduheguo* is the use of place names in Belize corresponding to earlier names found in St. Vincent. Examples include Masiraga, a community within the town of Punta Gorda, no doubt named after Masiracaw in southeastern St. Vincent. For more examples see Palacio (1999: 1-24).

Concurrence with place names leads to a remaining awareness of the "tribal" subdivisions in St. Vincent. A few persons in Belize can still identify themselves as originating from a given subdivision within the original Garifuna territory. The most popular is *Oreyuna,* no doubt a derivation from Owia, a community found in the extreme north of St. Vincent.

The vitality of the linkages around Chatoyer, *iduheguo,* and place names pales considerably in spotlighting the land relations that the Garifuna maintain in Central America. For a people who had been prepared to give up their life in St. Vincent, why did they not continue that zeal within their new locations? I would argue that their regard for land continued but that they were not given and have never been given the opportunity to exercise it in terms of ownership, inputs, and markets. As a poor, powerless, and black minority, the Garifuna could not compete with others for land within a political economy built on the ownership of land, preferably in large monopolistic portions. It is worth explaining that in the Caribbean coastal part of Central America, where the Garifuna are concentrated, the premium on land has traditionally been on its timber and large scale export agriculture carried out by multi-nationals. Such a political economy prevailed in both colonial and post-colonial Central America as well as colonial and post-colonial Belize. Differing political and cultural traditions notwithstanding, the one factor that Belize shares with its neighbours is an underlying public policy historically controlled and implemented by *latifundistas.*

The existence of the zeal for land ownership was so strong among the third and fourth generations of Garifuna arrivants in Belize that several formed a group and saved whatever little money they had to buy a little less than 900 acres behind Punta Gorda. Quite prudently they agreed that it would be held in trusteeship for the perpetual use of their descendants. One can even hear them say, "So that they may never suffer the indignity that our forefathers did at the hands of the British in St. Vincent."

Apart from this group effort, the Garifuna were allowed to buy a few acres for some farmlands. The vast majority, however, had to be satisfied with leasing plots that belonged to the state on reservations. There are many examples of their successful husbandry within the small portions available to them, especially when foreign markets were available. Traditionally, they have been allowed to use the beach facing their communities and some adjoining lands for common use of cutting wood for domestic purposes. Further below I will return to this vital question of land and cultural identity. My last comment on this point here is that the impossibility of earning a livelihood on the land led the Garifuna, after several failed efforts, to migrate in search of wage labour throughout northeastern Central America from very early. Several chroniclers remarked about their industry, dedication, and clannishness when compared with other ethnic groups in work gangs.

The final area of linkage to which I turn is one in which I have the least expertise. My discussion will, therefore, be more in a programmatic fashion indicating some questions for further research. It is the effect of St. Vincent on the personality of the Garifuna people. There have been observations about their facility to learn languages and engage in transcultural situations. Obviously, this came from their prolonged exposure to exactly these conditions from the very time of their first formation in the Eastern Caribbean. It became a prerequisite for their survival as a group.

But there are other traits that are not so easily explained. They include an overwhelming commitment to social services in their jobs in education, medicine, the church, and the government service; and their cultural transcendence, i.e. an ability to deal simultaneously within three levels of reality, such as dedication to the ancestors, the problems of the living, and constantly projecting into the future for the welfare of their progeny. Thirdly, there is their very rich artistic expression in literature, music, folklore, dance, and the plastic arts–all done with minimal formal training. I am suggesting that persons with the appropriate expertise look at these qualities and see why a set of people have been able to excel in them as against other fields; and whether there are any historical explanations that could be proposed.

Lessons Learned for the Indigenous Peoples Movement

In 1992 the Garifuna applied for membership within the World Council for Indigenous Peoples based in Ottawa and were accepted. The acceptance was a political victory for them within a primary forum of the hemispheric indigenous peoples movement. It is necessary to emphasize this given the prevailing ambivalence toward blacks who claim Indian origins among a cross-section of the indigenous peoples of the Americas. In the case of the Garifuna they literally had to make a case for their admission. Where whites who claim Indian ancestry can be accepted, it is not easily so for their black counterparts. The larger victory for global acceptance was that the Garifuna were being vindicated for a claim that they had always made. We will recall that the 18th century British and French had given them such recognition, albeit for their own ends. In opening the door, other black Indians could follow suit and exert their rights of belonging among their forty-odd million brothers and sisters recognized as indigenous peoples in the Americas.

The case of the Garifuna amplifies in various ways the definition of indigenous peoples, a task that continues within the hallways of the United Nations, the Organization of American States, and state capitols throughout the Americas. There is a need to look seriously at the often repeated criterion of land-based communal solidarity. In the case of the Garifuna we have seen that this was important for their early formation but no longer in the portion of Central America where they are now found and where land ownership continues to be denied them. It is extreme for the Garifuna but they are not unique among indigenous peoples, whom history has now made *de facto* landless. As painful as it is to lose land, many indigenous peoples have shown that they could survive without its ownership and economic use. A similar conditionality of identity is tribal character where kinship and traditional leadership remain. Again there are varying degrees of the existence of this for indigenous peoples. For the Garifuna, as for many others, it is the considered intention to retain what they had lost after more than two hundred years ago. The important point is that as times keep changing, the viability of previous definition criteria changes but not the indigenousness of the people themselves.

More and more the social equity for indigenous peoples will not be land and tribal characteristics. It will be other pillars of anteriority, such as blood ties, hereditary traits, collective memories of previous experiences, and an inner worldview of cultural identity that lies in the domain of cosmology, spirituality, artistic expression and other intangibles, which are yet to be identified. I am in no way descrying the viability of current definitions. Rather I am advocating that we use them as starting points that will lead us further to better know ourselves. As my hypothetical Garifuna listener said earlier, "We are people no different than others but who are share both Indian and African roots." The pronounced inclusivity among indigenous peoples will continue to challenge purists, who at given moments will feel that they have finally figured out completely who indigenous peoples are.

These exciting and challenging times call for more social scientists from among the indigenous peoples to study their own peoples. It is a cry that continues to be raised in the literature and which many are answering. In my own opinion the reward is an enriching of the various scientific disciplines, as new sets of researchers–differently grounded than the previous set–challenge conventional wisdom and introduce new methodologies that are truly indigenous (see Purcell 1998: 258-272).

As we get more involved in the study of our people, we could embark on another phase that has yet to unfold. It is a comparative analysis of phenomena occurring among two and more of our peoples. My own limited comparison between the Seminole and Garifuna, itself taken from a study done earlier (Bateman) was very exciting. At the least it pointed out to me strategic differences that account for specificities in the evolution of my own people. I would not have been able to arrive at this conclusion otherwise.

This paper started with the question of continuing the struggle to comprehend cultural identity left over from the last century. It has attempted to do so taking as its focus the very core of interculturalism. Furthermore, it has raised the complimentary question of fine-tuning perspectives and methods in the study of cultural identity.

References Cited

Bateman, Rebecca B. 1990. Africans and Indians: a comparative study of the Black Caribs and Black Seminole. Ethnohistory 37 (1): 1-24.

Gullick, C.J. M. R. 1985. Myths of a Minority – the changing tradition of the Vincentian Caribs. The Netherlands: Van Gorcum.

Gonzalez, Nancie. 1959. West Indian characteristics of the Black Caribs. Southwest Journal of Anthropology 15: 300-307.

Gonzalez, Nancie. 1988. Sojourners of the Caribbean – ethnogenesis and ethnohistory of the Garifuna. Chicago: University of Illinois Press.

Haslip-Viera, Gabriel et al. 1997. Robbing Native American Cultures: Van Sertima's afrocentricity and the Olmecs. Current Anthropology Vol. 19 (4): 4-19.

Kirby, I.E. and C.I. Martin. 1972. The Rise and Fall of the Black Caribs. St. Vincent.

Marshall, Bernard. 1973. The Black Caribs – native resistance to British penetration into the Windward side of St. Vincent 1763-1773. Caribbean Quarterly 38 (3): 419-441.

Palacio, Joseph O. 1998. Reconstructing Garifuna oral history – techniques and methods in the study of a Caribbean people. Journal of Eastern Caribbean Studies 34 (1): 1-24.

Purcell, Trevor. 1999. Indigenous knowledge and applied anthropology: questions of definition and direction. Human Organization 57 (3): 258-272.

Van Sertima, Ivan. 1976. They came before Columbus: the African presence in ancient America. New York: Random House.

Taylor, Douglas. 1951. Black Caribs of British Honduras. New York: Viking Fund Publications in Anthropology, No. 17.

Black Carib Bastion Of Freedom

Peter T. Muilenburg

These indomitable people maintained a stronghold of liberty on St. Vincent, despite waves of colonial oppression

Like so much else, it was Columbus's fault; he dislodged the pebble that set off the avalanche of demographic upheaval that first flung three races together--and at each other's throats--in the West Indies.

The Indians were already there, by turns peacefully or bloodily minding their own business. Then the Europeans arrived to decimate them and usurp their land and with them came a trickle of kidnapped Africans that became a torrent as the century wore on. The elements assembled, Euro, Afro, and Indio, were smelted into uniquely American alloys in a Caribbean furnace stoked to the melting point by monumental injustice.

Yet out of this bitter history came transcendent stories of freedom--such as that of the Black Caribs of Saint Vincent. Their tiny nation, an amalgam of Afro-Carib half breeds with runaways from plantation slavery and castaways from wrecked slave ships, was a beacon of liberty in a sea of slavery for nearly three hundred years. Against mounting odds they played their hand out with finesse, to the last card. And the ultimate twist to their fate holds out hope that all may yet be well in human affairs if might and greed can, in the end, be so side stepped.

From the first, many Africans who found themselves enslaved on a New World plantation, looked long and hard at the surrounding wilderness from which it had been cut and simply walked off the job--into the jungle, free once again. Although survival in the wild was anything but simple, nonetheless wherever the slaves had sufficient mountains and forests to escape to, there were Maroons--runaways living in the bush. Brazil, with its vast forests, had the largest Maroon nation, the Republic of Palmares, which spanned almost a hundred years and counted a population of twenty thousand. The Bush Negroes of Suriname re-created West African villages deep in the limitless interior of the Guianas. And in Jamaica the "cockpit country" gave the Maroons ideal terrain for successful guerrilla warfare.

But in the limited areas of the Lesser Antilles, runaways existed in perpetual apprehension of recapture--and never was the hypocrisy of the "civilizing mission" of Christian Europe laid more bare than in the satanic punishments it meted out to a recaptured Maroon--the pious Spaniards tied him to a stake in the town plaza and castrated him before a crowd of his peers, the refined French slow roasted him, the liberal Dutch hung him from a shark hook through the ribs, the scrupulous Danes pinched him with red hot tongs and lopped off a leg for good measure, the legalistic English broke his bones on a wheel. Despite such measures, marronage occurred everywhere; but in the Lesser Antilles, only the Black Caribs of Saint Vincent succeeded in making good their freedom.

Little is certain about the origin of the Black Caribs, but the first Africans in the Windward Islands--that we know about--were captives taken by the Caribs in raids upon the early Spanish settlements.

The Spaniards and the Caribs deserved each other. The Spaniards had exterminated, almost inadvertently, the peaceful Arawaks of Hispaniola and the Bahamas within thirty years after their arrival. The Caribs, however, were the original "warlike cannibals." From their strongholds in Saint Vincent and Dominica, the Carib warriors issued forth in their giant war dugouts eager for battle, women, and loot-just like the conquistadors (though the Caribs had the grace not to preach religion to those they were raping and robbing).

For 150 years after Columbus, the Caribs raided Spanish towns and plantations in the eastern Caribbean, then terrorized the English, Dutch, and French settlements. Their homeward-bound dugouts included captured African slaves. How many it is hard to say, but the presence of three hundred blacks on Dominica was reported by the governor of Puerto Rico in 1588 who had it from an eyewitness. It can be presumed that Saint Vincent would have had at least as many or more.

The Carib men fathered children with their African captives and set the African men at liberty, giving them Indian women. Such was the origin of the Black Caribs. The Caribs' motives can only be guessed at, but perhaps it was as simple as "the enemy of my enemy is my friend." The Africans, familiar with European defenses, language, and mentality, would have sharpened the Carib war effort. And since the Spaniards automatically enslaved any Carib they caught, there was a natural empathy for fellow victims.

This ready reception of Africans may also have had deep, pre-Columbian roots. Eighteenth-century missionary Abbe Raynal declared that when the first slave ship wrecked near Saint Vincent the survivors were received as "brethren." Given the prevailing drifts of wind and current, Saint Vincent, at thirteen degrees north latitude, would have been a likely landfall for trading and fishing dugouts from the great river deltas of West Africa that must have occasionally been disabled and blown across the Atlantic in the centuries before the Discovery. With no way home they would have intermarried with the Caribs--themselves great voyagers--thereby laying the groundwork for a future perception of kinship.

Castaways from the wrecks of slave ships boosted the Afro-Vincentian ranks at least twice that we know mishap of the sixteenth and seventeenth centuries, since nautical charts were incomplete, navigators unable to obtain longitude, their square-rigged vessels unable to work against the wind.

An important entrance to the southern Caribbean lies between Trinidad and Grenada. The passage is wide and deep, but should a vessel miss it and make landfall to the north it had to weave its way through the Grenadines, an archipelago of reefs, cays, and islets bounded to the north by Saint Vincent. Father Vasquez Espinosa, writing in the 1620s, mentioned the presence of five hundred Africans castaway on one of the Grenadines from a Portuguese slaver, "which for its misfortune blundered on that island ahead of its schedule. And they murdered the Portuguese."

Runaways became an important source of the Black Carib population after the mid 1620s, when the French and English began settling the Lesser Antilles, eventually forcing the Caribs back to their strongholds in Saint Vincent and Dominica. Sugar and slavery rapidly dominated the new colonies, particularly Barbados, whose level terrain was soon covered with verdant cane fields cultivated by a heavy population of Africans.

Barbados happened to be up wind and current from Saint Vincent. It didn't take long for the slaves to realize that a calabash raft, log, or stolen skiff set adrift off Barbados would generally fetch up on a windward beach in Saint Vincent within a couple of days; and that if they took that chance and won, they would stagger up the beach free.

Saint Vincent's windward side became a magnet for runaway slaves. They streamed there from neighboring Barbados and Martinique and the other islands all the way up the chain. By 1672 the English governor estimated there were six hundred runaway slaves with Caribs on Saint Vincent and Dominica. A few years later he reckoned that the two islands of Montserrat and Antigua had in two years alone lost thirteen hundred slaves to "either the French or the Caribs."

Besides the runaways/Maroons and a mixed group of Afro-Caribs from over a century's intermingling, the Caribs also held an increasing number of

Africans as slaves. At first when the numbers were small, it posed no contradiction since even the Maroons held some bondsmen. The Caribs' own wives were like slaves, so many of them having originally been captured from the Arawaks. Nevertheless, as in the surrounding white man's islands, the existence of a large body of slaves proved to be destabilizing. The enslaved grew restive; the Maroons needed females held by the Caribs. A nation was striving to be born.

The balance tipped in 1675 when another slave ship wrecked, on Bequia, an island eight miles south of Saint Vincent. The survivors were from a notoriously warlike tribe known as the Mocos and soon proved to be proud and refractory slaves. With their unwieldy addition the Caribs began to lose control over the minority group they had fostered in their midst. So they decided upon King Herod's strategy--putting to death all African males at birth, sparing the females.

This cruelty brought things to a head. The Africans rose in rebellion, killed the Caribs at hand, and fled to mountain fastnesses to join the free Maroons. Once established there, it was beyond the power of the Caribs to rout them out. From this time on the Black Caribs grew stronger while the Caribs grew weaker. Eventually they joined the general Carib exodus back to their ancestral homeland in Venezuela.

The Black Caribs, with no place else to go and surrounded by enemies, nevertheless flourished. They inhabited the windward side, wild and impenetrable, where the early runaways had fixed their redoubt, but also laced with rivers and fertile valleys. They hunted, fished, raised what crops they needed in the rich volcanic soils, and traded in their dugouts with the French islands.

They retained a great deal of Carib culture, partly the natural result of their Carib heritage, partly to separate themselves from slaves being brought into the island by French planters who bought land from the Indians. They called themselves Caribs, spoke Carib, flattened the foreheads of their infants as the Caribs did, and buried their dead sitting up in the grave according to Indian custom. Like the Caribs, they were excellent swimmers and divers. Also like the Indians, they were a democratic society, without rank or hierarchy, every man the equal of the next, but with leadership implicitly accorded to exceptional men.

Unlike the Caribs, and more typically West African, they spoke other languages with facility, and besides Carib and Arawak and a wide range of

African tongues, knew French fluently, as well as English, Spanish, and Dutch in consequence of having been enslaved by Europeans.

They also won widespread respect as skillful, tough fighters who handled firearms expertly and excelled at hand-to-hand combat. Their life in the mountains and on the sea, its egalitarian stimulus, their hard-won independence from whites and reds, all made them vigorous and self-reliant. Tough and wily, they trusted no one but themselves and with their backs to the wall they defended their land, their families, and their freedom.

They were put to the test in 1719 when a French plot was hatched to invade Saint Vincent to reduce the Black Caribs to their "original state of slavery." The backers of this scheme would gain vast plantations and slaves to work them through a swift stroke of violence and treachery. The governor of Martinique approved, and a private army of four hundred adventurers set sail for Saint Vincent to get rich quick.

It should have been a cue to the French that although the red Caribs were invited to join the expedition, they politely declined and stood on the sidelines; but no, inflamed with the prospect of easy pickings, the whites disembarked and marched off into the bush hot on the trail of the Black Caribs. Thereby they made a mistake subsequently made by others-assuming that a ragtag bunch of illiterate Negroes wouldn't pose much opposition to well-armed and trained Europeans.

The Black Caribs lured them to a spot particularly suited for ambush and loosed a devastating volley of musketry and arrows. The leader of the expedition fell dead to the ground, along with many of his men. The survivors did an immediate about face and beat it back to the ships, thence to Martinique, without further encounters. The Black Caribs were apparently content to make their point and drop the matter. The French hushed up the incident.

Despite the attack, the Black Caribs rather liked the French, carrying on a brisk trade with them; many of them spoke French and adopted French names. French priests brought the Catholic faith to a receptive people. But they burned down any building near their boundaries and allowed no white man into their territory without special permission. They also demanded from the French settlers payment for the lands they had occupied on the Caribs' half of the island. When the colonists exclaimed they had already paid the Caribs for them, and waved a deed to prove it, the Black Caribs waved in reply an arrow. In the words of Abbe Raynal, "In this manner did a people who had not learnt to read, argue with those who had derived such consequence from knowing how to write. They made use of the right of force, with as much assurance, and as little remorse, as if they had been acquainted with divine, political, and civil right."

In 1763 the English finally annexed Saint Vincent by agreement with France, and the island saw an influx of English colonists eager to buy land and plant sugarcane. Needless to say, the Black Caribs' interests were diametrically opposed to those of the English. The latter wanted to clear-cut the primeval forest and plant money-making crops on plantations, all connected by good roads upon which cannon could be wheeled.

This same forest was the Black Caribs' security. For hundreds of years their tribe's origin and tradition was rooted in the dense foliage. They held the land in common and only cultivated small portions of it-leaving the virgin forest mostly intact. This was anathema to the English. They made sententiously hypocritical pronouncements about "obligations to cultivate the earth" and that a people had "no right to appropriate more than they could cultivate." They wound up proposing that the Black Caribs should leave their lands and take up residence elsewhere. They would be compensated monetarily for the lands they left, and the English officials promised them "every proper indulgence." The Black Caribs response was to suggest it would be safer for the speaker if he left their sight and their lands immediately.

Trying to appear reasonable as they gave these savages the shaft, the English came back with a pronouncement that, like it or not, the Black Caribs would have to accept their sovereignty and agree to a series of restrictions. It was clear that the whites were setting the stage for the use of force, so the Black Caribs adopted a delaying measure. Half of the nation, led by the paramount chief, Chatoyer, told the commissioners that they were willing to abide by the proclamation, but that others of their people were still opposed to the idea. According to Sir William Young's account, "appearing divided amongst themselves was a settled design of the Charaibs; and it was the most artful that could be devised," since it gave their opposition hope that the rest would follow suit, given enough time. But as the negotiations with the reluctant ones dragged on, the English sent in surveyors to mark out the route for a road. The Black Caribs allowed them to proceed until they reached the boundary of their land, where it was made clear to the English that to proceed further would require the assistance of soldiery. And the one who delivered this menacing ultimatum was the very Chatoyer who had previously been the most amenable to the English proposals.

The English waited awhile and then sent the surveyors back, this time with forty soldiers. The Caribs, three hundred strong and well armed, surrounded the hill where the soldiers were posted, and cut them off, even from water. They then made the offer to liberate the detachment on condition that the English commissioners give up any plans to interfere within their country, including the making of roads. The commissioners, fearing a massacre of their troops, agreed--with no intention of abiding by their promise--received the forty soldiers, and wrote an urgent letter to England.

While a reply was awaited, the Black Caribs procured arms and munitions from the French islands. The English, becoming aware of this, sent an armed cutter to patrol the channel. One August day in mid channel between Saint Lucia and Saint Vincent, the cutter bore down on four large canoes, each with about twenty men and loaded with kegs of gunpowder. When ordered to approach the cutter one at a time, they rushed it simultaneously. The cutter fired a warning shot, which was answered by a volley of musketry. The cannon then splintered the leading dugout but its crew, undeterred, clenched cutlasses between their teeth and started swimming toward the cutter. One after another the dugouts were disabled, but the Black Caribs kept coming. Suddenly aware that his cutter was in danger of being boarded and his crew overwhelmed, the captain sailed the cutter off, leaving close to eighty Caribs in the sea, claiming in his report that they all must have drowned. Considering that the dugouts still floated, being all wood, and that the Caribs swam like seals, one has cause to doubt. After all, a log in the sea had been a traditional conveyance of runaways to Saint Vincent in the first place.

Eventually, Saint Vincent's white population did get its military force and the Black Caribs were forced to accede in 1773 to England's sovereignty and to a network of roads and military posts in their territory. But when war broke out between France and England, the Caribs rose and fought alongside the French and took the island in 1779. A few years later the French gave it and the Black Caribs once again had to abide under the rule of the English.

Another war with the French loomed up at the end of the eighteenth century, and suspecting that they would attempt the island, various individuals were sent to sound out the Black Caribs' intentions. According to Charles Shepherd:

"The utmost astonishment was expressed by the Caribs at the suspicions entertained against them. They said `they had been once already deceived by the French, and their misconduct during the late war had been generously canceled, and since the peace the utmost kindness and humanity had been displayed towards them; no possible advantage could arise by their making war against the English, and no pardon could be expected, should they attempt it.'"

Yet, on Tuesday following, these very men were foremost in attacking, plundering, and demolishing the very plantations where they had with the greatest apparent sincerity made these professions.

This second alliance with the French in twenty-five years, and the obvious hatred that the Black Caribs bore the English proved, to be the last straw. Orders to remove the Black Caribs to British Honduras on the opposite side of the Caribbean were carried out.

It may have seemed a defeat, but in retrospect it was a victory--the best they could hope for. They escaped slavery, and, aside from casualties in the war, they lost few of their number. They lost their land, but they were given other lands, where, as time went on, they prospered. Hardworking, determined to acquire an education, they pulled themselves up into solid middle-class status and provided many of the educated professionals for British Honduras, now called Belize. And they had congenial neighbors not far down the coast.

Balboa, en route to verify the existence of the Pacific Ocean in 1513, was forced to detour around the territory of a tribe of blacks who had shipwrecked on the Darien Peninsula. Evidently one of the first slave ships to the New World missed its destination. How refreshing it is--how restorative of one's faith in God, man, history, and fate--to consider that among the first fruits of the infamous slave trade was the creation of a fanatically free people who drove an intractable thorn into the side of those who had presumed to be their masters--for these must have been the ancestors of the Cimarrons, who gave crucial assistance to Sir Francis Drake's spectacular ambush of the Spanish silver train in 1575, and whose descendants, intermarried with the Indians, inhabit the Mosquito Coast to this day.

The Black Caribs must have felt right at home.

Peter T. Muilenburg is a professional sailor and writer who has previously contributed to Americas. Illustrations are from Wild Majesty: Encounters with Caribs from Columbus to the Present Day, Peter Hulme and Neil Whitehead, eds. (New York: Oxford University Press, 1992), except the drawing on page 19, which is from Cannibal Encounters: Europeans and Island Caribs, 1492-1763, by Philip P. Boucher (Baltimore: Johns Hopkins University Press, 1992).

Books about Garífuna

The Rise and Fall of the Black Caribs, by I. E. Kirby and C. I. Martin

The Black Caribs of British Honduras, by Douglas Macrae Taylor

The Sojourners of the Caribbean, by Nancy Solien Ganzalez

An Historical Account of the Island of St. Vincent, by Charles Sherpherd

Anthropological Genetics of the Black Caribs, by Charles Crawford

History of the West Indies, by Thomas Coke

An Account of the Black Charaibs in the Island of St. Vincent's, by Sir William Young

Conversamos en Garifuna, by Salvador Suazo

Yurumeingien Daga Rubadan, by Salvador Suazo

The People's Garifuna Dictionary, by E. Roy Cayetano

Aspects of Carib/Kalinago Culture

© Lennox Honychurch

Carib was a name used by Europeans to describe those people who inhabited the islands of the Lesser Antilles at the time of Columbus' second voyage in 1493. This was not what the people called themselves. The repeated use of the name for over five centuries however, has made it widely adopted even by the descendants of the people themselves. The French missionary Raymond Breton, visiting Dominica in 1642, recorded that the "Caribs'" name for themselves was *Callinago* in the "men's language" and *Calliponam* in the "women's language", while *Callinemeti* was "a good peaceful man". This has now led to the adoption of the word Kalinago and Karifuna by cultural groups, anthropologists and historians to describe the Caribs. The "Black Caribs" of Belize, who are descended from ancestors in St. Vincent, call themselves the "Garifuna".

Kalinago: The Carib word for the Carib people. As Father Breton, who lived among the Kalinago in Dominica off and on between 1642 and 1653 says in his dictionary: "This is the real name of the Caribs of the islands." He wrote it as "Callinago", but the usual phonetic writing today is "Kalinago". "Kalinemeti" means "A good, peaceful man".

Carib Reserve: A district on the north east coast now more popularly called the Carib Territory. It is an area of some 3,785 acres bordered roughly on the north by a ravine called Big River, to the west by the centre of the Pagua Valley, to the south by a line leading inland from the Aratouri Ravine and on the east by the Atlantic Ocean. This was the rugged unoccupied part of the island to which the majority of Caribs retreated after the colonisation of the rest of Dominica by the French and British. However many other Caribs remained in their previously occupied zones and mixed with the newcomers. For years during the 19th century the district was known as the Carib Quarter. In 1902 the British Administrator Henry Hesketh Bell, influenced by Victorian anthropology and a personal desire to preserve "the last of the tribe", persuaded the British government to give him permission to declare the area as reserved for the Caribs. This was done on 4 July 1903. The plan of the Reserve was based on a tracing of the Byres map of 1776 but no actual survey was ever carried out and there has been continuous controversy over the boundary lines. Bell officially recognised a Chief of the Caribs. In 1952 local government introduced a council system and in 1978 a Carib Reserve Act was passed to further formalise the affairs of the Territory.

Carib: As a place name, there are some areas outside of the Carib Territory that are called Carib as a result of being places which were occupied by Caribs during the colonial period. Pointe Carib between Bagatelle and Stowe was one such place, known to the Caribs themselves as Ouycala. Others were Carib at Pennville and Carib at Delices and Point Carib at Boetica. The Indian River near Portsmouth is so named because of a well-documented settlement of Caribs that existed on the upper banks of the river.

Kaire, (Acaera): For many years this was mistaken to be the indigenous name of Dominica. It is also claimed by Trinidad. It is the Arawakan word for "an island". The mistake arose during the second voyage of Columbus when the Spanish first sighted and named Dominica. When they reached neighbouring Guadeloupe (Karouacaera), a writer on the voyage, pointing across to Dominica, asked one of the women what was the name of the first place that they had sighted. She apparently replied in Carib, "acaera", which, like kaire in Arawakan, simply means "an island". In his journal the writer noted down "Ceyre…is the first [island] we saw but did not visit". This report, based on a mistake, led to the belief that the island, Dominica, was called Kaire. Some one hundred and fifty years later Father Breton found out that the Carib name for the island was actually *Ouaitoucoubouli*, now written *Wai'tukubuli*.

Wai' tukubuli   Tall is her body

Ouaitoucoubouli: The original spelling of the Carib name for Dominica used by Father Raymond Breton in 1665, but now more popularly spelt: Wai'tukubuli. It means, "Tall is her body", alluding to the mountainous nature of the island. The construction of the word is as follows: ouaitumti = *it* *is tall.* nocoubou = *my body.* li = *her,* (Tall-body-her). If you were an inhabitant of Dominica, you were a *Ouaitoucoubouliri.*

Karifuna: (C) The Carib word for Carib women. Father Breton says: "The women are called Calliponam". Some linguists say that this is the name of the Caribs "in the women's language". There is also confusion over the pronunciation of the letters "L" and "P" in the Carib language. In many cases these letters were actually pronounced as "R" and "F" respectively, so Breton's Calliponam may actually be Carifunam, which became Karifuna. The Black Caribs of St. Vincent who were expelled by the British in 1797 to Rautan Island off Belize, and who now live in southern Belize, call themselves the "Garifuna". The main Carib cultural group in Dominica, established in 1978, call themselves The Karifuna Cultural Group.

The main indigenous art forms of the Carib people in Dominica were:

Architecture
All materials used by the Carib/Kalinago people came from the land around them. Their houses were of several types.

Ajoupa: The basic ajoupa, which was a shed-like or "lean-to" structure made for sheltering a cooking or cassava making area of a shelter easily put up in the forest as a camp for hunting and canoe construction. This was made of about four stout posts anchored in the ground and held up by two other posts and a cross-beam. Thin laths of wood were placed across this frame which then was covered with balizier leaves or various types of forest palm leaves. The buildings were tied together with maho bark rope.

Maho: The Caribs grouped plants according to their uses and any plant with a bark capable of making rope was described as a "maho". The French took the word and wrote it in their own way: "mahaut". Since there were no nails or wire or bolts, everything was tied together with maho. House posts, roofing thatch, hammocks, head straps for carrying load, for attaching things to canoes, anchor ropes, net ropes and for hauling, all depended on maho. As Father Breton writes in his Carib Dictionary, "In short, I do not think that they could exist without maho". In Western scientific botany the Mahaut is found in divers plant families: *Cordia* (Boraginaceae), *Pavonia* and *Hibiscus* (Malvaceae), *Triumfetat* (Tiliaceae) and *Sterculia* (Sterculiaceae).

Karbay: Also written in French as "Carbet". A term used by the French to describe the main meetinghouse and settlements of the Caribs. The Caribs themselves called this house "Taboui", but the French settlers had picked up the name "Karbay" when they had lived among the Tupi-guarani tribe of Amerindians in Brazil. The French had also brought many Tupi-guarani people from Brazil to work for them in Martinique, Dominica and Guadeloupe. These people used their own language to describe familiar things that they saw in Dominica. Several words that today are passed off as

Carib have their origins in the Tupi-guarani language. This word "Karbay" is one of them. It was used so often in the new French/Carib/Tupi-guarani/Creole language that was emerging, that succeeding generations of Caribs abandoned their own word "Taboui" and adopted "Karbay". It has been used for so long by the Caribs, that today it is considered by them to be a Carib word.

The Karbay was a large building, in most cases about 60 feet long and thirty feet wide. It was made of tall round wood posts and was of an oval shape with a tall steep roof. The posts which supported the roof were also used to tie hammocks for sleeping. The roof was thatched with palm leaves or the leaves of "roseaux" reeds.

Roseaux: (*Arundo saccharoides*) Wild Cane in English. This tall reed grows throughout tropical America. It is found on Dominica mainly along stream banks and its French name was given to the capital of the island. Among the Carib/Kalinago people the name was bouleua, "arrow, pierce" and mabulu. It was used in numerous ways. The hard main stem was used as wattle work for the sides of houses and for lathes or thatching rods for the roof. The fan-shaped leaves were used as thatch.

The young shoots of unopened leaves were used for shampoo. The light, straight, mature upper stems on which the flowers grew were used for the shafts of arrows. The young main stem was stripped and used in certain parts of basket making. The midrib of the leaf is also peeled, bleached and sun-dried to be plaited and sown for the making of hats. Recently, some people have returned to using the main stem of the roseaux reeds as decorative work in hotels, bars and guesthouses. Much could still be made of this product today.

The Karbay was divided into different zones for family hammocks, visitor hammocks and a central place for gatherings and for eating and feasts.

Music

The Carib/Kalinago music was based on percussion instruments made of wood and gourds or calabashes. There were no animals such as goats and cattle with which to make drums and so the main instruments were in the form of wooden gongs made of hollowed out logs of wood, which were beaten with sticks. The shack-shack of small calabashes filled with stones or seeds and with a long wooden handle was also an important instrument. This rhythmic music was accompanied by chants in the same way that tribes in the Amazon region of South America still perform.

Painting

The pottery of the Carib/Kalinago people was painted with earth-based colours that were grinded from red, ochre, white and other earth-toned rocks. Finely ground charcoal was used to make black paint and to darken other colours. All painting represented mythical symbols associated with their beliefs.

Roucou: (C) (*Bixa orellana*) Annatto, a shrub native to South America and widespread on the islands. It is used mostly as a vegetable dye for food. In the past, annatto was used by the indigenous people of Dominica mainly as a protective ornamental paint and as warpaint on the body. As a body paint it was sometimes mixed with powdered charcoal to darken its colour. Mixed with oil it also served as a sun and insect lotion.

Baskets

Oualloman: (C) The reeds used for making the Carib baskets, tables, cassava squeezers and other utensils woven by the Caribs. By the time that the French settlers had Creolized the word, it became *l'arouman*, the word that even Caribs use today. The scientific name is *Ischosiphon arouma*. The plant is found from the Amazon River, north to Guadeloupe and was brought to the Antilles by the indigenous people some two thousand years ago. The stems are cut after having grown to a height of 12-15 feet. They are then stripped into four segments during which most of the pith is removed. They are spread in the sun to dry and during this time acquire a reddish brown colour. A black colour is obtained by putting the strands into mud holes for a few days. Creamy white strands are obtained by using the underside of the brown strips. Thus three colours are available for weaving the various traditional basket designs: brown, white and black.

Kaklin: (C) (*Clusia venosa*). This is the dominant tree of the Elfin Woodland, found on the highest peaks of Dominica's mountains. It is also sometimes found in the Littoral Forest along the east and north east coast clinging to cliffs and to the sides of ravines. It has thick rubbery leaves, which can withstand the wind and almost constant rain or sea spray. It bears a glossy deep purple coloured fruit. Its hanging aerial roots are used to make the frames of certain types of baskets.

Pottery:

Pottery was made out of clay from different parts of Dominica. Different pots were given different names according to their use.

Canari: A large earthenware bowl made by the Caribs to ferment and store their cassava beer called *ouicou*. The original word was *Canalli*, which was adapted by the French and Africans to Canari. In Creole it means any large earthenware pot, but the Caribs had many different names for each type of pot according to its use. It is also the name of a stream, Layvyè Canari, at Castle Comfort.

Sculpture:

Carvings were made in stone, wood and bone. Bas-relief carvings were done on the side of big rocks. These are called petroglyphs and are found on many Caribbean islands.

Stone tools:

The types of stone best suited for making particular tools such as mortars and axe-heads, *hoücoue,* were categorised by uses (Breton,1665:239). Flakes of jasper were necessary for making graters, *takia kani*, for shredding cassava tubers. The identification of jasper deposits was crucial for this process as were types of rock best suited for making into particular tools and other objects. Some of these are recorded by Breton with their Carib names and are identified in some cases to have been common to particular islands (Breton 1665:195):

tebou - stone
couléhueyou - firestone, for lighting fire
coyébali itágueli - smooth stone
taoüa - white stone
coyláya - black stone
ouroúali - pumice stone, with which they polish their 'auirons'
cherouli - pumice stone from Marie Galante
méoulou - pumice stone from Martinique
teukê oúbao - precious stones

tlimáparacola balou balou - green stone for the men
tácaoüa, tacoúlaoüa - green stones which serve as jewels for the women
macónabou - counterfeit green stones (Breton,1666:291,292).

Dance

The dances were representative of the spirit world of ancestors and nature. Some dances represented hunting and fishing or the stories of the creation of the Kalinago universe, the constellations of stars and the changes in the seasons. The dances were choreographed in circles and lines of dancers similar to those still danced among the indigenous people of South America today. As they danced they chanted in time with the music and many dancers carried and played shack-shacks as they danced.

Some Kalinago History

The people of Ouhayo

Prince Rupert's Bay at Portsmouth in the north of Dominica was an ideal setting for the pre-Columbian people of Dominica. It possessed all the requirements of the island-bases tribes who roamed the Caribbean from 5 000 BC: the sheltered bay, fresh water, reefs and fishing banks, land for cultivation and abundant forests bearing all the wood, thatch, bark, fruit and herbs which they needed for their self-sufficient existence. They called the bay Ouhayo and the island Wai'tukubuli.

Hardly any archeological study has made of the area, but through the years visiting experts and enthusiasts have picked up clues which indicate that settlements existing here following the pattern of other Amerindian habitation in the Lesser Antilles. When the Spaniards first reached Prince Rupert's Bay, first without landing in 1493 and then more effectively in 1502, they found the area inhabited by Indians who spoke Cariban, a language, which like Arawakan, is widespread in eastern South America. The material culture of these people belonged to the final pre-Columbian age, or period of development, in the Caribbean area; that age is know as the Neo-Indian. This means that the Caribs, like the Arawaks on other islands, made pottery. They also knew the art of farming and were skilled mariners.

It is probable that bays such as Prince Rupert's were populated by man early as 5 000 BC. We know about the Arawake from their finely decorated pottery chards and also from artifacts on other islands, but about the Caribs of Prince Rupert's Bay we have the more definite reports of Spanish, French and British visitors who called here after 1493.

The Carib villages along the Bay were each made up of a small number of house with the carbet or communal longhouse in the midst of the dwellings. Reports indicate that these dwellings were on firm ground out of the reach of the swamps. Missionaries and other visitors in the 17th century described the giant carbet of the chief of Ouhayo on the bank of the Indian River.

This was a splendid site for a major village. The canoes entered the river from the sea, paddling up to the firm ground some 300 metres upstream. Here, surrounded by smaller dwellings was the longhouse of Ouhayo, the big meeting place where the men assembled. It was 40 to 50 metres long and could hold some 150 hammocks slung from the several stout posts supporting the roof. This vaguely oval building was thatched with cachibou leaves tied down with mahoe bark cord.

The men were the fishermen, hunters, warriors, boatbuilders and basket makers. The women's work was plant, prepare and cook food. They also spun thread, wove hammocks and made clay vessels for holding food and liquid.

This pattern did not change as soon as a single Spanish caravel rounded the Cabrits point November 3, 1493, circled the bay and then sailed out again. Dominica, through the Caribs and its terrain, resisted colonization for a longer period than any other island of the Caribbean. Although many visitors called at Ouhayo during the next 250 years, the Caribs still held sway over the area until about the 1740's

Carib Warner: c1635-1674. The name that was given to the half-Carib son of Sir Thomas Warner, the English coloniser of St. Kitts. Carib Warner's name was also Thomas. His mother was a Carib woman from Dominica who was living in St.Kitts at the time of the English settlement. The boy grew up among his father's family, but at about the age of thirteen, his father died and his English stepmother wanted him out of the house. Along with other Caribs he retreated to Dominica where he rose to be a chief along the west coast in the vicinity of the present day village of Massacre. He used his knowledge of European ways and his Carib ancestry to the fullest, playing the French against the English in an effort to retain Dominica for the Caribs. The English in Barbados favoured him as an ally and the Governor Willoughby made him a colonel and Lieutenant Governor of Dominica. In 1666, Carib Warner was captured by the French and imprisoned. On 9 December the following year, Willoughby procured his release and reinstated him as governor of Dominica. In February 1668 a peace was agreed between the English and the Caribs through the medium of Carib Warner. But the English in Antigua did not see the Caribs in the same light as those in Barbados, and were angry at continued Carib raids on the Leeward Islands. Carib Warner's English half-brother, Phillip, led a force against him from Antigua, murdered him and massacred his village. The French gave the name Massacre to the site.

Garifuna Religion

The Garifuna are an ethnic group numbering roughly 300,000 with communities in some 40 villages dotting the Caribbean coasts of Nicaragua, Honduras, Guatemala, and Belize. Their traditional ancestor-focused religion presents a multilayered confluence of Amerindian, African, and Roman Catholic influences.

History

The Garifuna are descendants of Africans and Amerindians (Carib and Arawak) who shared the island of Saint Vincent beginning in the second half of the seventeenth century. *Garifuna* is properly the name of their language, which is affiliated with the Arawak linguistic family. The term is derived from *Kalinago*, the ethnic title used by Island Carib Amerindians to describe themselves but misrecognized by Christopher Columbus as "Carib." Europeans called the Garifuna "Black Caribs" because of the group's apparent African ancestry. That appellation was in common usage until the shift to Garifuna as a standard ethnic name after the middle of the twentieth century.

The African presence on Saint Vincent derived in part from survivors of a slaver shipwreck near the island dated to 1635. Most probably, then, their African origins derived from the slave trade out of the ports of west central Africa. The African presence also derived from Carib raids that carried slaves from European colonies and from the arrival of fleeing African maroons from neighboring Barbados and elsewhere. By 1674, according to accounts from the Jesuit missions, the "Black Carib" numbered as many as the "Red" Island Carib on Saint Vincent. Reports from 1700 indicate that they had already founded settlements separated from the Island Carib Amerindians.

After 1783 Saint Vincent became a permanent British colony and was slotted for sugar production. Following a period of military resistance in the Second Carib War (1795–1797), a British naval convoy deported approximately five thousand Garifuna to Roatan, an island just off the coast of Central America. Though half of those deported died in transit, their survivors settled the Central American coast early in the 1800s. This became the new homeland, the site of their reconstitution as a distinct ethnic group with its own specific set of religious practices.

Religious Transculturation

Garifuna religion provides a stunning example of the religious transculturation that occurred throughout the Caribbean Basin during the colonial period. Seventeenth-century missionary accounts of the Island Carib Amerindians describe religious leaders known as *piaye* or *boyé*. These were shamans who used gourd rattles and tobacco to cure patients of illnesses attributed to malignant spirits through their mastery and mediation of tutelary ancestral spirits. They are also recorded as performing divination. The "Black Caribs" adopted this religious office and techniques from their Saint Vincent hosts. Garifuna religion continues to rely upon the leadership of such shamans, still called by the similar title of *buyei*. They orchestrate and direct sophisticated ritual performances under the influence of the helping spirits of benevolent ancestors *(hiuruha)*. Other aspects of early Island Carib Amerindian religion, like the belief that a person is constituted by multiple souls, including the "heart-soul" *(uwani)* as the seat of agency and will and the "spirit double" *(afurugu)* that may wander during dreams and after death, remain a vital part of contemporary Garifuna religion as well. These bear witness to the legacy of Island Carib Amerindian societies, many of them now nearly assimilated or extinct, in Garifuna religious life.

Traditional west central African religious practices also left their mark on Garifuna religion. The most elaborate ritual performances, called *dügü*, utilize three drums to guide dances that culminate in spirit possession by returning ancestors, called *gubida*, who are feted as they dance and consult with the living. Drummers' use of polyrhythmic meter for dances like the *punta*, once a funerary dance, and the *junkunnu*, a mask dance, punctuate and offset the use of mono-rhythms like the *amalihani*. These complex drumming patterns recall in music and dance the west central African legacy.

Catholicism also played a key role in Garifuna religion as it assumed its current form after 1797. All traditional Garifuna religious actors also consider themselves to be Catholic, and Catholicism provides the overall mythic structure within which the ancestor religion is maintained. Malignant *(mafia)* spirits, for example, typically associated spatially with "the bush" *(el monte)*, are considered manifestations of the devil, while positive spirits are regarded as agents of the high God *(Bungiu)*. Postmortem rituals (see below) begin with "masses" *(lemesi)* adapted from official Roman Catholic liturgy and continue with novenas (ninth-night masses) and anniversary masses performed to remember and appease the dead. Catholic saints are prominent on Garifuna altars, and specific saints like Esquipula and Anthony are called upon as sources of solace and assistance.

Small-Scale Ritual Events

Since the overall mythic and ethical structure of Garifuna religion is provided by Roman Catholic Christianity, the distinguishing characteristics of Garifuna religion are found in its sophisticated complex of ritual practices. Moreover since specific beliefs and ethical postures vary widely in relation to popular adaptations of Catholicism, correct ritual practice is particularly crucial to Garifuna religious identity. Myths and belief remain largely implicit, embedded in ritual performance.

In general, rituals are focused on the problem of death and the transfer in status from living human being to exalted ancestor *(gubida)*. Though the dead remain a source of power for the living, they must also be helped by living family members as they take the steps from this world to their status as recently departed spirits *(ahari)* and then to one of finally becoming *gubida* in the otherworld. The otherworld is called *Sairi*, the home of the ancestors, and is often physically located on Saint Vincent. The postmortem journey is simultaneously one of progressive spiritual advance and one of geographic traverse, or return, to the lost homeland. The ritualization of death is therefore in part an expression of diasporic consciousness, a means of looking back to a paradise lost.

Insofar as the ritual obligations to the dead are not adequately performed by the living, ancestors register their complaints through signs experienced by the living as nightmares, bad luck, accidents, and unexplained illnesses. Garifuna religion is in this sense rigorously this-worldly. It is concerned with alleviating concrete material problems by contemplating them and acting upon them as ruptures in the relations between of the living and the ancestors. These crises are addressed through a sequence of ritual interventions that demand progressively more serious investments. The ability to prosper in the material world is therefore understood as directly related to and contingent upon the attention devoted to the family ancestors' "advance" through the spirit world.

Veluria

When a member of the community dies, the corpse of the deceased is placed in a coffin and laid out in his or her house for public viewing. Candles are lit and placed at each corner, and near the coffin a simple altar is erected on a low table, including holy water and statues of Catholic saints. Crepe-paper streamers are hung in a canopy over the body. Friends and relatives arrive at the wake and hold vigil through the night, drinking coffee and rum *(aguardiente* or *guaro)*, playing cards, and talking. At dawn the corpse is interred in a graveyard that is nearby yet spatially removed from the village. The burial is accompanied by wailing laments and the pouring of rum into the grave by family members and friends.

Amuidahani

Between six months and several years after the death, the family "bathes" the deceased. A small pit is dug immediately adjacent to the home, and a fresh change of clothes for the departed is suspended above it. Family members and intimate friends pour liquids into the pit, variously including freshwater, saltwater, strained cassava water, herbal infusions, and favored beverages like coffee and rum. Tobacco and favorite foods may be offered as well. Following the "bathing" of the deceased, the pit is closed. The ritual is small and intimate in nature, of short duration, and does not require the presence of the *buyei* as officiant.

Lemesi

Around a year following death, as well as later if called for by the ancestor through divination by the *buyei*, a "mass" is held for the spirit of the deceased *(ahari)*, who is viewed as still present in the village. The occasion marks the end of a period of mourning for the spouse who survives the dead and, as an occasion marking the return to everyday life, is conspicuously festive. Food and beverages are served, and the celebrative *punta* dance is drummed and danced in the yard. The *punta* is typically comprised of a circle into which a man and a woman enter in pairs, two at a time. The dance entails the rhythmic oscillation of the hips while holding the upper body perfectly still and the facial expression calm. It celebrates both the life of the deceased and the ongoing force of the community despite the loss of one of its members.

Women gathered for the purpose sing "women's songs" *(abaimahani)*, standing in a line with little fingers linked and thrusting the arms forward in rhythmic concert, a gesture suggestive of shared labor. The song lyrics recall the struggles of family life and loyalty and sometimes speak from the perspective of the ancestors, pleading to not be forgotten. Men's songs *(arumahani)* are ideally presented in similar fashion, though since the twentieth century it has become increasingly challenging to find a choir of males able and willing to perform the old songs. This is because of a common male pattern of leaving the village for long durations in order to find work. The lyrics of men's songs often recall the necessity and dangers of travel for labor far from home and the longing to return.

In addition traditional tales *(úruga)* may be told, often humorous trickster-like narratives. The festivities continue until dawn.

Major Ritual Events

While the foregoing are required in all cases, the most elaborate postmortem rituals, the *chugu* and the *dügü*, are called for only when specifically requested by an ancestral spirit. When a family member suffers unusual misfortune, recurring nightmares, or unexplained illnesses or pains, he or she may consult a shaman *(buyei)*. With the patient seated before the *buyei*'s altar *(gule)*, the *buyei* lights a candle, smokes his or her pipe, and summons his or her tutelary spirits *(hiuruha)* by blowing the vapor of rum from the mouth over the altar. This activates it. Blowing smoke over the head of the patient, he or she consults with his or her spirits to "read" the nature of the problem at hand, depending on the movement of the smoke and the insights granted by tutelary spirits *(hiuruha)*. This ritual act is called *arairaguni*, "bringing down the spirits." If the problem is one caused by the ancestors *(hasandigubida)*, he or she negotiates with the afflicting spirit to decipher what it requires.

This may be a *misa*, a *chugu*, or in the most serious of cases, a *dügü*. Together with the patient, and taking account of the family's financial resources, the shaman then plots the course of action.

Chugu

The *chugu*, literally the "feeding" of the dead, is a one- to two-day ceremony officiated by a *buyei*. In addition to all of the elements included in a "mass," it entails the assembly of a greater number of relatives and the preparation of large quantities of food offerings, including roosters *(gayu)* offered for sacrifice. Since a more intimate communication with the dead is required than in a "mass," the *buyei* erects his or her personal altar *(gule)* in the house where the *chugu* will take place. There he or she places the symbols of his or her key helping spirits as well as the implements of the shaman's vocation: the maracas *(sirisi)* used to call the spirit, the wand *(murewa)* used to communicate with and control the spirit should possession trance occur, and bottles of rum and tobacco used to purify the room and to activate, or "heat," the altar. Traditional foods are prepared, including most importantly the sacrificed roosters *(gayu)* and cassava bread *(ereba)*, to present an abundant table to the dead. Women's and men's songs are performed at length, and the spirit may also be celebrated with *punta* dancing. Much rum is consumed to create the atmosphere of exuberance and generous abundance believed to be favored by the ancestors.

At the conclusion of the day's events, the *buyei* concocts a nog of beaten eggs and hot rum *(furunsu)*. Each participant places his or her full cup upon the altar while making requests of the ancestor before exchanging the cup with another participant. The exchanged communal drink unites the group. Finally, the *buyei* "burns the table," pouring rum over its surface and igniting it in flame. A strong blue flame reveals the ancestor's approval of the offering and indicates that the precipitating symptoms of bad luck or illness that evoked the *chugu* should subside.

Dügü

Just as the *chugu* contains all the elements of the "mass," the *dügü* contains all the elements of the *chugu*, such that the larger ritual encompasses the smaller in the style of Chinese boxes. *Dügü* is short for *adugurahani*, "mashing down the earth," perhaps referring to the long periods of dance that are required of participants. It is regarded as the fullest expression of Garifuna religion and is a major ritual event that is prepared for a full year and performed over a week's duration. It typically occurs many years after the death of a family member and only when mandated by a *buyei* and his or her spirit helpers. Announcements about the *dügü* circulate for at least a year to insure that sufficient funds can be raised for sacrifices of roosters, pigs, and sometimes a cow and to feed a crowd of participants that may number in the hundreds for a week's time. All family members, even those residing in the United States, are obligated to attend. Indeed the ritual's efficacy depends on a complete demonstration of family unity to resolve the perceived crisis. It is arguably the emotional dramatization of family unity itself that provides in part the experience of the ritual as a healing cure.

First, a ceremonial house (*gayunere* or *dabuyaba*) must be constructed in "traditional" palm-thatch style on the beach. The *dügü* formally begins with the "return of the fishermen," a group sent three days prior to catch fish in the "traditional" way in the offshore cays. They arrive at dawn, attired as Garifuna ancestors wearing helmets of woven palm, and are greeted with exuberant songs by family members attired in matching red-dyed uniforms. They are given rum and cigarettes and are laid in hammocks, just as the ancestors will be later in the ritual when they are incorporated in living bodies of dancers through spirit possession.

Over the next two days follows a sequence of dances both to honor the ancestors and create the conditions for their arrival in possession. First are the *amalahani*, dances to honor the ancestors. These continue for up to four hours at a time, brought to crescendo by the shaman, who exhorts the large group until some are possessed by ancestors. Transformed into known figures from the past, they make requests and are soothed with rum and food. Living family members may ask questions, in response to which the ancestors give counsel.

Throughout the second and third day, the food offering *(chugu)* is prepared. Roosters—one required from each attending nuclear family—are sacrificed, massive amounts of rum assembled, and tables loaded with the most traditional Garifuna foods. The food is piled high on a wooden table and left for the ancestors' consumption. After the spirits "eat," the assembled participants also take their fill, rejoicing in the luxurious abundance far exceeding that of everyday life. At the close of the day, what remains of the spirits' food is buried in the ground or returned to the sea, taken by canoe and deposited in the deeps.

Finally, the shaman guarantees the ancestors' acceptance of the offerings. Pouring rum on the table, he or she feeds the flame and tips the table to all sides, as in the *chugu*. There is great joy, and all rush to wipe the sacralized liquor on their bodies as a balm for all pains. Reunited family groups run to enter the sea together in a temporary moment of *communitas*.

As the *dügü* summons and placates ancestors, it also reinforces family bonds among the living. This has become increasingly important as a third of the Garifuna have emigrated to the United States since the middle of the twentieth century. The *dügü* takes on new import and meaning for those residing abroad, serving the purpose of communicating the experience of home through the dense, compact form of ritual performance. Territoriality, or consciousness of place, is fortified above all in this central ritual performance. With increased migration, the *dügü* appears to be gaining in the frequency of its performance rather than suffering a decline.

New Developments

Migration to cities like New York has sparked a new identity consciousness of the Garifuna's African roots. Religious leaders in New York have begun to conceive of their traditional practices within the purview of other African diaspora religions like Cuban Santería and Haitian vodou. This new form of indigenous syncretism justifies a view of the Garifuna as a dramatically innovative religion, especially as it is reshaped in the new contexts of U.S. urban centers. As Garifuna religious leaders in the United States return periodically to perform rituals in Honduras, Belize, and Guatemala, they carry with them a new identity consciousness. This will likely have transformative effects on homeland religious performance as well.

The second key contemporary issue of Garifuna religion is the rise of evangelical Christian sects since around 1980 in homeland villages. Converts to the new churches disavow all connections to traditional practices, which are regarded as diabolical. The use of dance, tobacco, rum, and altars are vehemently rejected, leading to the dismissal not only of Catholicism but of virtually all traditional rites. This creates friction within families and between village factions and generates new conundrums for traditional practices like the *dügü*, since in that ritual all members of the family are required to be present. When evangelicals refuse to attend such events, they are accused of jeopardizing the rituals' efficacy and therefore also the physical safety of everyone in their kin group. While such disputes are divisive, they also serve as explanations of future accidents, bad luck, and illnesses. The disputes therefore incite ritual as much they compromise it.

Bibliography

Bianchi, Cynthia Chamberlain. "Gubida Illness and Religious Ritual Among the Garifuna of Santa Fe, Honduras: An Ethnopsychiatric Analysis." Ph.D. diss., Ohio State University, 1988. This dissertation goes to great lengths to show the rich detail of Garifuna postmortem rituals framed by an ethno-psychiatric approach to healing.

Coelho, Ruy. "The Black Carib of Honduras: A Study in Acculturation." Ph.D. diss., Northwestern University, 1955. Chapter 5 provides an important mid-century look at Garifuna religion in Honduras. Much of the literature gives attention to English-speaking Belize, giving added distinction to this source.

Conzemius, Eduard. "Ethnographical Notes on the Black Carib (Garif)." *American Anthropologist* 30, no. 2 (1928): 183–205. Possibly the earliest "modern" ethnographic description of Garifuna ritual.

Flores, Barbara. "The Garifuna Dugu Ritual in Belize: A Celebration of Relationships." In *Gender, Ethnicity, and Religion*, edited by Rosemary Radford Ruether, pp. 144–170. Minneapolis, 2002. A sympathetic and accomplished essay on the *dügü* ritual with special attention to the issue of gender.

Gonzalez, Nancie L. *Sojourners of the Caribbean: Ethnogenesis and Ethnohistory of the Garifuna.* Urbana, Ill., and Chicago, 1988. This is an important resource on Garifuna history and archaeology written by the preeminent Garifuna ethnographer.

Hulme, Peter, and Neil L. Whitehead, eds. *Wild Majesty: Encounters with Caribs from Columbus to the Present Day.* Oxford, 1992. This is a selection of descriptions of the Caribs, both Island Carib Amerindians and the "Black Carib," as represented by Europeans since the seventeenth century.

Jenkins, Carol L. "Ritual and Resource Flow: The Garifuna Dugu." *American Ethnologist* 10 (1983): 429–442. An important interpretation of the relationship between economic resources and ritual performance.

Johnson, Paul Christopher. "Migrating Bodies, Circulating Signs: Brazilian Candomblé, the Garífuna of the Caribbean, and the Category of 'Indigenous Religions.'" *History of Religions* 41, no. 4 (2002): 301–328. The essay compares types of religious dislocations and creative responses for the cases of Brazilian Candomblé and the Garifuna of Honduras and in New York City. The essay begins to elaborate and theorize the relation between migration and contemporary religious change.

Kerns, Virginia. *Women and the Ancestors: Black Carib Kinship and Ritual.* 2d ed. Urbana, Ill., and Chicago, 1997. A valuable text on Garifuna religion and ritual performance for its attention to women as the primary carriers and transmitters of tradition.

Melendez, Armando Crisanto. "Religious Elements of the Garifuna Culture and Their Connotations in the Americas." In *African Creative Expressions of the Divine*, edited by Kortright Davis and Elias Farajajé-Jones, translated by Dorothea Lowe Bryce, pp. 121–128. Washington, D.C., 1991. A short, descriptive account of Garifuna beliefs from an important Garifuna choreographer, historian, and cultural activist.

Sanford, Margaret. "Revitalization Movements as Indicators of Completed Acculturation." *Comparative Studies in Society and History* 16 (1974): 504–518. A provocative essay arguing that religious revitalization, including the

Garifuna case, is correlated with general acculturation or assimilation such that revivals are possible indicators of cultural distress.

Suazo, Eusebio Salvador. *Irufumali: La doctrina esotérica garífuna.* Tegucigalpa, 2000. A bilingual (Spanish and Garifuna) account of the *buyei's* knowledge from a Garifuna writer, acquired through interviews with practicing shamans.

Taylor, Douglas. *The Black Carib of British Honduras.* New York, 1951. The text offers several important chapters on Garifuna beliefs in relation to the soul and Garifuna ritual practices. Taylor brought rare linguistic depth to his descriptive task.

The Garifuna Flag

National Garifuna Council of Belize

History

The Garifuna flag consists of three horizontal strips of black, white and yellow, in that order, starting from the top. This flag has long been accepted internationally as the flag of the Garifuna Nation and the colours have been used in any forum where Garifuna people assert their Garifuna identity.

This flag represents an evolution that commenced with the Carib International Society (CIS) whose flag was made up of horizontal strips of red, yellow and black. Red (funati) stood for the blood of the Garifuna, black (würiti) the skin of the Garifuna and yellow (dumari) the food of the Garifuna. T.V. Ramos added the strip of white (haruti) in the middle, substituting it for the red, when he formed the Carib Development Society (CDS). Carib International Society, as the name implies, was international in scope and its development appears to have been facilitated by the convergence of Garinagu from the various countries in places like Puerto Barrios where they flocked in search of employment with the United Fruit Company. The area of operations of the Carib Development Society, on the other hand, was limited to Belize although the influence of its initiatives spread far beyond the borders of Belize and laid the foundation for the later emergence of its successor, the National Garifuna Council.

What is the significance of the colours of the Garifuna flag? This question has been asked quite frequently and some attempts have been made to answer it although I am not aware of any written explanation. I will now try to piece together what I have heard, with the hope that this will evoke some reaction that can contribute to a full and complete documentation of the significance of the colours. It should also be noted that it is people who give meaning to symbols. We, therefore, have the option of expanding on whatever meanings have been handed down to us by the originators of the CIS and CDS flags.

Black

The black strip, which is located at the top, represents the black ancestry of the Garifuna people. The people have always acknowledged the African input into what became the Garifuna people, a phenomenon that occurred in St. Vincent starting in the seventeenth Century.

This colour, at another level, recognizes the hardships and injustices that the people have had to endure, their struggles for survival and the odds that they have had to overcome in the course of their history. Apart from the experience of the Middle Passage, which we share with other black people of the Americas, there was the imprisonment on Balliceaux, the exile from our Vincentian homeland after the so called Carib Wars and the replay of the Middle Passage in the form of the mass forced relocation to Central America.

Tough though these experiences have been, they helped to strengthen our spirit and shape our spirituality which is based on the principle of reciprocity captured in the Malí song in the words "Aura buni Iyaya waü, amürü nuni" – I for you, Grandmother, and you for me.

Yellow

The yellow strip at the bottom of the flag symbolizes the other half of the ancestry of the Garifuna – the Amerindians or Yellow Caribs as they were referred to by Europeans. These were actually a mixture of Caribs and Arawaks and formed the host community in which the fusion of Africa and South America took place to give rise to the emergence of the Garinagu as a distinct group indigenous to the circum-Caribbean region.

In contrast to the hardships experienced in the course of history, the yellow symbolizes the hope and prosperity. Yellow is the colour of grated cassava, which is further processed to make ereba, one of our staple foods. It is the colour of cassava juice, a colour that is further brought out in the process of turning it into dumari, an additive for enhancing sauces, soups and stews. (It seems to have been an identifying feature of Garifuna people as it is the "tumali" that is referred to in the racial slur "Salt head Kerub, tumali water"). Yellow is also the colour of the rising sun, which brings new promise and much hope for a better life. Yellow, therefore, represents hope, plenty and prosperity, as well as the Carib/Arawak input into the Garifuna identity.

White

The white strip, located in the middle between the black and the yellow, reminds us of the role of the white man (Europe) in the history and formation of the Garifuna people – the forcible removal and enslavement of the African, the seizure of Garifuna land, which precipitated the Garifuna resistance, and the forcible removal of the people from St. Vincent. Even after the arrival and dispersal in Central America, it was still necessary to deal with the white man.

At another level, white symbolizes the peace that has eluded the Garifuna people for most of their turbulent history - the peace for which they continue to yearn.

Source: National Garifuna Council of Belize

Song and Ritual as a Key To Understanding Garifuna Personality

By E. Roy Cayetano
Fall 1974

This paper is based on two fundamental assumptions. The first is that in a culture where songs play such an important role, a study of the lyrics and behavior associated with the songs should reveal much about the people. Secondly, there is a tendency for people to seek to attain congruence between their beliefs and their behavior (and avoid cognitive dissonance). Ritual is a manifestation of a belief system and, since it is easily observable, it can be used to get at the underlying set of beliefs and the modal personality traits of the people who share those ritual observances.

Until about two decades ago the Garifuna were referred to by anthropologists as Black Caribs, partly because they are black and partly to distinguish them from the aboriginal Island Caribs whom Columbus encountered in the West Indies. These people, who call themselves Garinagu (derived from Island Carib Calinago), were the result of racial and cultural mixing between escaped African slaves originally from two shipwrecked slave ships (Taylor, 1951 pg.18) and the Island Caribs. Whereas the physical characteristics remained predominantly African, it seems reasonable to conclude on the basis of a number of similarities that can be found between the Caribs and a number of South American cultures from which the Island Caribs originated, that the Island Carib culture was retained almost completely and, in addition to some African influences, the extent of which has not yet been determined, later became subject to some influence from European cultures.

The Garifuna are today found only in Central America. Before 1797 they occupied the West Indian Island of St. Vincent and in that year following a series of clashes with the English who sought control of the Island, they were deported to the Central American Island of Roatan whence they spread south to Honduras and Nicaragua, and north to Guatemala, and British Honduras, now known as Belize.

In this paper I will concern myself mainly with the Garifuna of Belize since the material I am using was collected there. This is not to say, however, that what is said here will not apply to those in the other countries since those who hold on to their language and traditions from a fairly homogenous community that cuts across national boundaries. Some of the songs, although collected in Dangriga, a Belizean town, were composed in Honduras (Indura) or Guatemala (Wadimalu). Needless to say, the rites are basically the same throughout.

Religion and Ritual

Most of the Garifuna in Belize are Roman Catholics – at least nominally. Most of the others are Methodists while the rest, which constitutes an almost negligible proportion of the total population, are members of the Adventist Church or the Church of the Nazarene. So we see that the traditional belief system has not gone unchallenged by competing European religions who have until recently, and even today to a lesser extent, strongly discouraged its manifestation especially in the form of the Dügü rite. For example, quoting the Methodist Record as his source, Waddell (1961 pg. 68) writes that "Finding the Caribs practicing devil-worship, the Methodists extended their activities to Stann Creek, where they still retain a following …..". The missionaries, in spite of all the power they have built up in the area have not tried to understand the significance of the rituals but, while their condemnation of the native practices has been strong, Garifuna Religion has survived if not flourished. It appears in fact, that there has been "a steadily rising rebirth of interest in Black Carib ancestral rites". (Palacio 1973). This rebirth is interesting in itself and could be the topic of another study.

One question that comes to mind is this: Why should the Carib retain his traditional rites and belief system after three centuries of contact with influential missionaries and their western religion? Why should the Dügü rite and the Buyei retain importance in Garifuna life while the people profess to be Catholics, Methodists, or Nazarenes even though these practices are actively opposed by the Church leaders; and the other ethnic groups in the country regard these practices with suspicion, calling them such names as "Devil Dance" or "Mafia Dance"? And why should they be turning more and more to their traditional beliefs at a time when there is truly a national government (as opposed to a colonial type of government) and they are, if anything, playing a more active role in the day to day running of the country?

Whatever the full answer to those questions may be, whatever the external (and/or internal) pressures that are at work, it seems to me to be true that the traditional religion and the rites serve a function that continues to be necessary for the Garifuna and his adaptation – as an individual or as a group – to uncertain and changing times. This is a function that the foreign religions, which have been superimposed on Garifuna culture, cannot serve. If I am right, then I expect that by looking closely at the rites and the beliefs underlying them, by looking for parallels in the social organization and other aspects of Garifuna life, we might find indications of personality traits that are perhaps common to most Garifuna. Incidentally, we might also be able to suggest why these personality traits and the ritual system have persisted.

The main idea underlying Garifuna religion and perhaps their view of the world is that the spirits of the departed ancestors mediate between the individual and the external world. If the individual performs as he should, then all will be well with him. If not, then the harmony that one desires in his relationship with others and the rest of the external world will be disrupted. This disruption takes the form of persistent and recurring misfortune or illness that cannot be cured by ordinary known medical practices.

This religious or cosmological system implies that the living Garifuna and the ancestral dead have certain responsibilities and obligations to each other. It behooves the living not to neglect the ancestors. Food and drink should occasionally be laid out for them and, since the incorporation of Catholicism into the Garifuna way of life, masses have come to be one of the requirements. The ancestor may also indicate by appearing to the individual in dreams that he is desirous of certain food items, or a mass, and failure to comply with the request may result in the negligent progeny being struck by lamiselu (trouble) in some form. It is not clear exactly what the role of the ancestral dead is in the maintenance of harmony between the individual and the external world. It is not clear from my own observation, from Taylor's account (1951 pg. 102 – 137), or from Palacio's (1973) brief analysis whether the world is seen as inherently dangerous and the evil is warded off by the protective ancestral spirits, or if the world is seen as being inherently good and that the evil that befalls the individual is inflicted by the angered spirits as a punishment for negligence. But whether evil befalls the individual because the ancestral dead cause it, or because they allow it, the fact remains that they are seen as having some control over the living; similar to the control parents have over their children. This is not to say that the living live in fear of the dead, for the informality that prevails in the dügü temple would disprove that.

Garifuna religion requires the services of a specialist, a priest called buyei (derived from South America "paye"), to mediate between the living and the ancestral spirits. This is done with the help of spirit helpers (hiyuruha) who serve as a means of communication between the buyei and the individual ancestral spirits in Seiri, the place where souls go after death. In a ceremony called areiraguni (bringing down) the buyei goes into a trance, and finds out the causes of his clients' ailments and what needs to be done to make amends for past negligence.

There are three principal rites. The smallest and perhaps least important, the amuñadahani (the burying), which Taylor translates as "refreshing the dead", involves scattering cassava meal and water in a retangular hole and some singing. This is a family affair. The chugú (feeding of the dead) takes about a whole day and for this the buyei is required. Actually, the chugú is a mini dügü and unlike the amuñadahani is a propitiation rite. The dügü (the feasting of the dead) is the most important rite. The dügü proper lasts between 3 and 5 days but if one counts the preparatory stage which involves a number of people sailing to the cayes to collect sea food after being ritually prepared, even the smallest dügü requires a minimum of one week from start to finish.

One of the interesting and perhaps most important aspects of the dügü is that it involves not only the immediate family of the person on whose behalf the offering is being made, but all the relatives, no matter how remote, of both that person and the departed one to whom the dügü is being offered. This means that most people in a village are involved since, as noted earlier, the Garifuna of Central America can be said to constitute a community that cuts across national boundaries. Relatives usually travel from Honduras and Guatemala to participate in a dügü given in a Belizean village or town.

Just as living relatives from far and wide assemble in the dabuyaba (dügü temple) to join with their ailing or provisionally healed kinsman, so too, the ancestral spirit to whom the dügü is being offered is believed to invite relatives in the Seiri spirit community to feast with him. Thus the two communities – the living and the dead – are joined together during the dügü ceremony and this is manifested in visible physical terms when some of the ancestral spirits enter the bodies of some of their participating living relations, thus causing them to go into trance and to behave the way the ancestors did when they were alive. This takes place especially during those parts of the rite called ámalihani (placating the dead), when the drumming, dancing and singing, starting with a relatively slow pace, gradually builds up in pace and intensity.

The only musical instruments used are three huge drums, which are played by hand, and the buyei's sísira (rattle). The singing, the drumming and dancing are kept up for the entire duration of the dügü with only short breaks from time to time. Chickens and a couple of pigs and maybe turtles are slaughtered at prescribed intervals and these as well as the cooking, distribution, and offering to the dead, are done in the manner prescribed by tradition.

This has by no means been a complete description of Garifuna propitiation rites. This has been done reasonably well by Taylor (1951). My purpose so far has been to state the basic ideas that underlie these rites and to point out the salient features of the rituals, particularly the most important rite, the dügü. It only remains to add that at the conclusion of the dügü, the buyei in an araíraguni ceremony receives word from the ancestors as to whether the dügü was accepted or not. If it was not acceptable to the ancestor(s), he is told why and, at some time in the future, the whole procedure has to be repeated. Fortunately, this does not happen very often for a dügü requires many months, sometimes over a year, of preparation and, for many, the inconvenience of travelling, as well as the financial burden that it places on the shoulders of the family that is giving it.

Songs

Songs are a very important part of Garifuna culture. Indeed there are songs for just about every purpose. There are songs associated with grating cassava, the traditional food, there are songs that are associated with work and, of course, each of the many dances has its own type of song. It is not surprising then that there are usually many "composers" in each village or town. Although some are more prolific composers than others, it is as though even the most unlikely person has the potential and only requires some intense personal experience, like death, to open the door so that a song that he already had locked in his psyche could come out.

There are no Garifuna songs that deal with fictitious or imaginary events or feelings. All tell something about the "composer" or about some experiences he or she is having or has just had. Indeed, one can safely claim that one of the purposes of Garifuna songs, their reason d'etre, is to give expression to the feelings genuinely felt by the "composer" and shared by the people among whom the songs gain popularity because they have similar experiences or because the songs deal with themes that are among their main concerns or preoccupations.

Before considering the themes that are most common in the songs, it is necessary to state why I do not feel comfortable using the word "composer" with reference to the person who first sings a song and comes to be seen as the person whose song it is. Because the expression of one's feelings is the strongest motivating factor behind the emergence of a new song, an element of spontaneity, which the word "composer" does not convey, is involved here. This is important not only because of what it implies for my assumption that the songs tell us about the personality of the people, but also because of the claim that in many cases songs are ichahówarügüti (just given); that is to say that a person may be "given" a song in his sleep and he wakes up knowing it, (dügü songs are usually given by the ancestors in dreams), or it grows out of his thoughts and, without any conscious effort at creating it, it comes out as a complete song. Because of this, some composers do not regard certain of their songs as theirs. I am not qualified at this point to say anything further about this claim of ichahówarügüti beyond the observation that if the claim is true – and I have no reason to doubt it – then these songs, like dreams, constitute a valuable means of exploring the mind at the subconscious level.

One of the most common themes in the songs is death. Songs 1, 2, 3, and 4 tell of similar experiences and emotion. The singers of these songs, who incidentally are all women, have each just lost a loved one. In 1 and 3 a mother has just lost a daughter, in 2 a wife has lost a husband, and in 4 a husband has lost a wife, but this is being reported by a sympathetic female singer to whom he expressed his grief. The sense of personal loss and the feeling of grief are equally strong in all four examples and it is not merely co-incidental that the lines:

Ítara lian ra miseria, maga,
Ítara lian ra lamiselu
occur almost word for word in songs 2, 3, and 4. A free translation reads as follows:

"So grief is like this!
So this is what it is like to have troubles!"

However, there is an element of shocked surprise expressed by the morpheme ra which cannot be adequately captured by the English translation.

There are also several songs that deal with the dead. Numbers 5, 6, and 7 are good examples of this, but numbers 1 to 4 can be said to be about the dead as well as about death. In 5 the singer's father has been dead for nearly a year and in 6 we find what is perhaps a more typical situation: the dead exerting a guiding influence over the behavior of the living descendant. Just as a living parent corrects and reprimands an erring offspring, so too, the dead parent and others from preceding generations guide the living, speaking to them through their consciences. What seems to be happening is that the precepts and values inculcated in individuals by their parental and earlier generations continue to surface from the subconscious level long after the socializing agent has departed this life.

This leads us to the next theme, which is a feeling of dependence and helplessness. Parents and other relatives from preceding generations are seen as being endowed with more power, wisdom, and ability to cope with lamíselu (troubles and misfortune of all sorts). In the last verse of number 8, for example, the singer asks:

Where were the supernatural powers of my male ancestor? I would have anointed/equipped you with it, dear kinsman, before your departure; then I wouldn't be crying now.

In this song, the singer is grieving because the son has gone off to the war and it is feared that he will be killed. She feels an overwhelming sense of helplessness and feels that if she only had her ancestor's power and skills she would have been able to control the situation. Notice the striking similarities between this and the last verse of number 9, which suggests that God is conceptualized as just another mighty ancestor who can be called upon in such situations.

Méteñu is another important theme and is closely related to all those already mentioned. Méteñu is the state of being bereft of parents and close relatives. It is obvious that the state of méteñu is dreaded. Number 5 is a good example of this. Here the singer laments the fact that he cannot send a letter to his dead parents and complains:

When will méteñu leave me, my dear,
It has tied its hammock on me (i.e. It has made itself at home).
Although I'm already grown, I still feel it.

This idea is also clearly expressed in some of the other songs like number 10, which expresses the fact that the death of his kinsfolk has made this a sad world for him.

It is interesting that kinship figures prominently in the songs. In number 11 we get the words: She who has no sister is poor, She who has no mother is poor.

Death did it – Death took my male ancestor from me;
(Otherwise), I would not be crying.

In addition to the theme of méteñu, we get the idea that no matter what the rest of the world says about you, no matter how much you are slandered or how much lamiselu rains on you, you can always turn to these people for comfort. In 12, the signer, whose house has just been burnt down, fails to find this comfort and relief in her brother's house. Instead, it is her friend who does what she had a right to expect from her relatives. Hence the imaginary television in which she "have seen my friend here to be my relative".

It is necessary at this point to give a word of warning about the kinship terms that are found in the songs. Considering the importance of kinship ties in traditional Garifuna society, it is perhaps not surprising that kinship terms tend to be used rather loosely. For example, a daughter may be referred to as namúleluwa (my little sister) or núguchu (my mother) while a son or a younger relative may be called núguchi (my father), náti (my elder brother), namúlen (my younger brother) or wanwa (dear young male relative). This is usually done as a means of expressing affection and kinship affinity. Some terms are used in a similar fashion among people who are not so closely related and, as Taylor (1951, page 87) found, a girl may discourage a young man who is trying to flirt with her, by calling him náti, for this implies that she considers him a relative, and this in turn has implications concerning the type of behavior that he should display towards her.

It should be clear from what has been said up to this point that lamíselu – grief, misfortune and trouble of any sort – for the individual stand out as perhaps the most common single concern in the songs. As we have seen, there are many songs about death, grief, helplessness and méteñu. There are also a number of songs about sickness. Numbers 13 and 14 are examples of this.

This account would be unbalanced if I did not make mention of a less serious but nonetheless important group of songs which are concerned with slander, scandal and criticism. Unfortunately, most of these songs defy translation, even more so than the other songs, because many significant subtleties and nuances tend to be lost in translation, and what we are left with is at best only a rather crude approximation of the original lyric. Still, we can see in numbers 15 to 19 the essential points for our present purpose. In number 15, a young man had been the subject of gossip among a few women who criticized him severely because a girl had become pregnant by him, a teacher in the town. He chastises each one in turn: one had a child by a Spanish (muladu) from Honduras many year earlier; so who was she to condemn him? Another, "the charcoal", could afford to be self righteous for her being barren helped hide her own iniquities. Another was hump-backed and bow-legged; no wonder, for even the devil seemed incapable of putting up with her. In 16 a woman ridicules an unwanted man who dared to make advances at her; in 17 a woman accuses another of hypocrisy, for the discovery of the tell-tale hat was not congruent with the image of the good girl who was supposed to have been a virgin bride. Presumably, this attack was not unprovoked. Number 18 shows the singer getting back at some people who are gossiping about her because, having failed to keep other men she has had before, she has just taken yet another mate. Her method of attack is not unlike the one in number 15.

Number 19 is a little different. The násiun (i.e. the non-Garifuna foreigner) is praised for providing well for his wife and, therefore, for himself. He has just returned from a Mexican town where he bought her a number of silk underwear, embroidered and decorated with starch like a rich tablecloth or serviette. While the singer, his employee, is washing these, she hears the wife nagging as usual. To her Garifuna mind, it is unthinkable that such a good, thoughtful man should be treated in this way, or that he should tolerate it. Hence the advice that he should Stamp your foot to her,Pound your chest to her...

Finally, a song may be thought of as iyawaü (an image or picture) of a person or event. The iyawaü of a person may be a tribute to a loved or respected person or a stinging attack as we have seen. The point is that Garifuna songs provide an avenue for the release and expression of emotion and gives the individual a way to get even, but equally interesting is the idea suggested by the notion of iyawaü that people and events can be recorded in songs like little pictures which become public property and remain, long after the former become a matter of history, to give comfort to those who sing them. And, incidentally, I am reasonably certain that one could piece together a history of the post Saint Vincent Garifuna on the basis of the songs alone, although I suspect that the brighter side would be missed in such a reconstruction because of the singers' choice of topics for their songs.

Personality and Behavior

It is clear from the above account of ritual and song that certain patterns of thought and behavior occur in high frequency and can thus be seen as indictors of what one might call typical or modal Garifuna personality. However, it must be remembered that the generalizations made here do not apply equally well to all Garifuna persons. This is especially true of a few who have become so westernized, not merely through the impact of western type schools but especially through the effects of the religious indoctrination that invariably go with the education, with the result that they have come to regard the traditional practices with skepticism, if not something bordering on disdain. It must also be mentioned that in addition to non-participation in the ritual and belief system, people from such families are not known to be "composers" of songs.

In considering the personality traits and behavior patterns that are suggested by the material, I am reminded of what Eggan (1966, see LeVine 1974, pg. 267) had to say about weaning and the Hopi:

Weaning of course, when discussed in personality contexts, means more than a transition from milk to solid food. It is a gradual process of achieving independence from the comfort of a mother's body and care, of transferring affections to other persons, and finding satisfaction within oneself and in the outside world. Most people learn to eat solid food but many of us are never weaned, which has unfortunate consequences in a society where individual effort and competitive independence are stressed.

Eggan could just as well have been speaking of the Garifuna when she observes a few sentences later:

Weaning then was from the breast only, and as he was being weaned from his biological mother, he was at the same time in a situation that increased his emotional orientation toward the intimate in group of the extended family.

There can be no doubt that this runs counter to some of the aspirations of the individual. For example, the Garifuna are known, not only by others but by themselves as well, not to be able to make it in business (i.e. commercial enterprises), at least not on a large scale. The reason, as they are well aware, is that when one begins to show signs of prosperity he is expected to be more supportive of his less fortunate kinsfolk, an expectation that he does not have the disposition to ignore, and, as one might expect, the promising business concern soon begins to decline. This then, serves as a leveling mechanism so that unless the individual can break the ties that were welded into his being during his childhood socialization and escape the consequent feeling of guilt, it is unlikely that he can rise high above his fellows in terms of material wealth. This means that the group rises and falls, prospers and suffers bad times as a unit.

The evidence in the material I am using here also indicates that the average Garifuna is never completely weaned in the broader sense defined by Eggan. It is also true that instead of emphasis on the process of "finding satisfactions within oneself and the outside world", the individual's orientation is towards the kingroup. It is in the kingroup that the individual Garifuna finds his satisfactions. When one is faced with a situation with which he cannot cope, he turns to his mother, father, sister, brother, other kinsmen, or even the ancestors, for help.

Given this mutual dependence, one can understand why sickness and death should be among their main concerns and why a death in the family should prove to be such a traumatic experience for the individual. One can understand why méteñu (the state of being without parents and close relatives) should be dreaded so much. When a close relative dies it is like having some of the ground swept from under one's feet and when méteñu sets in, it is like having been deprived of the support that one relies on for his very survival. In the original lyrics, we find that one does not just die; rather he "dies from me" or "death took him from me". It is as though an integral part of one's being died, leaving him a less viable person.

But obligation is not uni-directional. Obligation is mutual along both horizontal and vertical lines. That is to say that one has obligations to relatives in one's own generation (e.g. siblings and cousins) as well as to those in preceding and succeeding generations, and they to him. The songs suggest that the strongest bond of mutual obligation is between parent, especially mother, and child. The traditionally oriented Garifuna cannot bear to fail in his obligations, and I expect that, seen from a psychoanalytic point of view, one could argue that failure to meet these obligations either through negligence, or because the parent or ancestor has died gives rise to guilt feelings. The propitiation rites would thus be seen as the means available for resolving this conflict. In any case, the "rites do provide a forum for the psychological release of the participants" (Palacio, 1973, pg. 6), and serve to reassure the participants of the unity not only of the kingroup but also of all Garínagu, past and present, be they in Seiri or on earth.

Since the Garifuna sees power as being diffused among the members of his lineage with a certain concentration at the top (i.e. among the ancestors), gradually reducing as one goes down the line, he considers himself as being relatively powerless. He may be more able than his juniors, like the mother in song number 20, but compared to his seniors he is powerless and has to be dependent the way the daughter addressed in the same song is expected to be dependent. Does this mean that the Garifuna is socialized to be dependent? In view of the evidence we find in the ritual and the songs, one would have to answer in the affirmative. However, my own observation is that the average person was brought up to be self reliant and independent in terms of meeting his subsistence needs by traditional means. Yet, with respect to his psychosocial adaptation, the evidence that he is socialized to be dependent is, to my mind, irrefutable.

A certain feeling of resignation, and perhaps even fatalism, is also evident. This is particularly noticeable in the songs dealing with sickness. Here the singers tell us that they have done their best, travelling abroad to obtain medicine and using up all the available medicine, but in each case we find a feeling of despair and resignation. It is as though personal effort is worthwhile only up to a given point, and when that point is reached one concludes that it had all been preordained, and that there is nothing left to do other than to let fate take its course.

But whereas we get this acceptance of one's lot, it is by no means a stoic acceptance. In song number 1, for example, the singer actually states, in the last line, that this lamíselu, the death of her beloved daughter, is "my share, I accept it", but this does not stop her from raising her voice in anguish. In fact, the songs leave no doubt that the people do not hesitate to show emotion. We can be certain that the songs are not the only socially approved outlet for expressing emotion, for if this were the case it is not likely that we would find reference to weeping, "raising my voice (in anguish)", and drinking "my own tears", among others. In addition, skeptics can also argue that onwehani, (going into trance), in the context of a dügü rite, is just another of the ample socially approved avenues available to the individual.

Considering everything that has been said up to this point, especially the most prevalent themes in the songs and the nature of the relationship that obtains between the living and the dead who mediate between the former and the external world, one would perhaps expect to find a sad, morose and frightened people. Yet nowhere in Taylor's ethnography (1951), in Palacio's work, or in any other reference to the Garifuna that I am aware of, has this observation been made. Seen on the ground, they are a happy people, with a culture that is very rich in song, music and dance. Very few outsiders can resist the beautiful rhythms of the native drums or fail to be fascinated by the beauty of the dances. This certainly seems to be inconsistent with the evidence that stare us in the face when we examine the ritual and songs.

In order to reconcile the two, that is, what is suggested by the material and what is actually found on the ground, one has to look more closely. To begin with, all the songs listed here are dance songs for punta and hüngühüngü, two dances that require vigorous movements and are associated with celebration and fun. Because the lyrics nearly all have sad themes, this fact appears to be contradictory to all but the Garifuna mind. How, one might ask for example, can one dance and celebrate to the tune of a song that treats of the death of a love one? One might also ask similar questions about the type of behavior that is found in the beluria (ninth night wake) (Taylor, 1951, pg. 99 – 100).

The beluria consists of prayers said for the soul of a departed relative every night for nine nights, beginning a few days after the death occurred. It is usually scheduled so that the ninth night falls on a weekend because this means that more people will be able to attend. While prayers and hymns may be kept up in one corner of the grounds, the beluria may be seen as a celebration or party given for the dead, for although real drums are not usually allowed, boxes are used instead and the people attending sing and dance. There is usually some story (úraga) telling, games, eating, and drinking. Their own explanation for this apparent contradiction is that "the rite is a sort of farewell party to the spirit-double of the deceased. The greater the gaiety and the number of those who attend, the better for all concerned .... The spirit of the dead person is pleased and satisfied, and therefore more ready to depart and leave the living in peace" (Taylor, 1951, pg. 101).

My own conclusion is that the Garifuna are basically a serious people, as suggested by the songs and ritual. The gaiety and the mirth and what appears to be the carefree attitude that we find on the surface do not go far beyond the superficial level. Nevertheless, the surface manifestation is very important for the individual and the group as a whole because it makes life without the departed relatives more tolerable. It enables one to survive. It serves as a sort of distraction – a distraction which in the end is good for the individual, whether he is the dancer dancing to the drums and the tune of the sad song he composed about his lamíselu, or whether he is the surviving relative whose more distant relatives and friends have brought singing, laughter, dance and story telling to him.

Conclusion

We have seen that as well as indicating certain patterns of personality and behavior as being prevalent among the Garifuna, the belief system, as seen through the window of the ritual, and the songs also suggest explanations. I have tried to incorporate some of these into the preceding section, in some cases trying to make causal connections. However, I freely admit that the material can bear closer and more detailed analysis, which I hope to be able to do at some time in the future.

One fact that I doubt reanalysis will change is that the ritual and the personality patterns that have been identified here have been indispensable elements in Garifuna psychosocial adaptation. The socialization leading to the development of these patterns and the socioculture pressures that ensure their maintenance must have their psychic cost to the individual, but I believe that this is balanced by the benefits that he can derive through participation in the ritual system and by making use of the other means that are available to him for psychological release.

Seen from a historical perspective, one can see why such characteristics as group solidarity, interdependence and the consequent feeling of inadequacy (at the individual level, that is) or lack of self reliance, and even fatalism, had to be emphasized over the centuries. I strongly suspect, although admittedly without adequate supporting evidence, that the beginning must have come from the African side of their ancestry and became developed into their present form, as an adaptive mechanism, to meet the stresses of the chain of traumatic experiences they encountered over the last few centuries. These include, to name only the major ones:

a) The horrors of being uprooted from their African homeland and the passage through the machinery of the slave trade.

b) After they "became" Black Caribs through intermarriage and adoption of Island Carib language and culture, conflict with the Island Caribs who had not become mixed.

c) Prolonged, and in the end unsuccessful, resistance of English encroachment on their Saint Vincent lands.

d) Deportation to Roatan by the English in 1797.

e) Persecution as a result of having supported the Royalists in an unsuccessful attempt to reestablish Spanish rule in Honduras.

f) Suspicion and contempt with which they were regarded by white colonists and Creoles (non-Garifuna blacks) of Belize at the time they settled in that country.

The Garifuna, unlike his Island Carib counterpart, has been able to survive and increase in number, in spite of adverse conditions, precisely because he was able to find his satisfactions in the group. Although the individual is not wholly self reliant, the group, because its organization is predicated on mutual obligation and support, is as a whole independent and capable of surviving severe odds. This does not mean that the Garifuna is wholly resistant to change. Just as he is able to superimpose a happy exterior on to a basically serious disposition, he is able to adopt many foreign values, even a foreign way of life, without completely setting aside the basic structure which, after all, is an essential part of his adaptation and which he needs to be able to fall back on should that be necessary. This, I believe, explains why he can be an active member of his church living in a manner prescribed by Western standards and, especially at critical points in his life, go to the dabúyaba (temple) of his ancestors despite the objections of the church leaders.

References
Taylor, Douglas M. 1951 The Black Carib of British Honduras. New York: Johnson Reprint Corporation

Palacio, Joseph O. 1973 Carib Ancestral Rites: A Brief Analysis. National Studies Vol. 1 No. 3 Published by BISRA in Belize City

Waddell, D. A. G. 1961 British Honduras – A Historical and Contemporary Survey.
Oxford University press

Eggan, Dorothy 1966 Hopi Dreams in Cultural Perspective. In Robert A LeVine (ed.) Culture and Personality Contemporary Readings. Chicago: Aldine Publishing Company

Cayetano, E. Roy and Phyllis Cayetano Unpublished Collection and translation of Black Carib Songs

Black Carib Songs

1) I was just passing the time, having fun with you, Sini,
I was just attending a ninth night with you.
How awful the news that came to me that night,
I have raised my voice (in anguish).
Where will I run from troubles?

Troubles can't kill, Chona;
It would have killed me that night.
If I were a gurásuwe, I would have just flown away.
That is my share, I accept it.
  (Gurásuwe is the name of a certain bird in Carib)

2) How now, husband? On this trip of yours,
    Won't I go with you to Guatemala City?
    No, I ha, stay here waiting for me;
    If I don't return ....you will hear.

    So this is what having troubles is really like!
    So this is what misery is really like!
    No, papa, to whom do you leave Mama?
    You went and died from us in Guatemala.
    Oh, when will you return?

3) It has been played on the radio,
It has been announced on my behalf;
I have drunk my own tears.
"Go, Death", is what you should have told him, little sister,
"I won't go with you" is what you should told him.
I have drunk my own tears
"No, Death", is what you should have told him, little sister,
"I won't go with you", is what you should have told him.
That day was sad.
"No, Death", etc.
So misery is like this!
So death is like this!

I have drunk my own tears.
Go, Death, etc.

4) The mulatto has cried out, weeping;
"My wife has died from me", he says.
"To whom do you leave me?
I have been with you twenty years – I never beat her.
The earth has covered her from me today
And again I didn't sleep.

Dawn has again broken with me today
And again I didn't sleep,
Thinking only of her life with me.
So this is what death's sting is like!
You are not asking me questions;
My sister, pardon me, I'm talking to you;
I didn't know that this is what death hurt is like

5) My father, it seems, is about to complete a year (i.e. since he died)
Without my seeing him.

One can't send with the dead, my dear,
There is a letter here that I would send to my parents.

When will méteñu leave me?
It has tied its hammock on me.
I have grown old, but I still feel it.

6) I've dreamt my mother -
What do you want mother?
Please speak to me.

That mass that you gave me,
I did not accept it.
I would have accepted it
But a lot was lacking,
Much was wrong.

I did not send you to steal so
So you could give to me;
But when you find it(i.e. the money by legitimate means)
Don't be forgetful:
Give me my mass, dear young kinsman,
So I may find salvation.

7) I hear the voice of the Departed One
In my sleep, a-yae
"You will not quarrel, my child,
Close your mouth.
You will not argue, my child,
Close your mouth,

Christmas will again be coming, my kinsfolk,
We are about to celebrate it, a-yae.
We will sell songs as we go, my child,
For money to buy shirts.

8). I am expecting my letter from England
About my deceased.
I had prayed to my God for you
For you, my son,   To keep you from the enemy who are in the sea.

This sleeplessness that is on me,
You will feel it", my mother had told me.
Where is my female ancestor, where is my mother?
So she may take some of this grief from me.

Where were the supernatural powers of my male ancestor?
I would have anointed / equipped you with it, dear kinsman,
Before your departure;
Then I wouldn't be crying now.

9) Behold me, my dear sister,
Look at me, Chris' mother.
How heavy my burden on earth is, older sister;
I had already cleared a path before me older sister,
But to no avail.

God, my father, where are you?
Come to me with your hand;
Come to me with your hand, my God,
So I may rub it on my star,
So I may find luck there.

10) I won't laugh big (laughs) anymore
The world has become sad around me
After my kinsfolk (i.e. after they died).
So this is what it is like to have troubles:
So this is what misery is like!!

I won't laugh big anymore –
The world has saddened around me
After my kinsfolk (departed).

11) My name has been raining, my child,
The thunder has rolled, the world has rumbled
With my name, my child.

She who has no sister is poor,
She who had no mother is poor,
Death is responsible, Death took my male ancestor from me;
(Otherwise), I would not be crying.

12) I am going to tie my hammock on my friend's back;
My friend to be my swinger, to be my relative.
My friend has opened her door to me.

My burden has become heavy, I can't carry it anymore;
But I won't get angry about it.
I am in a television,
I am seeing a relative,
I have seen my friend here to be my relative.

13) What is wrong with you why do you weep?
What has happened to you?
Confess to me, dear male relative.
Let me talk with you.
You are about to die from me.

I have traveled all over the coast, dear male relative,
In search of the "kindness of your skin" (i.e. medicine).
I have caused the stores to go empty;
For your skin (i.e. your ailment), there is no medicine.

14) Sheila, my sister, Sickness is making fun of me.
I have roamed Honduras in search of medicine;
The supplies are exhausted.

My sister, you cry then as usual I will hear that its your pleasure.
Wipe your tears; my sister, save them.
The day for you to cry is coming.

Am I about to die leaving my sister behind?
It is in Livingston that I will be buried,
Among my ancestor's grandchildren
So I may see them before I am buried.

15) What's wrong with me that these people should despise me?
I haven't done wrong, mother of mullato.
What is the matter with that charcoal? (she is barren)
After all, she doesn't always have children like I can.

What tremendous disgrace his is in!"
What's–her–name reportedly said about me.
But what ;s the matter with *Lady Lemu-lemu Dege-dege?
The devil must have put a curse on her.
 *Lemu means to bend and dege is to open one's legs or to step. The
reduplicated from, used here as a proper noun, is an adjective indicating that
the referent walks with her back bent and legs spread wide. In order words,
she is hump-backed and bow-legged.

16) I have been wooed by a man who has been spat upon by women.
"Deo's mother, have an affair with me,
I love you, I will marry you". Is what he told me. "Have an affair
"Have and affair with me, I love you.
Deo's mother, have an affair with me, I love you.
I will marry you", is what he told me.

I am not coming here to have affairs, my brother,
I am coming here to work with the Company for my livelihood.

Marriage doesn't frighten me, my brother,
Ring, my brother? Veil, my sibling?
I've been wearing them since my childhood.

17) Why do you (pl.) fuss about me?
That's my key, it's with me.
If I fall I will get up by myself.

If you hear the words of the duck, friend,
She, unlike me has good luck;
She was married for her virginity.

But you have forgotten something, female:
What about that hat that was found in the house
While your husband was away at Orange Point?

18) Basia, I have again admitted a man,
I have made the world murmur.
I have admitted yet another man,
I have made the murmur:
They have never seen the like.

Basia, isn't pitiful the way they assault their own purity?
They were bitches
How their cleanliness was wasted!
They behave like dogs.
They have forgotten about that!
Basia, it's just that their deeds can't stain –
We all would have been stained by now:
Very few among us would have been left unaffected.

19) Stamp your foot to her, Pound your
     Pound your chest to her!
     You provide well for her.

     Silk, embroidered and decorated with stars
     Is the cover of his meat:
     He provides well for her.
     The foreigner provides well for himself,
     Yes, he provides
     Silk, embroidered and starry
     Is the cover of his meat;
     He/it is ready.
20) A meeting has been held about you, my child,
Your father has gone to a meeting about you.

But never fear, Pulá; God will help you.

Let the world speak (as it will),

I still am; you will lean on me, my child.

Garifuna Music

By Sebastian R. Cayetano

Garifuna music is a rich and creative amalgam of all the cultural traditions to which the Garifuna are heir. In addition to the Amerindian and African elements, early French, Spanish and English folk music contributed to their musical heritage. Other Afro-Caribbean peoples, such as Haitians, Jamaicans and Barbadians, have also contributed to the Garifuna musical stock.

Songs, dances, mime, plays, processions, storytelling, and poetry make up the branches of Garifuna performing arts. Everyone is encouraged to participate and full-time professional "stars" in the American commercial sense, do not exist. Locally, expert drummers, singers, dancers, and composers are well recognized and their fame spreads from village to village. Small children perform publicly with a mastery rare in cultures where musicianship is considered the special gift of a privileged few.

Music accompanies all sorts of activities, and song and dance may spontaneously erupt at any time or place while riding in cars, working in the kitchen, carrying loads from the bush, or cleaning fish. More often, large groups of Garifuna come together at holidays, family social events, and religious occasions, wherever the drums gather them. The audience is usually as active as the dancers.

Garifuna drums are typically made of hardwood, such as mahogany or mayflower. Using fire, water, and gouges, the wood is hollowed out into symmetrical cylinders. Skins prepared of the peccary (a wild bush pig), deer, or sheep are stretched across one end. Two-headed drums are also known. Thin metal wires or strings are strung across the drum head to serve as snares. Drums are always played with hands and mallets are not used. Some drums, especially those used in sacred music, are nearly three feet across and create a great humming sound when struck.

In secular dance music, two drummers are rule,

one the primero and the other designated as segunda. Each drummer play his own part, with the segunda acting mainly as a steady accompaniment to the more expansive and elaborate cross-rhythms of the primero player. Three large drums are used in sacred music. In addition to the drums, Garifuna commonly use rattles. These gourd shakers, known as sisira, are made from the fruit of the gourd tree, filled with special seeds, and fitted with hardwood handles. Other instruments, such as guitars, flutes and violins have also found their way into Garifuna music.

Many hundred songs are known and sung by the Garifuna today. Most songs are accompanied by particular dance forms and drum beats. One class of songs, known an uyanu, is sung without instrumental accompaniment and is gestured instead of danced.

Lyrical themes vary widely, depending on the type of song and whether it is usually composed by men or women. Many themes concern travel, expressing a desire to leave, or the loneliness of being far from loved ones. Other songs are written to commemorate an event, comment on someone's foolish behavior, or poke fun at some situation.

New songs are constantly emerging, often coming to the composer in dreams or visions. The Garifuna repertoire includes work songs for men and women, lullabies, hymns, healing songs, ballads, and many types of dancing songs.

1. **Punta** - The most popular dance, performed at wakes, holidays, parties, and other social events. Dancing as couples, men and women try to out-do one another with sexy movement and style. Everyone takes a turn and the competitive spirit is high. Punta lyrics are usually written by women.

2. **Hunguhungu** - A circle dance which appears to be a secular versionof the sacred dancing of the dugu, the Garifuna feast for the Ancestors. Drums play a simple three-beat rhythm and everyone sings in unison.

3. **Combination** - An exciting alternation of punta and hunguhungu rhythms.

4. **Wanaragua** - Also known as John Canoe, this masked dance was once performed throughout the Caribbean at Christmas time, one of the few events during the year when slaves were free to dance and party for an extended period of time. Dressed with fanciful head-dresses, knee rattles, and in whiteface, John Canoe dancers would visit the houses of their masters and receive food and drink in return for riotous entertainment In Belize and other areas of the Garifuna domain, parties of John Canoe dancers roam from houseyard to houseyard, scaring children and collecting payments during the Christmas season.

This custom has died out in the rest of the Caribbean. Wanaragua masks were once made of basketry but are now cleverly constructed of metal screen and painted with a stylized face, either male or female. Some costumes include a skirt, completing the female disguise. Wanaragua songs are composed and led by men and danced in a thoroughly African style.

5. **Abaimajani**- This semi-sacred women's song is sung without instrumental accompaniment. Standing in lines, linked by their little fingers, women gesture rhythmically to a musical form of irregular meter. This song type is clearly derived from the Carib Indian heritage of the Garifuna and is closely related to many Amerindian, and ultimately, Siberian song styles.

6. **Matamuerte**- This mime dance depicts a group of people finding a body along the beach and poking it to see if the person is alive, perhaps with too much enthusiasm.

7. **Laremuna Wadauman** -- Men's work songs, usually sung when men work cooperatively at a strenuous task, as for example, chopping down large trees and hauling the logs down-river and out onto the beach in order to make sailing dories, or canoes.

8.**Gunchei** - A graceful dignified social dance, in which each man dances with each woman in turn.

9. **Charikawi**- In this mimed dance, a hunter meets up with a cave man and a cow

10. **Sambai** - After a short salute from the drum, each dancer jumps into the circle to display some fancy footwork.

11. **Eremwu Eu**- Sung and composed by women for accompanying the tedius work of grating the manioc root to make cassava bread.

12. **C h u m b a** - a highly accented polyrhythmic song, danced by soloists with great individualized style. This dance is probably related to the chumba found in other parts of the Caribbean where, as in Grenada and Carriacou, some people claim to be descended from the Chumba, a people of eastern Nigeria. This performance includes a wide range of Garifuna music, some of which is rapidly disappearing in many communities.

A Survey of Garifuna Musical Genres with an Emphasis on Paranda

Liam McGranahan
Masters Paper
Brown University,
Department of Music
May 2005

Walking to the Garinagu[1] temple in Punta Gorda, Belize for the first time I had no idea what to expect except that I knew that Paul Nabor, a parandero whose music I had heard on a recently released CD, lived there. When I arrived I was greeted by Mr. Nabor himself. In mid-June heat and humidity he was cutting the grass in the front of the temple with a machete. I was straining and sweating in the heat just from walking and the idea of any physical activity, nonetheless one so taxing as Mr. Nabor's, was almost unthinkable. I was 21 years old. Paul Nabor was 75.

Paul Nabor, known endearingly as "Nabi," is a legend in his own time. He is a paranda musician as well as a buyei (a Garifuna religious leader) and his songs are known throughout Belize. Though Mr. Nabor himself will tell you that he feels the effects of aging he still retains his physical and mental strength as is more than evident in his heartfelt performances. I have had the pleasure of seeing Paul Nabor play on several occasions, at times alongside leading Garifuna punta rock musicians, and without fail it is always he who receives the most enthusiastic ovation. When the first notes of his beloved song "Naguya Nei" are strummed a cheer shoots through the audience and his voice is almost inaudible over the collective audience singing along.

What follows is an account of Garifuna music broken into three sections. The first section consists of a description of the Garinagu journey from their origin on St. Vincent to the present day. This section is based on a review of the major ethnographic works on the Garinagu.

The second section is a description of Garifuna musical genres as well as a review of all currently available literature on Garifuna music. Though the information in this section is predominately drawn from other sources, there exists nowhere else in the literature a comprehensive list and description of all Garifuna musical styles. In this section I have taken what are often vague and sometimes contradictory pieces of data from many sources and synthesized them into as coherent a form as possible.

---

[1] Garinagu is the plural form of Garifuna and refers specifically to the people. Garifuna is the term for one Garinagu as well as the name of the language. Additionally Garifuna is used as an adjective as in Garifuna art or Garifuna music.

The final section is a detailed description of one genre of music: paranda. The existing literature on paranda is generally lacking and many questions of primary importance (origin, name, structure, rhythm, etc.) have gone unanswered for too long. I have answered these questions and in so doing have provided the most complete description of paranda to date. The section begins with a survey of what has previously been written on paranda and ends with my observations and clarifications based on my own fieldwork and interviews. I have made three trips to Belize. The first in June, 2002, the second in June 2004, and the most recent in March 2005. I have spent the majority of my time in Punta Gorda and Dangriga the two largest towns with a sizeable Garinagu population. The interviews cited in this paper are with paranderos Junior Aranda in Dangriga from 2004, and parandero Paul Nabor in Punta Gorda from 2005.

Through looking at their music and history it will become clear that the Garinagu are simultaneously a unique group with their own history and a model of creolization that is reflective of the entire Western hemisphere. Their uniqueness comes from the fusion of African and Amerindian that makes up this people. In many places in the Western hemisphere Africans and indigenous peoples came into contact through European slavery and colonization, but it is much less common that these two groups intermarried and created a new people. This intermarriage brings us to creolization, the creation of a new people from the meeting and mixing of two or more distinct peoples. Creolization is a process that has occurred throughout the Americas predating the arrival of Europeans. If there is one thing that all the Americas share in common it is that all Americans, to some extent, are the product of creolization. The Garinagu represent creolization at its apex. Looking at their musical styles we will see that there is a total synthesis of the Amerindian and African traditions. But the synthesis does not stop there. Garifuna music has incorporated aspects of European, North American, Latin American, and other Caribbean musics, and continues to evolve and synthesize constantly. The cultural processes that are at work in creating the music of the Garifuna are central to an understanding of "American" life (North, Central, and South).

Socio-history

The origin of the Garinagu is complicated and contested. It will be helpful to start this discussion with the popularly accepted origin story. There are slight variations but the story generally follows along the lines of this example from Dan Rosenberg's liner notes to *Paranda: Africa in Central America*,

> Centuries ago a slave ship crashed near the Caribbean Island
> of St. Vincent. These African men and women, and some

escaped slaves from nearby islands (and even some Pre-Colombian Africans living in the Caribbean) lived in St. Vincent for some generations. They mixed with native Carib and Arawak Indians... In March 1797, after a war over land (to make room for more tobacco and sugar cane plantations), the British exiled the entire Garifuna population from St. Vincent to Honduras... Since then, the Garifuna spread along the coast of Central America (1999).

The explanation presented above seems convincing and straightforward. However, various scholars have called into question nearly every aspect of this story.

To come to a better understanding of the origin of the Garinagu it is important to start with an overview of the first peoples of the Caribbean. Until fairly recently the standard view was that several different Amerindian groups had migrated to the Caribbean region at different times. Charles Osgood writes, "From the linguistic and historical point of view, three major groups, the Carib, the Arawak, and the Ciboney, appear to have occupied the Antilles in the pre-Columbian times" (1942, 2). Osgood also makes the case that the three groups migrated to the Greater and Lesser Antilles from the South American mainland (most likely the area around Venezuela) (1942, 1). Though there was not yet clear evidence of a timeline Osgood suggested that the Arawak arrived on the islands first and spread out the farthest. Following the Arawaks were the Caribs who displaced the Arawaks on the Lesser Antilles through force. This Carib migration was thought to have occurred relatively shortly before the arrival of Europeans (1942, 2). The Ciboney, according to Osgood's survey of existing work, were the most geographically restricted Amerindian group. The Ciboney were only found in significant numbers on Cuba and clearly distinct from both the Carib and the Arawak (1942, 3).

Over the 50 years since Osgood's writing a considerable amount of archaeological work has been done in the region and has challenged some of the earlier beliefs. In the anthology *The Indigenous People of the Caribbean* editor Samuel Wilson writes,

> Noticing the differences between the people of the Greater and Lesser Antilles, the Europeans joined these observations with half understood stories the Taino told them about other islanders. What emerged was a view of the Caribbean as having two kinds of people – Caribs and Tainos (Arawaks). What now seems more likely is that in 1492 the Caribbean contained many different ethnic groups, spread out through the Lesser Antilles, Greater Antilles, and Bahamas. Nearly

all of these people were speakers of Arawakan languages, probably mutually unintelligible, and nearly all of them were descendants of the Saladoid immigrants (1997, 7).

The fundamental difference is that were Osgood and his contemporaries saw three distinct groups of people, current scholars conceptualize one group with descendants organized into various different ethnic groups. This does not negate the idea that there were different groups of Amerindians, but rather than biologically distinct peoples from different places, the new theories conceive of them all originating from the same area.

Additionally a new timeline has been suggested. Scholars like Samuel Wilson now believe that the Caribbean islands have been inhabited for nearly 6,000 years (Wilson, 1997, 2). The migration is thought to have happened in three waves. The first wave took place sometime between 4,000-3,500 B.C.E. from either the northeast coast of South America or the Yucatan region of Central America to Cuba, and Hispaniola. This group appears to have been hunter-gatherers without agriculture. The second wave took place sometime before 2000 B.C.E. and consisted of a migration out of northeast South America to the Lesser Antilles and Puerto Rico. These people were also not agrarian. The final migration took place between 500-250 B.C.E. from the Orinoco valley around what is now Venezuela and into the Lesser Antilles and Puerto Rico. This final group of people, named the Saladoid people after an archaeological site in Venezuela, is thought to be the ancestors of what have come to be known as the Taino/Arawaks and the Caribs (Wilson, 1997, 5). These "Saladoid" peoples then spread from the Lesser Antilles to all of Puerto Rico, Cuba, Jamaica, and Hispaniola between 500-1000 A.C.E. As for the previous inhabitants of the Greater Antilles, "The hunting and gathering people who already lived in many of these areas were apparently incorporated into the newly emerging society, for there are some similarities in style between artifacts of the hunter-gatherers and those of the new migrants" (Wilson, 1997, 6).

There is still much that is unclear. For instance Wilson uses the term Taino to refer to the Amerindian group that inhabited the Greater Antilles at the time of European arrival. However, throughout the anthology that he edited, the terms Taino and Arawak appear to be interchangeable[2]. Arawak also refers to a language group that appears to have been spoken in some form by all the Amerindians on the Caribbean islands. While advances have been made and the picture of the pre-1492 Caribbean is becoming clearer there is still no real

---

[2] In the literature on the Garinagu I have never seen the term Taino used in this way and so for the purposes of this paper I will use the term Arawak.

consensus as to who settled where and when and how to define one group as distinct from another.

So what of St. Vincent? Garinagu scholars Myrtle Palacio and Sebastian and Fabian Cayetano assert that Arawaks initially inhabited the island and that Caribs arrived sometime around 1200 A.C.E. (Palacio, 1993, Cayetano, 1997). This view is shared by many Western scholars (Conzemius 1928, Taylor 1951, Kerns 1983, Gonzalez 1988). However this assumption is based on very minimal archaeological evidence. Carl Roessingh writes, "The Island Caribs had no written language. Furthermore, there are no remains of buildings that have stood the test of time... This led to an important role for the analysis of material recorded by missionaries" (2001, 61). Roessingh continues, "The descriptions of the Europeans were so ethnocentrically tinted that it could even be suggested that the first European 'artists' may have created the Island Caribs themselves" (2001, 61). In fact Christopher Columbus believed that the Caribs were the servants of Khan the Emperor of China, thus proving (he hoped) that he was on the Asian continent (Porter, 1984, 61).

C.J.M.R. Gullick had arrived at a similar conclusion to Roessingh's in 1985. Based on the lack of evidence in the archaeological record and the ambiguity of the minimal findings Gullick wrote, "It is still debatable whether various finds can be attributed to the Caribs or Arawaks and it is even debatable whether (i) the Caribs replaced the Arawaks in one fell swoop, (ii) lived together with them, or (iii) are themselves really Arawaks" (1985, 25-26).

Despite the problematic grounds for the argument, it has been taken for granted by most that the Arawaks arrived on the island first and were followed by the Caribs. The relationship between the Arawaks and Caribs on St. Vincent is another subject of controversy. Myrtle Palacio, Cayetano and Cayetano, and Edward Conzemius argue that the Carib arrival on the island constituted an invasion and that the Carib proceeded to kill off the Arawaks. Writing in 1928 Conzemius characterized the Carib and Arawak as oppositional groups, "The Carib were very warlike, more or less nomadic, and had little agriculture... The Arawak were peaceable and depended chiefly upon the products of the soil" (186). The outcome of their meeting would not turn out well for the Arawak, "These islands [the Lesser Antilles] were invaded by the Carib from South America, who in the course of a long and primitive warfare conquered these peaceable original inhabitants, killed off the men and appropriated their women... The new people, sprung from a mixture of Carib men with Arawak women, became known as 'Island Caribs'" (Conzemius, 1928, 186).

Some scholars see the Garifuna language as the outcome of Caribs killing off Arawak men and taking Arawak women. Cayetano and Cayetano write, "The Arawak males were killed, but the Arawak women were carried away to become wives of the Caribs. In due course the Carib-Arawak offspring evolved a spoken language with two versions: the female Arawak version, and the male Carib version, each distinct yet mutually understandable by both" (1997, 10). Pillich makes a similar argument saying of the Carib and Arawak relationship, "Vestiges of that history are alive today in the form of the modern Garifuna language... This can clearly be seen in the dialects based on gender differences" (2000, 31).

However, the issue of language is not so simple. While some see the Garifuna language as the result of a particular mixture between Carib men and Arawak women, other scholars are not quite so sure. Taylor writes, "Much attention has been paid to the fact that the speech of the Island Carib men differed from that of their women; but little notice has been taken of... [the] virtual lack of grammatical differentiation between the two" (1951, 44). Taylor continues to point out that the form of Garifuna currently spoken is "common to both sexes"(1951, 45). It is also interesting to note that Conzemius, a proponent of the theory that Caribs killed off Arawak men and took Arawak women for their own, makes no mention of any gender differences in the language (1928, 185).

Many of the hypotheses above take for granted that the Carib were warlike conquerors. However, drawing on accounts from European missionaries and explorers, Douglas Taylor disputes the characterization of Caribs as warlike writing, "Independent reports certainly do not vindicate such assertions of Carib cruelty and ferocity. In 1596 Sir Anthony Sherley, some of whose crew were sick, landed on Dominica, where he met with 'kind Indians' who showed him hot springs to bathe, and helped to cure the diseased sailors" (1951, 16). Taylor asserts that the notion that the Caribs were cruel and warlike stemmed from the Spanish attempts to portray any indigenous peoples who put up resistance as savage and fierce, "Breton, who was certainly one of the first white men to know the Island Carib intimately, speaks with unveiled sarcasm of the Spaniards' accusations against them... All our French sources agree in characterizing them as: reticent, taciturn, melancholic, fanciful, and fearful... but none who knew them well accuses them of cruelty" (1951, 17).

Did the Caribs kill off the Arawaks? Where the Caribs and the Arawaks on St. Vincent actually one and the same? No answers present themselves and the hypotheses in the literature are based on shaky archaeological evidence and extremely biased first hand reporting from European colonizers and missionaries.

Leaving the Amerindian question unresolved, the next aspect of the popular origin story is the arrival of Africans on St. Vincent. Three methods of immigration have been suggested: the existence of Africans in the Caribbean pre-dating Columbus, runaways from neighboring islands seeking refuge, and the crash of a slave ship (often said to be Spanish).

The shipwreck, runaway slave, and captured slave theories have all been given a good amount of attention in the literature, but there is one hypothesis that has been for the most part ignored. The notion that there were already Africans in the Caribbean prior to Columbus remains controversial. It is interesting to note that the pre-Columbus contact between Africans and Caribs is mentioned in the liner notes to *Paranda: Africa in Central America*, which was produced in Belize. This makes sense in the context of Roessingh's comments that,

> Every Garinagu that I spoke to in Dangriga characterizes this model [the shipwreck theory] as a typical expression of Western science. In their view, there had been contact between the people from Africa and those from the Caribbean region since before Columbus. After all, both North and South Equatorial ocean currents pass by the West Coast of Africa and from there they head for the Caribbean region (2001, 58).

> There are several other hypotheses about the arrival of Africans on St. Vincent. It has been suggested by most scholars that runaway slaves from neighboring islands made their way to St. Vincent. Palacio writes of a "constant flow of runaway slaves from the nearby islands of Barbados, Martinique and Guadalupe" (1993, 3-4). Because St. Vincent is windward to these islands it would not have been a difficult trip. However, it is unclear if these immigrant refugees from the neighboring island were in fact refugees at all. Gonzalez writes, "Dominican Caribs frequently raided European settlements between 1558 and 1580, taking both whites and blacks as slaves... Du Tertre reported a complaint by Martiniquan planters that more than 500 of their slaves had been kidnapped by Caribs from nearby islands" (1988, 26).

The notion that Africans arrived on St. Vincent via the crash of a slave ship is the most frequently encountered. It is generally agreed upon that this crash occurred in 1635 (Cayetano and Cayetano1997, Gonzalez 1988, Gullick 1985, Kerns 1983, Palacio1993, Taylor 1951) although Conzemius believes that it occurred in 1675 (1928, 187). The story involves two Spanish ships that crash somewhere to the south of St. Vincent and for a long time was thought to be the first contact between the Island Caribs and Africans. In 1928 Conzemius writes, "In 1675 a ship with a load of Negro slaves destined for Barbados was wrecked in front of the small island of Bequia near St. Vincent," he continues that the Africans on this boat made their way to St.

Vincent, "where they formed a colony apart from the Indians with whom they intermarried" (187-88).

Over the past century this story has been told in several different variations with slightly different dates for the wreckage, different nationalities of the ships, and different locations for the crash. Despite the loose evidence that the claims for the shipwreck are based upon, this had been the most important, if not singular arrival theory for Africans on St. Vincent until quite recently. Writing in 1985, Gullick casts serious doubts on the date and nationality of the ships,

> If they were Spanish, they must have been transferring slaves from one Spanish Colony to another, as the Portuguese transported the Spaniards slaves across the Atlantic. Since St. Vincent was not near any Spanish trade route, this origin sounds unlikely, as does any slave boat being in the immediate area before 1640 when sugar and plantations were introduced (44-45).

The most recent ethnography of the Garinagu calls the whole incident into question, "Hardly any details on the incident are available. Things like how the slaves got off the ships are not clear. Where did they come from and how many were on board? There are too many questions to assume that the accident with the two ships is the primary cause of African influences on St. Vincent" (Roessingh, 2001, 64).

It is unclear exactly how, when or from where Africans arrived on St. Vincent. The fact remains that they did arrive and this raises the question of the nature of the relationship between the Africans and the Amerindians. Much like the record of Arawak/Carib relations there is little evidence and many conflicting ideas. All scholars agree that there was intermarriage (hence the Garinagu) but there is no consensus as to the nature of this marriage and each scholar seems to have their own version. Kerns writes, "The nature of the original meeting... is disputed. According to certain records... the Caribs welcomed the Africans; according to other sources, the Indians immediately enslaved them" (1983, 17). Because nothing close to a consensus has been reached (and barring the unearthing of new archaeological evidence it is unlikely that any such consensus will be reached) only the most obvious conclusions can be made. Africans and Amerindians did intermarry on St. Vincent, and either due to this intermarriage, or war, or disease, or some other factor, both the populations of "pure blood " Africans, and "pure blood" Amerindians shrank to the point of near, if not total, extinction.

Garinagu history after the arrival of Europeans is much more clear although heavily biased, as the reporting comes from the Europeans themselves. After Columbus happened upon the Caribbean in 1492 repeated attempts were made by both the French and the British to colonize the island. Though at several different points the island fell under European control the Afro-Amerindian population of the island put up constant resistance rebuking the European attempts several times. It was not until 1796 roughly 300 years after contact that the British were able to decisively take control of St. Vincent. Quickly thereafter the British began deporting the islands residents. Palacio writes, "Between July 21, 1796 to February 2, 1797 some 4,195 were first sent to the small island of Baliseau to prepare for the exile [to Roatan]... On March 3, 1797 only 2,248... were left to make the journey... On April 12, 1797, some 664 men, 720 women, 642 children totaling 2,026 arrived in Roatan" (1993, 4-5).

The history since deportation is not just a history of survival but of flourishing. The Garinagu now live in Belize, Guatemala, Honduras, Nicaragua, and the United States. Garinagu language, religion, music, and other cultural elements are still continuing and thriving today, and a people that arrived in Latin America totaling 2,026 a little over three hundred years ago now number 300,000[3]. Though equally as fascinating as their early history, the post-deportation history is not as central to this paper and will not be addressed herein.

Garinagu history involved constant movement, cultural contact, and creolization. Moreover, the Garinagu exist as the product of the intermarriage of two very distinct groups, Africans, and Amerindians. Not only do the Garinagu present a clear picture of a creole people, they would not exist were it not for the process of creolization.

Literature and Genre Review

Observations about Garifuna music are found in the very earliest writings about the Garinagu. In 1658 Cesar de Rochafort writes of the people of St. Vincent, "They are great lovers of Musick, and much pleas'd with such instruments as make a certain delightful noise, and a kind of harmony, which they accompany with their voices" (quoted in Hadel, 1972, 94). Unfortunately these observations, like the example above, are generally brief and provide little or no information beyond broad descriptions. It was not until the 1950s that serious attention was given to the music by outside scholars. In 1951 Douglas Taylor's ethnography of the Garinagu makes note of the importance of music to their cultural practices but omits any discussion of music except to urge that further research be conducted on the subject. Taylor writes, "The ritual songs and some of the work songs of the Black Carib have a great deal of charm, and it is to be hoped that a fair number of them may be recorded before it is too late" (1951, 7). Perhaps in

---

[3] This is the most recent population estimate by the Gulisi Garifuna Museum in Dangriga, Belize.

response to Taylor's plea Doris Stone and Folkways Records released the first record of Garifuna music in 1953. It is not until 1971, however, that the first substantial writing on Garifuna music is published in the form of an M.A. thesis by Emory Whipple for the University of Texas Austin. The next work, a dissertation, is published a year later in 1972 by Richard Hadel also at University of Texas Austin. Since Whipple and Hadel's works in the early 1970s there has been a small but steady amount of work published mainly in the form of MA theses and articles. The works published since Hadel and Whipple's have been much more specialized and focused on specific aspects of Garifuna music and as of yet no one other than Hadel and Whipple has attempted a comprehensive description of Garifuna musical activities. It is also important to note that until Marc Perry's 1999 thesis on second-generation Garinagu in the United States, and Gualberto Pillich's 2000 thesis on Garinagu immigrants from Honduras living in Los Angeles, all the literature was based on fieldwork done in Belize. There has yet to be anything written about Garifuna music based on fieldwork conducted in Guatemala, Nicaragua, or Honduras, with the exception of Doris Stone's recording and brief liner notes.

In what follows I will address all of the literature currently available through a discussion of the many genres of Garifuna music. Before launching into a descriptive account of the genres I would like to organize them into some broad categories. Emory Whipple divides Garifuna music into three categories of song: 1) song for dance, 2) guitar song, and 3) abeimahani (religious) song (1971, 39). These three categories are then subdivided. Song for dance is divided by rhythm, guitar song is divided in two by gender, and religious song is divided by function (use in wakes, rites for the dead, or for the sick) (39). Whipple focused on song because "Carib music always involves singing. Vocal melody may be accompanied by drums and rattles, or by guitars or it may be unaccompanied. But as far as can be observed, there does not exist today any type of Carib traditional music which is totally instrumental" (38). He further justifies his song-based categorization by stating that the "[Garinagu] themselves classify their different styles according to the type of song that is used" (39). Whipple's contention is backed up by Carol and Travis Jenkins who in their cantometric analysis of Garifuna music conclude, "Song (oremu) dominates the Garifuna musical domain" (1982, 18).

Though song style is clearly a large factor in the delineation of musical style for the Garinagu it is difficult to ascribe song style primary importance because most distinct song styles have accompanying rhythms and dance styles that share the same name. Whipple's assertion is further complicated by Hadel's suggestion that there are solely instrumental forms of dance music. Hadel wrote, "Contrary to Whipple's contention... there are several different occasions when Caribs dance to instrumental music alone" (1972,

114). Hadel points to a children's dance that is accompanied solely by fife and drum (115). Hadel's claim is also somewhat problematic however, as nowhere else in the literature is the fife mentioned as an instrument used by the Garinagu. In fact with the exception of the occasional use of conch shells in punta (Greene, 2002, 194) there is no other mention of aerophones in Garifuna music before the inception of punta rock in the early 1980s (Perry 1999, Greene 2002).

Hadel's claim that there were solely instrumental genres led him to categorize Garifuna music differently than Whipple. Hadel categorized the music into either dance music or non-dance music (1972, 95). These categories are then subdivided. Dance music is divided by music accompanied by song and music unaccompanied by song. Non-dance music is divided by music accompanied instrumentally and music without instrumental accompaniment (95).

For the purposes of this paper I propose a new categorization system. I will divide Garifuna music into two categories: 1) secular music (including processional and/or Christmas music), and 2) sacred music. By focusing on the context of the music rather than the style of the music the categorization is much simpler and allows for musical change and invention. The descriptions below are in alphabetical order for ease of organization.

Secular	Secular [4]	Sacred
Ahuruhani (Eremuna Egi)	Afeduani	Abeimahani (Uyanu)
Gunjei	Charikanari	Abelagudahani
Guitar song (Berusu)	Chumba	Amalihani
Hunguhungu	Corropatia	Arumahani (Uyanu)
Laremuna Wadaguman	Pia Manadi	Awangulahani
Mata Muerte	Sambai	Chururuti
Occasional Song	Wanaragua	Hugulendu
Paranda	Warini	
Punta		
Punta rock		

---

[4] These genres are processional and/or Christmastime music. For the purposes of this paper they are included with secular music. Although the Christmas music is arguably sacred it is not related to the genres used in Garifuna religious practice.

Secular Music

The Garinagu play music for a wide variety of secular occasions ranging from social dances to works songs. Though serving many different functions the majority of secular genres have the same instrumentation. The typical secular music ensemble requires two types of drums: a primero and a segunda (the Garifuna term for drum is garawoun but there seems to be only one term for both types of drum and most people use the terms primero and segunda). Both drums are constructed in the same manner the difference being the size. The primero is a smaller drum that takes the lead role improvising over the patterns of the larger segunda. Hadel (1972) and Foley (1984) have suggested that the primero player is following the lead of the dancers in their improvisation. The rhythmic patterns of the segunda are set and indicative of the particular genre being played. There is some question over whether the segunda patterns for one genre differ from community to community. Pillich suggested that the basic punta and paranda rhythms vary from one country to another (2000, 82). Whipple takes the opposite stance on segunda patterns. He writes, "[they] are identical in every Carib community" (1971, 77). Though I am skeptical of both of these claims (Whipple conducted his fieldwork exclusively in Belize, and Pillich conducted his in Los Angeles, never venturing to Belize or Honduras) I lean more towards Whipple's interpretation. While there is certainly the possibility that there is some difference in segunda rhythms it has not been demonstrated convincingly anywhere in the literature nor in any of the recordings that I have encountered.

> The improvisations of the primero are at times in a different meter than the segunda but only for quick periods leading Whipple to classify the typical secular drumming style as "simple polyrhythm" (1971, 41). Whipple writes, "Carib drumming is characterized by rhythmic conflict, but this conflict is seldom maintained for any length of time... this conflict seldom lasts for more than a few measures, until the solo drummer returns to mesh with the basic rhythm of the accompanying drums. Instead of multiple meter, Carib drumming seems to be characterized by internal 'cross rhythm'"(41).

While most secular music genres only require the primero and segunda drums, there are many other instruments used in secular music. Frequently rattles are added, as are conch shells, and more recently turtle shells. The shells, played on their underside, are struck with drumsticks and the different sections of the shell produce slightly different pitches. The turtle shell player will usually have two or three turtle shells strung on a line hanging from their neck. Though I have found no exact date, I believe that Pen Cayetano first used the turtle shells in the early 1980s in his groundbreaking group The Turtle Shell Band. In addition to the turtle shells, in recent Garifuna recordings the range of instrumentation has greatly expanded to include the whole gamut of instruments used in popular music from the United States and the Caribbean. In one recent recording of paranda (Martinez, 2004) several traditional instruments from the Caribbean region were also used (like the cuatro and the guitarron). In fact, on a recent trip to Belize, I witnessed two different groups using <u>claves</u> and playing the son clave pattern over the paranda rhythm (one of the groups was a traditional ensemble and the other was Aurelio Martinez's punta rock group). I spoke to one of the clave players who confirmed that she was playing the son clave and that it was borrowed from Cuban music. Unfortunately no one that I spoke with had any ideas as to when the clave was added. It also appears, though unconfirmed, that the claves play different patterns over different genres of music.

The gender participation in the dancing and singing varies by genre. However, it seems to be the case in that women do not customarily play the drums. In my own observations I have seen women playing either the claves or the shakers and singing. However, Whipple leaves open the possibility that women may play the guitar (1971, 51) and this was confirmed to me in an interview with Paul Nabor.

The following is a descriptive list of the many styles of Garifuna secular music.

Ahuruhani (eremuna egi)

Doris Stone was the first to note the ahuruhani (also referred to as eremuna egi) in her 1953 recording. She simply defines the genre as work song. In the case of the recording the song accompanied the building of a house. Hadel was the next to address what he calls eremuna egi, and notes that it is specifically women's work songs (1972, 122). Hadel further suggests that the songs are sung only when women are grating cassava (a very labor intensive step in making cassava bread, a staple of the Garinagu) and refers to the genre as "grating songs" (122). Jenkins and Jenkins back up Hadel's assertion and also label eremuna egi as grating songs sung by women (1982a, 3). It is unclear from the literature if eremuna egi are limited to only grating cassava. It is a possibility that ahuruhani and eremuna egi are two different genres, but again, this is unclear.

The Jenkins' attribute eremuna egi to the Amerindian influence in Garifuna music, "In typical Amerindian style, grating songs use frequent exclamatory vocables and repetition. Vocal tone is highly nasal" (3). This genre is an exception to the typical two-drum accompaniment as it is sung without instrumentation but to the rhythm of the work

Guitar Song (Berusu)

See Paranda.

Gunjei

Emory Whipple was the first to take note of the gunjei, though he calls it the tumba (1971, 46). As described by Whipple the gunjei is a simple song style, short (four or eight measures) in duration that is repeated with little variation (46). The rhythm of the gunjei is duple meter and "is basically running sixteenth notes" (45). Whipple asserts that the gunjei is "the only Carib rhythm that does not use some form of triple time (at the simple or compound level)" (83). This last claim is not addressed by anyone else in the literature. While there seems to be a consensus on the music there is some discrepancy regarding the accompanying dance. Whipple describes a solo exhibition dance (46); Hadel on the other hand writes that the dance "is similar to the wanaragua but performed by a man and woman together" (1972, 114). Jenkins and Jenkins agree with Hadel, "The gunjai is a partner dance staged in a circle in which partners switch at the call of 'Sarse'" (1982a, 4). This description fits well with Cayetano and Cayetano's assertion that the gunjei is "a graceful dignified social dance in which each man dances with each woman in turn" (1997, 129). Pillich claims that the dance is a solo dance, except in Honduras where "it is a couples dance in which the couples dress formally" (2000, 41). Additionally Pillich claims that the gunjei is "a rite of passage for young Garifuna women" (41). No further explanation is given, nor is any background provided as to why he makes this claim.

Hunguhungu

The hunguhungu is in triple time with the segunda playing on every beat and accenting the one. The singing style, according to Whipple, is usually call and response though the melody of the songs can vary substantially (1971, 44). Lyrically Whipple suggests that the hunguhungu often addresses some type of repetitive action like "rocking a hammock, or grating cassava" (45). Hadel disagrees with Whipple's contention that the hunguhungu is generally call and response. In fact Hadel believes that there is no call and response in hunguhungu, "The other singers must listen to the leader to catch the first word or two of the line so that they may know what to sing, but they do not wait until the leader has completed a particular part before responding" (1972, 105). Hadel asserts that rather than call and response hunguhungu is sung in unison (105). Hadel also adds some new information claming that the songs of the hunguhunu are composed entirely by women and that there is no specific occasion that calls for a hunguhungu (103). However, Jenkins and Jenkins suggest that the hunguhungu is a "favorite type of song for processionals, especially on such occasions as Carib Settlement Day

(November 19)" (1982a, 2). Hadel writes that the hunguhungu is "a secularized version of the sacred dancing that takes place at the dugu" (103). More information is given on this subject by Jenkins and Jenkins who assert that the hunguhungu dance step and rhythm are secularized versions of the hugulendu (1982a, 2). Pillich has a slightly different take; he claimed that the hunguhungu and the hugulendu are in fact the same thing but in different contexts (2000, 88). This claim is very suspect as there is a definite distinction made by the Garinagu between sacred and non-sacred music. In fact as Oliver Greene points out, "The playing of ritual drums (including the rhythmic motives that accompany dugu songs) is forbidden in non-ritual context" (1998, 174).

Laremuna Wadaguman

This genre is first addressed relatively late in the literature. It is not until Kenan Foley's 1984 MA thesis that laremuna wadaguman is mentioned. Foley writes this about the genre, "These are men's work songs, usually sung while men work cooperatively at arduous tasks, such as chopping down large trees for the making of canoes or when they are fishing" (23). The only other mention of laremuna wadaguman is by Cayetano and Cayetano who give nearly the exact same description as Foley's (1997, 1299). I have not come across any recoded example of these songs. The scarcity of information could be related to changing work patterns for Garinagu men. At least in the Garifuna communities of Belize that I have visited, most men are engaged in some type of wage labor and fishing appears to be more an individual activity.

Mata Muerte

Only Cayetano and Cayetano who described only the dance address Mata muerte. They write, "This mime dance depicts a group of people finding a body along the beach and poking it to see if the person is alive, perhaps with too much enthusiasm" (1997, 129). On one occasion I saw this dance being performed for tourists in Dangriga, Belize. Cayetano and Cayetano left out the more humorous aspect of this dance which is that upon realizing that the body is dead the dancer comically mimics being overwhelmed by the smell. It is unclear whether or not the mata muerte is its own genre or just a dance style. Cayetano and Cayetano list it as a musical genre but when I saw the mata muerte performed it was danced to a punta, which leads me to believe that it is not its own musical genre, but rather a dance style.

Occasional song

Only Hadel discusses occasional song. He writes, "This is something of a non-descript class of songs. Either men or women may compose them and they have no generic name in Carib. The compositions are not intended for performance on any special occasion... but just occasionally, as the composer desires" (1972, 123). Hadel continues claiming that occasional songs were generally memorializing someone or some event, and that it is not important how often they are performed or to whom, but just that they are composed at all (123).

Paranda

Known variously as paranda, parranda, guitar song, and berusu, this genre is distinct in its guitar accompaniment. There has been a back and forth in the literature on what to call this genre with some scholars asserting that guitar music comprises more than one genre. Paranda has been discussed since Doris Stone's recordings in 1953 but there has been no consensus reached in the literature as to the music's origin, form, instrumentation, context, function, rhythm, or accompanying dance style. In the third section of this paper I will clarify much of this confusion.

Punta

Punta is the most popular of the secular musics (or was until the advent of punta rock) among the Garinagu (Whipple, 1971, Hadel 1972, Cayetano and Cayetano, 1997). Consequently the punta is also one of the most well documented secular genres. The dance that accompanies punta is a representation of courtship and was described first by Douglas Taylor in 1951, "The Punta dance... is danced by a man and a woman who evolve separately in a circle formed by the spectators... The step is a sort of minute and rapid shuffle...The figure varies with the ingenuity of the dancers but always represents the evolution of a courtship in which first the man pursues, and then the woman, while the other retreats" (100). This description is generally accepted in the literature although Jenkins and Jenkins suggest that the dance is based on the courtship of a rooster and hen. They also suggest that the dance can be performed by two women who will "exhibit their skills at mock combat" (1982a, 4). Alternately Pillich suggests, "As early as 1797 the original name of the punta was *landanu*. Because the dance was danced primarily on the balls of the feet and toes, the Spanish referred to this dance as being executed on the 'punta' (tips) of the toes" (2000, 44). Pillich's assertion is highly questionable. Though punta is clearly a Spanish word (and therefore would likely have come into use after 1797), the Garifuna punta is not danced on the toes or the "tips" of the feet.

Musically, Whipple describes the punta as having a wide range of melodic content and lyrical themes (although the text is often concerned with love or strife between couples) (1971, 49). Whipple notes that the melody is usually sung in unison by the entire ensemble with a changing verse and set chorus.

At times, according to Whipple, this will be in a call and response form with the verse sung solo (49). Hadel modifies Whipple's model. According to Hadel the basic structure of the song is a call and response that is repeated and then a refrain that is repeated. Hadel writes that the call is ideally sung solo by a leader but that others often join in, the response is sung by the chorus, and the refrain by the leader and the chorus (1972, 100). Hadel asserts that the chorus sings in unison and does not use polyphony. He further notes that the form of the call is "a half-sentence, which the response completes" (100). The leader determines the amount of time that a particular song is sung and "if the leader decides to change songs she simply introduces a new call at the appropriate moment without requiring a break in the rhythm of the drum" (101). Hadel also adds two more observations about the punta. Though performed at many different occasions, Hadel notes that the punta is a requirement at belurias (wakes). Hadel also notes only women compose punta songs (97). The rest of the literature on punta does not differ in any substantial way from the descriptions above.

Punta rock

Punta rock is (or was originally) a variation of the punta. The duple meter segunda rhythm of the punta is the same as that of punta rock but the punta ensemble has been added to considerably with predominately western electric instruments. Marc Perry was the first to write about punta rock, "Stylistically, Belizean Punta Rock frequently incorporates strong West Indian Soca and Reggae elements into its sound" (1999, 83). According to one of Perry's interviews with a Garifuna musician from Dangriga, punta rock was invented by Pen Cayetano in Dangriga in 1981 and its creation was in part a response to the death of Bob Marley (1999, 84). Oliver Greene also attributes the first performances of punta rock to Pen Cayetano and suggests that the first performances of punta rock took place around the time of Bob Marley's death possibly as a tribute (2002, 200).

With the exception of Perry's brief comments, Greene is the only scholar to address punta rock. Greene expands the definition of punta rock, rather than solely a variation of the punta he wrote that punta rock is, "An adaptation of punta, from which its name is borrowed, and to a lesser extent paranda" (190). Greene points out that rhythmically punta rock is very similar to both punta and paranda and that lyrically punta rock songs are many times adaptations of older Garifuna songs, though there are also many new songs dealing with contemporary life (190). Greene also notes several changes in punta rock over time. He shows that the turtle shells, snare drum and electric lead guitar were added early on and gradually more and more electronic instruments were added as well. Greene writes, "With the advent of synthesized instruments, the drum machine has replaced the segunda in most punta rock bands" (196). Greene also adds that whereas women composed most punta songs the punta rock music is generally composed and performed entirely by men (196). One of the important observations that Greene makes is that, in terms of classification, no new forms of Garifuna music have been invented since punta rock. Greene writes, "All recordings of Garifuna music that have employed electric instruments since the development of punta rock have been classified as such, regardless of the indigenous genre from which they were derived" (205). This quote is important not just for punta rock but I believe that a parallel situation exists for paranda, as I will discuss later.

Secular Music for Processionals and/or Christmastime

This sub-category is rather undefined. With the exception of the wanaragua there is not a lot of written or recorded data on these genres. However, in the limited information available there are stylistic, and/or performance similarities and in the literature they are all said to be similar to one another.

Afeduani

Only Doris Stone mentions the afeduani. She writes, "Women singing. Each person dances alone. This is done at Christmas time and at special celebrations" (1953). There is no more information provided other than the recording that I was not able to identify as belonging to any other genre.

Charikanari

Hadel is the first to discuss the Charikanari and claims that it is a version of the wanaragua for boys rather than adult men. Hadel writes that the accompaniment is with drums and fife and without singing (1972, 115). As for the dance Hadel writes, "When the music begins, each boy takes a turn dancing solo. The movements resemble those of wanaragua but are much slower... Finally, after everyone has had a turn dancing, the whole troupe jumps into the ring and dances together, signaling the end of the performance" (115). Cayetano and Cayetano provide only a one-sentence description, "In this mimed dance, a hunter meets up with a cave man and a cow" (1997, 129). The only other mention of Charikanari is from Whipple who writes that it is one of "four varieties of processional ceremonies which are performed by the Caribs of Belize during the Christmas holidays" (1976, 1).

Chumba

Chumba is another genre that has not been discussed much in the literature. Hadel first mentions chumba in 1972, but only writes that it appears similar to the wanaragua and has ""fanciful movements"(114). Hadel's description suggests that chumba is related to the processional dances (like wanaragua).

Jenkins and Jenkins' description of the dance is much more complete. They write, "One of the oldest dances known today the chumba requires subtle communication between drummers and dancers. Solo dancers come before the drum saluting them with staccato movements which often descend by stages to a level where the dancers' backs are on the floor" (1982a, 2). Cayetano and Cayetano are the only others to comment on chumba, they describe the chumba as, "a highly accentuated polyrhythmic song, danced by soloists with great individualized style... This performance includes a wide range of Garifuna music, some of which is rapidly disappearing in many communities"(1997, 129),

Corropatia

The only reference to corropatia is from Stone (1953). She describes it this way, "The name is taken from the Mexican *Jarabe Tapatia* and the participants are clad in all sorts of costumes in the manner of a masquerade. Only men generally do it, but sometimes women join as well. It is danced alone within a circle of people" (1953). From her description of the dance and regalia the corropatia would seem to be related to the wanaragua (discussed later), but it is rhythmically different. Unfortunately as no other reference is made to this genre Stone's brief description and recording are the only information available.

Pia manadi

Taylor is the first to discuss pia manadi and believes that Pia and Manadi are two of the characters of the wanaragua. Taylor writes, "Pia (a man) and Manadi (literally 'manatee,' in the masquerade a man dressed to represent a woman) are the two figures of fun in this entertainment. Pia, whatever his significance to the Black Carib, is a Guiana Carib hero, genius of the forest, and one of the twin children of the sun" (1951, 8). Whipple disagrees with Taylor's assertion that Pia and Manadi are two characters in the wanaragua. In his article "Pia Manadi" Whipple describes the pia manadi as a separate Christmastime processional musical play (1976). Related to English mumming, the pia manadi is accompanied by fife and drums, and is a processional play that moves from house to house telling a story involving the Devil and a doctor through dance. The pia manadi is performed between the Christmas and New Year's (Whipple, 1976).

Sambai

Sambai is given very brief treatment in the literature. Only Hadel, Jenkins and Jenkins and Cayetano and Cayetano address sambai and none spend more than a few sentences describing it. Hadel comments simply that it is similar to the wanaragua, danced only by men and one at a time (1972, 114).

Jenkins and Jenkins write, "The sambai is rarely performed today. Its beat seems related to the wanaragua, but both men and women dance it with a stomping step. The song is a simple call-and-response" (1982a, 4). Cayetano and Cayetano's description is similarly vague noting the use of "fancy footwork" but making no mention of gender (1997, 129).

Wanaragua (John Canoe)

First mention of the wanaragua, also called the John Canoe (the origin of either name is not found in the literature), is made by some of the earliest westerners to write accounts of the Garinagu. These accounts focus mainly on the costumes worn by the dancers. Costume is a distinctive element of this genre (Taylor, 1951, 7). Wanaragua dancers wear "macaw feather and crepe paper crowns, cowrie-shell kneebands, and whiteface masks made of molded and painted metal screen" (Jenkins and Jenkins, 1982a, 3). The wanaragua is performed from Christmas to New Year's Day (Hadel, 1972, 107) and is danced entirely by men though some are dressed as women. Additionally, according to Hadel, only men compose the songs although sung by both men and women (1972, 109). The dance is in the form of a procession. A group of dancers, drummers and singers move from one house to the next performing and receiving food and drink in return (Cayetano and Cayetano, 1997, 128). Whipple has suggested that wanaragua like other processional genres is related to English mumming (1976). Many scholars have argued that wanaragua is related to Christmastime dances that were once widespread in the Caribbean, especially Jamaica and Trinidad, and were one of the few occasions that slaves were allowed to dance and play music (Whipple, 1971, Jenkins and Jenkins, 1982a, Cayetano and Cayetano, 1997).

Warini

Only Hadel and Whipple have discussed the warini. Hadel writes that it is "identical to the wanaragua in dance style and song but dancers wear old, tattered clothes; danced as a prelude to the wanaragua" (1972, 114). Whipple only mentions the warini in passing noting that it was on of the Christmastime processionals of the Garinagu (1976, 1). It appears from this limited information that the warini is a form of dress rehearsal for the wanaragua, why Hadel and Whipple have separated the two is unclear.

Sacred Music

The sacred genres of Garifuna music are found in several settings, the most important of which is the dugu. The dugu is an ancestor honoring and placating ceremony that requires a year of preparation and lasts for two weeks (Jenkins and Jenkins, 1982b, 2). A dugu is called for when an ancestor becomes angered at having been ignored. This anger is manifest in sickness and misfortune among the living family members. Cayetano and Cayetano write,

> The Gubida [ancestor for whom the dugu is being held] is endowed with human qualities for the duration of the Dugu by all those participating... The Ancestor Spirit is asked to drink, eat and dance as he wishes. At tense moments during the ceremonies, one or more of the participants may loose consciousness, and... assume the characteristics of the Gubida Ancestor being honored. At the end of the ceremonies, the ancestor is asked whether he acknowledges receipt of the Dugu. Depending on what he says the ceremonies may have to be repeated (1997, 139).

The dugu ceremony is led by a buyei, a "shaman, herbalist, and traditional spiritualist" (Greene, 1998, 169), who mediates between the living and deceased family members.

Music and dance are found throughout the dugu, and indeed all Garifuna ritual. The instrumentation of the sacred genres are varied but less so than secular music. The instrumental ensemble always consists of three segunda drums. One of the three segundas is called the lanigi garawoun, or heart drum and is responsible for signaling changes in the rhythm (Greene, 1999, xxix). In addition to the drums there are several shakers. One shaker called a sisira is made of a calabash gourd filled with seeds and is used by the buyei, there are other shakers called variously maragas, shakers, shekere, and shakkas in the literature that are not restricted to the buyei only. It is unclear whether these different terms actually refer to different types of shakers. Drums, shakers, and voice are the only instrumentation for sacred music and are used in different combinations. Additionally some sacred music called uyanu is not accompanied instrumentally.

Although there are times during the dugu when secular music is played for entertainment, there is a clear line between sacred music and music for any other occasion. Sacred music is not found in any context other than religious ritual and its performance is prohibited in any non-sacred context (Greene, 1998, 147).

Abeimahani (uyanu)

The abeimahani is the female version of uyanu. Uyanu is unaccompanied gestured song. The singers, all female in the case of abeimahani, stand in a row clasping hands and singing while swaying back and forth. The first written notes on abeimahani come from Doris Stone, "This type of song is considered the property of the individual female who composes it or, to whom it appears in a dream. It is first sung in a dogo rite to honor the request of a dead relative and is sung by a group of women either with or without drums" (1953, 3). Stone's assertion that abeimahani is sometimes with drums is incorrect. There is an implied pulse as Whipple writes, "[a] definite durational relationship between the notes, there is an absence of a strictly recurring metrical system. A beat is maintained... but it is not as spectacular as in other metrical styles of the Carib" (1971, 58). On the rhythmic quality of uyanu Kenan Foley agrees that though in free meter there is a basic pulse. Foley also adds that uyanu songs are through composed with longer phrases than other genres and that the form is open ended with verses repeated any number of times (1984, 72). The texts of uyanu are, according to Foley, either about a direct experience of the composer or of a historical nature concerning the origin of the Garinagu and are given by the ancestors in dreams.

Abelagudahani

A description of the abelagudahani appears only in the liner notes to Jenkins and Jenkins' album of sacred Garifuna music. They describe the abelagudahani as "gathering in" music that is played while people are gathering and entering the dugu ceremony (1982b, 2). It is clear then that this music is played at the beginning of the dugu and is accompanied by drumming, and in at least one example the singing and sisira playing of the buyei (Jenkins and Jenkins, 1982b).

Amalihani

Amalihani is one of the dance/song styles of central importance to the dugu. The first writing on the amalihani comes from Jenkins and Jenkins who describe it as "the most sacred dance of the Garifuna" (1982b, 3). The dance consists of the participants of the dugu in a line behind the buyei, facing the drums. This group then moves around the temple stopping at the cardinal points and the drummers (who are also walking, not seated) one by one bow towards the ground (Jenkins and Jenkins, 1982b, 3). The bowing by the drummers is an act of supplication towards the ancestors. Cayetano and Cayetano refer to the amalihani simply as "a song and dance of supplication" (1997, 139). The above description is agreed on in the literature. There is a dispute however over when possession occurs. Jenkins and Jenkins assert that ancestor possession will often occur during the amalihani. Oliver Greene in his dissertation on dugu and spirit possession disagrees writing, "Onwehani [possession] does not occur during amalihani, the central rite of the dugu as previously reported. It usually occurs as the procession ends, while drummers return to the bench... This is the location from which they drum during chururuti and awangulahani" (1999, 262).

Arumahani (uyanu)

Arumahani is the men's version of uyanu, the counterpart of abeimahani (see above). This genre appears to be waning in popularity. In 1971 Whipple calls it "all but a dead tradition" (58), and in 1972 Hadel claims to be able to find only one man who knew how to sing arumahani (122). However in 1984 Foley suggests that rather than fading out all together it may just be fading out as a men's genre. He writes, "Nowadays women often sing arumahani and the tradition appears to be maintained for the most part by the women" (48). It is unclear what, if anything, other than the original gender distinction separated abeimahani from arumahani. This is made more difficult as primarily women now sing both.

Awangulahani

Awangulahani is another of the dance songs of the dugu. Cayetano and Cayetano write simply, "A dance of rejoicing" (1997, 139). Greene describes the awangulahani similarly adding that it takes place on the morning of the last day of the dugu and is a way that the participants bid each other farewell (1999, 302). Greene also concurs with Jenkins and Jenkins who describe the dance this way; "People grab each other by the arm and swing with all their might, trying to spin the person into dizziness. At this time, many spirits arrive for the last dance, i.e. many persons go into short trance. The whole awangulahani is very joyous and wild and even the buyei, who rarely dance, takes a spin or two with participants" (quoted in Greene, 1999, 302-303).

Chururuti

Chururuti is mentioned only by Greene who writes" Although chururuti is not a specific musical genre, it is the twenty-to-thirty-minute period of dancing, drumming singing and occasional rattling during which the onwehani most frequently occurs" (1999, 262). Greene then goes on to analyze two songs performed during the chururuti, but they are not related musically so much as they are related in their both being played in the same context. Though there is no evidence that marks churututi as a distinct genre I have included it because of its importance to the dugu in terms of onwehani.

Hugulendu

As mentioned above the hugulendu is the sacred form on which the hunguhungu is based. Marilyn Wells gives the first detailed description of the hugulendu, ""Four components are constant: 1) it is a circular formation, 2) presentation of ritual foods are associated with the circle, 3) progress around the circle is labored, and 4) the direction of the circle alternates"

(1980, 4). Jenkins and Jenkins add that the dance step is a tightly bound shuffle (1982b, 1). Nowhere in the literature is there any description of the music of hugulendu apart from general statements that refer to all sacred genres.

Paranda, Guitar Song, and Berusu

Paranda, guitar song, and berusu are all terms that have been used to describe Garifuna music with guitar accompaniment but paranda is the term most commonly used. Paranda is a guitar-based music with a rhythm that is very similar to the punta rhythm (though paranda can be played with or without rhythmic accompaniment and is often played over different rhythms). Generally paranda is sung solo with the singer accompanying himself on the guitar. However there are many variations in paranda especially in the more recent recorded examples which have greatly expanded the genre's instrumentation and form. Paranda originated as a caroling music at Christmastime and is strongly linked to Latin America. Though still played at Christmastime, paranda is now played year round as secular entertainment.

There has been a lot of confusion in the literature over what the distinctions are between these terms and what if anything classifies the genre of guitar accompanied Garifuna music. To begin I will turn to the literature, which is limited, and show how this genre has been presented. After this literature review I will present my own conclusions based on fieldwork in Belize and specifically interviews with two of Belize's most well known living paranderos Junior Aranda in Dangriga[5] (5/19/2004) and Paul Nabor in Punta Gorda (3/25/2005).

The first recording of the music and the first written mention of guitar-accompanied music are from Doris Stone in 1953. Stone, who was working in Honduras, calls the music parrandatinu and writes, "The Black Caribs call this type of song a parrandatinu, a word taken from the Spanish paranda signifying 'spree.' This type of song however is better interpreted in English as a serenade. Both the idea of the serenade as well as the instruments used, the guitars, are borrowed from their Spanish-American neighbors" (4). Serenade here (and elsewhere) refers to music played in courtship. Though it is unclear wear the suffix "tinu" comes from parranda is clearly taken from Spanish and paranda is merely the English spelling. To this day it is not uncommon to see a recording from Honduras with the parranda spelling.

The next to address guitar music was Emory Whipple who calls the genre guitar-song which, he claims, is what the Garinagu call the genre (1971, 50).

---

[5] Many thanks to Ken Bilby who co-interviewed Junior Aranda with myself (and whose questions proved to be far more insightful than my own) and kindly recorded the interview as well. Also many thanks to Francis Swaso for arranging the interview and performance with Mr. Aranda.

Whipple bolsters Stone's claim regarding the Spanish influence on the music, "[Guitar-song] is the Carib style most influenced by the music of Spanish-speaking Latin America, some tunes being merely translations or realizations in the Carib language of pre-existing Spanish songs, with the melodies more or less unaltered" (1971, 50). Whipple goes on to make a distinction between men's and women's guitar-song. He claims that women's guitar-song is generally at a slower tempo than men's and that men's guitar-song "is usually a bit 'racy' in content and in some cases the lyrics are as filthy as possible, though many have no sexual connotation at all" (1971, 52). Whipple outlines some lyrical themes that are often found in guitar-song: love, death, sickness, and injury, and adds that a common theme in women's guitar-song is a reprimand "where a man desiring love is put in his place" (52).

On the form of the music, firstly Whipple claims that guitar-song does not require a guitar and is often performed without one when there is no guitar available. However, in order to be guitar-song it must have some existing accompaniment that would be played if there were a guitar available (1971, 50). Secondly, Whipple makes the claim that guitar-song is the "only Carib song form accompanied by a harmony instrument" (1971, 50), which may have been true before the advent of punta rock. On the guitar playing style Whipple describes it as rhythmic and agitated, saying that, "The technique is similar to if not the same as, that used in much of the guitar (and other stringed instrument) playing of the Spanish Latin Americans, and the Caribs undoubtedly borrowed this technique from them" (1971, 55). He continues giving a fuller description,

> "Full chords are played on the instrument, but the guitar accompaniment often seems more important for its rhythmic assistance, than for what it contributes harmonically… the accompaniments are identical to their rhythmic style… The accompaniment is mainly on one chord, with changes to others coming predominantly between song phrases. A few guitar-songs were heard (in British Honduras [now Belize]) where the accompaniment was an attempt at harmonization of the melody, but the rhythm was the same as in the other accompaniments" (1971, 55).

Whipple does not mention any drumming, or other rhythmic accompaniment. He does provide a transcription of a guitar-song in 2/4 but it is only a transcription of the guitar part (1971, 138).

Hadel is the next to address what he calls "beresu" (the standard spelling is now "berusu"). It is clear that though he renames it Hadel is speaking of the same genre as Whipple. Hadel asserts that though men and women play berusu, it is composed exclusively by men (1972, 117). He agrees with Stone and Whipple that the berusu is heavily influenced by Latin American and Spanish musics writing, "melodies of beresu are clearly Western, but the text is in Carib" (1971, 117).

Hadel is very brief on the musical form, saying only that there is some stylistic variation between guitar players/villages, "One of my guitarist friends assured me that he could recognize the Carib village from which a particular guitar-player was from just by hearing him play, for each village has its own distinctive style of strumming" (1972, 117). Hadel does not delve any further into these potential differences and provides little more information on the music. In fact Hadel seems to give up describing berusu writing, "I could determine no structural components that might characterize this genre of song... the beresu allows the composer a great deal of freedom" (1972, 117).

Ten years after Hadel, Carol and Travis Jenkins are the next to write about, and also to record, Garifuna music with guitar. They are the first to use the term paranda to distinguish this genre, but they also record and describe a berusu song. On berusu they write, "Berusu are usually sung solo and accompanied by guitar with a listening, instead of a dancing audience. As a type of song used for general entertainment on social occasions, they are frequently played at wakes" (1982a, 3). Their description of paranda is in line with what Stone, Whipple, and Hadel had described as parrandatinu, guitar-song, and berusu, "A type of party song, likened to a serenade and usually composed by men. Apparently developed under Hispanic influence" (1982a, 3). However, Jenkins and Jenkins add something new writing, "Paranda is the vehicle men use when composing songs of social criticism" (1982a, 4). In addition to adding the element of song as social critique, the Jenkins' are the first to separate paranda and berusu. They assert that the two are separate musical genres making the distinction based on drum accompaniment; berusu is solo whereas paranda is not.

The suggestion that there are two different genres of guitar music confuses the picture presented by in previous scholarship. Were Whipple, Stone, and Hadel describing paranda or berusu? For instance much of what Hadel writes about what he calls berusu fits with what Jenkins and Jenkins write about what they call paranda. Since no one prior to Jenkins and Jenkins made any mention of the drum accompaniment, or lack thereof, it is difficult to try to determine which genre they were addressing using the Jenkins' distinction. On the other hand, it is possible that the Jenkins' are simply wrong in asserting that there is more than one genre of guitar music.

It is not until 1999 that paranda is again mentioned in the literature. This time it Oliver Greene very briefly summarizes paranda in the glossary to his dissertation on sacred music. Greene writes, "[Paranda is] a secular song-and-dance-form which displays the influence of Hispanic musical genres. A serenade-like social commentary song traditionally played by men" (1999, xxx).

Also in 1999 the album *Paranda: Africa in Central America* was released and Dan Rosenberg gives a very succinct description of the music in the liner notes,

> Paranda is both a Garifuna rhythm and a genre of music. The basic rhythm can be heard in Garifuna traditional drumming styles that date all the way back to St. Vincent and West Africa. The Paranda became a genre itself in the 19th century, shortly after the Garifuna arrived in Honduras. It was there were they first encountered Latin music, and incorporated the acoustic guitar, a touch of Latin and Spanish rhythms into the music. The Paranda reached its prominence in the early part of the 20th century, and has changed little since. Its instrumentation is totally acoustic, "Garifuna Unplugged' (1999).

In 2000 Gualberto Pillich offers another explanation. Pillich suggests that paranda grew out of berusu (45). Pillich also suggests that berusu is generally performed solo without drums, "Now virtually extinct, on the rare occasion that the guitar-song [berusu] is performed, it is primarily sung by a solo voice with guitar accompaniment. However, it is often embellished with percussion instruments consisting of everyday objects such as wooden boxes, bottles, cans, and tools as well as shakka-shakkas (maracas)" (2000, 45). Pillich also agrees with Jenkins and Jenkins that berusu is designed for sitting and listening rather than dancing (2000, 45). However, Pillich claims that berusu was originally a serenade song used in courtship (2000, 46), which contradicts Jenkins and Jenkins who believe that this is how paranda, not berusu, started.

Pillich, like Whipple, divides berusu into men's and women's versions and cites the same textual differences as Whipple (though he does not cite Whipple specifically). On the musical form Pillich writes, "The vast majority of songs in this genre use a simple two chord formula, tonic to sub-dominant (I-IV) or tonic to dominant (I-V). The guitar serves not only as harmonic support for the melody but has a strong rhythmic role to play in the song. The guitar style often includes the technique of dampening the strings while being struck by the right hand to create a percussive effect" (2000, 45).

Pillich devotes much less time to discussing the musical differences that set paranda apart from berusu. He writes, "Paranda is an outgrowth of the guitar-song [Pillich uses guitar-song and berusu interchangeably] genre, often with wooden boxes used as percussive accompaniment" (2000, 46). This is somewhat contradictory as it is nearly the exact same description that he has given for berusu. Pillich does suggest that paranda has become both a rhythm and a couples dance and gives a description of the dance style that sounds nearly exactly like punta dancing (2000, 46).

Oliver Greene again addressed paranda in 2002 (the most recent written work by any author that deals in any length with guitar music). He adds to his earlier description that the rhythm of paranda is nearly identical to that of punta, and reinforces the belief that paranda was originally a type of serenade (2002, 196).

Drawing from my own fieldwork and specifically on interviews with two of Belize's most well-known and respected paranderos I will clarify the murky picture that currently exists in the literature. The name of this music is a good starting point. As is clear from the above descriptions of parrandatinu, berusu, guitar-song, and paranda, there is no consensus in the literature as to the name of this genre of music or even whether it is one or two genres. Though unclear in the literature I have found no confusion in my own fieldwork. The people that I have spoken to, most importantly the musicians, refer to only one genre of music and refer to it as paranda. In my interview with Junior Aranda he did speak occasionally of guitar-song, but this was only as a description of paranda. Furthermore Mr. Aranda was clear that paranda could be with or without drums and made no mention of any other name (like berusu) for solo guitar music. Paul Nabor was equally clear in stating that there is no guitar music other than paranda. I asked him about berusu and he was not familiar with any style of music by that name. Mr. Nabor also emphasized that paranda could be played with or without rhythmic accompaniment though he mentioned that paranda is ideally accompanied with drums and shakers.

In Oliver Greene's 2002 article on punta he points out that since the advent of punta rock all Garifuna music with electric instruments falls under the category of punta rock. This is the case regardless of the rhythm or genre that the song may be based on. I believe that this is also the case with paranda. All acoustic music (or predominately acoustic music) with guitar accompaniment is now called paranda. The most recent paranda release, *Garifuna Soul* by Aurelio Martinez (2004) demonstrates this point. Several of the tracks on the album are based on non-paranda rhythms and use a variety of instruments (as mentioned above). The common element that brings these songs together is a solo singer and primarily acoustic instrumentation with a focus on the acoustic guitar. Therefore most, if not all, new Garifuna music falls into one of two categories, punta rock or paranda (the exceptions to this rule are traditionally non-Garifuna genres like hip hop that are now performed by some Garinagu).

It has been suggested in the literature that paranda was originally a type of serenade. There is no doubt that for some period of time paranda was used as music for serenading (both Paul Nabor and Junior Aranda confirmed this).

However, it seems (from both the literature and my own work) that paranda is no longer used in this way. Though the serenade was an earlier use of the paranda, paranda was not originally serenade music. Paranda was originally a music played on Christmas from house to house (and was in fact performed at the same time and even alongside the wanaragua according to Junior Aranda). The use of paranda as a Christmastime music has not been mentioned anywhere in the literature. Paranda is still played as a caroling music on Christmas day (at least in Punta Gorda). Both Mr. Nabor and Mr. Aranda said that paranda was originally Christmastime music and that the music was the same then as it is now. Mr. Aranda mentioned that he did not know any parandas that were about Christmas or that were specifically for Christmastime. His statement leads me to believe that the songs that are played at Christmas are the same songs that are played at any other time of the year.

The origin of paranda as a Christmastime music performed from house to house points further to the Hispanic influence on the music. In several Spanish-speaking countries including Venezuela and Puerto Rico there is also caroling at Christmas known as "parranda." Paranda also exists as caroling elsewhere in the English speaking Caribbean like Trinidad and Tobago, where it is called parang and thought to have come through Venezuela (Liverpool, 1994, 198).

Questions still exist about the form of the music. Since rhythm is one key factor in distinguishing between Garifuna musical genres this is a good starting point. Most scholars have either not included a description of the paranda rhythm or have been very vague. Greene was correct in writing that the paranda rhythm is nearly the same as that of punta but he does not include an example of the paranda rhythm. The paranda rhythm is:

Whereas the punta rhythm is

The similarity of the two makes for an easy transition between the two genres. In my experience the combination punta/paranda appears to be a popular song form moving fluidly from punta to paranda and vice versa. On one occasion I saw Paul Nabor playing with a group that played several punta/paranda combinations and the guitar part remained the same over both rhythms. It is also apparent from my fieldwork that the paranda rhythm can be and is played without guitar accompaniment and is still referred to as paranda (though the common definition of paranda is any acoustic guitar music). It is also important to reemphasize that though there is a rhythm that is called paranda to which the majority of parandas are played, paranda can also be played to other rhythms or without any rhythmic accompaniment at all.

The style of guitar playing is also something that has received some attention in the literature. For the most part the descriptions are accurate. The guitar playing often follows along with the rhythm playing arpeggios one note per beat. However this is not always the case. Additionally at times the guitar will not play arpeggios but will instead strum whole chords often on the upbeat. It should be noted that in more recent paranda recordings the role of the guitar has taken on different forms and with influential artists like Aurelio Martinez an element of virtuosity has been added (though I have not encountered any parandas with a guitar break/solo, artists like Martinez have made the guitar accompaniment more and more intricate).

The chordal harmony of paranda songs typically consists of the tonic, subdominant, and dominant[6], though it is not uncommon for a song to use only the tonic and subdominant, or tonic and dominant as Pillich suggests (see above). Whipple suggests that the guitar will stay on one chord for the entire verse and any chord changes will occur between phrases. This is true of some songs but in my experience it is more common that chord changes will occur throughout the song not just during breaks in singing.

Finally, there has been a suggestion made that there are distinct men's and women's styles of paranda. Though it may be the case that men and women may have a tendency to sing about different subject matter, I have never heard of any formal distinction between men's and women's paranda. From my experience, and the available recordings of paranda, it seems to be uncommon that women sing lead or play guitar though Paul Nabor was quite specific that women can and do fill these roles in the music. It has also been suggested that only men compose paranda, I have never encountered this and it would seem in opposition to the general means of composition for Garifuna music. Typically paranda (and other) songs are composed either by an individual (as in the case of songs for social commentary), or are given to an individual in a dream.

Conclusion

It is evident from their history that the Garinagu emerged as a new people from the mixing of several distinct groups. Rex Nettleford defines creolization as, "The evolution of a native born-and-bred culture pattern with its own inner logic and consistency different from the feeder sources" (1972, 10). Nettleford's definition is clearly applicable to the Garinagu and their musical styles provide the evidence.

---

[6] It is interesting to note that one Garinagu that I spoke with compared paranda to blues music. His comparison was based on lyrical content and performance and expression style, but the comparison also works on the harmonic level.

On Garifuna music Myrtle Palacio writes, "The Garifuna music, chants and dances are a rich and creative combination of Amerindian and African elements" (1993, 13). Cayetano and Cayetano add, "In addition to the Amerindian and African elements, early French, Spanish, and English folk music contributed to [their] musical heritage. Other Afro-Caribbean people, such as Haitians, Jamaicans, and Barbadians, have also contributed to the Garifuna musical stock [ex: wanaragua, paranda, etc.] " (1997, 127).

Much of the literature has focused on Garifuna sacred songs, in particular the abeimahani, a style sung by a group of women unaccompanied by instruments. On abeimahani, Hadel writes, "It more than any other genre, seems to bear resemblance to American Indian music" (1972, 92). Several aspects of the abeimahani are extremely close to forms found in Amerindian music. The use of vocables, the melodic contour, the vocal ornamentation, and the physical arrangement of the performers have all been linked to Amerindian music.

Vocables (often referred to derogatorily and incorrectly as "nonsense" or "meaningless" syllables) are a common part of abeimahani singing. Hadel writes, "Although meaningless syllables are found in dance songs also, they are far more common in the abaimahani; this tempts one to locate their origin in the New World rather than in African tradition. Bruno Nettl writes that 'meaningless syllables occupy an important role' in American Indian music" (1972, 93).

Here it is helpful to turn to some descriptions of Amerindian music as found in South America, specifically the Guiana Amerindians in Surinam. To begin with it should be reemphasized that the Amerindians who settled on St. Vincent are believed to have come from the Orinoco Valley north of the Amazon Basin. This is the same geographic area inhabited by the Guiana Amerindians (Agerkop, 2001, 42). There are two traits in the abeimahani that seem to directly correlate to the music of the Guiana. One is melodic contour. Hadel and others have noted that a prominent feature in abeimahani songs is a descending melodic contour (Hadel 1976, Foley, 1984). Terry Agerkop writes of Guiana songs, "The melodies… nearly always, have a descending final cadence to the lowest basic tone" (2001, 33). Additionally Pillich writes of abeimahani, "Another element of this song type that points to a probable Amerindian connection is the ornamentation used to color the melodic shape. Liberal use is made of glissandi, a 'moaning' sound, and glottal shakes" (2000, 42-43).

The arrangement of the performers is another similarity shared between the Garifuna abeimahani and the Guiana song styles. In the abeimahani performance the singers clasp hands and stand in a semi-circle and make swaying and bending movements while their feet remain in place (Hadel 1972, Taylor 1951, Whipple 1971). This same performance style (it would appear to be almost the exact same) is seen in the <u>sambura</u> dance style in Surinam (Agerkop, 2001, 34-35). There is another striking similarity between the two performance styles, Agerkop writes, "Sambura singing and dancing is always accompanied by the intake of large quantities of kasili (a lightly alcoholic beverage based on fermented bitter manioc)" (2001, 34), of the abeimahani Pillich writes, "When performing abaimahani songs, the women stand in a row or in a semi-circle and pass aguardiente (beer made from cassava [cassava is another name for manioc])"(2000, 43).

Based on linguistic evidence there is one final connection that can be made between the Guiana of Surinam, whose singing is representative of the whole style of song found north of the Amazon Basin (Agerkop, 2001, 42), and the Garifuna. One of the groups of Guiana Amerindians that Agerkop writes about is the <u>Kalinha,</u> and another is the <u>Wayana</u> (2001, 31). Cayetano and Cayetano have shown that the current word Garinagu comes from the root word <u>Karina</u> (1997, 13). Though not the exact same word, Kalinha, and Karina bear a striking similarity.

The case with the Wayana is even more striking. As mentioned above Wayana is the name of a particular group of Amerindians in Surinam whose songs are very similar to Garifuna abeimahani. As discussed earlier, abeimahani songs fall into a category known by the Garinagu as uyanu. Wayana, and uyanu are not exactly the same but given the musical connections and the fact that until the 1900's neither of these languages were written (therefore spelling of words is not uniform and varies from scholar to scholar) it is hard to discount the possible connection.

Much less has been written about the African elements of Garifuna music and the accounts are frequently not specific. Pillich writes, "The Garifuna people maintain a musical tradition that is a hybrid of several influences. The most prevalent of these are the drumming styles of West Africa and the melodic style of the Arawak-Carib Indians of South and Central America" (2000, 4). Carol and Travis Jenkins analyzed Garifuna music using cantometrics and came to this conclusion regarding the African component of the music,

> African influence is present in the instrumental component of secular music, especially in its rhythms and several vocalization patterns, such as the degree of rasp, the vocal rhythms, the scant presence of glottal shake, and tremolo. Also associated with Africa is the common diatonic melodic interval and a prominent position of women in both ritual and non-ritual song performance (1982, 22).

There are two other aspects of Garifuna music that have been problematically labeled as African: call and response, and the timbre of the drums. As for the call and response pattern found in much Garifuna singing, Whipple suggests that call and response may have existed in the Americas before Columbus and could be an Amerindian trait (1971, 43). The Jenkins' concluded, based on their cantometric examination, that, "Unlike most West African call-and-response patterns, there is little space for vocal elaboration by a soloist in Garifuna song" (1982, 20).

The timbre of the drum has been likened to instruments found in Africa. Garifuna drums are not complete unless they have a snare that is attached across the top of the drumhead. Cayetano and Cayetano write, "Thin metal wires or strings are strung across the drum head to serve as snares... Some drums, especially those used in sacred music, are nearly three feet across and create a great humming sound when struck" (1997, 127). Pillich makes the case that this is an Africanism,

> What might sound at first like electronic distortion or 'overload' in a sound recording is actually the characteristic sound of the wires or snares vibrating on the surface of the drumhead. This 'buzzy' affect is reminiscent of the buzzing sound found in the mbira of the Shona people of Zimbabwe and many of the balafons of Central and West Africa. This is possible further evidence of an African connection in the music of the Garifuna (2000, 57-58).

Pillich's argument is convincing. However, turning again to the Guiana Amerindians we find that the Kalinha also have a snare drum. Agerkop writes, "A snare extends on one of the skinheads and a palm leaf nerve is inserted in it, which produces an extra vibration and timbre. This extra vibration produces a drone-like effect on a fixed tone" (2001, 34). Agerkop's "drone" could be similar in character the "humming" that Cayetano and Cayetano describe.

Currently it would seem that there is more evidence pointing to a link between Amerindian and Garifuna music than with the musics of Africa. This may be the case, but if anything it is likely due to the disproportionate amount of work done on abeimahani songs as compared to other Garifuna musical genres. Additionally, some scholars maintain that Garifuna music is primarily African influenced with some Amerindian influences. Bruno Nettl writes, "Despite their Afro-Indian heritage... the [Garifuna] culture and music are mostly derivative of West Africa" (quoted in Pillich, 2000, 4). Carol and Travis Jenkins privilege the African element of Garifuna music by writing, "Garifuna music stands alone in the world of Afro-Caribbean music in having a strong Amerindian component" (1982, 23).

It is misleading and problematic to claim that Garifuna music is either or African or Amerindian. This reductive tendency has surfaced in much scholarship on Garifuna music. Such proclamations do not allow any explanation for the existence of musical traits that are neither African nor Amerindian. An example is paranda music. Paranda music adds the Western guitar and chord progressions to secular Garifuna drumming and singing. Other examples abound in newer styles of Garifuna music such as punta rock, which utilizes keyboards, drum machines, and other electric instrument developed in the West.

Simply calling Garifuna music or Garinagu people African or Amerindian, or even implying that they are mainly one or the other is a dead end. This type of theorizing does not account for the historical and musical examples that are so varied. Instead of attributing a single origin it is more helpful to view the Garinagu as a people born out of creolization and a continuing process of cultural syncretism with all the peoples whom they come into contact.

In the above three sections I have attempted to provide a clear and comprehensive record of Garifuna history and a description of their musical styles. Though much of this paper is a review of the work of others, nowhere else does there exist a comprehensive listing and description of Garifuna musical genres and the pertinent literature.

I was drawn to the Garinagu through paranda, specifically Paul Nabor's song "Naguya Nei." Since I first heard that song I have made several trips to Belize and met with Mr. Nabor and other musicians and paranderos in an effort to better understand and appreciate paranda. I am honored to have the ability to present the thoughts of Paul Nabor and Junior Aranda as well as contribute my own thoughts on this genre and to expand and enhance the understanding of a beautiful form of music and an important group of people.

Bibliography:

Agerkop, Terry. 2001. "Some Remarks on the Guiana Amerindian Songstyle." *Latin American Indian Literatures Journal* Vol. 5, No. 2. 31-42.

Cayetano, E. Roy. 1993. *The People's Garifuna Dictionary*. Dangriga, Belize: The National Garifuna Council of Belize.

Cayetano, Fabian and Sebastian Cayetano. 1997. *Garifuna History, Language & Culture of Belize, Central America and the Caribbean*. Dangriga, Belize: The National Garifuna Council of Belize.

Conzemius, Edward. 1928. "Ethnographical Notes on the Black Carib (Garif)." *American Anthropologist* Vol. 30, No.2. 183-205.

Foley, Kenan. 1984. *Garifuna Music Culture: An Introduction to Garifuna Music Practice With Emphasis on Abaimahani and Arumahani Songs*. Thesis, Southern University.

Franzone, Dorothy. 1994. *A Critical and Cultural Analysis of An African People in the Americas: Africanisms in the Garifuna Culture in Belize*. Dissertation, Temple University.

Gonzalez, Nancie. 1988. *Sojourners of the Caribbean: Ethnogenesis and Ethnohistory of the Garifuna*. Chicago: University of Illinois Press.

Greene, Oliver. 1998. "The 'Dugu' Ritual of the Garinagu of Belize: Reinforcing Values of Society Through Music and Spirit Possession." *Black Music Research Journal* Vol.18, No. 1-2. 167-181.

Greene, Oliver. 1999. *'Aura Buni, Amuru Nuni', 'I Am for You, You Are for Me': Reinforcing Garifuna Cultural Values Through Music and Ancestor Spirit Possession*. Dissertation, Florida State University.

Greene, Oliver. 2002. "Ethnicity, Modernity, and Retention in the Garifuna Punta." *Black Music Research Journal* Vol. 22, No.2. 189-216.

Gullick, C.J.M.R. 1985. *Myths of a Minority: The Changing Traditions of the Vincentian Caribs*. Assen, Netherlands: Van Gorcum.

Hadel, Richard. 1972. *Carib Folk Songs and Carib Culture*. Dissertation, University of Texas at Austin.

Hadel, Richard. 1976. "Black Carib Folk Music." *Caribbean Quarterly* Vol. 22, No. 2-3. 84-96.

Jenkins, Carol and Travis Jenkins. 1982. "Garifuna Musical Style and Culture History." *Belizean Studies* Vol.10, No. 3-4. 17-24.

Jenkins, Carol and Travis Jenkins. 1982a. *Traditional Music of the Garifuna (Black Carib) of Belize*. Folkways Records FE4031.

Jenkins, Carol and Travis Jenkins. 1982b. *Dabuyabaragu: Inside the Temple Sacred Music of the Garifuna of Belize*. Folkways Records FE4032.

Kerns, Virginia. 1983. *Women and the Ancestors: Black Carib Kinship and Rtiual*. Chicago: University of Illinois Press.

Liverpool, Hollis. 1994. "Researching Steelband and Calypso Music in the Brittish Caribbean and the U.S. Virgin Islands." *Black Music Research Journal* Vol.14, No.2. 179-201.

Martinez, Aurelio. 2004. *Garifuna Soul*. Stone Tree Records STR026.

Olawaiye, James. 1980. *Yoruba Religious and Social Traditions in Ekiti, Nigeria and Three Caribbean Countries: Trinidad-Tobago, Guyana, and Belize*. Dissertation, University of Missouri – Kansas City.

Osgood, Cornelius. 1942. "Anthropology – Prehistoric Contact Between South America and the West Indies." *Proceedings of the National Academy of Sciences of the United States of America* Vol.28, No.1 . 1-4.

Palacio, Myrtle. 1993. *The First Primer on the People Called Garifuna: The Things You Have Always Wanted to Know!* Glessima Research and Services.

Perry, Marc. 1999. *Garifuna Youth in New York City: Race, Ethnicity, and the Performance of Diasporic Identities*. Thesis, University of Texas at Austin.

Pillich, Gualberto Simeon. 2000. *Juxtaposition, Adaptation and Dominance: Observations on Belizean and Honduaran Garifuna Drumming in Los Angeles*. Thesis, University of California Los Angeles.

Porter, Robert. 1984. *The History and Social Life of the Garifuna in the Lesser Antilles and Central America*. Dissertation, Princeton University.

Roessingh, Carel. 2001. *The Belizean Garifuna: Organization of Identity in an Ethnic Community in Central America*. Rozengracht, Amsterdam: Rozenberg Publishers.

Rosenberg, Dan. 1999. "Liner Notes." *Paranda: Africa in Central America*. Stone Tree Records 3984-27303-2.

Stone, Doris. 1953. *The Black Carib of Honduras*. Folkways Records FE4435.

Taylor, Douglas. 1951. *The Black Carib of British Honduras*. New York: Werner-Gren Foundation for Anthropological Research.

Taylor, Douglas. 1977. *Languages of the West Indies*. Baltimore: Johns Hopkins University Press.

Wells, Marilyn. 1980. "Circling with the Ancestors: Hugulendii Symbolism in Ethnic Group Maintenance." *Belizean Studies* Vol.8, No.6. 1-9.

Whipple, Emory. 1971. *Music of the Caribs of British Honduras*. Thesis, University of Texas at Austin.

Whipple, Emory. 1976. "Pia Manadi." *Belizean Studies* Vol.4, No.4. 1-18.

Wilson, Samuel, ed. 1997. *The Indigenous People of the Caribbean*. Gainesville: University Press of Florida.

Leremuna Indura

lasügüragüdün Ruben Reyes

Bufanidiran aban aruni
huaiñuruguna
Dürüwaguali lau arumaü kai diliti
Arihuwatu tidan tanigi
Seingü waruguma dingubeletu
Tidan lidaündana hamuriti barana
Lau luwainamun labaunhan
lataunigira
Lagadaburugugien lerebe wübürugu
Anurain aban woruguma lau igemeri
miriti

Lau biñü luma bumagadien barumuga
Baranahagien lagambuwa uremu
Dan balañu ban lidan bigolun
Ñei ladairabu afayahati
Auweguati dan larihini bubuidun
Siñagua lungua ladüga bumagadien
Lidingugan tun tuwenden banagun
Lau linsiñe lachürün labinirabu

Aban ubau le ñei lubai lahücha
weyu
Yagüraun luai lidingun Adülandi
Gawenedüladibu wügüri ligia
Aban lafuduragun bübügürü
Lidan biñiuruni larufan berebe
Lau memeniha lan buga banigi
Labugien lufubulian huariñu
Fayali aban idedei terenchati

Malati lun warau le hinsiñebai
bun
Ludin awüdbuha tau sun ligañi
Agawainalai warau lita
Lidan lilulin ariabu labulucha
Tidangien sun to asügürübaun lun
Murusunrügali uraga araiduwa
Aban umuahaü ibidiewafi
Luma lamana lerebe wübü

Ürüwañai sigulu haganbuni
birahüñü
Lagumadihan gabafuti aburemein
ürüwañai sigulu maganbun lan
bumalali
Lidaun lidingun huariñu
laferidira
Aban weyu buiti lidaun barigai
Laganbuwa hamuri haliagien
Yetegien dise luagien Adülandi
Afaguali ladürühan liñu

Faransu buga to tunguabaun tau
tanigi
Sigulu buri lau tuwenedü
tarumuguña
Tagagudun duarina abagarida
Lau liderebugu lalugun Danton
Faransu ounahaubaun lidaun
auweni
Labulugu uruwei gayarati
Raramati lau pantaü laubawagu
Bungiu irichaü luagu tebudina

Iñraguatibu giñe aü nagaira
Lidangien lilulin buwenedü
Arufudahatibu giñe lun ubau
Dan babauchaguni lagu güdngürin
Lidangienti wamuan lagadabun
Lichügüwagugien dabiara lira
Kai aban dunuru würitura
Itara liña haudin terenchana

Lun waraiduni idaündani lira
Wauweguba luagu wagaira
Larandaruba giñe wabunurun
Anhawa auwegua luagu binsiñe
Hangina me lau lineben
bufanidiran
Auburahauwaina lidan tubana
Gibebaña auwegutiñu Indura
Lauba pantaü haiguada sungubai

Leremuna Wadimalu

Hasügüragüdün Ruben Reyes labu German W. Francisco
A,rufudahatüu. Francisco Caballero labu Fernando Norales Avila

Wadimalu gundatu le baraini
Mañawürihan hamai
gafarahaditiñu
Ni adamuruti le heluti gürabu
Ni hañawüriti lun lasuerun
bigibuawagun

Haruga me le libinin bumuan
Lasiadurai terenchana
Hurabai giñe lirufungu
bufanidiran
Wawarun, wagañeirun odi
wauwegun

Laguyuha:
Hurabai giñe lirufungu
bufanidiran
Wowarun, wagafieirun odi
wauwegun
Lun bagaira lauba durumandei
Himei wauwen luba wadamurun

Lidangien binadü güjringürin
Badügai lau uhabu hereguti
Sun awauhani le wabunagubai
Tuma efeintei to asefuhabaun

Dü hamuti giñe wagübürigu
Durunguaina lau linsiñe agairaü
Abihaina mama lau hitaü
Afidirabu luagu laiano insiñeni

Laguyuha:
Abihaina mama lau hitaü
Afidirabu luagu lalana insiñeni
Lau agairaü le hürü tumalali
Labagarida unguahabuni.

Bufanidiran murusun sairi
Ladahirai durari liharun
Tigirun ti lun le ibidioguabai
au
Lauchun ladaseiruni tewegeirun

Tau hanigi birahüññü luma
düwürügü
Inebela deregüdaguaü haun
Manurahantiñu luai lidere
würibu
Luagu hagaira luma hauiñe

Laguyuha:
Manurahantiñu luai lidere
würibu
Luagu hagaira luma habiñe
To hanigi lisaminan hawani
Tebudina agairaü hebudina

Balañu luagu lidüwürügü Ande
Lidangien lamuri biña barana
Labugien larüna funati luma
golu
Barumuga lau lirufungu ketüsali

Dunuru achiguli to lidanbaun
bidaünda .
Auniri hangitu lau bufulasun
Ubugua lun dari me Ian
lahamachun
Iñu Ian luai kondoru luma garun

Laguyuha:
Ubugua lun dari me lan
lahamachun
Iñu lan luai kondoru luma garun
Iñuraina dari sairi tidan
larüna
Wadimalu biri le mauwedibai

Garifuna Orthography

Towards A Commongarifuna Orthography

By E. ROY CAYETANO

Uaragua Wamamuga Luagu
Labürüdüniwa Wererun

June, 1992

Preface

This paper is the result of a study done while I was a Pearson Fellow at the Ontario Institute for Studies in Education in Toronto, Canada. It was something of an aside since it had nothing to do with the Fellowship, but being in Toronto gave me easy access to the University of Michigan which I had left four and a half years earlier with two credit hours short of a Master's Degree in Linguistics. Having also done my undergraduate work in Anthropology and Linguistics there I had done just about all the Linguistics courses the University had to offer. That, coupled with being resident in Toronto, meant that I had to settle for an independent study course.

This work is something that I had always wanted to do but somehow never had the time to begin. There has long been a need to standardize Garifuna Orthography. This is a task that only Garifuna People can undertake for, as history has shown, the work done by others is not intended for our temporal benefit and has therefore not done us much good.

It was my hope when I completed this paper in the Winter of 1981 that it would serve to initiate the search for a common orthography and that it would serve as a major contribution to the process. To that end, I distributed it as widely as my means would allow especially to interested acquaintances from Honduras and Guatemala. Pamela Wright, an Anthropologist friend, even presented it on my behalf at a Linguistics Conference in England!!

Today, one decade later, the National Garifuna Council of Belize has unearthed the paper and I am confident that the Garifuna Nation which cuts across national boundaries, is ready to pursue the matter of a standard orthography as a part of the common concern for preserving the language, retaining the identity, and promoting the general welfare of our people. It is expected that the spirit of cooperation that is sure to pervade the Garifuna Summit to be held in Los Angeles in July, 1992, will move the process forward.

I wish to acknowledge my debt of gratitude to Professor Ken Hill under whose supervision I undertook this study, and to IDRC, the Canadian Agency that awarded me the Pearson Fellowship that enabled me to take on this 'side' project.

My compadre Dr. Joseph Palacio has also been supportive, giving honest feedback on my occasional humble efforts and, in this case, he even kept his copy thus enabling the National Garifuna Council to 'unearth' it for an orthography course sponsored by the National Garifuna Council Secretariat when I could not find my last copy which I must have given out as an indefinite loan. I also wish to thank my wife, Phyllis, whose patience and endurance have been stretched to the limit these past two decades and not just to satisfy my need for a 'naive' native speaker. Finally, I must acknowledge the indirect contribution of CODE. That organization's generous support to the Garifuna Dictionary Project of the National Garifuna Council has facilitated and given new impetus to Belizean literacy efforts in Garifuna.

Writing Garifuna

When the first Europeans arrived in the West Indies, a few of the islands of the Lesser Antilles were inhabited by some people who called themselves "Callinago" or "Caliponam"1 and spoke a language which, because of the preponderance of Arawakan elements, is classified as an Arawakan language (Taylor 1977). Later in Saint Vincent the natives gave refuge to some shipwrecked and escaped African slaves and as a result of some intermarriage and the incorporation of that African element into the population, a new breed of Black Caribs arose, who adopted the language and to a great extent the culture of the original population. The Caribs, black and "yellow", greatly valued their freedom and fiercely resisted the efforts of the English and the French to dominate them until 1797 when they were finally routed and forcibly relocated to Roatan and the other Bay Islands off the coast of Honduras. It is believed that just over 2,000 persons were shipped from Saint Vincent.

The Garinagu or Garifuna2, as the deportees and their descendants called themselves, did not waste any time in moving to the mainland of Central America, first to Honduras, then on to Nicaragua, Guatemala and Belize. By the end of the year 1802, they had spread and were very much present as far north as Belize, to the extent that one of the English settlers felt compelled to write to the Magistrate of the Colony complaining that "he sees great danger in the presence in this settlement, so far from any assistance, of numerous "Charibs", he believes to the number of 150" (Burdon 1934).

Today, the Garifuna live in a number of towns and villages scattered along the Central American coast from Nicaragua to Belize. There does not seem to be any reliable indication as to how many inhabit the area, but in the mid 1950's it was estimated that they numbered about 30,000 (Meyers 1965). There also exist today, sizeable Garifuna communities in inland cities like Tegucigalpa in Honduras, Guatemala City, and some American cities like Los Angeles, New York City and Chicago.

The Garifuna people have been exposed to a number of different linguistic influences during the last three centuries. There are many instances of Spanish and French loanwords in Breton's dictionary which he compiled while working as a missionary in Dominica between 1637 and 1654. Many additional lexical items borrowed from Spanish, English and French have found their way into the language since then, and even today the influence of non-Garifuna languages and cultural institutions continue to be felt on Garifuna language and culture. Most of the people today are at least bi-lingual. In Belize they invariable speak English or the English-based Creole which is the lingua franca there, while in the other Central America countries the other language is Spanish which is the official language of those countries.

But the intrusion of English and Spanish has gone even further. As far as language preference is concerned, a growing number of Garifuna people are speaking English/Creole or Spanish as a first language and losing proficiency in Garifuna. Furthermore, the writing systems of English and Spanish have contributed to the differences between orthographies developed in Belize and those emerging from work done in Guatemala or Honduras.

The question is often asked if Garifuna is a written language. This question can be interpreted in at least two ways so that one can ask, firstly, if the people are literate in their language and, secondly, if written material is available in Garifuna. We will now consider each of these two questions.

The Garifuna have always had high regard for education, at times undergoing great hardships and privations to ensure that their children make use of educational opportunities that exist. Until recently children were often sent from Honduras and Guatemala to live with relatives and friends or even non-Garifuna acquaintances in Belize so that they might attend school "in the Colony". This practice seemed to have stemmed from the assumption that education obtained in the colony was superior and that it was desirable, even in the Spanish republics, that people be literate in English. In addition, it appears that Belize was ahead of both Honduras and Guatemala in the provision of free and compulsory primary education.

In spite of what has been said about the preference for and greater availability of education in Belize, the Garifuna in Honduras and Guatemala have made great use of the educational facilities to which they have access. As a result, even in the absence of the relevant statistics, one can claim with some confidence that the Garifuna have for a long time been among the most literate people of the region. In fact, the pioneering work of Garifuna men in the early expansion of education in Belize is widely acknowledged. They, more than others, were willing to take up the challenge of accepting teaching positions all over the country and enduring the hardships involved in working even in the remotest villages in the country.

Unfortunately, the price that they have had to pay for involvement in education has been very high. No regard is given to their cultural background even in the few schools which, because of their location, cater exclusively to Garifuna populations. Indeed, stories abound of instances in which the use of the language was actively discouraged or frowned upon by religious and education workers (often one and the same). So the Garifuna was schooled so that he became literate in English or Spanish and in many cases learnt to disassociate himself with his own language which the school at best pretended did not exist. When the young men with the greatest intellectual promise were sent to other villages as school teachers, they and their dependents went not as Garifuna families but as representatives of an alien culture, to teach the language, the lore and the religion of a foreign dominant power. The results have been devastating as Joseph Palacio demonstrated in a paper entitled "Problems in the Maintenance of the Garifuna Culture".

The Garifuna, therefore, although reasonably well schooled and literate in English and Spanish, is generally illiterate in his own language. There are a few persons who are able to read and write the language but these are exceptions that exist in spite of the schooling received. Also, these are usually persons who have a special interest in some aspect of Garifuna life or are involved in the movement resulting from a recent rebirth of interest and pride in their Garifuna identity and heritage.

The second question has to do with the availability of written material in Garifuna. In so far as published material is concerned, there is very little, a fact which is not at all surprising given the traditional attitude of the educational institutions towards the language and the culture. The school just did not foster among teachers or students the sort of interest that would have had to precede attempts to write the language and the production of literature in it. Nor could the products of the educational systems concerned produce written material in the language even if they were so inclined, for they had not been taught to read, let along write it. The dearth of written material in Garifuna and the inability of the people (although literate in English or Spanish) to read and write their own language were mutually reinforcing, a state affairs which has generally lasted up to the present.

A great deal of anthropological fieldwork (mostly as research for Ph. D dissertations) has been done among the Garifuna, but not many studies have been done in the field of linguistics. Nonetheless, the work of three scholars is generally well known to linguists interested in the language. These are Douglas Taylor, Richard Hadel S.J., following on the work commenced by John Stochl S.J. at Saint John's College in Belize City, and Ilah Flemming who together with Lillian Howland work for the Summer Institute of Linguistics.

Douglas Taylor's work is perhaps the best known. Taylor did anthropological fieldwork in Hopkins, a village in Belize, and in 1951 published an ethnography entitled "The Black Carib Of British Honduras". His linguistic work includes a large number of papers on Arawakan and Cariban linguistics, among them several papers on different aspects of "Island Carib" and "Central American Carib", published in a number of reputable journals and other publications. Unfortunately, Taylor's work is of no use to the average Garifuna, partly because it was pitched to a scholarly audience specialized in linguistics, and partly because it did not include text that would be of interest to the people. In other words, Taylor did not write Garifuna; he wrote about it. And he did not write for the Garifuna; he wrote about them. He did not even give any thought to the matter of an orthography for Garifuna and was content to use the sound letter correspondences from his phonological analysis with no regard for other considerations as will be shown later. Taylor's work was not intended for Garifuna readers, his linguistic publications are generally not available in the area, and his best known work which is an ethnography, a monograph with a chapter on language and a glossary, has limited availability and is known only to a small number of Garifuna scholars.

Towards the end of the 1940's a group of Garifuna students at Saint John's College in Belize City, working under the supervision of Father John Stochl S.J., compiled a small Garifuna- English Dictionary. This was the first work that had the potential for stimulating interest and serving as a tool in promoting literacy in Garifuna. Yet this was not to be, for very few copies were printed (with a spirit duplicator) and the dictionary did not become available to the general public. Two decades later, Father Richard Hadel S.J., while doing anthropological fieldwork in Seine Bight, Belize, collected, with the assistance of Roman Zuniga, additional material and enlarged and re-designed the dictionary and had it published in three volumes in limited mimeograph edition again by Saint John's College. Again this work had the disadvantage of not being available for general consumption, firstly, because the cost was prohibitive and, secondly, because like the original edition not enough copies were printed. It is regrettable that this monumental work from Saint John's College could not have found its way to schools and libraries at least in Garifuna towns and villages, not to mention Garifuna homes, for this failure defeats whatever useful purpose it could have had for the people and relegates the work and the people to the status of mere curios to be viewed and examined for the sole purpose of satisfying the curiosity and the equally irrelevant (for the speakers of the language) academic needs of others.

Next to be considered is work done in Guatemala by the Summer Institute of Linguistics. The work is done by Ilah Flemming who, together with Lillian Howland, began studying Garifuna in Livingston, a Garifuna township, in 1952. Those familiar with the SIL know that it is an American based organization dedicated to bringing God to the "heathen" peoples of the world by making the bible available to them in their native languages. Thus the linguistic work done by the members of the organization is subservient to the higher goal of developing orthographies to translate the bible and making these translations available to the people. Garifuna material produced by the SIL is divided into two categories: the technical works and the vernacular works. The former are the works that would be of interest primarily to linguists and are invariably written in English or Spanish; the latter comprise material written for the speakers of the language and typically include translations of the books from the bible and a few folk stories thrown in for good measure. Quite a number of books with biblical translations in Garifuna have been made available to the people especially in Guatemala. There are also a few booklets that can be considered as readers with some úraga (Garifuna folk tales).

The SIL material has the distinction of being the only one of the three listed above to be intended for use by the people. It includes material that is written in the language and published and distributed in a manner, which, it is hoped, would make it easily available to whoever wants it. This follows logically from the objectives of the organization. However, the organization does not seem to be engaged in much direct effort to make the people literate in the language. The assumption is that if the bible is available to the people in their language it will be easier for them to receive the word of God. There are a few problems attendant on this position, however, at least where the Belizean Garifuna is concerned. Firstly, the vast majority of the people are Roman Catholic or Methodist, and only those who are converted into the "born again" churches are likely to develop a strong interest in the bible. Secondly, those who are motivated to read the bible in Garifuna are already literate in English or Spanish and would find it easier and less painful to read the English or Spanish version. Thirdly, the aim is cultural imperialism rather than the more desirable goal of cultural liberation which can be attained through literacy. It is my view that in spite of the abundance of vernacular works that have been produced by the SIL, it has failed to have an impact on literacy in Garifuna.

There have also been some lesser works produced in Garifuna. I refer to them as lesser works for several reasons. They lack international prestige, they are limited in their distribution, and scope, and are usually ad hoc in nature. The Roman Catholic Church in Dangriga, Belize, has commissioned several translations of masses and excerpts from the bible to be read in the mass, but these lack internal consistency both in terms of the orthography, and the quality or type of the translations. There was also an excellent anthology of Garifuna poems "Chuluha Dan", edited by Roy Cayetano, but this was a one-shot effort whose greatest value lies in making Garifuna readers aware of the sort of work that can be produced when people respond to the creative urge in their own language.

One major obstacle to the development of a body of literature in Garifuna is the lack of a standardized orthography. Practically each person who writes the language has to create his own, drawing on his own experience in writing (usually English or Spanish), with the result that there are nearly as many orthographies as there are persons who have attempted to write the language. Thus, we often find the same word written in several different ways; for example, the name of the most important religious ritual is written as dogo (Taylor), dugu (Wells 1980), and dügü (S.J.C.). To complicate the matter even further, anthropologists and other transients, in their written reports and other papers, record words some of which their foreign ears have not apprehended correctly, but which once written, carry the brand of authority usually accorded to scholarship and the printed word.

Nevertheless, a great deal of benefit can be gleaned from the work already done by what can be referred to as the three traditions mentioned above, namely, the Taylor, the Saint John's College (S.J.C.), and the Summer Institute of Linguistics (SIL) traditions. Although they all have their weaknesses when regarded from the point of view of the speakers of the language, each is the fruit of a great deal of linguistic knowledge and scholarship. Consequently, each is being regarded here as a contributor to what is hoped will emerge as a standardized orthography that will be available to writers of the language, at least in Belize but possibly elsewhere as well.

In the remainder of this paper, I will attempt to accomplish two tasks. Firstly, to review existing orthographies, that is to say, orthographies developed by or reflecting the three traditions. This will necessarily entail some examination of the assumptions and the phonological analyses and other considerations on which they are based. Secondly, the orthographies will be compared and elements tabulated to illustrate the points of convergence and divergence. Such a comparison will provide the basis for the real purpose of this exercise, which is to propose an orthography that will draw on the strengths, and hopefully overcome the weaknesses, of the three traditions.

But, one may ask, what practical benefit would this have for the Garifuna? After all, it will be recalled that the three traditions have been criticized on the grounds that their potential for utility for the people have not been realized. It is believed that this brief study is necessary and will be useful for several reasons. To begin with, it is one way of making up for the major disadvantage of existing work on Garifuna, namely, limited circulation. The review of the orthographies will make readers more aware of the existing orthographies and their semi-technical aspects. Because the means now exist for reaching a wider audience than ever before outside of the Garifuna Community, especially in Belize, reaching the majority of Garifuna teachers, scholars, and organisations is a more realistic objective than ever before. There are periodicals with fairly large circulation in Belize including "Belizean Studies" and, "The Journal of Belizean Affairs" which provide a forum for the exchange and dissemination of scholarly ideas. Some universities abroad subscribe to these periodicals. The review of the three traditions can therefore serve for many as a systematic introduction to Garifuna writing so that even if individuals continue to device their own orthographies, it is likely that the result would do more justice to the language and be more internally consistent.

The greatest benefit, however, resides in the fact that the final section can make a significant contribution to standardizing Garifuna orthography by proposing one that can gain widespread acceptance in the international Garifuna community, or serve as the basis for a dialogue involving different sectors of the community, thereby resulting in the development of such an orthography.

Those who are familiar with the socio-linguistic realities of Garifuna communities may question the utility of taking measures to make the people literate in the language, let alone to standardize the orthography. To support such a position a number of points, some of which have been mentioned above, can be raised as arguments. It can be argued that:

1 The majority of the people are already literate in at least one other language, the official language of their country of residence.

2 They do not need to be able to read and write the language to be able to communicate effectively in writing.

3 There is not much written literature in the language.

4 At the present rate of acculturation, it is not likely that there will be a Garifuna speech community after the next fifty years.

These and possibly a number of other such arguments are difficult if not quite impossible to refute, and some are even self-evident. Nonetheless, the Garifuna, although conscious and proud of their national identity as Belizeans, Guatemalans, or Hondurans, have, especially in recent years, become acutely aware and conscious of their cultural identity and heritage so that a new value is being placed on the distinctive elements of that heritage. As a consequence of this new awareness and the resultant revaluation, a number of movements and organizations have been developed, which because of the nature of their activities have found the ability to read and write Garifuna not only desirable but necessary for at least some of their members.

The National Garifuna Council is an example of an umbrella organisation in Belize that sponsors a host of Garifuna cultural events and activities including dance, drama, speech, poetry, and other talent contests. In these and other activities leading up to Garifuna Day Celebrations (observed throughout Belize on the 19th November) the need for literacy often arises, as in translating and preparing Garifuna masses, composing and teaching new hymns, writing and preparing speeches and poetry for publication or for use in contests, writing labels for items in exhibitions, producing leaflets and booklets for distribution, and making banners with messages in Garifuna, to name only a few.

Another area of endeavour and concern that requires literacy in the language preferably with the sort of consistency that can be offered by a standardized orthography is the area of cultural retrieval. Granted that the language may not survive the next fifty years, it becomes necessary for the sake of posterity that as much as possible of the language, culture and lore of the people be captured, collected or otherwise recorded using as many different media as are available. Among the items that can be recorded in writing are úraga (stories usually told in the context of wakes), songs, of which there are literally thousands, proverbs, and accounts by key persons, in their own words, of their roles, their activities, their history as a people, and different aspects of life in their villages. A number of persons are interested in this task of cultural retrieval and obviously their self-confidence would be bolstered considerably if they had some guidelines they could follow in attempting to write the language. It is also obvious that the more uniform the spelling system, the easier it will be to read or otherwise work with the material that is recorded, especially for persons who, as may be the case of the Garifuna of the future, do not have the linguistic competence of present day native speakers.

The Three Orthographic Traditions

The Taylor Tradition

Douglas Taylor is perhaps the one anthropologist who has collected the most data, done the most analysis, and published the most on what he calls Island Carib and Central American Island Carib (Garifuna). His work is generally quite thorough although it must be noted that his analyses are more often than not diachronic in nature. However, with regard to the language as it is today spoken in Central America generally, or even Hopkins Village specifically, his work should be viewed with caution, partly because his knowledge of earlier forms in the language keeps intruding on his perceptions of what the people were actually saying, and partly because of what I believe are errors in his transcription.

Consonants

Taylor lists the consonantal phonemes of Garifuna as follows (Taylor 1977):

```
m n - -
b d - g
p t c k
f s - h
- l r -
```

He describes these as being pronounced approximately as in English, except for /c/ which "varies freely between the sound of 'ch' in 'church' and that of 'sh' in 'shut'". Conspicuously absent are /w/ and /y/. Also absent is the palatal nasal ñ. It is with regard to these three that Taylor departs most dramatically from the other two traditions, and practically all other persons who have tried to write Garifuna. We will return to the glides when we consider vowels. As for the ñ, there is ample support for Taylor's position that there is no such consonantal phoneme in Garifuna. What do exist are nasal vowels and certain vowel sequences namely, ie, ia, iu, and io, which, when nasalised, sufficiently resemble sound sequences containing the palatal nasal to lead most people who write Garifuna to use ñ, which they are familiar with from Spanish, and write these sequences as iñe, iña, iño, and iñu.

Vowels

According to Taylor the simple vocalic phonemes include i, e, a, o, u, and v, which is the nasalized counterpart of any of the five oral vowels. The simple oral vowels /i/, /e/, /a/, and /u/ "have so-called continental values, as in Spanish, but vary from a close to a more open sound according to position and stress, /u/ being occasionally heard as a close 'o'; /o/ is a high back unrounded vowel ï ë". Taylor's /o/ is what SIL and S.J.C. write as /ü/. The ten simple oral and nasal vowels are listed below together with some words in which the vowels occur.

i ígiri (nose) anígi (heart)
e eméragua (to rest) eiéri (male)
a adúlu (porridge) arári (octopus)
o óho (pus) hóro (crab) óma (road)
u ubáu (world) uéiu (sun)
i híaru (woman) herígi (beach crab)
e gurétu (plantain porridge) eréga (say)
a ba (socks) fulásu (plank)
u su (all) gúfara (cohune leaves used for thatch)
o iróhere (fishing line) gaiógiru (she's still a virgin

In his concern for economy Taylor has failed to include / / (or some other representation of it) in his phonemic inventory, possibly because there are not many instances of its occurrence. Nonetheless, uh bu, k pu, b nu, f nu, and the ever present demonstrative/relative pronoun t , and names like M d d and D d must be accounted for by any orthography.

Compound Vowels and Semi-vowels

Taylor lists the following as compound phonemes. Examples of words containing them are given as well:

ie eiéri (male) faníe (basket) asíedu (plate)
ia iauára (cohune palm) iáiaua (pineapple)
io ioródo (hummingbird)
iu hiúruha (spirit-helper) saiu (sack)
Iurumai (St Vincent)
uo uori (woman) uobu (mountain)
ua luágu (on it) úati (there isn't) masíua (fish trap)
ue ueiu (sun) ueue (tree) agíueriha (to carve)
ui uira (calabash tree) hauaui (kingfish)

ei erei (strength) agolei (oil, fat, grease)
          isubusei (mirror)

ai sairi (After life) aiga (to eat) agai (womb,   container)
ao háo (ants) aronao (arm) halao (chair)
au áuca (to try) hanau ("old wife" - a fish)
   urinauga (yesterday)

The first eight compound vowels listed above are the ones involved in any discussion having to do with the status of [y] and [w] in Garifuna. Taylor argues that phonemically what we have in Garifuna are /i/ and /u/, and that what may appear to some as [y] and [w] are simply variants of the phonemes /i/ and /u/ respectively (Taylor 1955:241). But while this is all very well phonemically, in practice it does not make much orthographic sense. In fact, it creates problems that Taylor himself does not seem to be aware of. Those eight so-called compound vowels often behave like consonant -vowel sequences, in other words, as ye, ya, yo, yu, wo, wa, we, and wi. But because Taylor insists on treating /i/ and /u/ as vocalic phonemes at all times he ends up writing words like iaiaua and iáuara such that syllable boundaries are difficult if not impossible for any reader who is not already proficient in the language to distinguish. The importance of this becomes clear when one considers the rules of accentuation that Taylor uses and are outlined below. Thus one may rightly ask: In iáiaua, is the accent marked because ia is the first syllable? Or is it because ia is di-syllabic and the accent is intended to show that? In iauara, which is the second syllable? a? au? u? or ua? Notice that this would not be a problem if the words were written thus: yayawa and yawara. We will return to this matter in Chapter 3 when we will propose a means of reconciling the result of Taylor's phonemic analysis with regards to /i/ and /u/ on the one hand, and the orthographic usefulness of consonants as syllable boundary markers on the other.

Taylor perceives ei and ai as two separate compound vowels. This does not seem to be the case, though, for [ei] can be used to replace [ai] in each of its occurrences. Indeed, it appears that Taylor tends to use/ei/ in word final position and /ai/ elsewhere!

Finally, Taylor missed the /ou/ /au/ distinction. Because he uses au to represent what SIL writes as ou, he is not able to capture au as in nauba (it will be with me) as opposed to nouba (my side).

Nasalisation

Taylor says that "it (nasality) may adhere to a particular vowel or a given morpheme; or it may in other cases shift or be lost with a change of environment". Thus, according to his analysis, nasalisation is constant (i.e., it does not shift) in the first vowel of íu (high) and hiaru (woman) but not so in io (hymen) or lia (he says). In gaiógiru (she's still a virgin) and itara lia ti (it is thus), there is a loss of one nasalization and strengthening of another correlated with shift of stress. As further examples of the elusive nature of nasalization in Garifuna, Taylor gives the following:

1 In uí-ba (whistle!) ? íuira (to whistle nasalization moves from stem to prefix.

2 In ugúie leà gue leà (today, now) in slow and rapid speech respectively, it clings to the only remaining syllabic vowel.

3 In áha (yes, agreed) ? mahati (he is unwilling) and sú (all, every) ? ásura (to finish) it is completely lost.

4 In núi (my meat) ? úi (meat) bisabadu (your shoes) ? sabadu (shoes), it constitutes a morph.

These examples demonstrate some of the problems in Taylor's work and should not be left without comment.

1 íuira (to whistle) can also be written íuira, íuira or íuira, a fact that Taylor seems to have overlooked.

2 ugúie leà and gué leà are not identical in meaning. The former means today and the latter means now. One is, therefore, not necessarily derived from the other.

3 áha is not nasalized on the second vowel.

sú and asura are not related forms, so it should not be claimed that one is derived from the other.

4 núi and bisabadu do not end with nasalized vowels. The final vowels are strongly voiced and this is what may have been mistaken for nasalisation. The final vowels in sabadu and úi (as in a large number of words in Garifuna) are at best only slightly voiced.

However, the shifting and elusive nature of nasalization in vowel sequences and sometimes across syllables cannot be disputed, and a lot is lost when one tries, as Taylor does, to tie it to particular vowels. This can be done successfully only when one is dealing with simple nasal vowels unencumbered by proximity to other vowels as in sego (five), sadi (sickness), and arasera (to get ready).

Taylor does not posit the existence of a velar or a palatal nasal consonant, but points out that "a nasalized vowel may approximate, in some environments, to an oral vowel followed by a labial, apical, palatal or velar nasal consonant". He also notes that where the nasalized vowel i is followed by semi-vowel off-glide, as many speakers pronounce it as an oral vowel followed by "an incomplete palatal nasal ñ" as there are who pronounce it as a nasal vowel. (Taylor, 1955).

Stress

Stress is not predictable and is therefore phonemic. Taylor claims that "the functional yield of this opposition (stressed unstressed) is not great; and, as is the case with English 'adult adult', forms are to be found in whose pronunciation different speakers employ different accentuations". With regard to the first claim - that the functional yield of the opposition is not great - there are lots of minimal pairs apart from the few poor examples given by Taylor which suggest otherwise (Taylor 1955). Consider the following to which a large number of additional examples can be added:

águra (to throw)   agúra (touch)
ágüra (to bite)   agüra (to tie)
ábürüha (to fall)   abürüha (to write)
ámura (to defecate)   amüra (to arrive)

ádaha (to push)   adáha (to make forms)
áriha (to doze)   aríha (to see)
íbiri (waist)   ibíri (sibling)
úbaraü (finger or toe nails) ubáraü (place)
dúru (offence)   durú (thick, measles)
fùna (maybe)   funá (ripe)
híu (thorn)   hiú (cassava beer)
núma (with me)   numá (my friend)

Nor is it accurate to say that "different speakers employ different accentuations". What may appear to be arbitrary or idiosyncratic shifts in accentuation may well be grammatically motivated; for example:

fegébei bagu (open your eyes)
fége lianli lagu (he's just opened his eyes)

Taylor correctly points out that in most words having three or more syllables, the stress falls on the second syllable and then on every third syllable; e.g. sabadu, nisábadu; warígabagaba (butterfly), nuwárigabágaba (my butterfly). Words with two syllables are usually stressed on the first syllable, while monosyllabic words pronounced in isolation are invariably stressed.

The Sil Tradition

Unfortunately it has not been possible to obtain the phonemic analysis on which the SIL orthographic tradition is based. Indeed, it does not appear that such an analysis has ever been published by the SIL, so that our examination of this tradition will necessarily be confined to the orthography itself as employed in some published Garifuna texts and the very brief orthographic note in "According to our Ancestors" edited by Mary Shaw.

Because the SIL fieldworkers did their study of Garifuna in Livingston, Guatemala, they use Spanish pronunciation as a basis for comparison when explaining Garifuna phonology, and the orthography of Spanish has a definite influence on their choice of symbols in writing the language.

Consonants

The following are the consonants used in the SIL orthography:

b bena (door)
d darádu (agreement)
g giárati (possible)
p pasu (a walk)
t to (this)   tuei (from her)
ch chülüti (it arrived)
c,k,q catei (thing), laik (like), quei (like)
m mudún (Sheep)
n nugúferan (my compadre)
f funa (maybe)
s seru (expensive)
j jarúga (tomorrow)
l luja (it is swollen)
r arári (octopus)
ñ ñei (there)
w weyu (day, sun)
y yara (over there)

According to the orthographic note (Shaw 1971:308) these consonants conform to Spanish pronunciation with the exception of b, d, and g which are always voiced as in English (bed, dog, go). Also, n in consonant clusters represents not a consonant but nasalization on the preceding vowel(s). In the same way, perhaps ñ should not be considered a consonant since here again "it indicates a nasalized 'y' or 'i'".

With regard to the choice of symbols for consonants, the use of j for /h/; k, c, or qu for /k/; and ñ for /y/, or /i/, demonstrate the attempt to conform to Spanish orthography. However, it is difficult to find justification for the use of the different symbols to represent the phoneme /k/. Even though there may be variation in the pronunciation of the sound represented by these different symbols as in quei, catei and Maskin lus his chipskin, there is certainly no distinctive opposition to justify the use of three different symbols, and the only motivation for this seems to be the Spanish model where the first two are concerned, and the English model in the case of the third. If the explanation for the use of k in such words as Maskin, chipskin and laik is that these are borrowed and that the spelling should conform to the spelling in the source language, then one would expect the same principle to apply to amicsira from English to mix.

Another puzzling choice of symbol is the use of c instead of ch in a few words like jucu (to throw down) and lajucurunu (his throwing her down).

Vowels

The SIL list of simple vowels include:

i íweruja (to steal) lisímisin (his shirt)
e tebéneri (her doorway) le (this) egéyeda (to turn)
a abínaja (to dance) ádara (to push)
o to (this) ódi (or) mosu (must)
u úraga (story) murusu (a little)
u üruwa (three) ümada (on the road) sügüti (he passed)

Each of the above cited vowels also occurs as a nasalized vowel in which case it is written as follows:

in ínwira (to whistle) liábin (his coming)
en wen (twenty) sensu (money)
an lan (his) agánba (to hear) asánsira (to change)
on gónwere (basket tie-tie)
un lun (to him) sun (all) mudún (sheep
ün günta (she's tightened it) ladaürun (its striking)

The compound vowels include the following:

ie (ye) gürígie (people) yegü (my pet)
ia (ya) ligía (he) giára (able, possible) yara (there)
iu (yu) sabiu (wise person) yuga (sweet cassava)
   (yü) yürüdü (hummingbird)

ua (wa) tuágu (on her) garáragua (turn around) wama (with us)
ui (wi) wanúi (gossip) wira (calabash tree)
ue (we) gue to (now)   wewe (tree, wood)
  (wü) würi (female)

ei jawéi (from them) éibuga (to walk)
ai badáira (you find)

au bau (with you)   au (I) tauba (it will be with her)
ou touba (her side) bougudi (outside)

aü ñüraüraü (small) ladaüragun (his clothes)

In the orthographic note in "According to our Ancestors" it is clearly implied that the vowels listed above conform to Spanish pronunciation. Nothing is said about/ü/ although there is no such sound or symbol in Spanish speech or writing. This is most likely due to an oversight on the part of the author so we will not belabour the point. Suffice it to say that /ü/ is an unrounded high back vowel, the same as Taylor's /o/.

It will also be noted that, unlike Taylor, the SIL tradition allows for the existence of the round mid-back vowel / / for which the phonemic symbol /o/ is reserved. This tradition, therefore, has a six-vowel system and can therefore adequately represent such words as:

to (this), mosu (must) and fonu (thing), which are problematic for Taylor.

There are not many instances of /o/ (phonetic [o]) but, as shown above, it does exist and must be accounted for in any phonemic analysis of Garifuna. There are also not many instances of/en/ and /on/, but the investigator has to be careful not to confuse those sounds with the diphthongs /ein/ and /oun/ respectively. ([e] and [o] do not occur in Garifuna except as [ei] and [ou]). Even though pronunciation is admittedly not uniform in all Garifuna communities and there are consequently some phonetic differences between the Garifuna of Livingston and that of say Barranco or Hopkins Village, it is evident that the SIL investigators did on occasion perceive and record /ei/ as /e/, especially when nasalized as in: wen (twenty) and sensu (money) instead of wein and seinsu.

The SIL orthography captures a necessary distinction between /ou/ and /au/ as in touba (her side) and tauba (it will be with her). The other two traditions use /au/ in both instances. However, one wonders about the use of /ai/ as in adaira (to find), for this does not appear to be any more than a variant of /ei/.

Since it was not possible to obtain an SIL phonemic analysis of Garifuna, one cannot say whether this tradition regards [y] and [w] as being identical with phonemic /i/ and /u/ respectively. Nonetheless, whatever their position in this matter, it is possible, as will be demonstrated in the final section of this paper, to specify the conditions under which Taylor's /i/ and /u/ become y and w in the SIL (as well as the S.J.C.) orthographic tradition.

Nasalization

The SIL orthographic note on nasality is reproduced below:

n, when it occurs at the end of a syllable, indicates that the preceding vowel or vowel cluster is nasalized:

lidi is written lidin
nanagu is written nanángun
tidou is written tidoun

ñ indicates a nasalized 'y' or 'i':

ligiarügüyei is written ligiarügüñei
yei is written ñei
lubie is written lubiñei (sic)
tariagu is written tariñagun
jiáruraü is written jiñáruraü

The first rule, namely that of using n at the end of a syllable to indicate nasality on the preceding vowels is quite reasonable. This practice has the advantage of being flexible in the sense that it does not try to restrict nasalization to specific vowels, but rather recognises nasalization as a shifting phenonemon within a syllable or even across syllables depending on how "tightly sealed" the syllable boundary is. My own analysis shows that "hard" consonants seal syllable boundaries tightly, semi-vowels [y] and [w] less so, and in the absence of either a consonant or a semi-vowel, nasality can shift freely from one syllable to another in different utterances of the same word by the same speaker.

The use of ñ, to indicate nasality can be used equally well in at least some of those instances for which SIL uses ñ. For example: taríangun, lubien and jiánruraü instead of taríñagun, lubiñe and jiñáruraü. In the other instances where it replaces the nasal palatal glide "y", the use of n is more defensible on the grounds that the use of the first rule would necessitate the use of two symbols, y and n instead of just one, ñ. For example: ligíarügüyein instead of ligíarügüñei.

Stress

The only comment in the SIL orthographic note on stress is that "stress, unless marked otherwise, occurs on the first syllable of two-syllable words". Nothing is said about words with more than two syllables although a general rule can be formulated so that here again only the exceptions would need to be marked. (See above to compare with Taylor's conclusions, and see remarks on stress in Chapter 3 below). The SIL practice is to mark stress on all words with more than two syllables, and on words with two syllables if stressed on the second syllable.

The St. John's College Tradition

The Saint John's College orthographic tradition dates back to the latter part of the 1940's and Father John Stochl S.J. was the driving force behind it. About twenty five years later it was revitalized by Father Richard Hadel S.J. with the publication of his enlarged and revised version of the original S.J.C. English - Garifuna Dictionary in 1975. Like the SIL tradition it does not appear that the S.J.C. tradition is based on the kind of phonemic analysis that Taylor made and published. The newer edition of the dictionary devotes two pages to explaning the orthography: on the first page, the consonants and their English equivalents are listed, and the second page lists the vowels and provides a brief explication of nasalization and stress. Thus here again, because of the absence (or unavailability) of a phonemic analysis, our study of this tradition will necessarily be limited to an examination of the orthography as employed in the dictionary and other written texts.

There is a great deal of similarity between this and the SIL tradition. Consequently, we will be brief in dealing with this tradition, and thereby avoid unnecessary repetition. The points of convergence and divergence especially with SIL will be mentioned in passing.

Consonants

Page iii of the revised edition of the S.J.C. dictionary is reproduced below. It lists the symbols used for consonants in the orthography, their phonetic equivalents, and some English words to illustrate those phonetic values.

Pronunciation Consonants

Carib	Phonemic Symbol	English
b	/b/	bill
d	/d/	dill
f	/f/	fill

g	/g/	gill
h	/h/	hill
k	/k/	kill
l	/l/	lil
m	/m/	mill
n	/n/	nil
p	/p/	pill
r	/r/	rill
s	/s/	sill
t	/t/	till
w	/w/	will
y	/y/	yet
ch	/c/ /s/	chill shall
j (foreign loan words only)	/j/	Jill
ñ	/ñ/	-

Notice that like the SIL, S.J.C. includes /w/ and /y/ in its phonemic inventory. Indeed, except for the S.J.C. use of an addition symbol j to accommodate "foreign loan words" with [dz] and some minor differences in the choice of symbols, the two lists of consonants are identical.

The need for /j/ in the phonemic inventory is, to my mind, highly questionable. Historically, words containing that sound were changed to conform to Garifuna phonology and in the process [dz] ? [s]. I do not believe that a sound can be regarded as a phoneme of a language until it is accepted and tolerated in much the same way that a word cannot be regarded as a part of the lexicon of the language until it has been incorporated into the phonology of the language by undergoing the necessary changes. I cannot think of any word in Garifuna that would warrant the inclusion of /j/ among its phonemes. (Notice that this is not the SIL /j/, which is the Spanish equivalent of the English /h/).

Vowels

The S.J.C. orthography indicates that the language is analysed as having six simple oral vowels. These are listed on page iv of the dictionary as follows:

Carib Phonemic Symbol English
- a /a/ father
- e /e/ (mid-front, unrounded)
- i /i/ meet
- ü /i/ (lower-high central, unrounded)
- o /o/ boat
- u /u/ boot

With regard to the phonetic value of the vowels, the vowels are all somewhat lower than their supposed English equivalents. They are more comparable to the Spanish values as both Taylor and the SIL point out.

It will be noted that this vowel system is identical to the SIL version. The same is also true of the nasalized simple vowels, so nothing further will be said about them.

The following are listed as diphthongs: ai, ei, aü, au, ui, and ua. However, an examination of the material reveals that the following is a more complete set of compound vowels:

ie (ye) iérehani (scorn) iédeme (regret) yegü (my pet)
ia (ya) surúsia (doctor) niárati (my ability) ya (here)
   (yü) yürüdü (hummingbird)
iu (yu) yúdi (my meat)
   (wu) wügüri (man)

ua (wa) úati (there is none) wáti (he called) suámein   (to admire)
ui (wi) úi (meat) núi (my meat) wíri (our name)
ue (we) duéiti (debt) hasúere (adz) weréwere (housefly)

ei   abúleigua (to waste) ugúnei (boat)
ai   wáiriti (it is big) urúai (king)

au   laúba (its side) láuguati (it is not enough)
aü   iríchau (truth) huráraü (game) aürüda (to spread)

Like the other two traditions, S.J.C. orthography uses ei and ai as two distinct compound vowels. Since this issue has been discussed, it will be sufficient to repeat here that those two are not distinct in Garifuna and that, as they can be used interchangeably, there is no justification for retaining the two in any orthography for the language.

au is used for the compound vowel that SIL orthography represents as ou. This has the effect of making the ou au distinction difficult to represent in this tradition which ends up ignoring it. The words that the SIL tradition would write as touba (her side) and tauba (it will be with her), would both be written as tauba by S.J.C.

The remaining vowels in the list are identical to their SIL counterparts.

Nasalization

Two rules for nasalization of vowels are given and these are again reproduced below (Hadel 1975 :pg.iv):

298

1 (V) ñ V ? (V) ñ V (both the vowel preceding and that following ñ are nasalized, e.g. haña ? haña)

2 V N { } ? V { } (a vowel preceding a nasal followed by another consonant or word ending is pronounced as a nasalized vowel; the nasal consonant is not pronounced e.g. nun ? nu   lámbara ? labara   but, gumánana and bímena remain unchanged.

Actually, these are orthographic rules designed to show how nasalization of vowels can be recovered (in reading) and the difference between nasals used as consonants and those used as a means of indicating nasality on vowels. However, they are also of interest because of their phonological implications, especially in the absence of the phonemic analysis on which the orthography is based. The first rule, for example, indicates that /ñ/ is here considered a consonantal phoneme and that nasality on the preceding and succeeding vowels is conditioned; that is, conditioned by proximity to /ñ/. This position is markedly different from that of the other two traditions and, in my view, erroneous. The second rule reflects, and capitalises on, Garifuna word structure which tolerates very few consonant clusters and never allows consonants in word final position.

Even though the S.J.C. use of ñ stems from entirely different phonological assumptions, SIL and S.J.C. orthographic conventions with regard to nasalization are virtually identical. The only difference is that S.J.C. uses both n and m to indicate nasalization on vowels, while SIL employs n even when the following consonant is a bi-labial as in lanbara (wire). In view of this similarity, the remarks made concerning the treatment of nasalization in the SIL tradition are equally applicable to the S.J.C. orthography.

Stress

"Stress must be included among the phonemes of Carib since it is sometimes critical in determining the meaning of a word (compare English cóntent and contént): áriha 'doze' and aríha 'see'; ábürüha 'drop, fall' and abürüha 'write'".

The above quotation from the revised dictionary is all that the S.J.C. tradition has to say about stress in Garifuna. It must now be clear from Taylor's analysis and, to a lesser extent, from his treatment of stress, that this S.J.C. comment is certainly inadequate. Also unnecessary is the practice in this tradition of marking stress on every word, in view of the fact that general rules can be formulated to predict accentuation on most words on the bases of syllable structure and number of syllables. We will return to this in the next chapter when we make proposals for a new orthography.

Towards A New Orthography

Having taken a look at each of the three main orthographic traditions, we can now compare them and propose a new orthography that will incorporate the strengths of the three traditions and provide alternatives to what are perceived in Chapter 2 as their weaknesses. Each of the following aspects will be considered in turn: consonants, simple oral and nasal vowels, compound vowels and semi-vowels, nasalization, and stress.

Consonants

The following chart is a comparison of the three traditions in terms of the consonants they consider as existing in the language, and the symbols they use to represent those consonants. Also included are the symbols proposed for the new orthography (except those choices that require some explanation).

TAYLOR	SIL	S.J.C.	PROPOSED
b	b	b	b
d	d	d	d
f	f	f	f
g	g	g	g
h	j	h	
k	c, k, qu	k	
l	l	l	l
m	m	m	m
n	n	n	n
p	p	p	p
r	r	r	r
s	s	s	s
t	t	t	t
-	w	w	
-	y	y	
c	ch, c	ch	
j (in loan words)			
-	ñ (nasal semi vowel)	ñ	

There is agreement on eleven of these consonants: b, d, g, f, l, m, n, p, r, s, and t. These would therefore remain unchanged in the new orthography. This leaves a total of seven other possible consonants to which we will now turn our attention. In the case of three of these the disagreement lies not in the existence of the phonemes in question, but in the choice of symbols to represent them. The other four have to do with differences in the phonological assumptions that underly the orthographies.

TAYLOR	SIL	S.J.C.	PROPOSED
h	j	h	h, j
k'	c, k, qu	k	k
c	c	ch	ch
_	w	w	w
_	y	y	y
-	-	j (in loan words)	-
-	ñ (nasal semi vowel)	ñ	-

It is obvious that it is because of social reasons, specifically the influence of Spanish orthography, and the goal of acceptability to authorities in Guatemala, where the SIL studies of Garifuna were done, and Honduras, where the majority of Garifuna people live, that the SIL chose j as the symbol for the phoneme that Taylor and S.J.C. write as h. This must also be the motivation for the use of c in most instances, and qu in a few, instead of k which is used only in English loan or foreign words. But even though the importance of the social goals of orthographies cannot be ignored or downplayed, the aim of universality for the spelling system being proposed here requires that the larger social context, specifically the Garifuna social context, be considered. h does exist in the Spanish alphabet, although it is usually 'silent', so the symbol would not be new to persons literate in Spanish. What they would have to do would be to become accustomed to assigning it the value that they usually give to j when reading Spanish. On the other hand, if we chose to retain j it would pose more of a problem for persons literate in English, but not Spanish, since they associate that symbol with an entirely different sound. It is therefore proposed that h be used for the phoneme in question. However, this may turn out to be the most controversial grapheme and we may end up agreeing to use j in the sphere of Spanish influence and h elsewhere.

The choice between c, k, are borrowed by SIL from Spanish, but the fact that it does use k as well, albeit only in loanwords, indicates that it is perceived as a proper representation of the phoneme even within the spere of Spanish influence. It is proposed that k be used to represent all occurrences of the consonant and that c and qu be dropped.

ch is bound to be more acceptable than c for the consonant that Taylor describes as "varies freely between the sound of 'ch' in 'church' and 'sh' in 'shut'". ch is used in both Spanish and English writing.

It was pointed out in our discussion of S.J.C. orthography that [dz] does not exist as a phoneme in Garifuna. For this reason, and the possibility that j may be retained as an alternative symbol to h in Spanish speaking countries, j as an equivalent of [dz] will not be listed in our proposed alphabet. Foreign words, as opposed to loanwords, can be written exactly as they would be written in the source language.

w and y will be considered below as semi-vowels, and ñ will be given some attention when we look at nasalization. However, we can conclude on the basis of the current practice of the SIL and S.J.C. traditions, and in the interest of orthographic elegance, that w, y, and ñ will have to be retained whether they are phonemes, or simply variants of /u/, /i/, and /i/ as Taylor with some justification claims.

Simple Vowels

TAYLOR SIL S.J.C. PROPOSED

TAYLOR	SIL	S.J.C.	PROPOSED
i	i	i	i
e	e	e	e
a	a	a	a
-	o	o	o
u	u	u	u
o	ü	ü	ü

Both the SIL and the S.J.C. traditions posit a six-vowel system, and they use the same symbols. The only difference is that S.J.C. incorrectly ascribes to them the values associated with them in English, while SIL, as does Taylor, equates them with the vowels in Spanish. Taylor denies the existence of a phonemic /o/ in Garifuna and uses that symbol for the phoneme that SIL and S.J.C. write as ü. It was demonstrated in chapter two that / / is a phoneme in Garifuna and that the symbol o is needed to represent it in such words as kopu (cup), fonu (thing), to (this), and ino (no). ü is a more practical choice for the unrounded mid-back vowel, since unlike o it exists neither as a grapheme nor as a phoneme in English or Spanish.

Taylor, SIL, and S.J.C. all agree that the simple vowels all have nasalized counterparts. Therefore, six simple nasal vowels will be recognised and will normally be represented as in, en, an, on, un, and ün.

Compound and Semi-Vowels

TAYLOR SIL S.J.C. PROPOSED

TAYLOR	SIL	S.J.C.	PROPOSED
ie	ie	(ye) ie	(ye) ie	(ye)
ia	ia	(ya) ia	(ya) ia	(ya)
io		(yü)	(yü)	(yü)
iu	iu (yu)	iu (yu)	iu (yu)	
	uo	(wü)	(wü)	(wü)
	ua	ua (wa)	ua (wa)	ua (wa)

302

```
ui  ui (wi) ui (wi)  ui (wi)
ue  ue (we ue (we)  ue (we)

     ei  ei  ei  ei
     ai  ai  ai  ei

   au  ou au  ou
   au  au au  au
   ao  aü aü  aü
```

There is general agreement about the first eight compound vowels. The major difference lies in the fact that both SIL and S.J.C. re-write some of Taylor's i's and u's as y's and w's respectively. Taylor's position that there is no opposition between i and y or between u and w, and that one is simply a variant of the other appears to be correct. His refusal to use y and w are therefore supported by the general phonemic goal that "There should be a one to one correspondence between each phoneme and the symbolization of that phoneme" (Pike 1968, pg.208). Yet, it must not be forgotten that the purpose of that or any other orthographic principle that may be adopted is to make the language easy to write and read, and to make the orthography acceptable to the people who are expected to adopt it or encourage its use. I contend that there are too many unbroken vowel sequences in Taylor's orthography, and that such words as ueiu, huia, iaiaua, uaua, and uaibaiaua are easier to read if written thus: weyu, yeyawa, wanwa, and waibayawa.

Whether or not the founders of the SIL and S.J.C. orthographic traditions are aware of it, their conversion of Taylor's /i/ and /u/ to y and w respectively is not arbitrary but is rule governed. The rules can be stated as follows:

1 If /i/ or /u/ and the following vowel are mono-syllabic and occur in word initial position, the /i/ and /u/ are written as y and w respectively.

2 When /i/ or /u/ occur between two other vowels they are written as y and w respectively.

These rules make it possible to re-write many of the words from Taylor's script so that they appear to have more consonants, thereby making them easier to read. They also make it possible to account for the difference in the way the following words are written:

waráü (our child)
uáraü (madness)
úaraü (togetherness)
wara (our heat)

Taylor, SIL, and S.J.C. all concur on the existence of /ei/ and /ai/ as two separate compound phonemes and all represent them in the same way. Given this agreement, it is unfortunate that I am forced to disagree with their analysis and argue that there is no opposition between the two, and that all instances of [ei] and [ai] should be written as ei. It is difficult to explain how the identity of [ei] and [ai] could have escaped the followers of the three traditions.

Taylor and S.J.C. use au where SIL employs ou. The SIL choice is clearly preferable for two reasons. Firstly, ou is phonetically more faithful to the sound in question and, secondly, SIL, unlike the other two, is able to capture a necessary distinction between /ou/ and another compound vowel which can be better represented as /au/; e.g. touba (her side) and tauba (it will be with her).

Finally, in the choice between ao and aü, the latter has to remain in our orthography. It will be recalled that ü was considered preferable to Taylor's 'o' as a symbol for the vowel in question.

Nasalization

As we have seen, Taylor tries to deal with nasalization by indicating nasality on those vowels, by means of an inferior hook. This practice has two main disadvantages; firstly, it is not so easy to keep track of individual nasal vowels, a task which is not made any easier by the fact that nasality may also be environmentally conditioned. Secondly, there is something distasteful, even unnatural, about an orthography that has hooks sticking from underneath many of the vowels, a practice which the would-be users do not see associated with other writing systems that they are familiar with.

The SIL and S.J.C. traditions use a method that is more acceptable. Here a nasal consonant n (and also m in the case of S.J.C.) is used to indicate nasality of all simple vowels and most vowel sequences. The n (or m) is placed after the vowel or vowels, which is to say that it goes at the end of the syllable, and since the language tolerates very few consonant clusters, the n which is followed by a consonant can only be a signal for nasalizing the preceding vowel or vowels. Unfortunately, this neat arrangement is slightly complicated by the use of ñ as a consonant by S.J.C., and as a nasalized glide, y, by SIL, and also to indicate nasality in some vowel sequences, including ie, ia, iu, and iü, which are written iña, iñe, iñu, and iñu. The problem here is that the use of ñ in these vowel sequences is unnecessary since they can just as easily be written as ien, ian, iun, and iün. It is proposed that the use of ñ be restricted to those instances when it indicates a nasalized

[y] or where the use of an n to indicate nasality would require the use of y as well.

For example, yei (there), ayárein (there are), gayügiru (she's still a virgin), ligíarügüyei (he's the only one) can be written thus:

ñei   yein
añarein or ayanrein
gañugiru gayüngiru
ligíarügüñei ligiarügüyein

I believe that the second solution which uses n to indicate nasalization more faithfully captures the actual pronunciation of the words. In reading, the nasalizing effect of the grapheme n goes backward, so that the preceding vowels and, to a lesser extent, the preceding semi-vowel, are nasalized. On the other hand, ñ tends to be perceived as a hard consonant so that even when it is used as an equivalent of y so much of the nasality seems to be concentrated in it that it is not carried over sufficiently into the succeeding vowels which should be the true bearers of the nasal quality. Indeed it can be argued, and this is my position, that what the SIL tradition perceives as a nasal glide, y, and the S.J.C. tradition seems to view as a palatal nasal consonant, is actually an oral glide [y] which appears to be nasal because of the influence of the nasal vowels that follow.

But even though I contend that the second method which employs both y and n instead of ñ is a more faithful representation, it is proposed that ñ be retained for two reasons. First, ñ is so entrenched in Garifuna writing that there is bound to be much resistance to its elimination. It is perceived by the average person as a consonant. This makes it more visible than say ai (which it is argued should be dropped) and easier to deal with than a vowel or a semi-vowel with an elusive nasal topping! Secondly, ñ is only one symbol while the second method would require the use of two symbols. The additional symbol can make a disgusting difference when we are dealing with long words like ligíarügüyein/ligíarügüñei (he's the only one), or layoundaguarügüyan/lañoudaguarügüña (he's only kneading).

Stress

Of the three traditions Taylor gives the best description of stress in Garifuna. Basically he makes two statements that can be regarded as general rules for accentuation.

1 In words with two syllables, the stress tends to fall on the first syllable.

2 In words with three or more syllables, stress tends to fall on the second syllable and thereafter on every third syllable.

This means that the accent need be written in only in the case of the exception to these rules.

Summary Of Proposed Orthography

Consonants

b, d, ch, f, g, h, (or j), k, l, m, n, p, r, s, t, w, y, ñ

Vowels

Simple Oral Vowels: i, e, a, o, u, ü
Simple Nasal Vowels: in, en, an, on, un, ün
Compound Vowels: ie (ye), ia (ya), (yü), iu (yu)

(wü), ua (wa), ui (wi), ue (we)
ei, ou, au, aü

Semi-Vowels or Glides:

1. i ? y and u ? w when they occur between two other vowels.

2. When i or u occur word initially and   together with the succeeding vowel forms a mono-syllable, i ? y and u ? w.

Nasalization

1. n before another consonant indicates nasalization of the preceding vowel(s).

2. ñ is used in place of y which occurs under the same conditions as y in word initial or inter-vocallic position.

Stress

Stress tends to fall on the first syllable of two syllable words, and on the second syllable of longer words. Only the exceptions are to be marked.

Supplementary Bibliography

Hadel, Richard, 1975 Dictionary of Central American Carib. BISRA, St. John's College, Belize City

Language Policy Statement Of The Garifuna Nation

DRAFT (for CABO meeting Dec. 1997)

We, the Garifuna people, although living within the borders of various countries (including but not limited to Belize, Guatemala, Honduras, Nicaragua, St. Vincent, and the United States), represent a single, united ethnic community known as the Garifuna Nation. Our language is the Garifuna language. This language has a dictionary, a working orthography, and a corpus of literature and descriptive grammatical work.

The Garifuna people recognize the natural and inherent interconnectedness of language and culture and that our language is the primary vehicle for the transmission of our culture. We believe that our survival depends on both the preservation of our traditional language and on social and economic development. Therefore, language policies and goals described here also impact and are intimately connected with our economic development and cultural survival.

As an indigenous people, the Garifuna Nation has basic rights to autonomy and self-determination, and the right to maintain and preserve Garifuna language and culture. Further, the Garifuna Nation recognizes the right of the Garifuna communities and member organizations in each country to establish and implement local level language policies and development initiatives, and expects these rights to be guaranteed by local governments, as described by the United Nations Draft Declaration of the Rights of Indigenous Peoples.

We, the Garifuna Nation, declare that our ancestral language is Garifuna, and that Garifuna is the language of the Garifuna Nation, regardless of the level of individual competence.

Language Maintenance Policy

In order to ensure the survival of the Garifuna language, the Garifuna Nation adopts the following language maintenance policies. In the process, we expect recognition of the Garifuna language by the governments of Belize, Honduras, Nicaragua and Guatemala.

These policies are reflected in the thrust of the Garifuna National Language Program, and will result in the formation and execution of language preservation projects and initiatives at all levels within the Garifuna Nation. The Garifuna Nation encourages its various communities to develop local level language maintenance strategies which are tailored to the unique circumstances and needs of the given community.

Lexical expansion

Our Garifuna language is a modern language capable of expressing the complete range of human communicative intentions. Our language is also capable of lexical expansion into contemporary technical and specialized semantic fields, including mathematics, information technology, economics, politics, science, etc. We hereby mandate the formation of a special international Garifuna committee to develop and determine appropriate new vocabulary so that Garinagu may speak on any subject without resorting to the use of foreign lexemes. This committee will represent Garinagu from all the various geographic regions, and will meet on a regular basis in an on-going process of development of new vocabulary where needed.

Corpus planning

The Garifuna Nation is committed to the finalization and standardization of a Garifuna orthography which is acceptable to all speakers. Much orthographic work has already been accomplished, and the remaining linguistic and stylistic questions will be resolved and a standardized Garifuna orthography adopted in the near future.

The Garifuna Nation also mandates the training of teachers and other interested and appropriate individuals in the use of the new Garifuna orthography (reading and writing), in order to promote and promulgate the production of literature, plays, videos, and other cultural materials in Garifuna. Access to publication will also be secured for all regions. We believe that the acquisition of literacy in the ancestral language will expand the domains of use of the Garifuna language, and will allow contemporary Garinagu the maximum potential for creative expression in their language.

Language acquisition and use

The Garifuna Nation recognizes that the single most important factor in the survival of our language is its transmission to the children. Our goal is for all Garifuna children to learn the ancestral language in the natural way, in the home, and we call on Garifuna parents to reclaim Garifuna as the language of the home.

For Garifuna parents whose competence in the language is imperfect, local programs to help parents improve their mastery of Garifuna should be implemented.

The Garifuna Nation recognizes the need for greater opportunities to practice and use the ancestral language, and calls for the establishment of fora at all levels promoting use of the language. In addition, we realize that elder speakers are a valuable linguistic resource, and we encourage the consultation of elder speakers and their involvement with language learners. In turn, elder speakers should be encouraging and supportive of language learners.

Resources and funding

In order to put into action Garifuna language maintenance, preservation, and revitalization efforts, we require resources, both human and monetary. The Garifuna Nation welcomes all persons seriously interested in participating in or contributing to the Garifuna National Language Program. In addition, grant writing skills will be developed at various levels within the Garifuna Nation in order to secure necessary funds for the enactment of our goals.

Linguistic documentation

The Garifuna Nation is committed to the development of a comprehensive grammatical description of our language which can be adapted for use in the classroom, facilitating the formal instruction of our children in Garifuna.

In general, Garifuna people welcome the interest of linguists in our unique language. We expect, however, a high degree of cultural sensitivity and responsibility. In addition, we require copies of any work produced which deals with our language, and especially appreciate materials and other work which may also be utilized in our language preservation and revitalization efforts.

Status
The Garifuna Nation expects recognition of the Garifuna language by the governments of Belize, Honduras, Nicaragua and Guatemala.

Educational Policy

Through this statement, the Garifuna Nation makes known our intention to exercise greater control over the schools in our communities and over the education of our children, rights guaranteed to us in the United Nations Draft Declaration of the Rights of Indigenous Peoples, as well as other national and regional agreements and legislation.

The Garifuna Nation requires of national and local governments not only recognition of the legal right to maintain our language, but implementation of the effective right to maintain our language through the allocation of resources, personnel, funds and equipment.

Schools in all Garifuna communities will institute a curriculum teaching the history and culture of the Garifuna people, including the story of the origin of the Garinagu and the Garifuna language, aspects of Garifuna cosmology, traditional Garifuna foods, and Garifuna songs and dance.

The Garifuna Nation also expects to act on our right to educate our children in our traditional Garifuna language, through programs designed to meet the educational, linguistic, and cultural preservation needs and goals of each individual Garifuna community within the Garifuna Nation. As an indigenous people, the Garifuna Nation reserves the right for our children to be educated in their ancestral language as a first or second language.

In keeping with the historical Garifuna tradition of academic excellence, the Garifuna Nation expects for our children an education which is culturally sensitive and linguistically responsible, and also prepares our children for the wider social context. We assert that our children are fully capable of developing a high level of mastery in both their ancestral language and the national language, and expect the use of Garifuna as a medium of instruction to increase student success and performance, increase student awareness and knowledge of their culture and history, and enhance educational opportunity; in addition, we believe that the inclusion of our language and culture in the school program in our communities will reaffirm traditional Garifuna values and pride in each of the nation states of which we are a part.

In addition to the use of our ancestral language in the formal education of our children, the Garifuna Nation also calls for the initiation of Garifuna language instruction at all levels for any and all interested persons. These are to include courses of instruction for non-speakers of the language, as well as courses for Garifuna speakers who wish to acquire literacy in the language.

The Garifuna National Language Program

Goal

To facilitate and encourage the development and implementation of programs and projects with a view to ensuring the preservation, promotion, development and wider utilization of the Garifuna language.

Purposes

1) To facilitate the development of the Garifuna language.

2) To standardize the orthography of the Garifuna language.

3) To facilitate the publication of literature including language learning and teaching materials.

4) To facilitate the acquisition of Garifuna language skills.

5) To provide fora that promote the use of Garifuna language skills.

Expected Results

1. Language Development

The lexicon is expanded.

There is an international mechanism in place for the development of new words and its authority is recognized and accepted in the entire Garifuna Nation.

There is a mechanism for promulgating the agreements emerging from the language development efforts.

The Garifuna language is used in domains for which it is currently inadequate.

2. A Standardized Orthography

Orthographic agreements negotiated by influential persons from the participating countries and published and accepted everywhere.

An orthographic guide is published and widely disseminated.

3.The Acquisition of Garifuna Language Skills

Materials for teaching and learning Garifuna available.

A cadre of persons available in each participating country to deliver classes in Garifuna Language and Culture.

Schools participate effectively in the transmission of Garifuna language and cultural skills.

Programs in place in each country to encourage and facilitate the acquisition and use of Garifuna language skills.

Garifuna households are supportive environments for Garifuna language learning.

4.The Publication of Literature in Garifuna Publishing capability developed by at least one Garifuna organization in each country.

Assistance available to writers in Garifuna to improve their work and to get it published.

Writers are recognized and international awards given for outstanding achievement in writing in Garifuna.

Distribution network in place to market and make published works available in each of our countries.

5. Fora Promoting the Use of Garifuna Garifuna established as the primary language used in Garifuna sponsored events.

Periodic contests are held that require competence in Garifuna language and culture.

6.Secure Financial Resources Local sources of financial and other resources identified and commitments secured.

Financial support secured from external sources.

UNESCO Declaration

UNESCO recognized the Garifuna Culture as a masterpiece of the oral and intangible heritage of humanity. This designation means that it is an important culture that should be preserved, promoted, and celebrated.

The candidature form is in the following pages so that you can see why this culture is so special.

You can also go directly to UNESCO's website about the Garifuna culture. Garifuna Culture-UNESCO Masterpiece.

The form is divided into 6 sections:

Preface

Justification of Candidature

Garifuna Language

Garifuna Music and Dance

Future Plans

Appendix and Reference

CANDIDATURE STANDARD FORM

Proclamation of masterpieces of the oral and intangible heritage of humanity

i. Identification

a) Member State:

Belize

b) Name of Cultural Space or Form of Expression:

"Garifuna Language, Music and Dance"

c) Name of the Community Concerned:

The Garifuna People of Belize. There are ten Garifuna Communities in Belize and these are united as branch communities under the umbrella of an organization registered in the country as the National Garifuna Council.

d) Geographical Location of the Cultural Form of Expression:

Garifuna language, music and dance are found to varying degrees in the ten Garifuna communities of Belize as well as in several other Garifuna Communities scattered along the Atlantic coast of Central America from

Nicaragua to Belize. They can also be found in some cities in United States of America.

e) Geographical Location of the Communities Concerned: Following their exile from St. Vincent to Central America just over two hundred years ago the Garifuna dispersed along the Atlantic coast of Honduras and continued to populate the coast of Guatemala, Belize and Nicaragua. In Belize the original settlements were established south of the Sibun River, which until 1859 was the southern border of the British "Settlement at the mouth of the Belize River". Up until the 1950's there were five of these Garifuna Settlements, including the towns of Dangriga and Punta Gorda and the villages of Barranco, Seine Bight and Hopkins. After the devastation of Hurricane Hattie in 1961 some people from Seine Bight settled an area that they had been farming for a long time thereby establishing the first and only inland Garifuna Settlement in the entire region.

The Garifuna people of Belize have naturally been affected by social and economic factors. In the 1960's many people were forced by economic difficulties to migrate to other parts of the country and even abroad in search of jobs and other opportunities resulting in concentrations of Garifuna populations outside of the areas they traditionally occupied. As a consequence, there are now Garifuna communities in Belize City, the former capital, Libertad, which was then the center of the sugar industry, Belmopan, the present capital, and San Pedro, one of the principal centers of the tourist industry.

There are over thirty Garifuna Settlements in Honduras, two communities in Guatemala and three in the Pearl Lagoon area of Nicaragua. All of these communities in Belize, Guatemala, Honduras and Nicaragua are descended from the just over two thousand Garifuna people exiled from Saint Vincent in 1797. They are therefore one people who share the same history and a common tradition in language, music and dance among other things.

g) Competent Persons or Bodies:

The National Garifuna Council is an organization of and for the Garifuna people of Belize. It represents the interests of the Garifuna People and is authorized to act on behalf of the Garifuna people. The Mission of the NGC is "to promote the cultural Identity, economic develop and general wellbeing of the Garifuna People as well as interracial harmony, through means that ensure the sustainability of the organization, being mindful of the responsibility to protect the environment". In a Memorandum of Understanding between the Government of Belize and The National Garifuna Council signed in July, 1999, the Government recognized the NGC as the representative of the Garifuna people of Belize.

The goals of the Council are

1. To promote the general well being of the Garifuna people.
2. To enhance the status of the Garifuna people and their communities.
3. To nurture and promote the Garifuna culture and identity.
4. To make the NGC an effective, efficient and sustainable organization.
5. To forge linkages with Garifuna and other organizations and groups.

The NGC has the benefit of the involvement of a number of resource persons who will make a significant contribution to the project. Listed below are just a few:

a) E. Roy Cayetano, the Chief Executive Officer in the Ministry of Rural Development and Culture, is the current president of the National Garifuna Council. He is an educator, a linguist and an anthropologist. He has served as a consultant in the effort of the Government and the Garifuna people of Honduras to develop a Garifuna language programme for the schools of that country. He is also committed to the collection and preservation of songs as well as the promotion of various aspects of the culture.

b) John Mariano is a buyei, a spiritual leader, a shaman. He is knowledgeable about Garifuna rituals and the songs and dances done in that context. He is also a master of the Wanaragua (Jankunu) Dance which is usually done during the Christmas season. He is also a member of the Indigenous Spiritual Council.

c) The Ugundani Dance Company, based in Belize City has been in existence for more than a decade. This Dance Company has mastered a wide range of raditional Garifuna dances which they have choreographed. They have traveled and erformed extensively both nationally and regionally.

d) Jessie Castillo is a primary school teacher and a published writer. She writes in both English and Garifuna and has demonstrated an interest in the preservation and promotion of the Garifuna language as well as other aspects of the culture.

e) Reverend Jerris Valentine is an Anglican priest and former president of the Dangriga Branch of the NGC. He is a source of information about Garifuna language, songs, dances and spirituality. He has served as a teacher and principal at both the Primary and secondary levels. His membership in the clergy has not inhibited his involvement in Garifuna rituals and dances which he often takes the time to teach and write about.

f) Marion Cayetano is a planner who has served in both the public and the private sector. He has been involved in the elaboration of a macro-economic strategy for Belize.

g) Andy Palacio is a well known singer, composer, musician who has performed nationally and regionally. He is currently employed at the Ministry of Rural Development and Culture, Belmopan, Belize.

h) Phillip Zuniga is an attorney and has been a member of the NGC Board of Directors for at least ten years. His support and guidance on the legal aspects of the organization's activities is invaluable.

Even though the National Garifuna Council is expected to take the lead role, the Ministry of Rural Development and Culture and the Ministry of Education and Sports are expected to continue to be involved. It is no doubt significant that the Chief Executive officer in the former Ministry is the current President of the NGC and that the National UNESCO Commission is located in the latter.

Justification of Candidature

a) Value of the Cultural Space or Form of Cultural Expression: The Garifuna are a hybrid people resulting from a biological and cultural mixture between Caribs and Arawaks of the Caribbean and people of African origin. This process of hybridization, which took place in the Caribbean island of Saint Vincent, gave rise to a new group called the Garifuna or the Garinagu. After they lost the so called Carib Wars, which were essentially land wars fought against the British, those who survived a six month imprisonment on the rock island of Balliceau were, on 11th of March 1797, exiled to Central America where they arrived in Roatan on 12th April of the same year. From there they spread to the mainland and along the Atlantic coast of Central America from Nicaragua to Belize. The Garifuna are thus a unique mixture of African, Arawak and Carib origins resulting from a process that took place in the West Indian islands but ended up being transplanted to Central America.

Because it was on the West Indian island of St. Vincent that the Garifuna came into existence as an identifiable group, the Garifuna people of Belize consider themselves, and are generally acknowledged, indigenous to the Circum-Caribbean region. In addition, this group of people have traditionally identified more with their Amerindian ancestry than with their African origins, which the casual observer would invariably consider more consistent with their physical attributes. The history, origins and even the present geographic location of the Garifuna people are all elements that contribute to the uniqueness of Garifuna culture and argue for the promotion and preservation of its various elements.

Garifuna Language has several features that are of universal interest and therefore value. It is a language of South American and West Indian origin that, today, is only spoken by a black population in Central America. It has been determined to belong to the Arawakan language family although it also includes some lexical items derived from Carib and the European languages with which the people came in contact during their history, those European languages being French, Spanish and English.

It is reasonable to assume that the languages of the Africans who made an input into the mix that became the Garifuna must have had an impact on the language. Unfortunately, this aspect has not been studied so that it is not possible at this time to go beyond speculation. However, it is certain that this kind of study needs to be undertaken and that it can yield much information about language contact and development for the benefit of humanity.

Another rare linguistic feature that should be of universal interest is the fact that in this language, because of its history, there is some difference between male and common speech. Some forms and structures are marked for exclusive male use. This difference is eroding as fewer and fewer men master the use of these male forms thereby diminishing the richness of the language.

Garifuna communities are rich in úraga (stories) that are usually told in the context of the ninth night wake or other social gatherings. Story telling is an art that unfortunately is not taught and is not being learnt by younger folk who are becoming less and less competent in the language. This means that this art form which has interesting features like audience participation, sung refrains, exaggeration for the sake of effect, the skillful use of a staff as the only prop plus the masterful use of language is in danger of becoming irrecoverably lost. Through the power of literacy, translation and the new technologies this trend can be reversed and the benefits of this art form made accessible to a wider audience.

There is an intimate relationship between Garifuna language and Garifuna music and between the music and the Dance as can be seen in the paper entitled "Inventory of Garifuna music and dance". Garifuna Music essentially consists of various types of songs that are utilized for different purposes in the culture. The songs are poetry. They capture the history, the values, the aspirations, the concerns and the deepest feelings of a people who have been kept illiterate in their own language. The songs capture and express the totality of the Garifuna experience and in a sense serve as a literature that is waiting to be committed to writing and translated into other languages for our common benefit. As for the melodies and the rhythms, which again are a very interesting amalgam of African and Amerindian elements enhanced by simple instruments in traditional music or by more elaborate instrumentation in the more modern Punta Rock forms, the appeal is universal. They are already being owned by a wider audience in Central America, an audience that has begun to work its way into the North American market and beyond as we can see from the success of Paranda, (one of the CD's in the package) which has the advantage of worldwide distribution by Warner. One can also cite the example of the Garifuna song "Wata nege konk supu" which was composed by a Belizean artist from Dangriga named Chico Ramos. This song was stolen, partly translated into Spanish and popularized in North and South America by the Honduran Band La Banda Blanca under the title "Sopa de Caracol". There was a lawsuit and La Banda Blanca settled out of Court. This is significant in that it demonstrates the fact that Garifuna music has universal appeal. It also underscores the fact that there is a difference between traditional Garifuna music, which we submit is a common heritage of humanity, and the more modern Punta Rock, which it nourishes and is subject to restrictions like copyright laws.

Finally, Garifuna dance is just as varied as the types of songs. It has been shown in that the relationship between song and dance types is so close that the dance and the songs associated with it are known by the same name. Thus, one can sing or dance punta, hüngühüngü, gunjái, wanaragua, paranda, sambai, chumba, etc. In addition, the dancers are always expected to know the songs and to even help to "sing for their feet". One unique feature of some of the dances including the wanaragua, the chumba and the sambai is that there is an unusual relationship between the drummer and the dancer such that the dancer dictates to the drummer whose task it is to anticipate the moves of the dancer and drum accordingly. This means that in these dances the dancers take turn dancing one by one, that the drummer has at all times to have a clear view of the dancer, especially his/her feet, and that the drummer can never be replaced by recorded or electronic music. It is our view that this feature of Garifuna Dance is rare if not indeed unique. The other dances have some elements of this feature to varying degrees though not to the extent that they cannot be done by groups. Still, they all have an appeal as we can see from the fact that the punta has become one of the best known and preferred dances in the region among Garifuna as well as non Garifuna, a phenomenon brought about by the emergence of Punta Rock in the early 1980's.

b) Value of the form of Cultural Expression in terms of the number and importance of the bearers of expertise:

Garifuna Language, Music and Dance are not supposed to be limited to a particular age group or sector of the society. Where the language is concerned, there is an assertion in The Language Policy Statement of the Garifuna Nation that:

"We, the Garifuna Nation, declare that our ancestral language is Garifuna, and that Garifuna is the language of the Garifuna Nation, regardless of the level of individual competence."

Similarly, the music and dance have a place in the lives of all Garifuna people regardless of age, sex, occupation, status in the community or place of residence. It is desirable that all should have some competence in the language, the music and the dances seeing that these are all important in the daily lives of the people and, therefore, their identity as Garifuna. There is a place for language, music and dance in their secular as well as their religious activities.

c) Inventory of similar cultural spaces or forms of cultural expression recorded on the provisional list of the State concerned:

Belize is a multi-cultural society that acknowledges and celebrates each individual cultural group in the rich diversity that gives the nation its identity. Apart from the Garifuna, it includes three Mayan groups – K'ekchi', Mopan and Yucatec – as well as Creoles, East Indians, Mestizos (persons of mixed Hispanic and Mayan descent), Mennonites, Chinese and people of Middle Eastern origin. Each of these cultures has made and continues to make a contribution to the wider Belizean culture and identity and as such need to be nurtured in order to ensure that the homogenizing tendency of globalization does not wipe them out of existence.

The languages of three Mayan are among the twenty or more spoken in the region. Of these, Yucatec is without doubt the weakest as it is quickly being supplanted by the Spanish spoken by the Mestizos of the north and west of the country. K'ekchi' and Mopan are still quite strong but they, too, are becoming subject to the influence of Creole and English, a process that is aided and abetted by a school system that so far has not given these languages the place they deserve in the curriculum. The East Indians have long lost their language, although there are more recent immigrants who do speak Hindi or other Indian languages, while the Mennonites and the Chinese, because their communities tend to be quite closed, still speak German and Chinese respectively.

In terms of music and dance, it is perhaps true to say that it is only among the Mayas and the Creoles that a fairly strong tradition of music and dance has survived.

Projects that we wish to develop and propose within the decade are the following:

- Music of the Mayas – This would focus on the musical forms and the instruments of the three Mayan groups of Belize, and the transmission of the requisite skills to the next generation.

- Mayan Dance and Dance Festivals – The Mayas of Belize, especially the K'ekchi' and the Mopan, have a number of costumed mime dances that are done from time to time. These include, among others, the Cortez, the Moro, the Maash or Monkey Dance and the Deer Dance. We are not aware of any study having been done of these dances or of any effort to document them.

- Belizean Creole Stories and Story telling – This would include collecting and documenting stories and the promotion of the art. This can well be expanded to look at traditional stories and story telling in Belize generally so that the stories and the story telling art of other Belizean groups can be included.

- Traditional Healing Arts in Belize – As has been indicated elsewhere in this paper, Belize represents the coming together of peoples of several different origins. Each came with its healing traditions but as is to be expected, each has not been immune to the influence of the others. It is proposed that these various traditions be studied and documented, including their cosmological bases, the accompanying rituals and the pharmacology which invariably requires a knowledge of medicinal plants.

d) Comparative analysis of similar cultural spaces or forms of expression in the region:

Garifuna language, music and dance are essentially the same in all the Garifuna communities of the region. To be sure, there are bound to be minor variations here and there like dialectal differences in pronunciation or shades of meaning in some lexical items but certainly not enough to hinder communication or the ability to participate jointly in music or dance events.

There has been much cooperation where efforts at language development and promotion are concerned. Roy Cayetano, a Belizean and the only Garifuna linguist up to this time, was called upon by the Honduran Government at the insistence of Garifuna teachers in that country to provide technical assistance to their efforts at developing a Garifuna Language Programme for schools in Garifuna Villages. In addition, interested persons from the other countries were invited to participate in the lexicography workshops that provided input for the production of the People's Garifuna Dictionary by the National Garifuna Council. It is recognized, as stated in the Language Policy Document for the Garifuna Nation, that tasks like lexical expansion and the standardization of the orthography must be a collaborative effort involving a regional body with representatives from competent organizations in all the countries that have Garifuna communities.

In the area of music and dance, it is to be noted that songs composed in one country move freely from one country to another, sometimes undergoing some change as they are transmitted orally from person to person and from village to village. Thus the songs, singing and dancing at a ninth night wake in Dangriga, Belize, is no different from those at a similar event in Santa Fe (Giriga) near Trujillo in Honduras.

As for the relations between the Garifuna and other population is Belize and the region, it can be said that while the Garifuna are generally at a disadvantage economically, they are invariably perceived as having a vibrant culture which in a way makes them the envy of the others. Their music and dance are gaining currency among other populations with the result that entrepreneurs from other groups are capitalizing on their musical ability by financing and owning musical groups like the Punta Rebels and the Griga Boys of Belize and other similar entities in Honduras and Guatemala.

Perhaps the relations between the Creoles and the Garifuna deserve special mention. These two black populations were separated soon after the arrival of the Garifuna in Central America by the divide and rule strategy of the white settlers who, fearing the military prowess of the Garifuna and the influence that this free black population might have on their property, taught the slaves to see the Garifuna as inferior. The settlers also saw the Garifuna as another source of labour, which was very much in demand in the woodcutting industry. The result was that social interaction between the two groups was, until recently, very limited and the two populations developed apart. It appears that they shared several common African elements of culture but as these were lost by the Creoles they came to be seen a purely Garifuna. There is evidence that dances like the wanaragua (Jankunu or John Canoe), sambai and gunjai may have also been done by the Creoles but not any more except in the Village of Gales Point in the Stann Creek District. Today, Garifuna music and dance appear to be one of several factors contributing to the healing of that divide and facilitating the unification of people in the country and the region.

Finally, it must be pointed out that the competences of the Garifuna have always been recognized and exploited by the dominant elements in the society. It is recorded that the British settlers had hoped that the Garifuna would have, on arriving in Central America, offered their military skills a mercenaries in the defence of the settlement against the Spanish. Later, the missionaries, recognizing their linguistic and cultural versatility quickly pressed the brightest and the best young minds from Garifuna communities into service as teachers whom they sent to teaching posts where they served all the ethnic groups all over the country. Unfortunately, this had the effect of hastening the erosion of Garifuna culture as these teachers were in those communities as representatives of an alien culture and not in their own right as members of a particular culture.

e) Justification of the value of the form of cultural expression according to the selection criteria:

i. Its outstanding value as a masterpiece of the human creative genius Garifuna language is essentially an Arawak language, a language spoken by Arawak women in communities conquered and taken over by Carib men in the course of the Carib expansion first in South America and later in the Lesser Antilles. The men spoke Carib and women spoke Arawak. The language of the vanquished survived although the community had come to be seen as Carib. While the language was influenced by Carib and the European languages with which it came in contact, it survived. It survived the assimilation of the escaped African slaves, the consequent change in phenotype and the rise of the so called Black Caribs. It survived the exile from St. Vincent so that today, over two hundred years later, the language is spoken only in Central America by the descendants of the exiles. It is no longer spoken any where in the West Indies. There can be no doubt that the very existence of the Garifuna language as a language that is fully alive and integrated into the lives of the people is testimony to the indomitable spirit and the creative genius of the Garifuna.

As for the music and dance the story is similar to that of the language except that here we find a rich and unique synthesis of African and Carib/Arawak elements in which the former predominate. This fusion is indeed remarkable, especially when one considers that the people have always, for reasons of survival, identified with their Amerindian rather than their African origins, and again attests to the creativity of the people.

ii. Its roots in the cultural tradition or cultural history of the Garifuna community as can be noted from (i) above, the Garifuna language has always been spoken by the Garifuna people and permeates every aspect of Garifuna life and culture. There is a oral tradition that manifests itself in úraga (stories) and a plethora of songs that speak to every situation that one might encounter. The songs and the dances are also an integral part of the culture with a role in the secular as well as the ritual life of the Garifuna community.

There are songs that are associated with various types of work as well as for play and spiritual activity and as we have tried to show, there is a close relationship between music and dance, which also tends to be a must in entertainment and spiritual activities.

iii. Its role as a means of affirming the cultural identity of the peoples and cultural communities concerned, etc.

Garifuna language, music and dance are important elements of the cultural heritage of the Garifuna people. Indeed, their ability and willingness to speak the language can be used as a test to determine the extent to which they are comfortable with being identified as Garifuna and the strength of the language in a particular community appears to be in direct proportion to the level of skill in the mastery of the music and the dance. It has also been noted that in those communities where the people are making an effort to reaffirm their identity as Garifuna, as in Orinoco, Nicaragua, the demand the pleas for help are for assistance in learning the language music and dances. In October, 2000, the National Garifuna Council responded to a request from that community for a workshop in Garifuna language and spirituality. Included in the spirituality is the performance of rituals that dramatize the worldview of the people. How can one communicate with the ancestors in a language other than their own? And how can a ritual like the dügü or the chugú be done without drumming, singing and dancing? The people of Orinoco wanted to affirm their identity and they sought the help of the NGC in an exercise that was to culminate in a chugú, a ritual that had not taken place there in decades. It is instructive that in order to accomplish the objective, it was necessary to go beyond a mere explanation of the Garifuna cosmology and teach some reading (to serve as a tool for learning), drumming, songs, and dancing, since all of these had to be brought together in the ritual.

iv. Excellence in the application of the skill and technical qualities displayed
There is a plethora of skills that are involved in Garifuna language, music and dance. What we have found is that special efforts like language retrieval and cultural promotion programmes have inspired individuals to do excellent work and develop innovative approaches to problems that confronted them. We will offer just three examples.

a) As a graduate student of linguistics two decades ago, Roy Cayetano noted that the few people who wrote Garifuna each did so in his own way. Clearly there was the need to begin a dialogue that would lead to the establishment of a standard orthography. He undertook to a study of the main orthographic traditions and made a proposal for a common orthography that acknowledged the common features of those traditions, capitalized on their strengths and sought to overcome what he perceived as their weaknesses. That was the first and, so far, only study of the phonology of the language by a native speaker, and the resulting document became the basis for national and regional efforts at arriving at a standard orthography.

b) In the area of music, the drum is one of the few instruments traditionally associated with Garifuna Music. Drum making is therefore an important activity. Drums were originally made from logs made hollow by the controlled use of fire. Later, the gouge (a curved chisel) was used for that purpose. Austin Rodriguez, a drum maker in Dangriga, in seeking to eliminate the waste, devised a way to cut out the inside of the log using a chainsaw and to cut out several smaller drums from the resulting wood. He went further to use his wood working skills to improve the appearance of the drums so that today, there is a demand for those drums by locals and visitors alike.

c) Garifuna dances were not originally intended for a stage where the audience sits in an auditorium and the dancers perform on a stage. In their natural cultural context there is no distinction between audience and performer. In a ninth night wake, for instance, we find the drummers with the main singers standing behind them and the other people standing around so that there is a circular space available for dancing in front of the drummers. There is a certain fluidity so that the individual can participate to the extent that he or she wishes. Everyone can join in the singing, the two dancers in the ring keep changing as the man or the woman steps back into the crowd and is replaced by another who may have just been standing around or sporadically joining in the singing as the songs that he or she likes are sung. The Waribagabaga Dance Group was the first dance troupe organized to seriously take on the challenge of arranging the dances and perform them on a stage without doing violence to the dances and the culture. They set a very high standard that was enhanced by international exposure, which also demonstrated the universal appeal of Garifuna music and dance and inspired the formation of similar groups in other parts of the country and the neighbouring countries. One such group is the Ballet Folkloriko Garifuna de Honduras, a national dance company in Honduras. With financial support from government and foreign technical assistance that group has managed to reach a very high level in choreography and performance and is very much in demand in festivals around the world. That kind of support has never been available to our groups in Belize.

v. Its value as a unique testimony of a living cultural tradition
Garifuna language, music and dance are elements of a living culture. The language is Amerindian spoken by black population in Central America. Linguists like Douglas Taylor refer to it as Central American Island Carib

but it is neither of Central American origin nor is it Carib. It has unique features like words and expression that are marked for exclusive male use, voiceless vowels in certain environments as well as vowels that are not included in the phonetic inventory of languages commonly spoken in this region. The music and dances are also, without doubt, even in their raw state very captivating. The sound of the drums are irresistible, the message and functions of the song are powerful and the relationship between the drummer and the dancer in dances like wanaragua, chumba and sambai is unusual in that the drummer interpret the movements of the dancer rather than the other way around. These are just a few examples of the uniqueness of these elements of this living culture.

vi. The risk of its disappearing due either to lack of means for safeguarding and protecting it or to process of rapid change or to urbanization or to acculturation.

There has been some erosion of the Garifuna language and some other aspects of the culture in Belize due to a combination of factors. These include migration in search of economic opportunities not present in Garifuna communities, discrimination and the failure of the school system to even acknowledge the language and culture in the work of the school even in Garifuna communities. This cultural erosion is worrisome and the concern is expressed in all sectors of the Belizean Garifuna society - young and old. It is the view of the leaders that this erosion is having devastating results including threatening their value system, their very existence as a people, their self-esteem and their performance as a people. There is a need to take action to stem this erosion as quickly as possible.

The fact is that the language is still spoken and its use is widespread. However, it is only in one village - Hopkins - that young children still learn it as their native language as a matter of course. There is an awareness of the fact that this very important part of the identity is beginning to slip away. This awareness is coupled with a feeling of helplessness as parents are blamed for not speaking it to their children even while they use the language among themselves. In this climate, it is imperative that the National Garifuna Council take the lead in working out interventions aimed at arresting the loss of the language and other elements of the culture.

Garifuna Music and Dance suffer a similar fate. If conscious intervention is not done all aspects of the culture could be lost very quickly. Humanity would suffer a significant loss if that were to occur, bearing in mind that Garifuna culture, including the language, music and dance, is a rare amalgam or synthesis of Amerindian and African elements fused together in the crucible of the Caribbean.

Garifuna Language

iii. Description

a)Description of the form of Cultural expression

1. Garifuna Language

The Garifuna language belongs to the Arawak language family. It is the principal medium of communication in traditional Garifuna communities. Unfortunately, the young are not learning it to the same extent that they did in the past so that today in some communities competence in the language is limited to the people who are middle aged or older.

The language has a [C]VCVCV structure. What this means is that the word may begin with a consonant or a verb but that it invariably ends with a verb. There are words that end with voiceless vowels, usually in word final position following a voiceless consonant, and consonant clusters are usually not tolerated. This is very important point since it makes it possible to assign other values to the grapheme "n" when it occurs immediately before a consonant or in word final position. It is also a VSO (i.e., a verb subject object) language.

It has been pointed that the language has some words and expressions that are reserved for male use as opposed to the rest, which may be used by either gender. This phenomenon is the result of history as has been explained elsewhere in this paper.

Apart from the language being used for everyday communication, it is also used in songs, which among other things capture the hopes, fears, joys and pains of the people.

The Garifuna language has an orthography, syntax and rich vocabulary. A high level of accurate description and definition can be achieved using the Garifuna language. The Peoples Garifuna Dictionary provides a sampling of the Garifuna words and the document titled "Toward a Common Garifuna Orthography" discusses orthography and some other aspects of the language.

Much work has been done on the standardization of the orthography of the language in each of the countries that have Garifuna populations in the region. There has also been an effort to establish a regional commission with representation from each of the countries to facilitate collaboration in the tasks of language retrieval, lexical expansion and the promotion of the learning and use of the language. Unfortunately, that effort was suspended when people had to turn their attention to the rebuilding that was necessary after the devastation caused by Hurricane Mitch in 1998. The necessary financial resources are being sought so that the effort can be resumed.

Garifuna Music and Dance

2. Garifuna Music and Dance

Garifuna music and dance are closely related. It is seldom possible to speak of one without the other. In fact the name used for each type of dance is also the same name given to the type of music associated with it. For this reason, the music and the dances will be treated together.

Musical Instruments

Garifuna musical instruments are quite basic. These traditionally consist of drums, maracas and, more recently, the guitar and the turtle shells.

Drums

The drums are the primary musical instruments of the Garifuna and these are used for ritual as well as secular purposes. The drums are normally are made out of hollowed sections of tree trunks with antelope skin stretched tightly across one end and held in place by rope that can be stretched to tighten the instrument by means of wooden pins. Originally, the drums were hollowed out by means of controlled burning. Later, gouges were used for that purpose so the drums could be made more quickly and with less chance of failure. Today, the gouge continues to be the standard means of digging out the inside portion of the logs to make the drum but Austin Rodriguez, a drum maker in Dangriga has perfected a system that makes use of the chain saw. His system is so efficient that he can now make several drums in one day and in addition produce several drums from the same log that formerly would have only yielded one such instrument.

Two drums are normally used for secular music. These typically consist of a base drum that is usually the larger of the two and provides the basic rhythm. This drum is called the segunda. The smaller drum provides the embellishments and normally require a greater level of skill on the part of the drummer who in certain of the dances may have to improvise in order to rise to the demands of the dancer in dances like the wanaragua, the chumba and the sambai. This smaller drum is called the primero. There are times when two or more segunda drums are utilized but the use of more than one primero would be awkward if not impractical.

There is a third type of drum. This is generally larger than the segunda and reserved for use in sacred music associated with rituals like the dügü. Three such drums are played at the same time with the one in the center, called the lanigi Garawoun (the heart of the drum) taking the lead.

The Maracas

The maracas are rattles that are played in pairs. To make these the insides of two whole calabashes are extracted and replaced with the mature seeds of a plant called weinwein. A stick to be used as a handle is then forced through holes that had been made at the top and the bottom of each of the gourds.

The maracas are used for certain types of secular and sacred music but there are other types with which they are never associated.

These rattles may also have religious significance in that each buyei (Garifuna spiritual leader) invariably has at least one pair of large rattles that can be seen as a badge of his or her office. This maraga, as it is called, is used by the buyei in healing ceremonies like the dügü or the chugú.

The Guitar

It is perhaps safe to assume that the acoustic guitar was borrowed into Garifuna music after the exile to Central America some time during the last two hundred years. It is here that Hispanic influence manifests itself in Garifuna music. The association of the guitar with traditional Garifuna music is limited to the paranda, a name which itself is obviously of Spanish origin. More recently, with the emergence of Punta Rock, the guitar has joined other modern instruments as Garifuna lyrics and rhythms were repackaged for wider national, regional and international consumption.

The Turtle Shells

Minor instruments like conch shells, cow bells, and the mouth organ have long had a peripheral place in traditional Garifuna music as there was always the need for improvisation and adaptability as our musicians strived to meet the musical needs of the community. What is perhaps ironic is that it was in responding to the need to improvise that the turtle shells found their way into Garifuna music in Pen Cayetano's art studio at Moho Street in Dangriga in 1982 and it can be said that it was that happy accident that gave rise to the Turtle Shell Band and brought about the latest development in Garifuna music in the form of Punta Rock.

Songs and singing permeate just about every facet of Garifuna life. As a consequence, there is a wide variety of songs covering every mood, and circumstance imaginable. There are certain types of songs that are associated with work, some with play, some with dance and some that are reserved for prayer or ritual use. And even within those categories there are further subcategories as should be evident from the description given below.

Work Songs Leremun Egi (Cassava grating songs)

Cassava is one of the staple foods of the Garifuna people. Cassava or manioc is a tuber which comes in two varieties - sweet and bitter. Sweet cassava or yucca can be boiled and eaten. Bitter cassava, on the other hand, is poisonous and has to be transformed into cassava bread (ereba) by means of a process inherited from the Carib and Arawak ancestors who utilized the same technology in South America hundreds of years ago. The cassava fields are cleared by the men and subsequently worked by the women. Farm work is usually accompanied by singing which naturally makes the work light while allowing for reflection on the themes and events treated in the songs.

The making of ereba entails peeling, washing and grating the tuber, then straining, sifting and baking the meal. Much of the work especially the grating was traditionally done with volunteer help from neighbors and friends, a situation that lends itself to communal type singing. This is perhaps what gave rise to a special type of work song associated with cassava grating. The women would stand together with their graters around a rectangular wooden bowl and sing as they tackled the pile of tubers that need to be grated. As is to be expected, the rhythm of the singing matches that of the movements of the hands as the grating proceeds.

Talurún Guríara (Pulling unfinished dugout canoes)

Subsistence in Garifuna communities traditionally depended on fishing and farming. Farming was largely a female activity while fishing was almost exclusively the domain of the males whose association with the sea was very close. This meant that canoe making was very important activity. The canoes were always dug out in the forest where the tree suitable for that purpose was found and then had to be dragged to the village to be finished before being hauled down to the sea. Many hands are usually required to haul the unfinished canoe - sometimes a distance of several miles - to the shore for finishing. However, there was usually no difficulty in securing the required number of persons who are invariably attracted by the talurún guriara songs which make the activity a fun thing.

The songs used for pulling canoes are somewhat obscene. However, they are considered acceptable in that context and persons of varying generations including no-nonsense parents and their children may stand shoulder to shoulder singing the songs as they lend a voluntary hand to the canoe maker.

Tagurún Wewe (wood cutting)

The Garifuna arrived in Belize at a time when there was a growing demand for labour in the timber industry as slavery began to be phased out. As a result, many men were attracted to the forest where they earned wages for services rendered in woodcutting. Several of these men were also skilled woodsmen who cut and sawed timber for use in the village. There were songs associated with felling trees. These songs are hardly known today and require much research among the oldest men if they are to be recovered.

Abüdürühani (Making adobe houses)

Another activity that required many hands is the making of büdürü (adobe) houses. There was a preference for this type of house which was considered cooler in the summer months and warmer in the cool season. The construction of this type of house entailed the framing of the walls with wild cane and palmetto stems to be later filled with red clay that invariably had to be dug and carried to the site. The clay is then mixed with water and worked to the right consistency before being pac ked into the wall frame. It can be seen from this description that this is a lot of work which, even with a lot of help would normally take the better part of a day. By making use of abüdürühani songs and incorporating dance movements into the work, the drudgery is transformed into a fair atmosphere that attracts helpers from the entire village and its environs.

Abüdürühani songs are similar to the talurún guríara songs in that they are rather lewd but are acceptable for use in that context.

Hadibiri Irahüñü (Children's Play Songs, Rhymes and Jungles) Cradle Songs or Lullabies

Songs and rhythm are incorporated into Garifuna life from the earliest stages of a child's life. Parents or babysitters could be heard soothing babies with simple songs like:

1)
Atiri bei san niri huma ya   How many names will you call me ?
Ragü wama wabua ni ei   Let us hold on, my fellows
 Hagéi Doyo, hagéi Rome, hagéi So? Where's Doyo, Where's Romay, Where's   So?
Aguya baba, ka un bígirei   Goodbye father, To whom do you leave him?
 Do do do do do mayahua ba   Sleep sleep sleep sleep sleep, Do not cry
 Do do do do do míruda ba Sleep sleep sleep sleep sleep, Do not cry

Do do, papa,   Sleep sleep, papa, Anunte beiga fein Your bread is coming

Children's Songs and Jingles

As might be expected of children in a community where singing permeates daily life, the culture is rich in songs associated with children's activities. There are children's games into which specific songs are incorporated like:

Lugudi bágasu mágürügáli
Dun pepe dun pepe

or

Da rose is in the Julan Jay
Da rose is in the Julan Jay
Da rose is in the Julan Jay
Julan Julan Jay

Ei chubaba lindo Julan Jay
Chubaba lindo Julan Jay
Chubaba lindo Julan Jay
Julan Julan Jay

In songs like these, there is no concern about what the meaning might be. The focus is on the melody, the rhythm and the game with which it is associated.

Finally there are jingles that are associated with games like the following which is used to determine who should be "it" in bisabísa, a hide and seek game.

Nidin béyabu luma nouba   I went to the beach, I and my mate.
Laríenga nouba nu   My mate said to me
"Híngiti gege bau.   "You smell of faeces.
Samina boun tia, bra,   Think about it, friend,
Bianguañádiwa   It was two of us
Tau wéibugu gúñarü"   On our walk yesterday"
Mátara tin tin   Pig snout
Mátara tin tin   walk right
Huréi   out

The underlined words at the end of the English translation are sometimes used in this jingle, which does not have a tune but has a definite rhythm in the original Garifuna version that cannot be captured in any translation.

Traditional Music and Dance

As was indicated earlier, there is a very close relationship between music and dance. For every type of dance there is a corresponding type of song, which bears the same name. In addition, it is generally felt that the dancer should always, whenever possible, join in the singing because only so can the best performance possible be assured. In other words, the performance is usually at a higher level when the dancer knows and likes the song and can join in the singing - singing for his feet, as it is referred to.

The hüngühüngü, punta, gunjai and the paranda are what can be characterized as ordinary dances as the dancer has the usual relationship with the musician. The dancer listens to the music and dances accordingly. Another set, namely the sambai, the chumba and the Wanaragua are unusual in that the dancer dictates the patterns that the lead drummer (primero drummer) plays. In these dances the drummer has to have a clear view of the dancer's feet and translates the movements into sound.

b. Historical background, development and social, symbolic and cultural purpose:

The Social Function
Ichahówarügüti
I hesitate to speak of composers or ownership in relation to Garifuna songs. This is so because songs are generally Ichahówarügüti, i.e., just given (by the spirits) rather than composed or written. A song comes into existence without any effort on the part of the person who will often speak of having learnt it instead of taking credit for its coming into being. Also relevant is the fact that an expression like "John's song" can have any of several possible meanings including the following.

1. The song was given (by the spirits) to John.
2. The song is a favourite of John's.
3. The song is about John.
4. henever I hear it I think of John.
5. John was allowed to take credit for the song (by the one to whom it was given)

As one can imagine, copyright is never an issue in traditional Garifuna society as the songs are in effect collective cultural property which everyone is free to use at any time. This cannot be said for Punta Rock which belongs to another world and is, therefore, subject to another set of rules. Unfortunately, it is not always possible to keep the two worlds separate and distinct because Punta Rock has always been nourished by traditional punta and paranda, and Punta Rock artists routinely draw their material from the traditional pool and simply repackage and embellish it for international consumption.Songs serve a multiplicity of functions in Traditional Garifuna life apart from their obvious use in work, ritual and in play. These include but are not limited to a) social control b) social comment c) personal and emotional release d) the recording of historical events and e) the affirmation of values.

Social Control

The idea here is that one had better watch his behaviour and how he relates to his fellows. The composer's skill is a powerful tool that can be used to inform the public about indiscretions or unacceptable behaviour. In particular, one should watch his words since these can provoke the composer's ire.

In the following example, the composer was accused by her neighbour of interfering in her life causing two men with whom she had an affair to arrive at her door at the same time:

(Punta)
Wéiriya bounli nei tuni buban
Your doggish behaviour is too much for your house
Sian ba aramuda
You can't hide it any more
Wa tina tuni nubesina
I called my neighbor
 Dungua eyeriun yara múnada
 Men have met at your house
 Chará ba badügüni an bidaradun
 You missed in making your arrangements.

An san nuguyaba lubéi bírida?
Why do you blame me?
Igira bana gia núnigua, Jane, lubá nubungiute,
Leave me alone, Jane, to my God,
Ligía lámuga agumucha nau.
Let Him be the one to do away with me.
 Igira bana gia núnigua, Jeni,
 Leave me alone, Jane,
 Igira bana gia núnigua, Wana,
Leave me alone, Juana,
 Lubá nubungiute,
 Leave me to my God,
Ligía lámuga agumucha nau.
Let Him be the one to do away with me.

This is a punta song and as such is used for festivities of all sorts. The "composer" would normally teach the song to close acquaintances and others who would invariably be asked to be filled in on the background information. The song and the relevant information would normally be passed on until it reaches the beluria where it would find a wider audience. As can be appreciated, this means of transmission is more effective than a local newspaper can ever be.

Social Comment

There are times when the target of the song is the entire population as opposed to a particular individual. The song can be seen as a comment on the social realities in the society. In the following song the singer is obviously reacting to comments that may have been made by some persons about her situation and attacks them for their double standards.

(Hüngühüngü)
Basia, belugüda yadina eyeri, ma,
Basia, I have taken in yet another man
Gülülügüdá dina ubóu
I have made the world murmur.
Marihi gian libe
They have never seen the like.
Basia, lagamari harumani hara, ma,
Basia, isn't it pitiful how they assault their own purity?
Hounligugüdü hau
They were bitches.
Lagamari harumani hara, ma,
How their cleanness was wasted.
Hounligugüdü hau
They have behaved like dogs.
Bulíeiguaña luari.
They have forgotten about that.

Basia, madaseihadírügü ligía, ma,
Basia, it's just that their deeds can't stain;
Daseigádiwa hamuga
We all would have been tainted already.
Gaganarügádiwa hamuga.
Very few among us would have been left unaffected

Personal/emotional Release

In this category we find a number of songs that can be described as scandal or muck raking. Here the composer has somehow been hurt by words, a decision or an action of the subject. As a result, the singer needs to save face and does so by finding something uncomplimentary to say about the subject. The important thing here is not the rightness or wrongness of the subject who may have been perfectly justified in taking the position that the singer considered offensive. What is important is the emotional release that the singer gets by getting back at him or her.

(Paranda)
Numada raü waü, dada ta yanu to wawariyua,
My friend, let us leave this discussion
Aninte Biulu aü, aganba liánliwa.
Biulu is coming, he may hear us.

Chülü tina tumoun nóufuri amuriahoun tura tubuiduri tuma
I went to my aunt, to ask for her daughter's hand.
Máhatu tau nuni, níbegunu.
She refused to give her to me, my friends.

Tarienhere tura nóufuri, ma, Anuhein würi ya ladünatu maríei
My aunt said, "Here's a girl, fitting for marriage,
Busientina tubagü haña luéndeme túhobu, ladünama me taslirun
I want a ring for her, to decorate her hand and will befit her when she goes out.

Tarienhere tura nóufuri, ma, gíbeti katei huagu mariahówati,
My aunt said, "There is much about your kind, that is not seen.
Aganbahówati luagu hirasa luma higaburi.
Much is heard about your clan, and their ways,
Ida tuba me niráü huma hubien?
How will my daughter fare with you in your home?"

Maritagun/masamina ta nóufuri lubá tanabunina
How my aunt has fails to think before she speaks.
Túmari tibarimu, tibarimu túmari, túmari tibarimu
Her son in law is her mate; her mate is her son in law; her son in law is her mate.
An, bulati tari, tari hanóu
She has protruding teeth like an ale wife (a fish).

If the allegation of the girl's mother sleeping with her son in law was true, it certainly did not bother the singer when he went to ask her for her daughter's hand; nor did her ugliness - her protruding teeth. It only became a problem for him when she refused to sanction the union because of a perceived social difference between the two families or a negative family trait which gave rise to her concern that her daughter might not be able to cope. This shows that the focus here is on saving face and "getting his own back".

It can be argued that most if not all traditional Garifuna songs provide much needed emotional release for the singer. It is almost as if the singer has an obligation and will not rest or have peace of mind until the song comes into being. This idea is actually expressed in several songs almost as an apology, so again and again we get words like:

Meremuhadina nian yebe,
I had decided to not sing anymore
Chülüha dan, au neremuhaba.
But the time has come, I will sing.

Here is another example:

Uremese nígirali nian yebe, aweinamudáña nisanigu.
I had decided to quit singing, my children are now grown up.
Dan le narihi nuóugua, gíbeti mégeiti nuóugua;
When I look at myself, much is not right with myself;
Ligía eremagüdübadina
That is what makes me sing.

Record Historical Events

It has been asserted that Garifuna songs are snapshots of events, happenings or even persons as seen from the singer's perspective. This being the case, it is not surprising that major events in the lives of individuals or conditions that were prevalent at a particular point in time are captured in song. Thus we find references to great tragedies like hurricanes, fires, drownings, celebrations and murders, as well as information on the daily lives, issues and concerns of the people at the time the song came into being.

This example is about hurricane Hattie that devastated the Stann Creek and Belize Districts of Belize in 1961. Notice the very personal tone as the singer is expressing her very personal experience as she talks to her daughter, Sylvia, the morning after:

(Punta)
Wa ba bumalali, Sili, lanarime dan
You've raised your voice (i.e., you've wailed), Syl, how terrible the storm.
Wa ba bumalali, niráü,
You've raised your voice, my child.
Ünabuguá yali ubóu
The earth has been brought low,
Wa wama ferudun, wonweguá yebe.
Let us beg forgiveness, we nearly died.

Larugan aningira híruha ubóu
At dawn the earth lay in sadness.
Laramañahandügü wagía, giúngiuñahándügü wagía

We could only stand around, just sucking our teeth (stupesing?).
Higóu waban? Barüla Hati
Where is our house? Hattie has taken it.

Affirm Values

Many of the principles and beliefs that have guided the life of the Garifuna for generations are transmitted and passed on in songs even though the songs invariably treat their subject matter in a very personal manner. The following example shows the close relationship between parent and child and the mutual obligations that continue even after death. The dead mother continues to exercise her parental obligation of providing guidance, to admonish and even punish while her son has an obligation to make offerings that will assist her spirit in finding salvation.(Paranda)

Gewenedi naru núguchuru
I've dreamt my mother
Kasa babuserúnbei, Mama, dimureba gia?
What do you want, mother? Please speak.

Lemesi le bíchugubei nu tugurabuga
The mass you gave me the other day
Maresibiru numuti
I did not accept.
Resibi nei hamuga tia
I would have accepted it.
Gíbeti mégeiti, saragu mégeiti
A lot was lacking, much was wrong.
Móunaha nubadibu íweruha lun bíchugu nu
I will not send you to steal so you can give to me.
Po dan me le babihini mabulieidágua ba
But when you get it(i.e., by legitimate means) do not forget.
Ru bei nelemusuru nu, wánwaraü, sáluba námuga.
Give me my mass, my dear son, so I can be saved.

Fatalism is prevalent in Garifuna culture. There is the belief that certain conditions are given and that there is nothing the individual can do to change them because they were written in ones book or star at the time he or she came into this world. In this next example, the singer presumably in her old age or infirmity finds that she is being neglected by her daughter (the mother of her granddaughter, Chris) and that she is hardly ever visited by relatives. While she complains about it there is nothing she can do since it was something written into her book. Her only fault is that she accepted that book in the first place but even here we find the disclaimer that she did not know what she was signing for. So she can only plead to God to change her fate.

(Punta)
2. Anhein hamuga le subudi numuti itara lian la tila nigaradan
If I had known that this is the contents of my book
Masaini numutu hamuga
I would not have signed it,
Sansi bei gia nu, nubungiute, Kululu bei gia nuei ñeigien
Change it for me, my God, Erase it for me from there
Gaduhe námuga tau nigabana nei
So I can have relatives by my bed.

Mágura bana gia, niráü,
Do not throw me away, my child,
Mágura bana gia, túguchuru Crisi,
Do not reject me, Cris' mother.
Mágura bana nirü, búguchu nuguya,
Do not reject me, my child, I'm your mother.
Buguya ba gagurasun nubara
It is you who must be patient with me.

Notice that the obligation of the child to the parent is also affirmed in this song.

All of the Above?

This last example shows that one song can serve several of the functions at the same time. First, there is emotional release as in the opening lines the singer confirms his obligation to sing after having been given cause. He appears to have been rejected by the young lady so he is getting his own back. Secondly, his criticism of the young lady can be generalized and seen as a comment on those persons who, on the surface, appear to be paragons of virtue but in actual fact are not so chaste. Thirdly, the preference for a man from Panama or a sailor has historical significance because there was a time when men from Belize went to Panama to work and others got work on merchant ships that sailed the world. Those men would send money home to their women so that those women would enjoy a higher standard of living because of the remittances.

(Paranda)
Neremuha ya funa anihán ga lébuna
I guess I will sing again, here is a reason,
Nagúara yali funa iseri resun le
I guess I will again raise this new song
Gúnfuli námugei niri neremuhadi.
Thus will I confirm my name as a singer.

Magoubahábadina buma, nátiraü,
I will not walk beside you, my brother,

Magoubahábadina buma, nibiri ei,
I will not walk beside you, my sibling,
Mayara badibu luni nugunda.
You will not be able to satisfy me.

Irahü gídina lian tererun nu
I am still a child, is what she said to me,
Wabien gídina lian tererun nu
I am still at home, is what she said to me.
Ireme funa buga lúmari guririguaü
As it turned out, she was the wife of the crowd.

Naguraba gubeiba númari Panamana
I'd better wait for a mate from Panama,
Naguraba gubeiba númari mádulun aü
I'd look for a sailor to be my mate.
Eyeri gawarati, labureme larugoungan.
A man who is able, owner of the light.

c. Technical description, authenticity, style, genre, school, influences
To repeat what has been indicated elsewhere, Garifuna Language is an Arawak language, a large language family in northern South America. The lexicon is primarily Arawak but it also has some loan words originating from Carib, French, English and Spanish indicating the influence that those languages have had on the language as a result of the contact with populations that speak those languages. The Garifuna had contact with the Spanish, English, and the French prior to the exile in 1797 while there was a later period of contact with the English and the Spanish after the arrival in Central America.

The word order in the language is generally SVO.

The phonemic inventory of the language consists of six oral vowels, (including voiced and voiceless vowels), six nasal vowels and twenty three consonants.

The authenticity of the language is cannot be challenged. Douglas Taylor, probably the foremost authority on West Indian languages, spent time studying the Garifuna people and language in Hopkins in the Stann Creek District of Belize and wrote extensively about both.

Garifuna music and dance, which have been extensively described in section 3(b) above, are equally authentic. There is not anything like it among any of the other ethnic groups of this hemisphere although some elements may share common origins with some found elsewhere. It is believed, for example, that the Garifuna punta, the kumbia of Columbia and the kumina of Jamaica probably share common African origins while the hüngühüngü, on close examination, manifests some Amerindian features suggesting some South American origins. The paranda reveals some Spanish influence as this is where the guitar makes its entry into Garifuna music while the French influence is unmistakable in the Gunjai, a sort of square dance that utilizes songs, which abound with words that are reminiscent of French.

Future Plans

iv. Management

a) Body or bodies in charge of safeguarding the cultural space or form
The National Garifuna Council (NGC) is the lead organization that is responsible for safeguarding preserving and revitalizing of the Garifuna language, music and dance. Other players at the national level that could complement the work of the NGC include the Ministry of Rural Development and Culture and the Ministry of Education. At the Regional level the Central American Black Organization could also be of assistance.

The mission of the NGC is to promote the cultural identity, economic development and general wellbeing of the Garifuna people as well as interracial harmony through means that ensure the sustainability of the organization, being mindful of the responsibility to protect the environment. The NGC is registered in Belize under the Companies Ordinance, Chapter 206 of the Laws of Belize. Section 3 of the Memorandum of Association of the National Garifuna Council lists 20 reasons for which the NGC was established. Among those reasons are:

- To preserve the Garifuna Culture through its Language, music, food, dances, crafts, arts and rituals.

- To develop programs which will bring out the diversity and the richness of Garifuna

- To motivate Garifuna youth to take active part in the council's programmes and activities for the development of leadership skills

- To maintain contact with Garifuna communities outside of Belize and to cooperate in matters which will enhance and preserve the heritage of the Garifuna people

The Memorandum of Association lists the entire set. It is included in the candidature file that was submitted.

The NGC has its headquarters in Dangriga Town. It has been working on establishing a secretariat at the Pablo Lambey Cultural Center in that town. Resource constraints have limited the success of the secretariat to date. A taskforce is currently charged with developing the process to fulfill the institutional strengthening needs of the NGC.

The Board of Directors headed by the President provides leadership to the organization at the national level. The board made up of 20 people meets every two months. The national executive meets every month. There are 10 branches. These branches are located in communities where Garinagu live in Belize. Each branch has an executive that provides leadership. The strength of the NGC lies in its branches. It is at the branch level that programmes are executed and it is through the branches that the Garifuna people influence the work and thinking of the NGC.

Over the last 15 years, the NGC has been hosting an annual convention. That convention is the supreme decision making body of the NGC. Between conventions the branch executive make branch level decisions in collaboration with the people, and national decisions are taken by board of directors.

The key people in the organization at this time include the entire board of directors and the executive of each branch. In addition there are several resource persons that contribute to the operations of the Council. The people listed below are in addition to those listed in section 1a of this submission. Among them are:

- Ernest Castro, FCCA, is a well-known accountant in Belize his address is 27 Mango Street Belmopan, Belize.

- Phyllis Cayetano, Community leader and prominent Garifuna lady. She is recognized as a woman with influence and charisma. Isla Road, Dangriga Town, Belize

- Harold Arzu, Consultant, Inter American Development Bank

- Claudina Cayetano MD, is a psychiatrist and an active member of the NGC. Poinsettia Street Belmopan, Belize.

- Cecil Ramirez is an Attorney who has made significant contributions to the development of the NGC. His law practice is based in Belmopan.

- Bernard Palacio ACCA, is an accountant. Like Mr. Ramirez he has been making significant contributions to the work of the NGC.

  b) Measures taken or planned

- The Garifuna People of Belize, through the National Garifuna Council, has developed the Garifuna Agenda as the policy tool to develop the Garifuna people. The language policy and the statement on cultural identity support the Garifuna agenda. The agenda attempts to show that ultimately people influence what happens to them and around them. It also shows that it is up to the Garinagu to take action and protect those elements of the culture that have value to them including the language, music and dance. While they managed to survive the inhuman treatment two hundred years ago and continue to exist today as a distinct group it is their view that that survival is now threatened. The threat comes from themselves as well as from some of the modern day institutions that have a profound effect on their daily lives. The danger from within arises from the fact that the identity and cultural strengths that enabled our ancestors to resist great hardships and deprivations is eroding quickly. They learned and taught the history, language and culture of those that colonized us and are losing their own. Consequently their sense is that they have become vulnerable and allowed others to define them and their right in a manner that is marginalizing them. Clearly, this is something that has to be addressed with some urgency.

This country was educated to a great extent through the efforts of Garifuna teachers. While there are those who feel that this is something for which the Garinagu should be proud, the fact is that that service has been at a high cost to the Garinagu as an ethnic group here in Belize. This is so because They lost the services of our brightest and best minds who otherwise would have been available to take a leading role in developing and promoting Garifuna culture. Instead, they played a leading role in perpetuating the language, religion and culture of the colonizer and thereby helped in a big way to give momentum to the cultural erosion that is now evident everywhere.

Schools are a very powerful tool that has been used effectively to serve the dominant interests in the society. On the other hand, the language, history, spirituality, and other aspects of the Garifuna culture have never been given any serious attention even in the schools in towns and villages where they are the predominant population. The result is that there is currently an identity crisis among the young Garifuna people most of whom cannot speak, let alone read and write, their own language, and do not know where they came from or who they are. They, therefore, become vulnerable to the lure of the North and the subtle messages they see on the television screens featuring persons who look like them and, in their misguided minds, must somehow be them.

There are those who argue that it is the business of the homes to teach the ancestral language and culture of the children and that that is not a proper role for the school. To that the Garinagu respond by saying firstly, that when it is convenient they are often told that the school belongs to the community and that it should serve the community. Secondly, the school has such credibility that what it values is valued by the community and what it ignores or devalues is also automatically labeled as worthless. (The language, history and culture have long been ignored by the schools in communities where they live, and often when they do get attention it is only in a manner that is disparaging. Small wonder, then, that those who know our history and culture and can read and write the language are able to do so in spite, rather than because, of the school.)

Thirdly, if the school can be used as an instrument to teach foreign languages like English and Spanish to the extent that some of us are more comfortable using them than our own ancestral language, it is difficult to argue against the role of the school in halting and reversing a linguistic and cultural erosion that it has helped, albeit inadvertently, to bring about. Fourthly, it is interesting to note that all the countries of Mesoamerica are ahead of Belize where the introduction of bilingual intercultural education involving native languages is concerned. Consequently, the agenda argues that:

National and local education authorities must recognize that Garifuna children have a right to learn to speak, read and write their ancestral language. While the importance of English and Spanish as international languages is recognized they are strongly opposed to Spanish being given precedence over their ancestral language at the primary level. The history, culture and art of the Garifuna people must be given serious attention in the schools in our communities.

There is a need for scholarships at the highest level to study indigenous culture, folk medicine, folklore, language and archaeology so that the Garinagu can acquire knowledge that they can disseminate to their children, and lead in the development of various aspects of their culture.The Garinagu are aware that they will have to play a major role in the development of materials and the training of teachers where the Garifuna language and cultural aspects of an improved and more relevant school curriculum are concerned. To this end, the National Garifuna Council is already embarking on a language initiative aimed at preserving, developing and promoting the Garifuna language.

c) Machinery for Safeguarding the Cultural Space or Form

The Garifuna Agenda and the language policy are the two policy level documents that provide information on the position of the NGC and some of the actions that it will utilize to safeguard the Garifuna Language, music and dance. In addition the Garifuna people of Belize recognize the NGC as their official voice in Belize. Garinagu in other countries also see the NGC as an example and occasionally they call on it to speak on their behalf.

i. The Garifuna people will utilize ILO Convention 169 and other avenues open to indigenous peoples as legal mechanisms to safeguard our heritage

ii. In 1999 the NGC signed a Memorandum of Understanding with the Government of Belize. That MOU has ten points one of them being that the Government of Belize shall give due recognition to the social, cultural, religious and spiritual values and practices of the Garinagu in Belize.

iii. The Archives of Belize and the Archeology Department are two places where information of value about the Garinagu will be lodged. Materials will also be lodged at the Secretariat of the NGC in Dangriga

iv. Schools have been used as an instrument to teach foreign languages like English and Spanish. This has been so successful in Belize that some Garinagu are more comfortable these foreign languages over their own ancestral language. Schools have also proven to be of value in the development of a music and dance culture. It is difficult to argue against the role of the school in halting and reversing a linguistic and cultural erosion that it has helped to bring about, albeit inadvertently. It is interesting to note that all the countries of Mesoamerica are ahead of Belize where the introduction of bilingual intercultural education involving native languages is concerned. Consequently, the agenda argues that:

National and local education authorities must recognize that Garifuna children have a right to learn to speak, read and write their ancestral language. While the importance of English and Spanish as international languages is recognized they are strongly opposed to Spanish being given precedence over their ancestral language at the primary level. The history, culture and art of the Garifuna people must be given serious attention in the schools in our communities.

The Garinagu are aware that they will have to play a major role in the development of materials and the training of teachers where the Garifuna language and cultural aspects of an improved and more relevant school curriculum are concerned. To this end, the National Garifuna Council is already embarking on a language initiative aimed at preserving, developing and promoting the Garifuna language among school age children and among adolescents.

Finally, there is a need for scholarships at the highest level to study indigenous culture, folk medicine, folklore, language and archaeology so that the Garinagu can acquire knowledge that they can disseminate to their children, and lead to the development and revitalization of various aspects of their culture.

v. The Garinagu recognize that lifestyle changes over the last 30 years have eroded and in many cases eliminated traditional modalities and mechanisms for oral transmission of knowledge, skills and values. The kinds of games that children play have changed immensely. The community gatherings for social and festive and healing occasions have decreased considerably. Consequently attention needs to be given to developing new modalities and mechanism through which the knowledge, skills and values are transmitted. The Garinagu need to become creative in the use of new technologies to transmit the elements of the culture that make them successful as a people

d) Means of implementing protection

The Garifuna people recognize the natural and inherent interconnectedness of language and culture and that the language is the primary vehicle for the transmission of the culture. They believe that their survival depends on both the preservation of our the traditional language and other elements of the culture and on social and economic development. Therefore the language policies and goals also impact and are intimately connected with their economic development and cultural survival.

As an indigenous people, the Garifuna Nation has basic rights to autonomy and self-determination, and the right to maintain and preserve Garifuna language and culture. Further, the Garifuna Nation recognizes the right of the Garifuna communities and member organizations in each country to establish and implement local level language policies and development initiatives. It expects these rights to be guaranteed by local governments, as described by the United Nations Draft Declaration of the Rights of Indigenous Peoples.

e) Plan of Action

The erosion of the Garifuna language, music and dance in Belize is particularly worrisome and the concern is expressed in all sectors of the Belizean Garifuna society - young and old. This erosion threatens their value system and their existence as a people. There is a need to take action to stem this erosion as quickly as possible. The erosion of the culture and value system is seen to affect the self-esteem and performance as a people. As a result, they are alienating their traditional lands and are performing poorly in school.

Recently, Garifuna children have not been doing as well as they should in school. This means that they are not taking advantage of study opportunities. If this is allowed to continue, the skilled pool will become smaller over time. There is a definite need to build enthusiasm about education so that Garifuna children become motivated to succeed and to select fields of study that give Garinagu a competitive advantage.

The fact is that the language is still spoken and its use is widespread and the music and dance are still vibrant. However, it is only in one village - Hopkins - that young children still learn it as their native language. There is an awareness of the fact that this very important part of the Garifuna identity is beginning to slip away. This awareness is coupled with a feeling of helplessness as parents are blamed for not speaking it to their children even while they use the language among themselves. In this climate, it is imperative that the National Garifuna Council takes the lead in working out interventions aimed at arresting the loss of the language and other elements of the culture. The ten year action plan that they continue to develop will serve as the modality through which they will seek to preserve the language music and dance among other elements of the Garifuna Culture.

e) Durability and possible risks of disappearance, pressure or constraints due to

i. Economic and technological development: The lack of economic opportunities puts pressure on people to migrate in search of jobs. They move to urban centers in Belize as well as abroad as the opportunities present themselves. Very often the children become absorbed in the host culture and drift further and further away from their own cultural traditions that are not taught to them at home or in the school. As for technological development, it is our view that this can only help in transmitting and promoting the culture but only if easier access is facilitated and the technology made available for recording, storing, transmitting and disseminating cultural material.

ii. Climate change and pollution: Not applicable

iii. The development of tourism: The Garifuna people have not really benefited or been impacted upon by from tourism. However, the promotion of the language, music and dance as important elements of their culture and the impact that this can have on their self image can put the Garifuna in a position to capitalize on the economic possibilities offered by tourism on their own terms.

iv. An increase or decrease in population: This has not had an impact either.

v. Other factors: The people encountered racism from the time of their arrival in Central America. This did not have too much of an impact while they remained in their communities. However, as they have found it necessary to leave and seek opportunities elsewhere their self esteem and identity began to be affected and the culture began to erode. This is compounded by the fact that the use of the language and other aspects of the culture were even actively discouraged in some town schools.

The NGC is involved in several key projects at this time. The implementation of the Language Policy is one of these. Reviving the Garifuna folklore and ethic is an important complementary project. The Garifuna agenda and the Memorandum of Association provide the context for the planning process. The following section of the draft action plan is relevant to the safeguarding and revitalization of the Garifuna Language, Music and Dance:

Nurture and Promote The Garifuna Culture and Identity

Purpose: To nurture and promote the Garifuna culture and identity

Expected Results:

1. Establish a Garifuna Cultural Centre and Institute
2. Garifuna cultural elements including the language, music and dance are being utilised to promote the culture and the people.
3. Garifuna festivities and festivals that showcase the language, music and dance are being promoted.
4. Garifuna crafts are being celebrated and marketed

Expected Result 1. Garifuna cultural elements are being utilised to promote the culture and the people.

Indicators:

* Promotional exhibits are being used
* The Garifuna culture is being marketed
* The Garinagu are proud of their culture

Activities:

* Design and implement an exhibit that promote the Garifuna culture
* Co-ordinate the promotion and sale of Garifuna craft and music

Expected Result 2. Garifuna festivities are being promoted.

Indicators:

* An annual Garifuna Festival is conducted
* Other Garifuna Festivals are carried out

Activities:

* Establish a festival committee
* Design and carry out an annual Garifuna Festival
* Design an carry out promotional festivals

Expected Result 3. Garifuna music, arts and crafts are being celebrated and marketed.

Indicators:

* Arts and craft exhibits and displays can be viewed locally and internationally
* Musicians, artists and artisans are being promoted using the various media options

Activities:

* Design a Garifuna Heritage Park

* Build the Garifuna heritage Park
* Establish a marketing program

Development of Youth Leadership

Purpose: To motivate and work with Garifuna children and youth to develop leadership skills so that they can take active part in the development of the Garifuna people and culture.

Expected Results:

1. Programs that attract youth participation are in place and are being implemented
2. Garifuna youth groups are operational in communities where Garinagu reside
3. Youth are actively represented in the national headquarters of the NGC
4. Youth are acquiring skills and knowledge in the Language, Music and Dance of the Garifuna people

Expected Result 1. Programs that attract youth participation are in place and are being implemented.

Indicators

* Youth programmes and activities are carried out
* Youth are participating in the activities and programmes that are planned
Activities:
* Establish a youth committee
* Develop and implement a youth program

Expected Result 2. Garifuna youth groups are operational in communities where Garinagu reside

Indicators:
* Garifuna youth groups are operating in Garifuna communities
* Youth leadership is developing

Activities:

* Establish youth groups in Garifuna Communities where none exist
* Facilitate the development and operation of Garifuna youth groups where these exist

Expected Result 3. Youth are actively represented in the national headquarters of the NGC

Indicators:

* Youths are represented by an official delegate on the national headquarters
* Mechanism for the youth representative to report to his national constituency is in place

Activities:
* Establish a mechanism through which a youth can be selected to represent young people on the Board of Directors.

f) Administrative Machinery for safeguarding the space or form or cultural expression
The National Garifuna Council as described above will be the administrative machinery for safeguarding Garifuna language, music and dance.

g) Sources of Funding
The sustainability of the language, music and dance of the Garifuna people is an important concern for the NGC. To this end it would like to establish and have operate an autonomous Trust that has the ability to attract financing that will foster the development of Garinagu and their way of life. The Garifuna Council has developed a draft ten-year plan.

Financing for the action plan and its activities is limited. It is hoped that the declaration that is now being sought will help to attract attention and much needed resources that will help to assure the survival of this valuable cultural and intangible heritage.

h) Number of persons involved
The NGC as an organization is committed to the safeguarding of the language music and dance of the Garifuna people. The entire organization supports the efforts. Over the weekend of the ninth of March the NGC held its 17th Annual Convention. There was representation from all ten branches as well as from Honduras, Nicaragua and the United States. All participants supported the submission that has been made.

i) Human Resources
There are several well-educated Garinagu who believe in the work of the NGC and who give of their time to the work of the NGC. The Garinagu contend that there is still a long way to go, and this submission is one of several steps that is being taken to garner support for the effort of saving what they consider to be of value to them and all humanity.

Appendix and References

d. References

Language

Cayetano, E. Roy. 1992. Uaragua Wamamuga Luagu Labürüdüniwa Wererun. Towards a Common Garifuna Orthography. National Garifuna Council (compendium, 33p)

Cayetano, E. Roy. 1993. The People's Garifuna Dictionary. Dimureágei Garifuna. Belize: National Garifuna Council. (170 p.)

Taylor, Douglas M. 1977. Languages of the West Indies. Baltimore and London: Johns Hopkins
University Press.

Literature

Lumb, Judy & Fabian Cayetano, eds. 1994. Walagante Marcela. Marcella our Legacy. Poetry and Other Writings by Marcella Lewis. Belize: National Garifuna Council (75 p.)

Ramos, Adele. 2000. Thomas Vincent Ramos. The Man and His Writings. Belize: National Garifuna Council. (54 p.)

Anthropology

Cayetano, E. Roy. Song and Ritual as a Key to Understanding Black Carib Personality. A Research Paper in Anthropology. University of Michigan.

Taylor, Douglas M. 1951. The Black Caribs of British Honduras. New York: The Viking Fund Publications in Anthropology, No. 17.

Warigóun Barangun. Barranco Home-coming. August 3rd-9th, 1997. (booklet,30 p.)

Warigóun Barangun. Second Barranco Home-coming. April 20th- 26th, 2000. (booklet, 42 p.)

History

Gonzalez, Nancy L. Solien. 1988. Sojourners of the Caribbean. University of Illinois. (253 p.)

The Garifuna Journey. Celebrating the Resiliency of the Garifuna People and their Traditions. Study Guide. 1999. Belize:Leland /Berger Productions & NationalGarifuna Council. (49 P.) (also on video).

Kirby, I. E & C. I Martin. 1995. The Rise and Fall of the Black Caribs. UNESCO/Saint Vincent and the Grenadines Trust. 52 p.)

Audio & Video

4 video Cassettes:
The Garifuna Journey (overview of Garifuna culture and history)
The Garifuna Journey I
The Garifuna Journey II
The Making of the Paranda CD (music)

6 cd's:
Different examples of Garifuna music, professional productions

13 audio cassettes:
Mostly containing music, some also discussions

vi. Appended Documents

Contents of the Package

1. The Garifuna Heritage. This is a documentary film produced using selected material from the video footage collected for the project and serves as the centre piece of this submission. It addresses Garifuna Culture including ritual, music, dance and language.
2. Draft Ten Year Plan for the preservation, development and promotion of Garifuna language, music and dance as key elements of Garifuna culture.
3. The Garifuna Journey is a documentary film produced by Andrea Leland and Kathy Berger, two Chicago based film makers, in collaboration with the National Garifuna Council. It provides excellent background information on various aspects of the history and culture.

4. Warigóun Barangun is a commemorative booklet for an event, the Barranco Home Coming, that seeks to forge a collaborative relationship between the residents of this Garifuna village and its children who have been forced by economic circumstances to seek their fortune elsewhere.

5. The Garifuna Agenda is a document produced by the National Garifuna Council prior to the last general elections, after consultations with the various Garifuna communities in the country, to inform our discussions with the political parties contesting the elections. It captures the main issues and concerns of the Garifuna people of Belize.

6. Language Policy of the Garifuna Nation is another document produced by the National Garifuna Council and adopted by the Central American Black Organization (on behalf of Garifuna People everywhere) at its General Assembly held in Livingston, Guatemala, in December, 1997.

7. Towards a Common Garifuna Orthography is a paper written by E. Roy Cayetano in the early 1980's. This paper continues to inform work that is ongoing in the region aimed at standardizing Garifuna Orthography. 8. The Rise and Fall of the Black Caribs of Saint Vincent is a monograph written by Martin and Kirby. It tells the story of the Garifuna people up to the time of their exile from their homeland in St. Vincent in 1797. For a change, the story is told from the point of view of the people themselves. 9. The People's Garifuna Dictionary, the first work published by the National Garifuna Council.

10. Thomas Vincent Ramos - The Man and his Writings, the most recent work published by the National Garifuna Council. It is a modest attempt to provide information about the life and work of the founder of Garifuna Settlement Day.

11. Walagante Marcella is an anthology of poems written by Marcella Lewis, a Garifuna poet who is now over eighty years of age. This work was co-published by the NGC.

12. Six CD's with commercially produced Garifuna Music. Reggae Nuanee was originally produced as an LP record in the 1970's. Celebration is a CD commissioned by the Belize Arts Council and includes a couple tracks of Garifuna Music and shows the impact that Garifuna Music has had on Belizean music. Keimoun and Til da Manin are two Punta Rock CD's by Andy Palacio, one of our foremost Punta Rock artists. On Fire is a CD's by the Punta Rebels which is without doubt Belize's leading Punta Rock Band. Paranda is pure unadulterated Paranda that is professionally recorded. It represents the first attempt to introduce Paranda as a genre of Garifuna music as distinct from Punta Rock to the international market.

13. Twelve Audio Cassettes which represent a sampling of the material collected for the project. They include: Chumba, Arumahani, Abeimahani, Punta, Paranda, Hüngühüngü, Wanaragua discussion, Wanaragua music, Leremun Egi (cassava grating songs), Dügü music (two casettes), miscellaneous Garifuna songs (acapella) by Ernestina Fernandez and Uraga (stories) as told at a Beluria.

14. Twenty Photographs as shown below:

Photographs In The Package

1. Abeimahani
2. Wanaragua (Jankunu) Dr. Roy Lopez is a medical doctor with specialization in Internal Medicine and Psychiatry. When he lived and worked in the United States he came home to Dangriga every Christmas to dance Wanaragua.
3. Wanaragua dressing. Dr. Roy Lopez helping Rambibi.

352

4. Helping Cassian Nuñez, Mayor of Dangriga, get dressed. Mr. Nuñez also lived in the United States for many years and used to come home at Christmas time to dance.
5. Wanaragua from Livingston, Guatemala. Notice the difference in the dress.
6. Wanaragua from Livingston, Guatemala.
7. Wanaragua, Dangriga style.
8. Putting on the mask. The word "wanaragua" actually means mask, and it is from this that the dance gets its name. The mask is made of sieve pulled over a wooden mould to give it the shape of a human face and then painted. These masks are always painted pink, presumably to depict a white person's face.
9. Drummers
10. Wanaragua dancing in Livingston, Guatemala.
11. Christmas in Livingston, Guatemala
12. Scene from Dance Workshop
13. Another scene from Dance Workshop
14. Language Workshop
15. Teaching drumming at a Language and Spirituality Workshop in Orinoco, Nicaragua
16. Buyei singing for the hiúruha in delivering a food offering for the ancestors in Orinoco, Nicaragua
17. Food offering in the Dabuyaba at a dügü in Dangriga
18. Abeimahani while the food offering is on the table in Orinoco, Nicaragua (Language and Spirituality Workshop)
19. Scene from the Lexicography Workshop in Hopkins, an activity in the process of producing The People's Garifuna Dictionary.
20. A volunteer teaching the children at a Garifuna Youth Convention in Georgetown, Belize.

The life of the Saint Vincent Caribs today

As you drive along the village of Sandy Bay, you'll notice a few concrete houses in between the make shift shacks that the Caribs live in. The road is rugged and only a heavy duty vehicle could past. The road is lined with many coconut trees growing wild. Everywhere you look there is some sign of poverty, which the people are trying to fight. They have lost most of their culture and influence into the life of the English.

This village is populated by Caribs. The Caribs were at a disadvantage from the start of their settlement, from the Europeans who forced them out of their land, placed in an area of steep terrain and where got the worst destruction from the eruption of Soufriere. In 1812 when Soufriere erupted, the villages of the Caribs were destroyed. Some Caribs who could afford it, migrated to Trinidad, others stayed and tried to put back their ruins of their village into some workable order.

Most of the houses are board with galvanized roofs, if of a lower standard the roofs are thatched. The kitchens are outside, under a thatched shed. There is a fireside made out of three large stones. Wood has to be collected daily. the few richer Caribs living here could afford a kerosene stove and coal stoves inside their house. Huge iron pots covered with tar, are familiar utensils used by the Caribs. Pit latrines are familiar sites around the houses. The bathrooms are separate. the lives of the Carib here is rather secluded and primitive. Pipe water is rather rare and limited, electricity and telephone are not even available in these areas. Only a few could afford running water in their house.

Religion plays and important role in the Caribs life. Along the countryside, the roads are lit with churches from different sects, Catholic being the most dominant religion. It must be noted that the Methodist religion has not penetrated into the Carib Villages. Church is attended regularly, and the attire used are normal English clothes. The ministers of these churches do not always come on Sundays, due to the fact that the roads are not accessible, therefore a few villagers get together and keep worship. The doctor visits the villages periodically. Shops are rare and other Caribs from other villages often come to get supplies at Sandy Bay. this makes the cost of living expensive since the goods are more expensive due to transport.

Strips of cultivated land could be seen on the hillside of arrowroot, yams, eddoes, bananas and other crops. The popular means of transport here is the donkey and mule carts. Other means of transport are by foot. The trails are rough and rugged and often the Carib has to carry their produce from the mountains on their heads to their village unless they could afford a donkey.

An automobile is rare in these parts and is a treat to see one in the neighbourhood. The Caribs sometimes go from place to place on the coast by means of canoes.

The unemployment rate of the villages is very high. The men and the women have different tasks. The men hunted, did the craftwork, fished, did peasant farming and wage larbour. The women do the domestic chores, collecting firewood, weaving, hammock making and bartering the goods.

The income the Caribs have is rather low. Most of the parents want a better life for their children when they are born, therefore they give their children to other people who are well-to-do, to take care of them. It was some kind of "adoption" plan. Most of the children got to a primary level education. the girls are usually taken out of school after a primary school education unless they did really well, then they went on to Secondary school. The education level of the school is rather low with a few passes since they are small and crowded since the population is very high due to many teenage pregnancies. The teachers are not very experienced and equipment is very small. The girls are taken out of school to help take care of the house and smaller brothers and sisters. On "banana day" the school is empty since most children help their parents to pick and pack the bananas. This results in a lower education standard.

Marriages for girls are rather young, around the age of sixteen to eighteen. The girl chooses her partner. After marriage they live with the girl parents until they could afford a house of their own.

The village of Greiggs is similar to the villages like Sandy Bay except it is a little more developed since it is closer to the city.

Sarah Baptiste was born in Campden Park on the 18th of November, 1909. Her parents were from Sandy Bay. She was given to the Da Sliva's family to be taken care off.

She became a nanny and went to work for a relative of the Da Sliva's. She had an arranged marriage to a respectful young man from Sandy Bay. At forty she decided to end her marriage with a divorce, during this time she had one daughter who had already grown up. Any woman who was divorced in the village was looked upon has a failure, but she was able to built up her courage to forget her fellow woman sneers and work for her keep. She should be considered brave since such few women could built up courage to end a marriage at forty to gain happiness especially when at this age women began to accept their life. Most of the women stayed with their husbands for financial support, but Sarah Baptiste was able to be an independent person, to earn her money and ruled her own life although her salary was small. She worked as a domestic in the Fancy Estate.

One day, the Estate Manager asked Sarah if she would liked to be a nurse on his estate, she promptly answered yes although she was scared of trying to learn a new profession at her age and starting a new life. The next month Sarah Baptiste enrolled in a midwife training program at the Kingstown General Hospital. she was the oldest trainee. She was at first embarrassed of her age, being a domestic and a Carib. She learned how to swallow her pride. Younger girls commanded her to do the dirty duties such as cleaning the sewage. She always smiled outwardly, but in her heart she was troubled, she continued her training program because she was determined to become a nurse.

She returned to Sandy Bay, to start her nursing career after her training. she was a nurse for 25 years. The job was hard and demanding since little medical staff was there in the village. People came from different villages to see Sarah Baptiste. Sarah was sometimes stationed at different villages each week. She soon came to be trusted, and she was soon popularly called mother, since she was the one who mothered the village. She was always responded to people calls for her at all times. there was one case in which an expectant father had come to her 2:00 am in the morning to come and see about his wife. The man lived at Windsor Forest which was only accessible by boat. Sarah Baptiste immediately got up and jumped into the canoe and proceeded to Windsor forest. She was in time to see the child delivered.

She tried to teach women self respect and protection for themselves. In one instance, Sarah had been called upon by a young wife during one of her beatings by her husband to help her stop her husband from bruising her in which she did successfully by scolding the young man who respected her and stopped.

She was the person who tried to make her community better, she spear-headed the Girl Guides, the Mother's Union and the Church. She often took over the services at church when the minister couldn't make it due to the bad roads. she started Sunday School for the younger children so that they come closer to God in spirit. She often did the work of the doctor such as prescribing medicines for patients. It is incredulous to believe that such a woman as Sarah Baptiste through all her midwife experience never lost a mother in child birth or a baby through all the hundreds she helped bore.

Sarah Baptiste is considered an inspiration for the Caribs in that community and also the people of St.Vincent and the Grenadines.

The Caribs are part of the integral Vincentian society. Although most of them stick together in their villages they grew up in.

The Caribs have contributed many things to the Vincentians. They have a historical background that they share with their fellow citizens. This adds History to the country, making it a more interesting place to visit by tourists.

Their culture still exists in traces. They have passed down dishes to the community of the Vincentians such as their soups. There are still witch doctors that exist in St.Vincent that claimed to help a sick person. Their hammocks is something of their culture that has spread widely through the Caribbean and to the extended world.

Agriculture was on of the main things that the Caribs have passed down to the people of St.Vincent. Crops such as yams, cassava and corn have been widely used by the community, which the Caribs and other tribes first planted. The Caribs today are important since they contribute arrowroot and bananas to the export market. They also are small peasant farmers.

Most of the Caribs are into activities in their community such as Girl Guides, Boys Scout and sports. They often play cricket and football during the seasons against other villages.

Caribs have been able to educate themselves and become better. Some people have gone into the medical field like Sarah Baptiste and most schools around Sandy Bay to Fancy are taught by local Caribs.

The Caribs were smart enough to stick together to retain as much of their culture today, but today most of them have been influenced by other people in the society to become English-like, which they exactly did in some of their food, their dress code and religion. therefore it could be safely say since the Caribs and other races of St.Vincent have been influence by the English, the Caribs would have no problem in mixing with the other people.

The Caribs have integrating quite well with the people of St.Vincent although they live in a community by themselves. the person's . Sarah this The Caribs has a part of the Vincentian Society. to the oftourist attraction to foreigners who wishes to learn the Caribs culture. Therfore, indirectly the Caribs help to provide income for the counttry. whonill or get rid of any evil surrounding the personhave been widely used by the people of St.Vincent and the othe regions of the world. These hammocks are one of the traces of the Carib culture that has been able to be sustain.

Carib Customs

Discover St. Vincent and the Granadines Brochure

The Caribs or Callinagos, the early inhabitants of St. Vincent or Youroumei were a very disciplined and fiercely independent people, far from the savages they were though to be. What is known about their customs indicate that they were highly organized.

The Caribs lived on fish and wild animals they caught with lines and hooks and bows and arrows which supplemented their diet of fish, cassava, yams and pumpkins.

The Caribs did not practice an organized religion, but more private individual type. They believed that they had three souls, the main soul residing in the head and called Akamboue. It went to heaven after death and was though to be able to help living. There was a *Boyez*, a kind of priest, who could be consulted privately.

Men could take many wives, each wife was provides with a separate house and the husband shared his time with them.

The woman performed very definite roles in the community apart from being just partners to the men. They were responsible for looking after the domestic animals and growing the food. Mothers looked after the boys until they were two years old, after which the father took them over to be trained in the ways of the Carib men. The girls were brought up by their mothers and learned her skills.

Men were the hunters and fishermen and in times of war, warriors. The community was responsible for fishing, transportation and organizing feast after raids and on commercial occasions.

The Caribs showed spirited resistance to the British and French as they were fiercely independent and wanted to keep their island.

Early Peoples of St. Vincent and the Grenadines: The Caribs (and the Garifunas)

St.Vincent and the Grenadines today has a mixed population which can be clearly seen in the picture below. There are individuals of African, Asian, European and Native American heritage, and many have multiple ancestries. However, before the coming of the Europeans and the other groups, St.Vincent was settled by the Ciboney and then the Caribs, as well as, subsequently, the "Black" Caribs (known as the Garifunas). The descendants of these peoples live today on the Windward coast of St.Vincent (from Sandy Bay to Fancy) and at Greiggs (see map on our web site). The island today has very few pure Caribs, with most having intermarried with other groups, primarily, the descendant of the Africans who make up the majority of the population.

The first settlers of these islands were a group of hunter-gatherers, the Ciboneys, who explored and lived on the islands eating fruit and berries, seashells and the pink conch more than 5000 years ago.

More than 200 years before Christ, another culture traveling in 50 foot dugout canoes arrived in these islands. The Arawaks carried fire-burners, animals and plants. During a 1500 year period the Caribbean islands were peaceful.

The islands did not survive the invasion of the Caribs who killed the men and carried off the women. The Caribs were fierce fighters and strong swimmers. Captured Arawak women refused to speak the Carib language, but eventually the Tupi-Arawakian language died out along with the beautiful pottery created by these women.

Today, we know very little about these early settlements other than some petroglyps left on rocks and some pottery and tools found at archeological sites.

In St.Vincent and in other Antillean islands the Caribs lived on the coast. They preferred living near the sea because they relied mainly on fishing, and the sea also was their key means of communication with the Caribs on other islands. Living on the coast meant that it was usually easy to see an an oncoming attack from their enemies. They may have also avoided settlement on the larger islands because of the difficulty in penetrating the densely forested interiors and because they did not need vast amount of lands for farming.

Inter-island warfare seems to have been a large part of significant portions of Carib history. The windward side of many islands was developed so as to guard against attacks. The windward side of most Caribbean islands often has the roughest waters therefore it would have been difficult for an enemy to sneak up to Carib villages by means of the sea unless the coast was well known.

The Caribs life was thus heavily influenced by war, and they made success in battle a key part for manhood initiation and respect. The early Caribs' fighting equipment was rather simple— were made from wood, bone and stone. They had war clubs, bows and arrows that were poisoned so that even a scratch was fatal, fire arrows, wooden swords and knives made of sharp rock.

The Ubutu, the Carib's war leader, decided the day that the attack was to be made. Each Carib man would collect a stick and make notches in it to count the days until the attack. Their attacks were made under the cover of night. On the eve of battle the Caribs painted and armed themselves and then set out in their canoes or piragas. These canoes held up to fifty men and in fact, many battles actually occurred at sea. Attacks always attempted to catch the enemy off guard. They often started with a shower of fire arrows that immediately set fire to the thatched roofs of the enemy village. The surprised enemies would then attempt to exit their houses to meet the Caribs who meanwhile would have had their clubs and arrows at the ready. They kept no order when they fought. When the fighting was over, if victorious, the Caribs often piled the bodies of any dead warriors into the piragas because they refused to leave their dead and wounded behind. In the canoes were also the men and women they had taken for prisoners. They often sang songs of triumph as they sailed back home. Select warriors were awarded medals for special courage in battle. These medals were called caracolis, and were crescent shaped copper pendants to be worn around the neck.

The Making of the Garifuna

Recent research indicates that Africans probably came even before Columbus and settled in St. Vincent. The Caribs of St. Vincent were joined by Caribs fleeing Europeans attacks on other islands, and also by runaway African slaves and slaves who survived shipwrecks in the area. In the year 1635 two Spanish ships carrying African captives, believed to be Nigerian, were shipwrecked off the island of St. Vincent. At first, the Africans and Caribs fought one another but eventually intermarried.

News of the free men on St. Vincent spread throughout the islands. By 1676, it is estimated that 30% of the population of St. Vincent consisted of formerly enslaved Africans who had escaped. Women were scarce and the African men were fierce competition for the Caribs.

A new group of African and Carib heritage developed and became known as the "Black Caribs" or "Garifuna" as the subsequently named themselves— the word "Garifuna" means "cassava eating people." Eventually the Garifuna outnumbered the original inhabitants, the "Yellow Caribs." The Garifuna's population growth created political tensions with the outnumbered "Yellow Caribs" and so that at one point the Yellow Caribs even negotiated with French wanderers to settle on the islands in 1719—hoping to shift power away from the Black Caribs.

Social Structure, Religion and Culture

We don't have any real written record of very early Carib society, but by looking a their descendants in South America and from records made by early historians (mainly priests) we can infer a number of probabilities. The Caribs social structure was mobile. The social caste of the Carib community was:

    i) The war leader or Ubutu

    ii) Priests and elders

    iii) Warriors and hunters

All decisions for running the community was made by the men, therefore only men held the ruling positions. The Ubutu was always a male whose position was not hereditary. He was chosen by the elders of his village. He had to have been a good warrior, proved that he was physically strong, brave and highly skilled in battle. When he was chosen, he had to carry out a raid, if the raid was successful his positioned was permanent. The Ubutu had to do many things, including:

1) He was the leader for any raid.

2) He planned and decided when to carry out raids and which village or enemy it should be.

3) He distributed the medals and the loot from the raid.

4) He chose the commanders of the piragas.

In times of peace each district was ruled by a headman called a Tiubutuli Hauthe. The headman supervised the fishing and the cultivation of crops, beyond this he had a very little authority.

Most boys were trained to be warriors. The warriors were the ones who fought first in line, they were also the hunters for the villages. They were the common villagers. A small percentage of the boys were trained to be priests or Boyez.

The elders of the villages were well respected. They were taken care of by their families and their relatives. The elders were all ex-warriors. They were the ones who trained the warriors and looked for the qualities in the Ubutu since they were experienced.

The Carib males practiced polygamy. Marriages were arranged and girls married at an early age around sixteen to eighteen years. The husband provided a hut and furniture for each of his wives at the time of their marriage.

If the wife committed adultery it was punishable by death. It was a custom for an unmarried woman to wear a garter on her right leg, at the time of marriage the garter was removed.

They did not have a family unit but a communal way of living, they were separated based on their sex. The men lived separately in their carbets or houses and the women lived in huts. Boys at the age of four were taken away from their mothers and placed in the carbets, because the men thought that if the boys stayed with their mother too long he would become weak. The women were expected to bear a number of children. If she was barren she was considered a disgrace.

The Carib houses were rectangular shape. The houses were large about 40ft x 20ft. The furniture in the house was rather sparse. There were hammocks, amais, stools and tables. Outside the house there was a storeroom in which household utensils, weapons, tools and extra hammocks and beds were kept. The Caribs slept on hammocks. The hammocks had a small packet of ash placed at the ends that were thought to make it last longer. The stools were made from red or yellow polished wood. The tables were made from rushes. At nights the huts were lighted with candles that were made with a sweet, smelling gum.

The women and the men had different roles in the society. Men were supposed to be the warriors, priests, leaders, builders of houses and boats, craftsmen and hunters. The women were supposed to do the domestic chores, bring up the children, collecting firewood, bartering produce, weaving, hammock making and cultivating the land.

The Caribs believed in life after death, but they had no wish for dying. They preferred to stay on earth to enjoy the materialistic pleasures. They ate healthily and took their medicines regularly. When a Carib died, he/she was examined to see if they'd been the victim of sorcery. The body was then washed carefully and painted red. The hair was oiled and combed. The grave for the body was on the floor of he/she house. The grave was round. It was about four feet wide and six feet deep. The body was placed on a stool in the grave, for ten days relatives brought food and water at the grave and a fire was lit around it in order to prevent the body from being cold. At the end of the ten days the hole was filled. There was a ceremony in which, the Caribs danced over the hole. As a sign of mourning relatives cut off their hair. The dead person's possession was burnt. Later a feast was held over the grave, and after which the person's house was burnt.

The Black Caribs Of St. Vincent

Newsday Historical Digest

June 24, 2001

Page 28

She proudly showed me a picture of her mother and her aunt, two very good-looking black women, well dressed in the style of the 1910s.

They had handsome, regular features with bright, intelligent eyes that looked directly into the camera. I could not help but notice their hair. Both girls had luxurious, thick, wavy black hair, parted in the middle and arranged at the back in a bun. She looked across at me and smiled.

"Carib," she said.

"From St. Vincent?" I asked.

"Yes."

"One of the finest vistas in the Caribbean is that from Coke's View in the St. Vincent, looking down the rock-bound coast to the Grenadines; a view that is best on a day when the trade winds are freshening and the white foam breakers against the dark rocks and the sea seem to be racing towards Bequia," wrote Dr. Philipp Sherlock in a radio script, which he delivered one Sunday in October, 1963. Because there are so many Vincentians or people of Vincentian descent living in Trinidad today, and especially in memory of Mrs. Gittens, who showed me the photograph of her mother and her aunt, I will bring to you the text of Sir Philipp Sherlock's most interesting account of the Black Caribs of St. Vincent.

"Drive over the mountain ridge behind Kingstown, and you come to a very different view, as Mesopotamia valley opens up before you with some of the finest terracing of land in the West Indies. This fine sweep of cultivated land is in sharp contrast with the north end of the island. St. Vincent is as mountainous as Dominica, and the central ranges are so high and difficult that up to several years ago it was the only island that was not crossed by a road."

"Mount Soufrière itself rises to just over 4,000 feet, and it reaches this height within two miles. Flying over the crater, you could look straight down into a bleak, deep cup, sinister with its yellow lake 2,000 feet down in the centre. Perhaps Soufrière looks all the more sinister because it is one of the two active volcanoes remaining in the Caribbean. It's a fantastic location and holiday makers and groups of excursionists make their way down the inside of the crater. In 1902, Soufrière and its partner, Mt. Pelée in Martinique, erupted. Before that, Soufrière erupted in 1812, causing the most dreadful destruction and laying waste much of the island."

"This triggered a mass exodus from St. Vincent of entire families to Trinidad, a migration that continues to this day."

"The volcano is itself a reminder that the island is almost entirely volcanic in origin," writes Dr. Sherlock. "It is made up chiefly of ash and other broken material. It is not too fanciful to say that St. Vincent has had elements of the volcanic in its history also. It was a Carib stronghold. Columbus testified on the strength, courage and determination of the Caribs, and in his journal, when he advocated making slaves of them, he writes that - 'they are a wild people, fit for any work, well proportioned and very intelligent, and who, when they have got rid of their cruel habits...will be better than any other kind of slaves.'"

"The Caribs held St. Vincent in such strength that the island was one of the last of the lesser Antilles to be settled by Europeans and the first group of settlers, whether French or English, had to make treaties with the Caribs in order to get a foothold. The last of these treaties was made in 1773, ten years after the island became British."

"As in Grenada, so in St. Lucia, the French and English fought each other for possession of the island. The sharpest conflict took place in the 1790s, the period of the conquest of Trinidad by the British and the revolt of Fedon in Grenada. One of the most skillful of the revolutionary leaders in the Caribbean was Frenchman Victor Hugues, a man of extraordinary energy who stirred up the slaves and the Caribs against the English."

"In the years immediately before Hugues arrived in the Caribbean from France, the English expanded sugar production in St. Vincent in preference to cotton, with the result that sugar production rose from 3,700 tons in 1787 to over 14,000 tons in 1828. The increase in sugar meant an increase in the number of slaves, and where there is slavery, there is the fear of slave uprisings. Hugues knew well how to organise disaffection and he had considerable success. On landing in St. Lucia, he immediately proclaimed all slaves were free, organised a rising and recaptured the island from France."

"After St. Lucia, he stirred up the Black Caribs of St. Vincent. These Black Caribs were a mixture of African and Carib. You will find them in St. Vincent to this day."

Bryan Edwards wrote in his book of 1793, that origin of the Black Caribs of St. Vincent lies in the fact that a ship was wrecked in 1675 on Bequin, carrying slaves from the tribe of Mocoes in Benin. Together with runaway slaves from Barbados, the "Red Caribs" produced offspring with the Africans, who were subsequently called "Black Caribs".

The 1960 census showed that there were 1,200 Caribs in St. Vincent, most of these are in fact Black Caribs.

"Urged on by Hugues, the ancestors of these same people rose in rebellion and there was desperate fighting, so desperate that it looked at one time as if the French and their Carib allies would succeed in throwing the English off the island, as they had done in St. Lucia. In the end, the rebellion was put down, and large quantities of Black Caribs were carried away from St. Vincent and settled in the Bay islands, in Ruatan and Bonacca off the Mosquito coast of South America."

"Years later, some of these Black Caribs were allowed to leave Ruatan and settle in the southern part of British Honduras, and today you will find them among the most progressive and hardworking of the inhabitants of Belize. Some make a living cutting timber in the forests, others fishing, others are farmers. They number about 7,000. It is because of this transportation that the number of Black Caribs in St. Vincent is so small."

"After a period of turbulence, St. Vincent settled down to become a sugar island. England often exported criminals. Many "poor whites" came to the Caribbean and made a home for themselves at Dorsetshire Hill, northeast of Kingstown. Many Portuguese were settled there in the same way that many also came to Trinidad. West Indian immigration to Trinidad and Tobago over the last 150 years has contributed to an aspect of our cosmopolitanism in that tens of thousands of people, mostly of African descent, have come here, their origins at first very diverse, but in the melting pot of Trinidad and Tobago we all have become one people."

St. Vincent/Grenadines:Caribs Fight To Recover Their Culture

an inter press service feature
by Colin Williams

Sat, 5 Oct 1991 08:29:35 PDT

Kingston, Sep 30 (ips) -- it says "urau" instead of october and "ebedimu" where the english would say "november" -- all 12 months of the year and the seven days of the week are quoted in the garifuna language in the first Garifuna calendar here.

The calendar is one of many initiatives through which the yurimein association for rural development (yard) seeks to give back to the black caribs of Yurimein a language born, like its speakers, out of the forced encounter of peoples from different continents.

Yurimein is the carib name for st. vincent.

When european colonisation began to take root in yurimein, about two centuries after columbus came to the americas in 1492, africans were brought as slaves to this 389 km2 caribbean island.

Many escaped and joined the indigenous caribs. their offspring , who came to be known as "black caribs", fought against the europeans until the end of the 18th century, when some were exiled to belize, then british honduras, by the british.

It is these belizean 'Garifuna', who have managed to retain their dress, food, music, traditional dances and language, who are now helping their vincentian brothers and sisters to recover their culture. Through constant contact with the "creole" culture of the remainder of st. vincent's and the grenadines' 108,000 people of mainly african and afro-european origin, St. Vincent's 6,000 black caribs lost their language and much of their culture.

Though most live in a relatively small area in northeast st. vincent, there has always been social intercourse between the caribs and the rest of the vincentian population. A penpal exercise linking students from villages in st. vincent and in belize and a scholarship programme enabling students from each country to study at secondary schools in the other are among ways in which the cultural rebirth of st. vincent's black caribs is being fostered.

"With the penpal system, we have begun to introduce words and phrases so that the children can learn the basic things such as greetings", nelcia robinson, a social worker told ips.

(more/ips) St. Vincent/Grenadines: Caribs (2) Robinson is a major driving force behind 'yard', which has also published "in a calabash", a booklet of Garifuna foods and "yard talk" which details its activities.

She says her organisation hopes to have the St. Vincent/Grenadines national anthem translated into the Garifuna language. "that happens in belize", she said, "it is there in English and Garifuna".

But the black caribs' efforts to revive their culture is no isolated initiative. it is part of a wider movement spearheaded by the Caribbean Organisation of Indigenous Peoples (COIP), to which both branches of the Garifuna or black carib group belong.

COIP is an umbrella organisation of national associations of indigenous peoples in four anglophone caribbean countries, the other two being Guyana and Dominica. It represents some 75,000 indigenous people: about 25,000 mayas and garifuna in belize, 5,000 Caribs in Dominica and 6,000 in St. Vincnet and an estimated 40,000 Akawoio, Arawaks, Arecuna, Caribs, Macushi, Patamona, Wai Wwai, Wapishiana and Warrau in Guyana.

Enforced separation has long been a feature of the powerlessness of indigenous peoples in the english-speaking caribbean, according to coip coordinator Joseph Palacio of Belize. Writing quietely in the umbrella group's publication, "COIP indigi-notes", Palacio said there is a need to break down existing barriers "both those that have been imposed upon us as well as those we impose upon ourselves".

COIP is "strongly objecting to the idea of a celebration of the quincentennial of the coming of columbus", says robinson. the indigenous people in the caribbean, like those elsewhere in the americas, "have suffered tremendously" since 1492 and there has been no significant improvement in their lot.

The region's amerindians "remain first in being malnourished, unschooled, unemployed, unhoused, unclothed, disease ridden and politically disenfranchised", according to palacio. COIP intends to use 1992 to highlight the plight of indigenous peoples and intensify the thrust towards exchanges between them in an effort to recover their culture.(more/ips)

St. Vincent/Grenadines: caribs (3)

With support from the caribbean network for integrated rural development, coip is currently conducting research -- to be completed in 1992 -- in its four member countries on the indigenous people, where they live, their living conditions, their numbers and their economic status.

But 1992 "is also an opportunity to celebrate the victory and resistance ... because despite the tremendous genocide following the coming of columbus, the fact that indigenous people still survive today is itself a tribute to their resistance", Robinson said.

There has been a perceptible resurgence of pride in carib and other indigenous communities in the caribbean. In st. vincent and Dominica people have started giving their children carib names in much the same way as the growth of african consciousness led afro-caribbean people to adopt african names in the 1960s and 1970s.

There is also increased interest in research on and by indigenous peoples. researchers in Waitukubuli -- Carib name for Dominica -- are now in the field talking to the elderly, artisans, practitioners of traditional medicine under a project of the Waitukubuli Karifuna Development Centre.

The centre, a non-governmental organisation, aims to investigate and document aspects of the carib culture and ensure the continuity of their heritage and, well aware of the truth of the african proverb 'until lions have their own historians, stories of hunting will always glorify the hunter', the caribbean's indigenous peoples have also begun to take a new look at the region's history.

Background Note: Saint Vincent and the Grenadines

Unite State Department of State Bureau of Western Hemisphere Affairs

Profile

OFFICIAL NAME: Saint Vincent and the Grenadines

Geography

Area: 340 sq. km. (130 sq. mi.); slightly less than twice the size of Washington, DC. The Grenadines include 32 islands, the largest of which are Bequia, Mustique, Canouan, and Union. Some of the smaller islands are privately owned.

Cities: *Capital*--Kingstown.

Terrain: Volcanic and mountainous, with the highest peak, Soufriere, rising to 1,219 meters (4,000 ft.).
Climate: Tropical.

People

Nationality: *Noun and adjective*--Vincentian.
Population (2008): 118,000.
Annual growth rate (2006): 0.5%.
Ethnic groups: African descent (66%), mixed (19%), West Indian (6%), Carib Indian (2%), other (7%).
Religions: Anglican (47%), Methodist (28%), Roman Catholic (13%), other Protestant denominations, Seventh-day Adventist, and Hindu.
Language: English (official); some French Patois spoken.
Education (2004): *Adult literacy*--88.1%.
Health (2006): *Infant mortality rate*--17/1,000. *Life expectancy*--men 69 years; women 74 years.
Workforce (2006): 57,695.
Unemployment (2004): 12%.

Government

Type: Parliamentary democracy; independent sovereign state within the Commonwealth.
Independence: October 27, 1979.
Constitution: October 27, 1979.

Branches: *Executive*--governor general (representing Queen Elizabeth II, head of state), prime minister (head of government), cabinet. *Legislative*--unicameral legislature with 15-member elected House of Assembly and six-member appointed Senate. *Judicial*--district courts, Eastern Caribbean Supreme Court (High Court and Court of Appeals), final appeal to the Privy Council in London.

Subdivisions: Six parishes.

Political parties: Unity Labour Party (ULP, incumbent), New Democratic Party (NDP).

Suffrage: Universal at 18.

Economy

GDP (2006): $422.5 million.
GDP growth (2005): 4.9%.
Per capita GDP (2005): $3,594.
Inflation (2006): 3.0%.
Natural resources: Timber.
Agriculture: Mostly bananas.
Industry: Plastic products, food processing, cement, furniture, clothing, starch, and detergents.
Trade (2005): *Exports*--$40 million (merchandise) and $155 million (commercial services). *Major markets*--European Union (27.2%), Barbados (12.7%), Trinidad and Tobago (12.3%), Saint Lucia (10.9%), and the United States (9.2%). *Imports*--$240 million (merchandise) and $74 million (commercial services). *Major suppliers*--United States (33.3%), Trinidad and Tobago (23.6%), European Union (15.1%), Japan (4.2%), and Barbados (3.9%).
Official exchange rate: EC$2.70 = U.S. $1.

People

Most Vincentians are the descendants of African slaves brought to the island to work on plantations. There also are a few white descendants of English colonists, as well as some East Indians, Carib Indians, and a sizable minority of mixed race. The country's official language is English, but a French patois may be heard on some of the Grenadine Islands.

History

Carib Indians aggressively prevented European settlement on St. Vincent until the 18th century. African slaves--whether shipwrecked or escaped from St. Lucia and Grenada and seeking refuge in St. Vincent--intermarried with the Caribs and became known as "black Caribs." Beginning in 1719, French settlers cultivated coffee, tobacco, indigo, cotton, and sugar on plantations worked by African slaves. In 1763, St. Vincent was ceded to Britain. Restored to French rule in 1779, St. Vincent was regained by the British under the Treaty of Versailles in 1783. Conflict between the British and the black Caribs continued until 1796, when General Abercrombie crushed a revolt fomented by the French radical Victor Hugues. More than 5,000 black Caribs were eventually deported to Roatan, an island off the coast of Honduras.

Slavery was abolished in 1834; the resulting labor shortages on the plantations attracted Portuguese immigrants in the 1840s and east Indians in the 1860s. Conditions remained harsh for both former slaves and immigrant agricultural workers, as depressed world sugar prices kept the economy stagnant until the turn of the century.

From 1763 until independence, St. Vincent passed through various stages of colonial status under the British. A representative assembly was authorized in 1776, Crown Colony government installed in 1877, a legislative council created in 1925, and universal adult suffrage granted in 1951.

During this period, the British made several unsuccessful attempts to affiliate St. Vincent with other Windward Islands in order to govern the region through a unified administration. The most notable was the West Indies Federation, which collapsed in 1962. St. Vincent was granted associate statehood status in 1969, giving it complete control over its internal affairs. Following a referendum in 1979, St. Vincent and the Grenadines became the last of the Windward Islands to gain independence.

Natural disasters have plagued the country throughout the 20th century. In 1902, the La Soufriere volcano erupted, killing 2,000 people. Much farmland was damaged, and the economy deteriorated. In April 1979, La Soufriere erupted again. Although no one was killed, thousands had to be evacuated, and there was extensive agricultural damage. In 1980 and 1987, hurricanes devastated banana and coconut plantations; 1998 and 1999 also saw very active hurricane seasons, with Hurricane Lenny in 1999 causing extensive damage to the west coast of the island.

Government

St. Vincent and the Grenadines is a parliamentary democracy within the Commonwealth of Nations. Queen Elizabeth II is head of state and is represented on the island by a governor general, an office with mostly ceremonial functions. Control of the government rests with the prime minister and the cabinet.

The parliament is a unicameral body, consisting of 15 elected members and six appointed senators. The governor general appoints senators, four on the advice of the prime minister and two on the advice of the leader of the opposition. The parliamentary term of office is five years, although the prime minister may call elections at any time.

As in other English-speaking Caribbean countries, the judiciary in St. Vincent is rooted in British common law. There are 11 courts in three magisterial districts. The Eastern Caribbean Supreme Court, comprising a

High Court and a Court of Appeals, is known in St. Vincent as the St. Vincent and the Grenadines Supreme Court. The court of last resort is the judicial committee of Her Majesty's Privy Council in London.

There is no local government in St. Vincent, and all six parishes are administered by the central government.

Principal Government Officials

Head of State--Queen Elizabeth II
Governor General--Sir Frederick Ballantyne
Prime Minister--Ralph E. Gonsalves
Minister of Foreign Affairs, Commerce, and Trade--Sir Louis Straker
Ambassador to the United States and the OAS--La Celia Prince
Permanent Representative to the UN--Camillo Gonsalves

St. Vincent and the Grenadines maintains an embassy at 3216 New Mexico Ave., NW, Washington, DC 20016 (tel. 202-364-6730). St. Vincent also has a consul resident in New York.

Political Conditions

The People's Political Party (PPP), founded in 1952 by Ebenezer Joshua, was the first major political party in St. Vincent. The PPP had its roots in the labor movement and was in the forefront of national policy prior to independence, winning elections from 1957 through 1966. With the development of a more conservative black middle class, however, the party began to lose support steadily, until it collapsed after a rout in the 1979 elections. The party dissolved itself in 1984.

Founded in 1955, the St. Vincent Labour Party (SVLP), under R. Milton Cato, gained the support of the middle class. With a conservative law-and-order message and a pro-Western foreign policy, the SVLP dominated politics from the mid-1960s until the mid-1980s. Following victories in the 1967 and 1974 elections, the SVLP led the island to independence, winning the first post-independence election in 1979. Expecting an easy victory for the SVLP in 1984, Cato called early elections. The results were surprising: with a record 89% voter turnout, James F. Mitchell's New Democratic Party (NDP) won nine seats in the House of Assembly.

Bolstered by a resurgent economy in the mid-1980s, Mitchell led his party to an unprecedented sweep of all 15 House of Assembly seats in the 1989 elections. The opposition emerged from the election weakened and fragmented but was able to win three seats during the February 1994 elections under a "unity" coalition. In 1998, Prime Minister Mitchell and the

NDP were returned to power for an unprecedented fourth term but only with a slim margin of 8 seats to 7 seats for the Unity Labour Party (ULP). The NDP was able to accomplish a return to power while receiving a lesser share of the popular vote, approximately 45% to the ULP's 55%. In March 2001, the ULP, led by Ralph Gonsalves, assumed power after winning 12 of the 15 seats in Parliament.

In the December 2005 parliamentary elections, Prime Minister Gonsalves and the ULP retained their 12-3 majority over the NDP.

Economy

Banana production employs upwards of 60% of the work force and accounts for 50% of merchandise exports in St. Vincent and the Grenadines, with an emphasis on the main island of St. Vincent. Such reliance on one crop has made the economy vulnerable to fluctuations in banana prices and reduced European Union trade preferences. To combat these vulnerabilities, the Government of St. Vincent and the Grenadines is focused on diversifying its economy away from reliance on bananas. Recently, there has been a parallel reduction in licit agriculture and a rise in marijuana cultivation, making St. Vincent and the Grenadines the largest marijuana producer in the Eastern Caribbean.

In contrast to developments on the main island, tourism in the Grenadines has grown to become a very important part of the economy, and the chief earner of foreign exchange for the country as a whole. The Grenadines have become a favorite of high-end tourism and the focus of new development in the country. Super-luxury resorts, yachting tourism, and a commitment by the government to rehabilitate and protect the Tobago Keys as a national park have all contributed to strong tourism returns in the Grenadines.

St. Vincent and the Grenadines' currency is the Eastern Caribbean Dollar (EC$), a regional currency shared among members of the Eastern Caribbean Currency Union (ECCU). The Eastern Caribbean Central Bank (ECCB) issues the EC$, manages monetary policy, and regulates and supervises commercial banking activities in its member countries. The ECCB has kept the EC$ pegged at EC$2.7=U.S. $1.

St. Vincent and the Grenadines is a beneficiary of the U.S. Caribbean Basin Initiative that grants duty-free entry into the United States for many goods. St. Vincent and the Grenadines also belongs to the predominantly English-speaking Caribbean Community and Common Market (CARICOM) and the CARICOM Single Market and Economy (CSME).

Foreign Relations

St. Vincent and the Grenadines maintains close ties to the United States, Canada, and the United Kingdom, and is a member of regional political and economic organizations such as the Organization of Eastern Caribbean States (OECS) and CARICOM. St. Vincent and the Grenadines is also a member of the United Nations, the Commonwealth of Nations, the Organization of American States (OAS), and the Association of Caribbean States (ACS). St. Vincent and the Grenadines has chosen to recognize Taiwan instead of the People's Republic of China.

U.S.-ST. Vincent Relations

The United States and St. Vincent have solid bilateral relations. Both governments are concerned with eradicating local marijuana cultivation and combating the transshipment of narcotics. In 1995, the United States and St. Vincent signed a Maritime Law Enforcement Agreement. In 1996, the Government of St. Vincent and the Grenadines signed an Extradition Treaty with the United States. In 1997, the two countries signed a Mutual Legal Assistance Treaty.

The United States supports the Government of St. Vincent and the Grenadines' efforts to expand its economic base and to provide a higher standard of living for its citizens. U.S. assistance is channeled primarily through multilateral agencies such as the World Bank. The United States has 27 Peace Corps volunteers in St. Vincent and the Grenadines, working in business development, education, and health. The U.S. military also provides assistance through construction and humanitarian civic action projects.

A relatively small number of Americans--fewer than 1,000--reside on the islands.

The United States maintains no official presence in St. Vincent. The Ambassador and Embassy officers are resident in Barbados and frequently travel to St. Vincent.

Principal U.S. Embassy Officials
Ambassador--Mary M. Ourisman
Deputy Chief of Mission--D. Brent Hardt
Political/Economic Chief--Ian Campbell
Consul General--Clyde Howard Jr.
Regional Labor Attaché--Jake Aller
Commercial Affairs--Ian Campbell
Public Affairs Officer--John Roberts
Peace Corps Director--Margo Jean-Child (resident in St. Lucia)

The U.S. Embassy in Barbados is located in the Wildey Business Park, Wildey, St. Michael (tel: 246-436-4950 ; fax: 246-429-5246).

Other Contact Information
International Trade Administration
U.S. Department of Commerce
1401 Constitution Ave NW
Washington, DC 20230
Tel: 1-800-USA-TRADE
http://trade.gov/

Caribbean/Latin American Action
1818 N Street, NW, Suite 310
Washington, DC 20036
Tel: (202) 466-7464
Fax: (202) 822-0075

TRAVEL AND BUSINESS INFORMATION
The U.S. Department of State's Consular Information Program advises Americans traveling and residing abroad through Country Specific Information, Travel Alerts, and Travel Warnings. **Country Specific Information** exists for all countries and includes information on entry and exit requirements, currency regulations, health conditions, safety and security, crime, political disturbances, and the addresses of the U.S. embassies and consulates abroad. **Travel Alerts** are issued to disseminate information quickly about terrorist threats and other relatively short-term conditions overseas that pose significant risks to the security of American travelers. **Travel Warnings** are issued when the State Department recommends that Americans avoid travel to a certain country because the situation is dangerous or unstable.

For the latest security information, Americans living and traveling abroad should regularly monitor the Department's Bureau of Consular Affairs Internet web site at http://www.travel.state.gov, where the current Worldwide Caution, Travel Alerts, and Travel Warnings can be found. Consular Affairs Publications, which contain information on obtaining passports and planning a safe trip abroad, are also available at http://www.travel.state.gov. For additional information on international travel, see http://www.usa.gov/Citizen/Topics/Travel/International.shtml.

The Department of State encourages all U.S citizens traveling or residing abroad to register via the State Department's travel registration website or at the nearest U.S. embassy or consulate abroad. Registration will make your presence and whereabouts known in case it is necessary to contact you in an emergency and will enable you to receive up-to-date information on security conditions.

Emergency information concerning Americans traveling abroad may be obtained by calling 1-888-407-4747 toll free in the U.S. and Canada or the regular toll line 1-202-501-4444 for callers outside the U.S. and Canada.

The National Passport Information Center (NPIC) is the U.S. Department of State's single, centralized public contact center for U.S. passport information. Telephone: 1-877-4USA-PPT (1-877-487-2778). Customer service representatives and operators for TDD/TTY are available Monday-Friday, 7:00 a.m. to 12:00 midnight, Eastern Time, excluding federal holidays.

Travelers can check the latest health information with the U.S. Centers for Disease Control and Prevention in Atlanta, Georgia. A hotline at 877-FYI-TRIP (877-394-8747) and a web site at http://wwwn.cdc.gov/travel/default.aspx give the most recent health advisories, immunization recommendations or requirements, and advice on food and drinking water safety for regions and countries. A booklet entitled "Health Information for International Travel" (HHS publication number CDC-95-8280) is available from the U.S. Government Printing Office, Washington, DC 20402, tel. (202) 512-1800 .

Bibliography

Cayetano, Sebastian R. Garífuna History, Language & Culture of Belize, Central America & The Caribbean, pp.22. S & F Cayetano: Belize, 1997.

Garinagu Early History, Garífuna World, pp.1-3. 1997.

Garinagu Future. Garífuna World, 1997.

González, Nancie. *Sojourners of the Caribbean: Ethnogenesis and Ethnohistory of the Garífuna*, pp. 26, 82. University of Illinois Press: Urbana and Chicago, 1988.

Griffin, Wendy, "Garífunas prepare for 200 year anniversary bash in La Ceiba," pp. 1-2. Honduras This Week: 3/19/97.

Idiáquez, José. *El culto a los ancestros en la cosmovisión de los Garífunas de Honduras*. Instituto Histórico Centroamericano, Managua, Nicaragua, 1994.

Melendez, Armando Crisanto and Auyujuru Savaranga. *Adeija Sisira Gererum Aguburigu Gariganu: 'El enojo de las sonajas; palabras del ancestro, "* pp. 51-53. Graficentro Editores: Tegucigalpa, Honduras, 1997.

Cosminsky, Shelia

1976 Medicinal Plants of the Black Carib. 42nd International Congress of Americanists 6:535552.

1974 Davidson, William V.

Historical Geography of the Bay Islands, Honduras. Birmingham, Alabama: Southern University Press.

1976 Dispersal of the Garifuna in the Western Caribbean. 42nd International Congress of Americanists 6:467-474.

1966 Evans, David K. The People of French Harbour: A Study of Conflict and Change on Roatan Island. PhD dissertation, Anthropology Department, University of California, Berkeley.

1986 Macklin, Catherine L. Crucibles of Identity: Ritual and Symbolic Dimensions of Garifuna Ethnicity. PhD dissertation, Anthropology Department, University of California, Berkeley.

1993 Global Garifuna: Negotiating Belizean Garif4na Identity At Home and Abroad. In: GlobaUation and Development: Challenges and Prospects for Belize Pp. 162-173. Belize: SPEAR.

Palacio, Joseph 0.

1973 Black Carib History Up To 1795. Journal of Belizean Affairs 1:31-41.

1993 Global Garifuna: Negotiating Belizean Garifuna Identity At Home and Abroad. In: Globalization and Development: Challenges and Prospects for Belize Pp. 162-173. Belize: SPEAR.

Gullick, Charles

1976 The Black Caribs in St. Vincent: The Carib War and Aftermath. 42nd International Congress of Americanists 6:451-465.

Suazo, Pablo Inés Flores. Interview with Alejandro Tosatti, InCorpore Cultural Association.

Breton, Raymond (1877) *Grammaire caraibe, composée par le p. Raymond Breton, suivie du Catéchisme caraibe.* Maisonneuve, Paris. - from 1635 manuscript

Cayetano. Sebastian R Garifuna history, language and culture of Belize and C.A. November 1, 1989

Coke, Thomas (1970) History of the West Indies 3 Vols. London.

Davidson, William V. Historical Geography of the Bay Islands, Honduras.

Southern University Press, 1974.

Edwards, Bryon The History, Civil and Commercial of the British West Indies.

4 Vols. London, 1818-1819.

Gonzalez, Nancie L. (1988). *Sojourners of the Caribbean: Ethnogenesis and*

Gullick, C. J. M. R. (1985). *Myths of a Minority.* Assen: Van Gorcum Press.

Humphrey, Chris. (1997) *Honduras Handbook Ethnohistory of the Garifuna.* Urbana: University of Illinois Press. Moon Publications.

Kerns, Virginia (1983). *Women and the Ancestors: Black Carib Kinship and Ritual.* Urbana: University of Illinois Press.

Labat, Jean-Baptiste (1722) Voyage aux Isles de l'Amerique 2 Vols. Paris

Lehman, Jeffrey. *Gale Encyclopedia of Multicultural America.* 2nd ed., vol. 1. Gale Research, 1995

Ragatz, Lowell Joseph (1963) The Fall of the Planter Class in the

Caribbean, 1763-1783, New York.

Shepherd, Charles (1971) An Historical Account of the Island of St. Vincent., London.

Southey, Thomas (1968) Chronological History of the West Indies 3 Vols. London.

Taylor, Douglas Macrae (1967) The Black Carib of British Honduras, New York.

Van der Plas, (1964) Gualbart The History of the Massacre of two Jesuit Missionaries in the Island of St. Vincent., Kingstown.

Waters, Ivor (1964) The Unfortunate Valentine Morris, Chepstow, U.K.

Young, Thomas (1839, 1840, 1841) Narrative of a Residence on the Mosquito Shore during the years, London

Young, Sir William (1971) An Account of the Black Charaibs in the Island of St. Vincent's, London.

Whitehead, Neil L. (1988). Lords *of the Tiger Spirit*. Leiden: Foris Publications Holland

Bianchi, Cynthia Chamberlain. "Gubida Illness and Religious Ritual Among the Garifuna of Santa Fe, Honduras: An Ethnopsychiatric Analysis." Ph.D. diss., Ohio State University, 1988. This dissertation goes to great lengths to show the rich detail of Garifuna postmortem rituals framed by an ethno-psychiatric approach to healing.

Coelho, Ruy. "The Black Carib of Honduras: A Study in Acculturation." Ph.D. diss., Northwestern University, 1955.

Conzemius, Eduard. "Ethnographical Notes on the Black Carib (Garif)." *American Anthropologist* 30, no. 2 (1928): 183–205. Possibly the earliest "modern" ethnographic description of Garifuna ritual.

Flores, Barbara. "The Garifuna Dugu Ritual in Belize: A Celebration of Relationships." In *Gender, Ethnicity, and Religion*, edited by Rosemary Radford Ruether, pp. 144–170. Minneapolis, 2002.

Gonzalez, Nancie L. *Sojourners of the Caribbean: Ethnogenesis and Ethnohistory of the Garifuna.* Urbana, Ill., and Chicago, 1988.

Hulme, Peter, and Neil L. Whitehead, eds. *Wild Majesty: Encounters with Caribs from Columbus to the Present Day.* Oxford, 1992. This is a selection of descriptions of the Caribs, both Island Carib Amerindians and the "Black Carib," as represented by Europeans since the seventeenth century.

Jenkins, Carol L. "Ritual and Resource Flow: The Garifuna Dugu." *American Ethnologist* 10 (1983): 429–442.

Johnson, Paul Christopher. "Migrating Bodies, Circulating Signs: Brazilian Candomblé, the Garífuna of the Caribbean, and the Category of 'Indigenous Religions.'" *History of Religions* 41, no. 4 (2002): 301–328.

Kerns, Virginia. *Women and the Ancestors: Black Carib Kinship and Ritual.* 2d ed. Urbana, Ill., and Chicago, 1997.

Melendez, Armando Crisanto. "Religious Elements of the Garifuna Culture and Their Connotations in the Americas." In *African Creative Expressions of the Divine*, edited by Kortright Davis and Elias Farajajé-Jones, translated by Dorothea Lowe Bryce, pp. 121–128. Washington, D.C., 1991.

Sanford, Margaret. "Revitalization Movements as Indicators of Completed Acculturation." *Comparative Studies in Society and History* 16 (1974): 504–518.

Suazo, Eusebio Salvador. *Irufumali: La doctrina esotérica garífuna.* Tegucigalpa, 2000. A bilingual (Spanish and Garifuna) account of the *buyei's* knowledge from a Garifuna writer, acquired through interviews with practicing shamans.

Taylor, Douglas. *The Black Carib of British Honduras*. New York, 1951.

Stone, Michael C. (2006) Garifuna Song, Groove Locale and "World Music Mediation" Globalization, Cultural Identities, And Media Representations

CPSIA information can be obtained
at www.ICGtesting.com
Printed in the USA
LVHW022203020920
664947LV00012B/308